W9-BNZ-123

Microsoft®
Word 2019 & 365

COMPREHENSIVE

BEN LINFORD
Southwest Applied Technology College
and Southern Utah University

LABYRINTH
LEARNING™

Microsoft Word 2019 & 365: Comprehensive

Labyrinth Learning
PO Box 2669
Danville, CA 94526
800.522.9746
On the web at lablearning.com

President:
Brian Favro

Product Manager:
Jason Favro

Development Manager:
Laura Popelka

Senior Editor:
Alexandra Mummery

Editor:
Alexandria Henderson

Developmental Editor:
Sudha Putnam

Production Manager:
Debra Grose

Compositor:
Happenstance Type-O-Rama

Indexing:
BIM Creatives, LLC

Cover Design:
Sam Anderson Design

Bound book: 1-64061-063-4
ISBN-13:   978-1-64061-063-7

Loose-leaf: 1-64061-089-8
ISBN-13:   978-1-64061-089-7

Manufactured in the United States of America

GPP   10 9 8 7 6 5 4 3 2 1

Contents

Word Chapter 11:
Personalizing Word

Word Chapter 12:
Creating Custom Forms and Using Macros

Word Chapter 13:
Integrating Word with Excel, PowerPoint, and the Web

Preface

This textbook is part of our new approach to learning for introductory computer courses. We've kept the best elements of our proven, easy-to-use instructional design and added interactive elements and assessments that offer enormous potential to engage learners in a new way.

Why Did We Write This Content?

In today's digital world, knowing how to use the most common software applications is critical, and those who don't are left behind. Our goal is to simplify the entire learning experience and help every student develop the practical, real-world skills needed to be successful at work and in school. Using a combination of text, videos, interactive elements, and assessments, we begin with fundamental concepts and take learners through a systematic progression of exercises to achieve mastery.

What Key Themes Did We Follow?

We had conversations with dozens of educators at community colleges, vocational schools, and other learning environments in preparation for this textbook. We listened and adapted our learning solution to match the needs of a rapidly changing world, keeping the following common themes in mind:

Keep it about skills. Our content focus is on critical, job-ready topics and tasks, with a relentless focus on practical, real-world skills and common sense. We use step-by-step instructional design to ensure that learners stay engaged from the first chapter forward. We've retained our proven method of progressively moving learners through increasingly independent exercises to ensure mastery—an approach that has successfully developed skills for more than 25 years.

Keep it simple. Our integrated solutions create a seamless experience built on a dynamic instructional design that brings clarity to even the most challenging topics. We focus our content on the things that matter most and present it in the easiest way possible. Concise chunks of text are combined with visually engaging and interactive elements to increase understanding for all types of learners.

Keep it relevant. Fresh, original, and constantly evolving content helps educators keep pace with today's student and work environments. We reviewed every topic for relevancy and updated it where needed to offer realistic examples and projects for learners.

How Do I Use This Book?

Our comprehensive learning solution consists of a print textbook, a groundbreaking interactive ebook, and our easy-to-use eLab course management tool featuring additional learning content, such as overviews and video tutorials, and assessment content. Our interactive ebook contains learning content delivered in ways that will engage learners.

The eLab assessment solution includes Project Grader exercises for most chapters that are automatically graded by the system, in addition to clear feedback and analytics on student actions.

Included with Your Textbook Purchase

Depending on your purchase option, some or all of the following are included with your textbook:

Interactive ebook: A dynamic, engaging, and truly interactive textbook that includes elements such as videos, self-assessments, slide shows, GIFs, and other interactive features. Highlighting, taking notes, and searching for content is easy.

eLab Course Management System: A robust tool for accurate assessment, tracking of learner activity, and automated grading that includes a comprehensive set of instructor resources. eLab can be fully integrated with your LMS, making course management even easier.

Instructor resources: This course is also supported on the Labyrinth website with a comprehensive instructor support package that includes detailed lesson plans, lecture notes, PowerPoint presentations, a course syllabus, test banks, additional exercises, and more.

Student Resource Center: The exercise files that accompany this textbook can be found within eLab and in the Student Resource Center, which may be accessed from the ebook or online at:
labyrinthelab.com/office19

We're excited to share this innovative, new approach with you, and we'd love you to share your experience with us at: lablearning.com/share

Visual Conventions

This book uses visual and typographic cues to guide students through the lessons. Some of these cues are described below:

Cue Name	What It Does
`Type this text`	Text you type at the keyboard is printed in this typeface.
Action words	The important action words in exercise steps are presented in boldface.
Ribbon	Glossary terms are highlighted with a yellow background.
Note! Tip! Warning!	Tips, notes, and warnings are called out with special icons.
⚠	Videos, WebSims, and other ebook or online content are indicated by this icon.
Command→Command→ Command→Command	Commands to execute from the Ribbon are presented like this: Ribbon Tab→Command Group→Command→Subcommand.
≡ **Design→Themes→Themes** 🖼	These notes present shortcut steps for executing certain tasks.

Display Settings

Multiple factors, including screen resolution, monitor size, and window size, can affect the appearance of the Microsoft Ribbon and its buttons. In this textbook, screen captures were taken at the native (recommended) screen resolutions in Office 2019 running Windows 10, with ClearType enabled.

The Microsoft Office Specialist Exam and This Text

 This textbook has been certified and carries the ProCert Certified logo, distinguishing this courseware as a trusted and critical part of preparing for a certification exam. This solution meets all course objectives to prepare students to take the Microsoft Office Specialist (MOS) Core exam for this subject matter.

For more information on MOS certification, go to: certiport.pearsonvue.com/Certifications/Microsoft

CORE EXAM

OBJECTIVE		TEXT LOCATION
1	**Manage Documents**	
1.1	Navigate within documents	
	1.1.1 Search for text	pp. 14–15 Find and Replace *and* pp. 227–230 Advanced Find and Wildcard Characters
	1.1.2 Link to locations within documents	pp. 228–230 Bookmarks
	1.1.3 Move to specific locations and objects in documents	pp. 248–249 Creating a Table of Contents *and* pp. 226–230 Navigating Long Documents
	1.1.4 Show and hide formatting symbols and hidden text	pp. 23–24 Showing and Hiding Formatting Marks
1.2	Format documents	
	1.2.1 Set up document pages	pp. 130–131 Page Setup Options
	1.2.2 Apply style sets	pp. 192–193 Using Themes and Style Sets
	1.2.3 Insert and modify headers and footers	pp. 84–86 Inserting Headers/Footers, Comments, and Page Breaks *and* pp. 252–255 Multiple Headers and Footers
	1.2.4 Configure page background elements	pp. 137–138 Formatting the Page Background
1.3	Save and share documents	
	1.3.1 Save documents in alternative file formats	pp. 31–32 Saving Your Work in a Different Format
	1.3.2 Modify basic document properties	pp. 303–304 Document Properties and the Document Inspector *through* Controlling Document Access
	1.3.3 Modify print settings	pp. 57–58 Working with Print and Print Preview
	1.3.4 Share documents electronically	p. 7 Sharing Files via Email and with People
1.4	Inspect documents for issues	
	1.4.1 Locate and remove hidden properties and personal information	pp. 303–304 Document Properties and the Document Inspector
	1.4.2 Locate and correct accessibility issues	pp. 302–303 The Accessibility Checker
	1.4.3 Locate and correct compatibility issues	pp. 298–299 Compatibility Issues

4	Create and Manage References	
4.1	Create and manage reference elements	
	4.1.1 Insert footnotes and endnotes	pp. 88–92 Working with Footnotes, Endnotes, and Citations
	4.1.2 Modify footnote and endnote properties	pp. 88–92 Working with Footnotes, Endnotes, and Citations
	4.1.3 Create and modify bibliography citation sources	pp. 88–92 Working with Footnotes, Endnotes, and Citations
	4.1.4 Insert citations for bibliographies	pp. 88–92 Working with Footnotes, Endnotes, and Citations
4.2	Create and manage reference tables	
	4.2.1 Insert tables of contents	pp. 248–249 Creating a Table of Contents
	4.2.2 Customize tables of contents	pp. 248–249 Creating a Table of Contents *and* pp. 250–252 The Table of Contents Dialog Box
	4.2.3 Insert bibliographies	pp. 94–96 Working with Bibliographies
5	**Insert and Format Graphic Elements**	
5.1	Insert illustrations and text boxes	
	5.1.1 Insert shapes	pp. 124–126 Working with Shapes
	5.1.2 Insert pictures	pp. 128–130 Using WordArt and Inserting Pictures
	5.1.3 Insert 3D models	p. 128 Using WordArt and Inserting Pictures
	5.1.4 Insert SmartArt graphics	pp. 133–135 Working with SmartArt
	5.1.5 Insert screenshots and screen clippings	p. 18 Take a Screenshot *and* pp. 340–342 RYS W11-R1
	5.1.6 Insert text boxes	pp. 130–131 Using Text Boxes and Page Setup Options
5.2	Format illustrations and text boxes	
	5.2.1 Apply artistic effects	pp. 142–144 Artistic Effects and Wrapping Text Around a Picture
	5.2.2 Apply picture effects and picture styles	pp. 142–144 Artistic Effects and Wrapping Text Around a Picture
	5.2.3 Remove picture backgrounds	pp. 128–130 Using WordArt and Inserting Pictures
	5.2.4 Format graphic elements	pp. 128–130 Using WordArt and Inserting Pictures
	5.2.5 Format SmartArt graphics	pp. 133–135 Working with SmartArt
	5.2.6 Format 3D models	pp. 128–130 Using WordArt and Inserting Pictures
5.3	Add text to graphic elements	
	5.3.1 Add and modify text in text boxes	pp. 130–133 Using Text Boxes and Page Setup Options
	5.3.2 Add and modify text in shapes	p. 127 Adding Text and Formatting Shapes
	5.3.3 Add and modify SmartArt graphic content	pp. 133–137 Working with SmartArt
5.4	Modify graphic elements	
	5.4.1 Position objects	pp. 124–126 Inserting, Resizing, and Moving Shapes
	5.4.2 Wrap text around objects	pp. 142–144 Artistic Effects and Wrapping Text Around a Picture
	5.4.3 Add alternative text to objects for accessibility	pp. 336–338 Accessibility

6	**Manage Document Collaboration**	
6.1	Add and manage comments	
	6.1.1 Add comments	pp. 84–86 Inserting Headers/Footers, Comments, and Page Breaks
	6.1.2 Review and reply to comments	pp. 84–86 Inserting Headers/Footers, Comments, and Page Breaks
	6.1.3 Resolve comments	pp. 84–86 Inserting Headers/Footers, Comments, and Page Breaks
	6.1.4 Delete comments	pp. 84–86 Inserting Headers/Footers, Comments, and Page Breaks *and* pp. 316–317 RYS W10-R2
6.2	Manage change tracking	
	6.2.1 Track changes	pp. 275–278 Tracking Changes to a Document
	6.2.2 Review tracked changes	pp. 279–281 Reviewing Tracked Changes
	6.2.3 Accept and reject tracked changes	pp. 279–281 Reviewing Tracked Changes
	6.2.4 Lock and unlock change tracking	pp. 279–281 Reviewing Tracked Changes

EXPERT EXAM

OBJECTIVE	**TEXT LOCATION**
1 Manage Document Options and Settings	
1.1 Manage documents and templates	
1.1.1 Modify existing document templates	pp. 205–206 DYS W6-D7
1.1.2 Manage document versions	pp. 6–7 Saving Files
1.1.3 Compare and combine multiple documents	pp. 283–284 DYS W9-D6 *and* pp. 285–286 Comparing Documents
1.1.4 Link to external document content	pp. 374–378 Embedding and Linking Excel Objects
1.1.5 Enable macros in a document	pp. 355–357 Automating Tasks with Macros
1.1.6 Customize the Quick Access toolbar	p. 4 The Quick Access Toolbar *and* pp. 358–359 Running Macros from the Quick Access Toolbar
1.1.7 Display hidden Ribbon tabs	pp. 350–355 Preparing to Add Content Controls
1.1.8 Change the Normal template default font	pp. 207–208 Customizing the Default Font
1.2 Prepare documents for collaboration	
1.2.1 Restrict editing	pp. 304–305 Restrict Editing
1.2.2 Protect documents by using passwords	pp. 308–309 Passwords and Encryption
1.3 Use and configure language options	
1.3.1 Configure editing and display languages	pp. 338–339 Global Content Standards and Language Options
1.3.2 Use language-specific features	pp. 338–339 Global Content Standards and Language Options

Acknowledgements

Many individuals contribute to the development and completion of a textbook. We appreciate the careful attention and informed contributions of Jane Bauer of Northcentral Technical College, Deb Pheris Blencowe of Collin College, Marcio de Paula Wai of Martinez Adult School, Kimberly Duffey of North County Community College, Tracy Foreman of Huntington Beach Adult School, Lynne Kemp of North County Community College, Olivia Kerr of El Centro College, Theresa Loftis of San Bernardino Adult School, Nataliya O'Neil of North County Community College, Suzanne Wright of Francis Tuttle Technology Center, and Claudia Young of Ventura Adult School, for their assistance in the development of this book.

We are also deeply grateful to the instructors and professionals who reviewed the text and suggested improvements for this first edition.

This book has benefited significantly from the feedback and suggestions of the following reviewers:

Jessica Akers, *Tennessee College of Applied Technology*

Vickie Baldwin, *Piedmont Technical College*

Colleen Barela, *Hacienda La Puente USD*

Elaine Beam, *Lehigh Career & Technical Institute*

Dixie Becker, *Reading Area Community College*

Bentley Beckles, *Advantage Caribbean Institute*

DeAnne Bowersock, *Ohio Business College*

Gary Brown, *Western Technical College*

Brenda Bryant, *the gayle group*

Jason Clawson, *Goodwill of the Olympic and Rainier Region*

Kristine Condon, *Kankakee Community College*

George Coss, *Macomb Community College*

Elaine Davis, *Carroll Community College*

Dolores Dominguez, *Beckfield College*

Kevin Edwards, *CALC Institute of Technology*

Debra Farrelly, *El Paso Community College*

Janet Fisher, *Delaware Technical Community College*

Bethany Flanagan, *Winston County Board of Education*

Taryn Fletcher, *Eastern Washington University*

Joyce Hill, *Mississippi Band of Choctaw Indians*

David Hoffmeier, *Gordon Cooper Technology Center*

Terri Holly, *Indian River State College*

Tony Hunnicutt, *College of the Ouachitas*

Judy Hurtt, *East Central Community College*

Kyle Kelly, *Lake Michigan College*

Grace Laphan, *Rowan College at Burlington County*

Gabriele Lenga, *Truckee Meadows Community College*

Helane Littles, *Brooklyn Educational Opportunity Center*

Dan Luna, *John A. Rowland High School*

Kim Mapes, *Lackawanna College Towanda Center*

William Mathis, *CollegeAmerica-Denver*

Cynthia Moody-Paige, *Erwin Technical Center*

Tamar Mosley, *Meridian Community College*

Nancy Nibley, *Simi Institute for Careers and Education*

Tatyana Pashnyak, *ABAC-Bainbridge*

Mary Peterhans, *Elgin Community College*

Tom Rose, *Kellogg Community College*

Samuel Said, *Volunteer State Community College*

Alva Santiago, *Workforce Computer Training*

Theresa Savarese, *San Diego City College*

Arthur Schneider, *Portland Community College*

Albert Spencer, *North Salinas High School*

Pamela Taylor, *Los Angeles Unified School District/L. A. High School*

Karen Tuecke, *Northeast Iowa Community College*

Raji Visvanathan, *Freemont Union High School District - Adult School*

Laura Way, *Fortis College*

Jim West, *Computer Systems Institute*

Alexis Wilcox, *Sandusky Career Center*

Claudia Young, *Ventura Adult and Continuing Education*

Peter Young, *San Jose State University*

1 Introducing Microsoft Office and Using Common Features

I n this chapter, you will be introduced to Microsoft Office and given an overview of the various versions of the software. Understanding what is offered in each will help you make the best decision about which version meets your needs. You'll also practice using some of the features that are common across the Office suite. Once you learn how to use a feature in one application, you can use the same or similar steps in the others.

LEARNING OBJECTIVES

▹ Describe similarities and differences between Office 2019 for the desktop, Office 365, and Office Online

▹ Identify uses of cloud storage

▹ Identify parts of the Office user interface

▹ Use the spelling checker and other review features

▹ Identify Office features available through Backstage view

▹ Use the Office Clipboard

▹ Format text in Office applications

▹ Search for Help within Office applications

▹ Capture a screen in an Office application

Introduction to Microsoft Office

Microsoft Office is a software suite that enables users to create, format, revise, collaborate, and share files quickly across multiple devices. The Microsoft Office 2019 software suite for Windows includes Word, Excel, Access, PowerPoint, Outlook, OneNote, Publisher, and Skype. A software suite is a collection of applications generally produced by the same manufacturer and bundled together for a better price. Being produced by the same manufacturer also means that each application offers the same user interface. Examples of features shared among the different Office 2019 apps are the Ribbon, Quick Access toolbar, a spelling and/or grammar checker, and collaboration tools.

What Devices Will Microsoft Office Work With?

Microsoft Office works on desktops, laptops/notebook computers, and all-in-one PCs and Macs, as well as Windows, Android, and iOS smartphones and tablets (though some apps, like Publisher and Access, work only on PCs).

If you are writing a paper or preparing a business plan, you probably want to create it on a desktop, laptop, or all-in-one computer. If you want to open, read, share, or make simple changes to a Word document, you could select any device. This chapter assumes you will be using a desktop, laptop, or all-in-one computer.

To learn more about the operating systems (Windows, Android, macOS, or iOS) and types of devices (all-in-one computer, desktop, laptop, smartphone, or tablet) that will run Microsoft Office, do a web search for *Microsoft Office 2019 products*.

What Storage Does Microsoft Office Provide?

Microsoft OneDrive is the cloud storage location included with Microsoft Office 2019 and Office 365, and it provides a convenient way to save, store, and share files, photos, and videos via your computer, smartphone, or tablet anytime, anywhere, and on any device—provided you have an Internet connection or Wi-Fi access. Depending on the Microsoft Office product you use or purchase, you will receive anywhere from five gigabytes to five terabytes of OneDrive cloud storage.

You may want to use cloud storage as your primary saving method so you can access your files at home, at school, at work, or anywhere. Or you may decide to use cloud storage as a backup for your files located on your computer's hard drive or your flash drive. Instead of emailing files to yourself, use OneDrive as a faster way to store something in the cloud. To learn more about OneDrive, do a web search for *OneDrive*.

Which Microsoft Office Should I Use?

You may have heard others talk about Microsoft Office 2019, Office 365, and Office Online and are not sure which one is right for you. Base your decision on the apps and features you need, in addition to the pricing structure.

▸ **Office Online:** This version is free and requires a Microsoft account. It includes limited versions of Word, Excel, PowerPoint, and OneNote. No software is installed on your computer, as the apps are accessed and run in a web browser. The apps are not the same as the full-version apps in the other variations of Office and lack many features of those full versions. This version requires an Internet connection. Office Online is great for simple tasks, like writing a short letter or creating a basic slide show presentation.

- **Microsoft Office 2019:** This version is software that is purchased once and installed on one PC. It does not require an Internet connection to run. It does not have all the features of Office 365, and you must pay for future major upgrades. Choose from a variety of plans that may include Word, Excel, PowerPoint, OneNote, Outlook, Publisher, Access, and Skype.

- **Office 365:** This version requires users to pay a monthly or annual subscription fee for installing and using the software on one or more devices (PC/Mac and mobile devices). All upgrades are included, so you always have the latest-and-greatest version, and all Office 2019 apps are included. Microsoft says the Office 365 apps can include features not present in the Office 2019 apps, as Office 365 is updated more frequently than Microsoft Office.

While Microsoft Office has three distinct formats—Microsoft Office 2019, Office 365, and Office Online—and the examples provided in this chapter can work in each of the Office formats, this book assumes you are using Office 2019 on the desktop or Office 365 in a subscription-based plan, as well as Windows 10. Remember that Office 365 can change at any time. If you are using Office 365, keep in mind that your screen may not match all the illustrations in this book. Changes made to Office 365 after publication of this title may result in additional differences between your book and the software.

What Are the Microsoft Office Apps?

In this chapter, you will learn about four of the Microsoft Office applications included in the Microsoft Office suite: Word, Excel, Access, and PowerPoint.

Application	What It Is Used For
Word	Word-processing software used to create, edit, format, and share documents, such as letters, reports, essays, and business plans.
Excel	Spreadsheet software, arranged with rows and columns, used to perform calculations and analyze numerical data. Use Excel to prepare a budget or income statement, or to determine the amount of interest paid on a loan.
Access	Database software that stores and helps you quickly retrieve data. In Access, you create and enter data into a table and then use forms, reports, and queries to display the desired results.
PowerPoint	Presentation software used to create, edit, format, and share slides designed to tell a story; market a product; or explain a concept.

The Microsoft Office suite includes the following additional applications:

Application	What It Is Used For
OneNote	Note-taking software used to organize notes (handwritten or typed), audio recordings, screen captures, or sketches you have collected or created to share with others.
Outlook	Personal information management software used to create, send, and receive emails, record tasks, maintain one or more calendars, schedule meetings and appointments, manage contacts, and take notes.
Publisher	Desktop-publishing software used to design and lay out text and images, often for newsletters or brochures.
Skype	Internet communication software used to share audio, video, text, messages, files, or desktop screens.

Microsoft Accounts

A Microsoft account provides you with access to your Microsoft settings, files, contacts, and more. A valid Microsoft account can include Hotmail, Bing, MSN, Office, OneDrive, Outlook.com, Skype, Store, Windows, or Xbox Live. Once logged in to your computer, you can log in to your Microsoft account from any Office app. If you do not have a Microsoft account, you can create one for free by doing a web search for *Microsoft account*.

Common Features in Microsoft Office Apps

The Office 2019 applications share some frequently used features. These include the Ribbon, Quick Access toolbar, and common commands.

The Ribbon

Within each application, you will find the Ribbon displayed along the top of the window. The Ribbon contains tabs and commonly used buttons and other icons that are specific to the application. The buttons are arranged in groups within each tab. While the Ribbon changes with each application, some tabs, groups, and commands are common throughout the Microsoft suite. In this chapter, we will look at the Word Ribbon and, specifically, the Home, Insert, Design, Layout, References, Mailings, Review, and View tabs.

(!) View the video "Ribbon Overview."

The Quick Access Toolbar

Each application has a one-line Quick Access toolbar located, by default, in the top-left corner of the application window. This helpful toolbar contains some frequently used commands to help you be more efficient as you work. You can customize the toolbar with the buttons you use most frequently. The settings for each application's Quick Access toolbar work independently; therefore, you need to customize the Word, Excel, Access, PowerPoint, and Outlook Quick Access toolbars separately.

(!) View the video "Quick Access Toolbar Overview."

Undo/Redo

Within any application, you may type text or perform a command or action and then change your mind about what you did. As long as you have not exited the application, you may be able to undo the action.

 Some actions, such as saving or sharing, cannot be undone.

You may want to redo an action you just undid. Sounds confusing, right? Use the Redo button to undo the undo, or to reapply the action. This puts the command or action you just undid back into effect.

Undo and Redo on the Quick Access toolbar

 Quick Access toolbar→Undo 🔄 *or* Redo ↪

DEVELOP YOUR SKILLS: O1-D1

In this exercise, you will use the Undo and Redo buttons.

1. Log in to your computer, start Word, and tap [Enter] to accept the default template, Blank Document.

2. Type the following and then tap [Enter]: **My favorite word-processing feature is inserting citations.**

3. Now, type this text: **I also like how the Quick Access toolbar can be customized with buttons I frequently use.**

4. Drag with the mouse pointer over the phrase **Quick Access toolbar** to select it.

5. Choose **Home→Font→Bold** B to apply bold formatting.

6. Now apply **Italic** I formatting to the phrase *inserting citations*.

7. Follow these steps to undo more than one action at a time:

Ⓐ Click the **Undo menu** button ▾.

Ⓑ Point to the second step, *Bold*, to select it and everything above it, and then click the mouse button.

8. Click the **Redo** ↻ button two times to reapply the bold and italic formatting to the phrases.

9. Click the **Undo** � button once to remove the italic formatting from the first sentence.

10. Keep Word open.

Unless otherwise directed, always keep any files or programs open at the end of an exercise.

Common Features on the File Tab

In this section, you will learn about the features on the File tab that are used in a similar manner throughout multiple Microsoft applications, including Word, Excel, and PowerPoint. Here you will use Microsoft Word 2019 to save, close, share, and print a file, and to open a template.

Backstage View

When you are working in your file and open the File tab, the Backstage view displays. Think of your Backstage view as your personal manager for the open file and application. Use the Backstage view to update file information, select account settings, view program options, open new files, save, print, share, export, provide feedback to Microsoft, and recover unsaved files. These are the "big-picture" items you do to your file and not the specific tasks you perform using the other tabs on the Ribbon.

Program Options

Microsoft provides preference settings that you can customize for each application (that is, Word or Excel) so they are automatically applied each time you use the application on your device. To change your preferences, use the Options feature on the File tab. Some custom options include adding your username and initials so they automatically display in some downloaded templates, displaying formatting marks, correcting spelling, and saving files to a default file location.

Word Options

General	
Display	**Customize how documents are saved.**
Proofing	
Save	**Save documents**
Language	Save files in this format: Word Document (*.docx) ▼
Advanced	☑ Save AutoRecover information every 10 ⬍ minutes
	☑ Keep the last autosaved version if I close without saving

The Save options allow you to set defaults for the file format and the frequency with which documents are automatically saved.

≡ File→Options

Saving Files

As you work in your file, you should save frequently to prevent data or information loss. Some people prefer to save important files every few minutes, while others save at less frequent intervals.

The saving commands are found on the File tab, and you'll see different options, including Save and Save As. You can use the Save command the first time you save a file, and when you do, the Save As screen will appear.

 Word can automatically save your file as you work. Toggle this feature on/off using the AutoSave button just to the left of the Quick Access toolbar.

 View the video "Using Save and Save As."

You may choose to save files to your device (for example, on the hard drive in the Documents folder), to your flash drive, or to the cloud in OneDrive.

View the video "Saving Files to Multiple Locations."

You can even set Word to save your work automatically whenever a specific interval of time has elapsed. A good rule of thumb is to save as often as you can afford to lose data. If you can only afford to lose one minute of data, save your file every minute!

≡ File→Save *or* Save As

DEVELOP YOUR SKILLS: O1-D2

In this exercise, you will use Save As to store a Word document in a new folder.

Before You Begin: *Download the student exercise files from your eLab course or the Student Resource Center (labyrinthelab.com/office19) and determine your file storage location before beginning this exercise.*

1. In your open Word document, choose **File** to display the Backstage view and then click **Save**.

   The first time you save a file, the Save As screen displays. Otherwise, choosing File→Save updates the file with the same name, location, and file type.

2. Click the **Browse** button and navigate to the **Overview** folder in your file storage location.

3. In the Save As dialog box, click the **New Folder** button.

   The New Folder button is to the right of the Organize button, just under the address bar.

4. Type **My Overview Files** for the new folder name and tap Enter twice.

5. Click in the **File Name** box and type: **01-D2-Features**

6. Verify that *Word Document* displays for Save as Type and click the **Save** button.

   If the Save As Type box displays something else, click the arrow at the right end of the box and select Word Document.

7. Close the file.

Finding, Searching, and Opening Files

Files can be opened within an application by using the Open dialog box, choosing from a recently saved files list within the application, using File Explorer, or typing the filename in the Windows Search box. Within Windows 10, as well as previous versions of Windows, you can use File Explorer to locate and manage your files. Located on the taskbar, you can click the File Explorer icon and then search for files located on your PC, flash drive, or OneDrive.

 View the video "Opening Files."

Sharing Files via Email and with People

You can share open files directly from the application to either email or OneDrive. Sharing a file directly to email is usually faster than opening an email application, such as Microsoft Outlook, locating the file to send, and then attaching it. When someone shares a file with you from an application to OneDrive, you will receive a link (in your email account) to access the file.

View the video "Sharing Files via Email."

If the Automatically Share Changes option is set to Always, once the file is shared, anyone who has editing rights to the file can make changes to it.

Tip! *You can also use the Share* ⏷ Share *button located in the top-right corner of the application window.*

☰ File→Share→Email 🖳

☰ File→Share→Share with People 👥

DEVELOP YOUR SKILLS: 01-D3

Complete this exercise via the online WebSim.

In this exercise, you will share an open Word file by using the Share with People option that saves to the cloud.

1. In your web browser, go to: **labyrinthelab.com/websims/W19-00-D3**

   If your classroom is using eLab, you can complete this exercise in your eLab course.

2. Follow the onscreen instructions to complete this exercise.

Printing

If you are connected and have access to a printer, you should be able to print. Before printing, you should save your file, run Spelling & Grammar (Word) or Spelling (Excel and PowerPoint), proofread your file, verify formats, and review the file to see if you have used the fewest possible number of pages. Use the Print Preview feature to browse the pages in your document prior to printing so you don't waste time or printing resources and use the options in the Settings area to adjust elements such as page orientation, paper size, margins, and more.

Keep in mind that you can print to paper or to PDF if you want to be eco-friendly.

View the video "Printing Files."

☰ File→Print

Templates

A template is a document, worksheet, or presentation that has the fonts, paragraph styles, and page layout settings such as margins, orientation, and size already built in. Instead of selecting these settings each time you prepare a similar file, you may opt to use a template to save time when you need to add new text, images, and additional formats specific to the file.

Usually an application includes sample templates that are stored on the hard drive of your computer when you install the software. You can also search for online templates using the Search feature available in the New tab of the Backstage view. Templates are arranged according to categories; for example, by business, personal, and industry.

☰ File→New

DEVELOP YOUR SKILLS: O1-D4

In this exercise, you will open a prebuilt Word template.

1. Choose **File→New**, search for and select the **APA Style Report (6th Edition)** template, and click **Create**.

   Scroll through the Word document to view the types and formats of items that you may want to include in your report.

2. Choose **File→New**, search for and select the **Resume (Color)** template, and click **Create**.

   You may have to scroll down to find the template. Review the document to locate what is automatically filled in based on the Word Options settings, as well as text placeholders that request your input.

3. Choose **File→New** and then search for and select the **Welcome to Word** template or another template of your choice.

   Notice the document formatting and review the text contained in the file.

4. Close all open files without saving and leave Word open for the next exercise.

Common Features on the Home Tab

In this section, you will learn about the features on the Home tab that are used in a similar manner throughout multiple Microsoft applications, including Word, Excel, and PowerPoint. You will use Microsoft Word to Cut, Copy, and Paste with the Office Clipboard, format text, use the Mini toolbar, and find and replace text.

DEVELOP YOUR SKILLS: O1-D5

In this exercise, you will open a file created from a Word template and become familiar with Word.

1. Start Word and click the **Open Other Documents** link under the Recent menu at the left side of the window.

2. Click the **Browse** button, navigate to the **Overview** folder in your file storage location, and open the **O1-D5-Clipboard** file.

3. Click **Enable Editing** in the Protected View bar at the top of the screen, if necessary.

   The Security Warning bar may display the first time you open a file. If you know the file sender and trust the content, open the file.

4. Scroll down to display the bottom of the document and then scroll back up to the top.

5. Scroll down to section 1 at the top of page 2. Click anywhere in the paragraph below the section 1 header to place your insertion point.

> ### 1. Use live layout and alignment guides
>
> Click the image below and drag it around the page. With images that have text wrapping, the text moves around the picture so you get a live preview of the new layout. Try to line the image up with the top of this paragraph to see how the alignment guides can help you position it on the page. Click the Layout Options button next to the image to change how it interacts with the text.

The Office Clipboard

Located at the far left on the Home tab, the Clipboard group contains the Cut, Copy, Paste, and Format Painter buttons. Selecting the Clipboard dialog box launcher opens the Clipboard pane, which displays at the side of your application. The Clipboard contains thumbnails (small images) of what you have recently cut or copied from your Microsoft Office file(s) during your Windows session, with the most recent item at the top of the list. You can use the Clipboard to quickly paste text, pictures, images, or charts into your file. You can paste all items on the Clipboard into your file(s) as many times as desired, and you can clear all items from the Clipboard.

The Cut feature in the Clipboard group functions much like a scrapbook in which you cut out information, such as newspaper articles about yourself, and then paste it on the desired page(s). When data is cut, the original selection is removed from the source location and is pasted at the target location. When data is copied, the original selection remains in the source location and a new selection is pasted at the target location.

View the video "Clipboard Overview."

CLIPBOARD FEATURES

Feature	What It Does
Cut ✂	**Cut:** Removes the original selection from the source location and places the selection on the Office Clipboard.
Copy 🖹	**Copy:** Creates a duplicate of the original selection, which remains in the source location, and places a copy of the selection on the Office Clipboard.
Paste 📋	**Paste:** Inserts a copy of the most recent item found on the Office Clipboard at the target location, or destination. Depending on the application, there are usually at least three paste choices: Keep Source Formatting, Merge Formatting, and Keep Text Only. **Keep Source Formatting:** Pastes the text and the formatting (bold, italic, underline) of the selection from the source location to the target location. The selection pasted retains the original formatting from the source location. **Merge Formatting:** Pastes the text and formatting (bold, italic, underline) of the selection from the source location to the target location and combines it with any formatting that is already at the target location. The selection pasted has formats from both the source and target locations. **Keep Text Only:** Pastes the selection from the source location to the target location. The selection pasted takes on the formatting of the target location.
Format Painter 🖌	**Format Painter:** Applies the character and paragraph formatting from the source selection to any characters or text selected. Double-click the Format Painter to apply formats to multiple selections. Click the Format Painter button or tap Esc to turn it off when you are finished.

≡ Home→Clipboard→Cut ✂ | Ctrl + X

≡ Home→Clipboard→Copy 🖹 | Ctrl + C

≡ Home→Clipboard→Paste 📋 | Ctrl + V

DEVELOP YOUR SKILLS: O1-D6

In this exercise, you will use Word to copy text from the source destination to the target destination (another area of the document) and cut data from its original location and paste it into the target location.

To begin, you will navigate to the desired location in the document and find the text to be copied. Depending on the size of your monitor, you may or may not need to scroll.

1. Follow these steps to select a specific section of text in the first paragraph:

> **A**
>
> Click the image below and drag it around the page. With images that have text wrapping, the text moves around the picture so you get a live preview of the new layout. Try to line the image up with the top of this paragraph to see how the alignment guides can help you position it on the page. Click the Layout Options button next to the image to change how it interacts with the **B**

    A Click to place the insertion point just before the word *With*.

    B Press and hold the ⟨Shift⟩ key and click just after the period of the sentence ending with *page*.

2. Release ⟨Shift⟩ and notice that the entire section between both clicks is selected.

> Click the image below and drag it around the page. With images that have text wrapping, the text moves around the picture so you get a live preview of the new layout. Try to line the image up with the top of this paragraph to see how the alignment guides can help you position it on the page. Click the Layout Options button next to the image to change how it interacts with the text.

3. Choose **Home→Clipboard→Copy** .

The copied text is placed on the Office Clipboard and is ready to be pasted in a destination location. The copied text also remains in its original location.

4. Scroll down to section 3 at the bottom of the page and place the insertion point at the end of the paragraph.

> ## 3. Insert Online Pictures and Video
>
> Add and play online videos inside your Word documents. Add your pictures from online photo services without having to save them first to your computer. Click **Insert > Online Video** to add a video to this document.|

5. Choose **Home→Clipboard→Paste** to place the copied text.

Cut and Paste

6. Scroll down to section 4 and select the **first sentence**, making sure to include the period at the end.

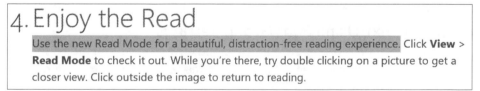

7. Choose **Home→Clipboard→Cut** ✂.

8. Place the insertion point at the end of the section 4 paragraph, after the period.

9. Choose **Home→Clipboard→Paste** 📋.

10. Choose **File→Save As** to save the file in your **My Overview Files** folder as: `O1-D6-Clipboard`

Drag and Drop

If you want to cut or copy text and then paste it in a different location on the same page, try using drag and drop. Whether you want to cut or copy text, the first step is always to select the desired text. The difference between cutting and copying in this method has to do with the ⌈Ctrl⌋ key. That is, to copy, you hold down ⌈Ctrl⌋ while moving from one location to the next; when cutting, you do not use ⌈Ctrl⌋.

⚠ View the video "Using Drag and Drop."

DEVELOP YOUR SKILLS: O1-D7

In this exercise, you will use drag and drop in Word to cut, or move, data from one area of the document to another.

1. Choose **File→Save As** to save the worksheet in your **My Overview Files** folder as: `O1-D7-Drag`

2. If necessary, scroll until you can see items 2 and 3.

3. Hover the mouse pointer in the left margin and select the header and paragraph by clicking and dragging from the level of the header down to the level of the last line of the paragraph.

> 3. Insert Online Pictures and Video
>
> Add and play online videos inside your Word documents. Add your pictures from online photo services without having to save them first to your computer. Click **Insert > Online Video** to add a video to this document. With images that have text wrapping, the text moves around the picture so you get a live preview of the new layout. Try to line the image up with the top of this paragraph to see how the alignment guides can help you position it on the page.

4. Hover the mouse in the selected area and then click and hold the mouse button, drag it up to the beginning of the header in section 2 before the word *Collaborate*, and then release it.

   Using drag and drop to cut removes the selected text from the original location and pastes it in the new location. Notice also that the header numbering changes as well.

5. Choose **File→Save** to save your changes.

Formatting Text Using Font Group Settings

To make your selection more visibly appealing and easy to read, you may want to use some or all of the font formats available in the Font group or in the Font dialog box. To apply the formats, you must first select a word or group of words.

Use the Font dialog box launcher to open the Font dialog box.

The Format Painter applies formats found in one piece of text to another piece of text within the application. Think of the selected text's original location as your paint can. You apply the formats found in your paint can to another piece of text with the help of the paintbrush, or Format Painter. Whatever text you click gets the formatting. You can use Format Painter to format multiple pieces of text by double-clicking the Format Painter button. To turn off the multiple-use feature and stop "painting," tap the Esc key.

DEVELOP YOUR SKILLS: O1-D8

In this exercise, you will increase the font size, make text bold, remove the bold, change the font color, launch the Font dialog box, and use the Format Painter.

1. Use **Save As** to save the worksheet in the **My Overview Files** folder as: **O1-D8-Format**
2. Scroll to section 1 and select the text **Layout Options** in the fourth line.
3. Choose **Home→Font→Increase Font Size** A‸ two times to increase the font size of the selection to 14 points.
4. Choose **Home→Font→Bold** B.

   Bold is used to add emphasis to text. When a format such as bold is applied, the button on the Ribbon displays a dark-gray background. To turn the format off and remove the dark-gray background behind the button, click the button again. This is known as a toggle *format.*

5. With the **Layout Options** text still selected, choose **Home→Font→Font Color** A menu **button** ▾ and then select **Red** under Standard Colors.
6. Click the **dialog box launcher** at the bottom-right corner of the Font group on the Home tab to open the Font dialog box.
7. Select the **Small Caps** setting under Effects and click **OK**.
8. With Layout Options still selected, choose **Home→Clipboard→Format Painter** .
9. In section 2, select the text **Insert→Online Video** starting at the end of line 2 and going into line 3.

   Notice that the font size, small caps, red font, and bold formatting applied to the piece of text in section 1 are now applied to the piece of text chosen in section 2.

10. Place the insertion point anywhere within the two pieces of text that now have the custom formatting applied and double-click the **Format Painter**.
11. In section 3, select the text **Simple Markup** in the first line.
12. In section 4, select the text **View→Read Mode** in the first line.

    The custom formatting is now applied to pieces of text in sections 1, 2, 3, and 4.

13. Tap the Esc key to toggle the Format Painter off.
14. Save the file.

The Mini Toolbar

The Mini toolbar is a floating toolbar that contains some of the more commonly used formatting buttons found on the Home tab and specific to the application. The Mini toolbar appears at various times in all the Office applications, giving you a convenient way to choose the most commonly used commands. If the Mini toolbar does not display, right-click the mouse.

The Mini toolbar in Word (left) and Excel (right)

File→Options→General→check Show Mini Toolbar on Selection

DEVELOP YOUR SKILLS: O1-D9

In this exercise, you will use the Mini toolbar in Word to apply formatting.

1. Use **Save As** to save the worksheet in the **My Overview Files** folder as: **O1-D9-Toolbar**
2. Scroll to section 1 and select **Click**, the first word in the paragraph.
3. Hold Ctrl and then select the word **drag** a few words later in the first line; then release Ctrl. *Notice that both nonadjacent words are now highlighted.*
4. If the Mini toolbar is not already showing, right-click either of the selected words to display the Mini toolbar as well as the context, or shortcut, menu.
5. In the Mini toolbar or on the Ribbon, click the **Bold B** button.
6. On the Ribbon, select **Home→Font→Font Color A menu button ▼** and select **Green** under the Standard Colors row.
7. Click anywhere else in the document to close the Mini toolbar.
8. Save the file.

Find and Replace

Within a document, worksheet, database, or presentation, you may need to locate text quickly. You may also need to substitute one word or phrase, or formatting, for something else. The Find command is used to search for characters, symbols, numbers, words, phrases, or formats that meet the criteria. The Replace command first finds whatever meets the criteria and then replaces it with what you desire.

DEVELOP YOUR SKILLS: O1-D10

In this exercise, you will use the Find command to locate the word page and then replace each occurrence with document.

1. Use **Save As** to save the worksheet in the **My Overview Files** folder as: **O1-D10-Replace**
2. Choose **Home→Editing→Replace**.
3. Type **page** in the Find What box.

4. Click **Find Next** two times.

   The first click finds the first occurrence. The second click finds the next occurrence.

5. Type **document** in the Replace With box.

6. Click **Replace All** to change all three occurrences of the word *page* to *document*.

7. Click **OK** in the Microsoft Word message box.

8. Close the Find and Replace box.

9. Save your file and then close Word.

Common Features on the Review Tab

In this section, you will learn about the features on the Review tab that are used in a similar manner throughout multiple Microsoft applications, including Word, Excel, Access, and PowerPoint. You will work with Microsoft Word to use the Spelling and Thesaurus features.

Spelling & Grammar

Whether you are working in a Word document, an Excel worksheet, an Access database, or a Power-Point presentation, you should use the Spelling & Grammar button before you share the file with anyone. The Spelling feature reviews the file for misspelled words or words that do not match the Microsoft dictionary for that computer. A red, squiggly line below a word indicates that the word is not recognized in the Dictionary file on your computer. Right-click the unrecognized word and choose the correct spelling from the context menu or add the word to the Dictionary.

DEVELOP YOUR SKILLS: O1-D11

In this exercise, you will open Word, create a new document, and use the Spelling feature.

1. Start Word, locate and select the **Welcome to Word** template, and then choose **Create** to open the document. If the help panel appears on the right side of the screen, close it.

2. Preview the document by using the scroll bar to scroll up and down.

3. At the top of the document, click at the end of the word *Welcome*.

4. Tap ⌷Backspace⌷ two times and type: **em**

5. Click anywhere in the text below the first line.

   Notice the misspelling of Welcome *displays with a red, squiggly line below it.*

6. Right-click the misspelled word and choose **Welcome** from the context menu to correct the spelling.

7. Place the insertion point at the beginning of the first paragraph, before the word *Unlike*.

   instructions you

   |Unlike old-school user guides
   teach you some basics about
   so you can learn by doing.

8. Type **Parctice makes prefect** and tap ⌷Enter⌷.

   Yes, you are deliberately typing misspelled words so you will have a document that can be spellchecked in the next few steps!

9. Type **Mispllings are notticable** and tap ☐Enter☐ again.

10. Place the insertion point at the top of the document, before the word *Welcome*. Choose **Review→Proofing→Spelling & Grammar** ✅ to launch the Spelling pane at the right of the screen.

11. Click the correct spelling of **Practice**. Be sure to select the capitalized version of the word.

    The spell checker will automatically jump to the next misspelled word.

Suggestions	
Practice Repetition, Habit, Perform	⌄
practice repetition, habit, perform	⌄

12. Continue correcting two more misspelled words (*Misspellings* and *noticeable*). For the remaining entries, continue clicking **Ignore All** until the spellcheck is complete and then click **OK** in the Microsoft Word message box.

13. Scroll back to the top of the document, double-click **prefect**, and type: **perfect**

    Since prefect *is a word, it was not identified as a misspelled word when running the spelling checker. You must remember to proofread your work!*

14. Use **Save As** to save the file to the **My Overview Files** folder as: **O1-D11-Word**

Thesaurus

There are times when you end up using a word over and over and over again! Instead of using the same word, you could use a synonym. The Thesaurus provides definitions, word forms, synonyms (words with similar meanings), antonyms (words that are opposite in meaning), and word forms in other languages when dictionaries of other languages are installed on your computer.

DEVELOP YOUR SKILLS: O1-D12

In this exercise, you will use the Thesaurus feature in Word to replace a word with one of its synonyms.

1. If necessary, scroll to the top of the page and place the insertion point anywhere inside the word **edit** in the second line.

2. Choose **Review→Proofing→Thesaurus** 📖.

3. At the right side of the window, in the Thesaurus pane, click **revise** to see a list of synonyms for that word.

4. In the Thesaurus pane, hover the mouse pointer over the word *modify*, click the **menu** button ▾, and then choose **Insert** to replace *edit* with *modify*.

5. Close the Thesaurus pane.

6. Use **Save As** to save the file to the **My Overview Files** folder as: `01-D12-Proofing`

Other Common Features

In the preceding exercises you learned about features found on multiple programs' Ribbons. Here are three additional common features that are available no matter what Ribbon is displayed in Microsoft Office.

Help

When you are working in Microsoft Office, you may need to find out more about a topic as it relates to the application. Located to the right of the last tab on the Ribbon is the *Tell Me What You Want to Do* box. This box provides a quick way to access help or learn more about a feature in the application. When you click the box, suggestions related to the application display. Use the text box to enter words or phrases describing what you would like to do or locate next in the application. You can use the Tell Me... box to research or explain the meaning of a term with Smart Lookup. To view a list of Help topics, tap the ⌑F1⌑ function key on the keyboard.

Another Help feature is the *Tell Me More* link that may display at the bottom of a button's help tip. When you click the link, the Help window displays with more information about the specific feature. Using this method, you learn more about the feature without typing any search text.

Some buttons display robust help tips with a *Tell Me More* link when you point to them.

Smart Lookup with the Insights Pane

Smart Lookup is available within an application on the context menu. In the Insights pane, you can view and listen to pronunciations, look at word forms and definitions of selected text, and view results of wikis and web searches related to your selected text. Using the Smart Lookup feature can be especially helpful, as it saves you the time of having to retype the same selection in your search engine.

Take a Screenshot

The Take a Screenshot button is used when you want to remain in your Word, Excel, PowerPoint, or Outlook application while capturing a screenshot of the entire window or part of a window. In PowerPoint, once the screenshot is captured, it is temporarily placed as a thumbnail in the Available Windows gallery located with the Take a Screenshot button in your open application. If you open another application, such as Word, the thumbnail displays in the Available Windows gallery. Once you close the PowerPoint application, the screenshot will no longer display in the Available Windows gallery in Word.

DEVELOP YOUR SKILLS: O1-D13

In this exercise, you will use the Tell Me More help link and the Tell Me What You Want to Do box to learn more about the Insights feature. Then, you will use the Screenshot feature to copy what you found onto a new document.

1. Save the document in the **My Overview Files** folder as: `O1-D13-Help`
2. On the Ribbon, go to **Home→Clipboard**.
3. Point to the Format Painter button to see the name of the button, the keyboard shortcut, a description of the button, and the Tell Me More link.
4. Click the **Tell Me More** link to learn about using the Format Painter in Word; close the Help window.
5. On the Ribbon to the right of the View tab, click in the **Tell Me What You Want to Do** box and type: `Insights pane`

   💡 Tell me what you want to do

   Observe the options that Microsoft displays in the Tell Me... box.
6. From the displayed list, point to the Get Help on the "Insights Pane" option to display its suboptions.
7. Click **Get Insights into What You're Working on with Smart Lookup** or a similar option.
8. Read about the Insights pane.
9. Scroll to the bottom of the Help pane and click **Read Article in Browser**.

   Your web browser opens to the Microsoft website and displays the help page.
10. Click the **Word** button on the taskbar to return to Word.
11. Place the insertion point before the word *Practice* in the first line below the page headers, tap ⎵Enter⎵, and then tap the up ⎵↑⎵ arrow key to place your insertion point at the beginning of the blank line.
12. Choose **Insert→Illustrations→Screenshot** 📷.
13. Click **Screen Clipping** to display the browser window and then drag over a portion of the browser window to take a screenshot of it.

    You are returned to Word, and the screenshot is pasted where the insertion point had been placed.
14. Save the file and then close Word and any other open applications.

1

Creating and Editing Business Documents

I n the employment world, few skills are more valued than effective formal writing. Business-to-business communication is an essential element of the employment network; it's the oil that keeps the whole machine running. You can help further your company's goals by crafting effective business letters that are formal, succinct, and engaging. Of course, in our digital age, simply writing a letter is only half the picture; skills in digital word processing are just as critical. In this chapter, you will create and format a well-crafted business letter that is perfect for the digital age.

LEARNING OBJECTIVES

▸ Navigate in a document

▸ Enter, select, and edit text

▸ Create numbered and bulleted lists

▸ Use document views

▸ Save documents as different file types

📂 Project: Creating a Well-Formatted Business Letter

School is over, and it's time to line up some interviews. You are seeking a position in the technology field. You've scanned lots of ads and websites, and found a few job openings you're interested in. You know the hiring process will be competitive for most of these positions. To give yourself an edge, you'll need to draft a stellar cover letter—one that will get you noticed right from the start.

Elements of a Professional Business Letter

There are several acceptable styles of business letters. All business letters contain similar elements but with varied formatting. The block style, as shown in this image, is the most common business letter style.

Date: two inches from top of page but may vary based on letterhead

November 24, 2021

Inside address: two to four lines below the date

Mr. Blake Carter, Hiring Manager

Global Computer Sales and Service

347 Wellington Street

San Francisco, CA 94123

Salutation: Followed by a colon

Dear Mr. Carter:

Body

I am applying for the position of Retail Computer Sales Representative advertised on your website. I am a recent Computer Science graduate from Case Western University, where I attained a 3.9 GPA. During the summers, I worked as a sales intern at Best Computers in Cleveland. I am extremely interested in discussing your sales position, which aligns well with my education and sales experience.

My education provided me with the following technical skills that will allow me to make a positive contribution to Global Computer:

- An understanding of real-world computer needs
- An awareness of the latest technologies available
- The ability to analyze problems and apply the suitable hardware and software solutions
- Hands-on experience with a wide variety of computer equipment

My experience at Best Computers provided me with the following sales-related knowledge that would benefit Global Computer:

- Skill in using consultative sales abilities to learn about clients' needs
- Adeptness in analyzing client requirements and addressing their business issues
- Competence in clearly stating solutions and demonstrating product benefits to the client
- Proficiency in handling objections
- Ability to provide a training and implementation plan that ensures high customer satisfaction

I am impressed with your excellent products and reputation. I am confident that I am a strong candidate, and I will contact you in the near future to arrange an interview.

Complimentary close: Followed by a comma

Sincerely,

Signature

Stella Martin

📖 What's Important in a Cover Letter?

Now that you know the fundamentals of a proper business letter, you will explore the best approach to creating a cover letter that, along with your résumé, is sure to impress hiring managers. Keep the following points in mind:

▶ *Purpose:* Use a cover letter to introduce yourself and explain why you fit the job requirements.

▶ *Application Tracking System (ATS):* The first review of your application documents (cover letter and résumé) is likely to be done by an ATS software program. You may wish to conduct an Internet search to learn how best to write your documents so that they will not be overlooked by an ATS.

▶ *File Types:* Some file types work better than others relative to an ATS, and some employers may request that you submit your documents using a specific file type.

▶ *Audience Awareness:* Study the job description and conduct an online search of the company to learn as much as you can.

▶ *Beginning, Middle, and End:* Introduce yourself and include an attention grabber; highlight, but don't duplicate, outstanding points from your résumé; close the letter expressing your enthusiasm for the company and position.

▶ *Importance of Fresh Eyes:* An error in your documents could cause an employer to eliminate you. Ask friends or colleagues to proof your documents.

Navigating in a Document

If you are working in a multipage document, it's helpful to know various techniques for moving through it quickly. You can navigate using the scroll bar at the right side of the screen, or you can use keystrokes.

Navigating with the Scroll Bar

The scroll bar lets you navigate through documents; however, it does not move the insertion point. After scrolling, you must click in the document where you want to position the insertion point. There are two ways you can use the scroll bar. You can click the up and down arrows at the top and bottom of the scroll bar to scroll one line at a time, or you can drag the scroll box to move quickly through a multipage document. By clicking in the gray area above or below the scroll box, you'll be able to move up and down the document one screen at a time.

When the mouse pointer is in the text area, it resembles an uppercase "I" and is referred to as an I-beam. The insertion point is positioned at the location where you click the I-beam and it begins flashing. Wherever the insertion point is flashing is where the action begins.

☁ **View the video "Using the Scroll Bar to Navigate."**

Keyboard Navigation Tips

Whether you use the mouse or the keyboard to navigate is up to you. Navigating with the keyboard always moves the insertion point, so it will be with you when you arrive at your destination. Here are some handy keyboard navigation tips:

▶ The right and left arrow keys `→` and `←` move the insertion point one character to the right or left, while the up and down arrow keys `↑` and `↓` move the insertion point one line up or down.

▶ `Ctrl`+`End` moves to the end of the document.

▸ [Ctrl]+[Home] moves to the beginning of the document.

▸ [End] moves to the end of the line.

▸ [Home] moves to the beginning of the line.

DEVELOP YOUR SKILLS: W1-D1

In this exercise, you will use the scroll bar and keyboard to navigate in a document. When you use the scroll bar, you have to position the insertion point. When you use the keyboard, the insertion point moves with you.

1. Start Word.

2. Click the **Blank Document** template on the Word start screen.

3. Make sure the Word window is **maximized** ▣.

   Next you will open an existing document so you can practice navigating.

4. Choose **File→Open** to display the Open screen in Backstage view (which is another name for the contents of the File tab).

5. Navigate to your **Word Chapter 1** folder and open **W1-D1-MyVirtualCampus**.

6. Move the mouse pointer through the text in the body of the document and notice that it looks like an I-beam ⌶.

7. Move the mouse pointer into the left margin area and note that now the white selection arrow ⬧ is visible.

Navigate with the Scroll Bar and Keyboard

8. Click the gray area below the scroll box to move the document down one screen.

   Notice that the insertion point has not moved.

9. Move the mouse pointer back into the document text and click the **I-beam** ⌶ anywhere within the text to position the insertion point.

   The insertion point appears where you clicked. If the background is highlighted, you accidentally selected the text by double-clicking. Deselect by clicking the I-beam somewhere else within the text.

10. Drag the **scroll box** down and position the insertion point after the last period at the end of the text.

11. Drag the **scroll box** to the top of the scroll bar and position the insertion point before the word *My* at the top of the document.

12. Tap the down arrow ⬇ on your keyboard to move the insertion point down into the top line of the first paragraph.

13. Tap [End] to move the insertion point to the end of the line and then tap [Home] to move the insertion point to the beginning of the line.

14. Press [Ctrl]+[End] to move the insertion point to the end of the document.

15. Choose **File→Close**, and if you are prompted to save changes, click **Don't Save**.

The Word interface now shows a blank gray screen.

Entering Text

When you type using the keyboard, the text will appear wherever you've set the flashing insertion point. Therefore, you must position the insertion point at the desired location before typing. When you insert text, existing text moves to the right as you type. Also, text automatically wraps to the next line when you reach the right-hand margin, meaning that you do not need to tap [Enter] when you reach the end of a line. This feature is known as Word Wrap.

Using the Enter Key

You use the [Enter] key to begin a new paragraph or to insert blank lines in a document. Anything that ends by tapping [Enter] is considered to be a paragraph. Thus, short lines such as a date line, an inside address, or even blank lines themselves are considered paragraphs.

Tapping [Enter] inserts a paragraph symbol in a document. These and other symbols are visible when you show formatting marks.

Showing and Hiding Formatting Marks

Although formatting marks appear on the screen, you will not see them in the printed document. Viewing these symbols can be important when editing a document. For example, you may need to see the formatting marks to determine whether the space between two words was created with the [Spacebar] or [Tab].

Paragraph symbols appear when you tap [Enter].

```
¶
¶
Mr.·Blake·Carter,·Hiring·Manager¶
Global·Computer·Sales·and·Service¶
347·Wellington·Street¶
San·Francisco,·CA··94123¶
¶
Dear·Mr.·Carter:¶
¶
I·am·applying·for·the·position·of·Retail·Computer·Sales·
```

Dots appear between words when you tap [Spacebar].

To toggle the formatting marks on and off, you can use the Show/Hide button.

☰ Home→Paragraph→Show/Hide ¶

In this exercise, you will turn on the Show/Hide button to show formatting marks. Next you'll type a paragraph, allowing Word Wrap to end lines automatically at the right-hand margin. Then you'll use the Enter *key to end the first paragraph and start another paragraph.*

1. Choose **File→New**.
2. Click the **Blank Document** template to start a new document.
3. Choose **File→Save As** and navigate to your **Word Chapter 1** folder.
4. Name the file **W1-D2-CoverLtrTips** and then click the **Save** button at the bottom of the dialog box.
5. Choose **Home→Paragraph→Show/Hide** ¶ to show formatting marks.

   All new documents contain a paragraph symbol directly to the right of the insertion point; you won't see it if you don't turn on the Show/Hide feature. Paragraph symbols carry formatting in them. In this example, the Blank Document template formatting includes the default Calibri font and 1.08 line spacing.

 Feel free to turn the Show/Hide button on and off as needed.

6. Type the following text and let Word Wrap do its thing:

   Your cover letter may be the first impression a company has of you. You want to be certain it's a good impression. Research the company on its website before preparing a cover letter. The more you know about what a company is doing, the better you can explain how you can contribute to the company.

   If you make a typo, use Backspace *or* Delete *to remove it. Remember to position the insertion point next to the typo.*

7. Tap Enter to create a new paragraph.

   Notice the paragraph symbol ¶ *. Also notice the extra space between the end of the paragraph and the insertion point. That is due to the default line spacing of 1.08.*

8. Type the following text:

   Proofreading is critical. Errors in a cover letter will likely eliminate you. Don't go it alone. Ask others to proof your letter as well.

9. Save and close the file.

   The document window is blank once again.

Selecting Text

You must select (highlight) text if you wish to perform an action on it. Suppose you want to delete a line. You select the line first and then delete it. Whether you use the mouse or the keyboard to select text is up to you.

The most common way to select text is to click and drag the I-beam through the text you wish to select, but there are more efficient methods:

▸ To select a single word, double-click that word.

▸ To select a paragraph, triple-click it.

▸ To select a single sentence from the first letter to the period, hold Ctrl and click anywhere within the sentence.

▸ To select single lines of text, hover your mouse in the left margin and click to the left of the line you wish to select.

▸ To quickly select multiple lines, click and drag.

Note! *The Mini toolbar appears when you select text. It contains frequently used commands. You can choose a command or ignore the toolbar; if you ignore the toolbar, it will fade away.*

View the video "Selecting Text with the Mouse."

Here are some handy mouse and keyboard combinations for selecting text:

▸ Press click+ Shift +click to select awkward amounts of text, such as the end of one line and the beginning of the next. Simply click at the beginning of a text block, hold down Shift , and click at the end of the text block.

▸ Press Ctrl +click to select a sentence.

▸ Press Ctrl + A to select the entire document.

Tip! *If you're ever working with the Mac version of Microsoft Office, simply use the cmd key in place of the Ctrl key, and most of the shortcuts will work in exactly the same way.*

DEVELOP YOUR SKILLS: W1-D3

In this exercise, you will practice various selection techniques.

1. Navigate to the **Word Chapter 1** folder in your file storage location and open **W1-D3-CoverLtr**.

2. Follow these steps to select text using the left margin:

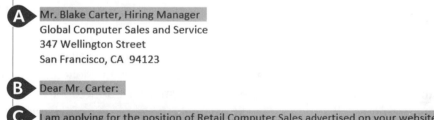

A Place the **selection arrow** in the margin to the left of the first line of the inside address; click to select the line. The Mini toolbar appears; you can ignore it for now.

B Use the **selection arrow** to select this line. (Notice that the previously selected line is no longer selected.)

C Select this paragraph by double-clicking the **selection arrow** in the margin to the left of the paragraph; deselect by clicking anywhere in the document text.

3. Using the **selection arrow**, drag down the left margin to select text.

4. Click anywhere in the body of the letter to deselect.

5. Triple-click with the **selection arrow** anywhere in the left margin to select the entire letter, and then deselect it.

6. Double-click any word to select it.

7. Double-click a different word; notice that the previous word is deselected and then deselect the latest selection.

Select Nonadjacent Text

You can select multiple locations simultaneously.

8. Double-click to select one word.

9. Press and hold Ctrl as you double-click another word; release Ctrl.

   Both selections are active. You can select as many nonadjacent areas of a document as desired using the Ctrl *key.*

10. Move the **I-beam** I to the start of the first main paragraph, click to position the insertion point, and then hold down Shift and click after *Sales*.

> I am applying for the position of Retail Computer Sales advertised
> Computer Science graduate from Case Western University, where
> summers, I worked as an intern in the sales department at Best Co
> interested in discussing your sales position, which aligns well with

11. Click to deselect.

Using Numbered and Bulleted Lists

Numbered and bulleted lists are effective in drawing your reader's attention to items of interest. You can turn them on before you begin typing or apply them after you have typed the list. Numbered lists are automatically renumbered if you insert or delete an item. A good example of when to use a numbered list is when sequence is important, as in a series of steps in a procedure. Items in a bulleted list have no sequence.

Once you've created a list, each time you tap Enter, a new list item will appear. Tapping Tab once you've created this new item will demote the item, indenting it to the right and creating a subitem. Shift+Tab will do the opposite: promote an item by moving it back to the left. Items can be demoted multiple times, allowing the user to create up to eight levels of subitems.

Note! *Be sure to check whether the ATS used by a prospective employer can read numbered and bulleted lists.*

View the video "Promoting and Demoting Lists."

≡ Home→Paragraph→Bullets ▤

≡ Home→Paragraph→Numbering ▤

In this exercise, you will create and format numbered and bulleted lists. Because correctness is important, you'll also work with proofreading tools.

1. Choose **File→Save As** and save your letter as: **W1-D4-CoverLtr**
2. If necessary, choose **Home→Paragraph→Show/Hide** ¶ to display formatting marks.
3. Position the insertion point at the end of the last line in the first body paragraph.
4. Tap Enter twice and type this text:

   My college education provided me with the following technical skills that will allow me to make a positive contribution to Global Computer: Enter

Type a Numbered List

5. Choose **Home→Paragraph→Numbering** ☷ to turn on numbers.
6. Type this text, tapping Enter at the end of each item to generate the next number:

   1. An understanding of real-world computer needs Enter

   2. An awareness of the latest technologies available Enter

   3. The ability to analyze problems and apply the appropriate hardware and software solutions

   Notice the arrow formatting marks following the numbers. They represent tabs, which were automatically generated by the numbering system.

7. Begin typing the last item, purposely misspelling *experience*, but don't tap Spacebar yet:

   4. Tab **Hands-on experence**

8. Now, as you tap Spacebar, watch how AutoCorrect fixes the misspelling for you.

   This proofreading tool makes corrections automatically. It also fixes common punctuation errors and capitalizes the names of days and months if you do not.

9. Finish typing the fourth item: **with a wide variety of computer equipment**.

   4.→ Hands-on·experience·with·a·wide·variety·of·computer·equipment¶

10. Tap Enter three times at the end of item 4: once to generate the next number, once to turn off numbering, and once again to add space between paragraphs.
11. Type this text:

    My experience at Best Computers provided me with the following sales-related knowledge that would benefit Global Computer: Enter

Continue a Numbered List

12. Choose **Home→Paragraph→Numbering** ☷.

    Notice that numbering restarted at 1. The system assumes you are starting a new list. There may be times when you want to continue numbering even though some regular text is entered within the list.

    A smart tag *pop-up appears next to the number.*

13. Click the **AutoCorrect Options** ⚡ smart tag and then click **Continue Numbering** to continue the previous list with the number 5.

    Another smart tag appears.

14. Right-click where the insertion point is flashing to the right of the number *5*. From the menu that appears, choose **Restart at 1**.

Remember that numbered lists are typically used when sequence is important. In this example, the items you type are not in sequence, so you will change to a bulleted list.

15. Choose **Home→Paragraph→Bullets** :≡ .

16. Type the following list:

- `Skill in using consultative sales skills to learn about clients' needs`⌷Enter⌶
- `Adeptness in analyzing client requirements and addressing their business issues`⌷Enter⌶
- `Competence in articulating solutions and demonstrating product benefits to the client`⌷Enter⌶
- `Proficiency in handling objections`⌷Enter⌶
- `Ability to provide a training and implementation plan that ensures high customer satisfaction`

Because numbering is typically used when sequence is important and in this case the list is not in sequential order, you decide to use bullets for the first list as well.

17. Move the mouse pointer to the left margin next to the first numbered item, press and hold down the mouse button, and drag down through the fourth item.

18. Choose **Home→Paragraph→Bullets** :≡ to apply bullets.

19. Click in the body to deselect the bullets and then save your letter.

Editing Text

There are many tools for editing documents, allowing you to insert and delete text. Remember, you must position the insertion point before you begin typing. You can use ⌷Backspace⌶ and ⌷Delete⌶ to remove one character at a time. If you select a block of text, you can use ⌷Backspace⌶ or ⌷Delete⌶ to remove the entire block, or you can type over the selected text to replace it.

Spell checker and grammar checker automatically help you edit text as you type by placing a squiggly red line under words that might be misspelled and a double blue line under words that may be grammatically incorrect. Right-clicking on underlined words presents options for correcting the potential error. Spell checker and grammar checker are only editing aids; you must use your own good judgment when deciding what action to take.

You can look up synonyms from within the document you are editing in order to enhance your word choice. You can view a list of synonyms by right-clicking a word and choosing Synonyms from the menu. For a more extensive list, choose Thesaurus from the submenu to open the Thesaurus task pane.

DEVELOP YOUR SKILLS: W1-D5

In this exercise, you will insert and delete text, and you will use the pop-up menu to find synonyms.

1. Choose **File→Save As** and save your file as: `W1-D5-CoverLtr`

2. In the first line of the first main paragraph, click the **I-beam** $\boxed{\text{I}}$ in front of *advertised* to position the insertion point.

> I·am·applying·for·the·position·of·Retail·Computer·Sales·advertised·
> Computer·Science·graduate·from·Case·Western·University,·where·

3. Type **Representative** and then tap $\boxed{\text{Spacebar}}$.

4. In the third line of the first paragraph, position the insertion point between the *a* and *n* in *an*.

> I am applying for the position of Retail
> a recent Computer Science graduate fr
> the summers, I worked as an intern in

5. Tap $\boxed{\text{Delete}}$ to remove the *n* and then tap $\boxed{\text{Spacebar}}$.

The a is underlined in blue indicating a grammar error, but you can ignore it, and it will eventually go away.

6. Type: **sales**

7. In the third line of the first paragraph, drag the mouse pointer across **in the sales department** to select (highlight) the words.

> I am applying for the position of Retail Computer Sales Representa
> a recent Computer Science graduate from Case Western University
> the summers, I worked as a sales intern in the sales department at

8. Tap $\boxed{\text{Delete}}$ to remove the selected words.

9. In the first line of the second paragraph, double-click **college** to select it and then tap $\boxed{\text{Delete}}$ to remove it.

10. In the third bullet point in the second bulleted list, double-click **articulating** to select it.

> • → Adeptness·in·analyzing·client·
> • → Competence·in·articulating·so

11. Type **clearly stating** in its place.

Work with Synonyms

12. In the third bullet point in the first bulleted list, right-click **appropriate** to display the pop-up menu.

13. Follow these steps to choose a synonym:

> | Smart Lookup | e.¶ |
> | Ⓐ ▶ Synonyms ▶ | suitable Ⓑ |
> | Translate | fitting |

    Ⓐ Hover the mouse pointer over the menu at *Synonyms*.

    Ⓑ Move the mouse pointer over to the submenu and choose **suitable** from the list of synonyms.

The word suitable *replaces* appropriate.

14. In the second bullet point in the second list, right-click the word **Adeptness** and then follow the same steps to replace it with the word **Expertise** from the Synonyms menu.

15. Save your document.

Working with Views

You can view your documents in several ways. Each view is optimized for specific types of work. The views change the way documents appear on the screen, but in most cases they do not impact the appearance of printed documents. You can choose views from the View tab or from the status bar at the bottom right of the screen.

DOCUMENT VIEWS

View	Description
Read Mode (View tab) Read Mode (status bar)	This view provides a book-like reading experience with pages laid out side by side. The Ribbon disappears to display more of your document. You navigate horizontally as in a book.
Print Layout (View tab) Print Layout (status bar)	With this default view, your documents look similar to the way they will look when printed. You can see graphics, headers and footers, and multi-column layouts.
Web Layout (View tab) Web Layout (status bar)	This view displays your document as it would look as a web page. It appears as one long page without page breaks.
Outline (View tab)	Outline view is useful for organizing long documents.
Draft (View tab)	This view simplifies page layout by eliminating elements such as headers and footers and graphic elements. This view is useful when you want to focus on content.

 View the video "Using Views."

DEVELOP YOUR SKILLS: W1-D6

In this exercise, you will try out various views.

1. Locate and mouse over the View buttons on the status bar at the bottom right of the screen and notice the ToolTips that appear.

2. Click the first button, **Read Mode** 📖, and notice how the look of your letter has changed.

3. Click the **arrow** at the right side of the window to move to the end of the document.

 Depending on your screen's resolution, both pages may already be visible, in which case the arrow on the right side is not active.

4. Click the **Print Layout** ▤ button on the status bar to return to the previous view.

5. Choose **View→Views** on the Ribbon to display all available views.

Notice that additional view options, which do not appear in the status bar, appear in the Views group.

Saving Your Work in a Different Format

You can save a document in many different formats. Prospective employers may ask you to send your application documents in one of several different formats. The format of a file is specified by the extension added at the end of the filename.

 You may or may not see a file extension in your filenames. There is a default Windows option to hide extensions.

Document Files

Earlier versions of Word saved documents in the *.doc* file format. The current version uses the *.docx* file format. When using *.doc* formats, users may not be able to read files in the *.docx* format. However, you can choose to save your document in the older *.doc* format so users of these earlier versions can read the document.

When you open a document created in earlier versions, the title bar displays *[Compatibility Mode]* next to the title. This means features not compatible with older versions are turned off while working in the document.

PDF Files

Using a PDF file (**.pdf*) is great when sharing files with others. If you're not sure what hardware and software the other person has, save your document as a PDF file; the layout and fonts will look the same on various types of computers, software, and operating systems. A prospective employer may ask you to submit your employment application documents as PDF files.

Saving a Document for ATS Analysis

Text files (**.txt*) contain very little formatting, and thus they may be the best format when you are submitting employment application documents that are likely to be scanned into a computer. ATS software can read text files. It's always a good idea to check with prospective employers if they haven't specified a particular file format.

It's great to have nicely formatted, paper-based documents to hand to an interviewer, if necessary. In addition, many prospective employers may ask to receive your documents electronically. In this exercise, you will assume the employer has asked to receive the document as a PDF file.

1. Choose **File→Save As** and navigate to your **Word Chapter 1** folder.

2. Click the **Save As Type** field toward the bottom of the dialog box to display the list of possible file formats.

Ⓐ Default format

Ⓑ Older document versions

Ⓒ PDF format

Ⓓ Plain Text format

3. Choose **PDF (*.pdf)** from the menu.

   Remember, you may or may not see a file extension in your filenames. There is a default Windows option to hide extensions.

4. Change the filename to **W1-D7-CoverLtr** and then click the **Save** button at the bottom of the dialog box.

   Your document now appears in Adobe Acrobat Reader if you have it installed. If not, it may appear in a browser instead, like Microsoft Edge. In addition, you may be prompted to choose how to open the file. If so, choose Adobe Acrobat Reader.

5. Click the **Close** button in the upper-right corner of the Adobe screen or whichever application automatically launched the document.

6. Click the **Close** button in the upper-right corner of the Microsoft Word screen to exit Word. If prompted to save the file before closing, click **Don't Save**.

Self-Assessment

Check your knowledge of this chapter's key concepts and skills using the Self-Assessment in your ebook or online (eLab course or Student Resource Center).

Reinforce Your Skills

Create an Informal Letter

In this exercise, you will create a letter from Kids for Change to local residents, announcing an upcoming recycling pickup. Because this does not have to be a formal business letter, you will use a more casual style. You will also practice selection and navigation techniques.

1. Start Word.
2. Create a new document based on the **Blank Document** template and save it as:
   W1-R1-RecycleLtr
3. Type the return address and then tap Enter twice.

   Kids for Change Enter

   159 Park Boulevard Enter

   Atlanta, GA 30313 Enter

   Enter

   Enter

4. Type **Nove** to begin the date, use **AutoComplete** to finish entering the month by simply tapping Enter, and then complete the date as: **November 19, 2021**
5. Tap Enter twice.

6. Complete the letter shown in the following illustration, tapping `Enter` wherever a paragraph symbol appears.

Notice when you type the website address in the second paragraph that it is automatically recognized and formatted as a hyperlink.

Current Resident`Enter`

123 Peach Blossom Lane`Enter`

Atlanta, GA 30313`Enter`

`Enter`

Dear Neighbor, `Enter`

`Enter`

I am the recycling representative for Kids for Change, and our motto is Think Globally, Act Locally. We know that recycling large objects takes extra effort since they do not fit in your city-provided recycle cans. We would like to give you a hand.`Enter`

`Enter`

On November 22, we will collect recyclable objects in your neighborhood. Visit http://recycleatlanta.org to ensure you are following the city's recycling guidelines. Please place your recyclables at the curb in front of your house before 9:00 a.m.`Enter`

`Enter`

Thank you for caring about our planet!`Enter`

`Enter`

Sincerely, `Enter`

`Enter`

`Enter`

`Enter`

Tania Tulip`Enter`

Recycling Representative

7. Use `Ctrl`+`Home` to position the insertion point at the top of the document.

8. Use the **selection arrow** in the margin to select the return address at the top of the page.

9. When the Mini toolbar appears, click the **Bold** `B` button to bold the return address.

10. Click the **Zoom Out** button enough times to see the entire page.

| `−` |━━━━━━┃━━━━━ `+` 100% |

11. Click the **Zoom In** button enough times to return the screen to 100% and then use `Ctrl`+`End` to position the insertion point at the bottom of the letter.

| `−` ━━━━━┃━━━ `+` 100% |

12. Use ⎡Ctrl⎤+⎡Home⎤ to position the insertion point at the top of the letter.

13. Save and close your letter.

Edit a Document

In this exercise, you will edit a letter from Kids for Change to local residents, inviting them to celebrate Mother Nature Day at Camp Cuyahoga. The group has planned many exciting activities. In the letter, you will create lists and use proofreading tools. You will then save the letter in an older version of Word.

1. Open the file **W1-R2-CuyahogaCamp** and save it as: `W1-R2-CuyahogaCampRevised`

You can see the wavy red and double blue lines, indicating typos and grammar errors. The double blue line in the inside address indicates that there are two spaces between the state and zip code. This format is recommended by USPS guidelines.

2. Instruct the grammar checker to ignore the double space by right-clicking the underlined state and zip code and choosing **Ignore Once**.

3. Correct the spelling of *leeding* by right-clicking on it and selecting **leading** from the menu that appears.

4. In the second line of that paragraph, right-click on the word **receiving** and replace it with **be receiving**.

5. In the first line of the next paragraph, replace **convening** with **be convening** using the same tool.

6. Correct the spelling of *buug* using the same tool.

7. In the same line in which you corrected bug, right-click **important** and then select **vital** from the Synonyms list.

Create a Bulleted List

8. In the second line of the first paragraph, delete the comma following *scheduled* and type a colon in its place.

9. Use an **arrow key** to position the insertion point in front of *including* and then tap ⎡Enter⎤.

10. Click the **Bullets** ⊞ button.

11. Delete *including* and the space following it.

12. Delete the *h* in *hiking* and replace it with an uppercase **H**.

13. Delete the comma and space following *Hiking* and then tap ⎡Enter⎤.

14. Continue editing the list of activities until it looks like the illustration:

- Hiking
- Bird watching
- Tree planting
- Bug hunting

15. Display the document in **Read Mode** 📖 and then return to **Print Layout** 🗐 view.

Change Document Format

Some recipients will get the letter as an email attachment. For those who may not have the latest version of Word, you will save the letter in an older format.

16. Choose the **Save As** option in Backstage view and navigate to your **Word Chapter 1** folder.

17. Use the Save as Type field to save the file in the **Word 97-2003 Document (*doc)** format and then click **Save** at the bottom of the dialog box.

Notice [Compatibility Mode] *in the title bar.*

18. Save and close the letter.

REINFORCE YOUR SKILLS: W1-R3

Edit a Letter and Navigate in a Three-Page Document

In this exercise, you will create a letter for Kids for Change members, announcing a fundraiser to adopt a seal. Donations help to fund research and educate the public about ocean health. In the letter, you will work with lists and proofreading tools. You will save your letter as a PDF file and then you will navigate in a longer document.

1. Start a new document using the Blank Document template and save it as:
W1-R3-Fundraiser

2. Begin typing the letter.

Remember to use AutoComplete to help with the dates and let Word Wrap do its thing.

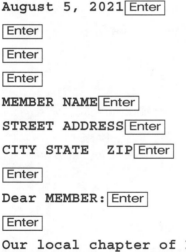

August 5, 2021 Enter

Enter

Enter

Enter

MEMBER NAME Enter

STREET ADDRESS Enter

CITY STATE ZIP Enter

Enter

Dear MEMBER: Enter

Enter

Our local chapter of Kids for Change will hold a car wash fundraiser to collect $300 to adopt a seal at the Center for Seals. We are scheduling the car wash for August 17. The next monthly meeting will be a planning session. Here are some things to think about before the meeting: Enter

Enter

Enter

Use Numbering and Bullets

3. Type the following list using the **Numbering** ☷ feature:

   1. Choose a location. Our options are the parking lots at the following businesses: Jake's Gas Station, Beulah's Diner, or Dick's Grocery Store. `Enter`
   2. What hours can you volunteer on August 17? `Enter`
   3. Let me know if you can supply any of the following: hose, vacuum, soap, brushes, sponges, or rags. `Enter`
   4. Should we set a price or request a donation? `Enter`
   5. Can you design a flyer for the car wash?

   Now you will demote, or indent, some of the items in the list.

4. In the first item, position the insertion point in front of *Jake's*, tap `Enter`, and then demote the line by tapping `Tab`.

5. Position the insertion point in front of *Beulah's* and tap `Enter` to generate the next item.

6. Continue modifying the list, deleting extraneous punctuation and words as shown.

   > 1. → Choose·a·location.·Our·choices·are·the·parking·lots·at·the·following·businesses:·¶
   >   a. → Jake's·Gas·Station¶
   >   b. · Beulah's·Diner¶
   >   c. → Dick's·Grocery·Store¶

7. In item 3, position the insertion point in front of *hose*, tap `Enter`, and then demote the line.

8. Organize the list as shown, deleting unnecessary punctuation and words. If Word automatically capitalizes the words in each line, correct this and make everything lowercase.

   > 3. → Let·me·know·if·you·can·supply·any·of·the·following:·¶
   >   a. → hose¶
   >   b. → vacuum¶
   >   c. → soap¶
   >   d. → brushes¶
   >   e. → sponges¶
   >   f. → rags¶

   Remembering that numbering is typically used only when sequence is important, you decide to change to a bulleted list.

9. Select all list items, including the demoted lists, and apply **Bullets** ☷ to the selected text.

10. Position the insertion point at the end of the last bulleted item and then tap `Enter` three times to turn off bullets and create a blank line.

11. Type the following sentence, intentionally making the typo as shown:

    We're looking forward to a great planning sassion. See you at the meeting!

WORD

Proofread Your Letter

12. Correct the spelling error in the last line.

13. Right-click the word **options** in the first bullet point and choose **choices** from the Synonyms menu.

14. Move the insertion point to the end of the document, tap `Enter` twice, and then type the letter closing.

`Sincerely,` `Enter`

`Hobert Chan` `Enter`

`Kids for Change`

Save the Letter in PDF Format

15. Save the file in PDF format and then close Adobe Acrobat Reader (or whatever program launches to view the PDF once saved).

16. Save and close the Word file.

You've discovered a document that gives some helpful hints on car washing, and you plan to include it with the letter to the members.

17. Open the three-page document named **W1-R3-HowToWashACar**.

18. Using the following notes, navigate through this longer document:
- Use two keystrokes to position the insertion point at the end of the document.
- Use two keystrokes to move the insertion point to the top of the document.
- Use an arrow key to move down one line.
- Use one keystroke to move to the end of the line and then use one keystroke to move to the beginning of the line.

19. Use the following text selection techniques:
- Position the insertion point at the top of the document and use mouse clicks to select **Introduction**.
- With *Introduction* still selected, select **How** and **Wash** in the next heading and then click to deselect.
- Use two keystrokes to select the entire document.

20. Use the following notes to observe the document in various views:
- Position the insertion point at the top of the document.
- Display the document in **Read Mode** 📖, using the status bar button, and then page through the document.
- Display the document in **Web Layout** 🖳 using the status bar button.
- Switch back to **Print Layout** 🗐 view using the status bar button.

21. Close the document and exit Word. If it asks you to save changes, click **Don't Save**.

Apply Your Skills

Create a Business Letter

In this exercise, you will create a letter from a Universal Corporate Events representative inviting the sales winners at Reukert Enterprises to an orientation meeting for their Paris tour. You will work with proofreading tools and use navigation and text selection techniques.

1. Start Word, create a new document using the Blank Document template, and save it as:

    W1-A1-LeeLtr

2. Create the following letter, using AutoComplete with the dates and intentionally making the spelling and grammar errors indicated.

    Note that the company name, Reukert, is correctly spelled, but it is not in Word's dictionary. You can ignore the red underline in this case.

    September 2, 2021

    Mrs. Suzanne Lee
    Reukert Enterprises
    8445 Princeton Street
    Chicago, IL 60628

    Dear Mrs. Lee:
    Congratulations on your outstanding sales achievement. Universal
    Corporate Events is orginizing your Paris tour, which will
    departs October 8 and return October 18.
    Please plan to attend the orientation meeting on September 14 in
    the Lake View conference room at 10:00 a.m.
    We are looking forwared to making your trip a memorable event!

    Best Regards,

    Jack Bell
    Universal Corporate Events

3. Correct the spelling and grammar errors.

4. In the first sentence, use the Synonyms feature to replace *achievement* with **attainment**.

5. Use the following navigation techniques:

Scroll Bar	Keyboard
• Move down one screen. • Move to the top of the document and then position the insertion point at the beginning of the first main paragraph.	• Use two keystrokes to move to the end of the document. • Use one keystroke to move to the beginning of the line. • Use one keystroke to move to the end of the line.

6. Use the following selection techniques:

- Use the **white selection arrow** to select the first line of the first paragraph.
- Use the keyboard to select the entire document and then click anywhere in the document to deselect.
- Use the **white selection arrow** to select three adjacent lines and then click anywhere else in the document to deselect.
- Select three nonadjacent words simultaneously and then deselect.

7. Save and close your letter.

APPLY YOUR SKILLS: W1-A2

Work with Lists and Make Editing Changes

In this exercise, you will create a letter from a Universal Corporate Events representative to a client, suggesting ideas for side trips during its annual kickoff meeting in San Francisco. You will create a bulleted list and make editing changes. Then you will save the letter in the older version .doc format.

1. Open **W1-A2-SFTours** and save it in the older **.doc** format as: **W1-A2-SFToursRevised**

2. Position the insertion point at the end of the letter and type the following bulleted list:
- **Yacht Charters**
- **Napa Valley**
- **Sausalito**

3. Tap Enter twice to turn off bullets and create a blank line.

4. Use cut and paste to rearrange the list in alphabetic order.

5. Position the insertion point after *Napa Valley*, generate a new bullet, and then demote the bullet one level.

6. Add to the list as shown:
- **Napa Valley**
  - **Napa Wine Train**
  - **Hot air balloon rides**
  - **Top-ranked restaurants**
- **Sausalito**
  - **Ferry boat ride from San Francisco**
  - **Docks and marinas**
  - **Boutiques and art galleries**
- **Yacht Charters**
  - **Sunset cruise**
  - **Sail under Golden Gate Bridge**
  - **Alcatraz and Angel Island**

7. Position the insertion point at the end of the document and type the closing:

```
Sincerely,


Geoff Simons
Universal Corporate Events
```

8. Make the following changes:
   - In the first line of the first paragraph, select **needs regarding your** and replace it with: **annual**
   - In the second line of the same paragraph, insert **San Francisco** to the left of *meeting*.
   - In the first bullet point under *Yacht Charters*, insert **dining** between *Sunset* and *cruise*.

9. Display your letter in **Read Mode** 📖, page through to the end if your screen resolution allows it, and then return to **Print Layout** 📄 view.

10. Save and then close the file.

APPLY YOUR SKILLS: W1-A3

Edit and Format a Letter

In this exercise, you will draft a letter to a Universal Corporate Events employee, detailing his responsibilities relative to the Vaughn Storage Device's Kauai event. You will use proofreading tools and add a bulleted list to a letter. You will use navigation and selection techniques and save the document in PDF format. Finally, you will work with different views.

1. Open **W1-A3-WilliamsLtr**, save it as **W1-A3-WilliamsLtrRevised**, and then correct the spelling error.

2. In the first line of the first paragraph, use the Synonyms feature to change *ambassador* to **representative**.

3. In the same line, select **Hawaiian** and replace it with: **Kauai**

4. At the beginning of the second paragraph, insert **and Martin** between *You* and *will*.

5. At the end of the second paragraph, change *entertainment* to: **entertainers**

6. Move the insertion point to the end of the document and add the following text:

```
The side tours will take place on September 13, 14, 15, and 16.
Here's a list of the side tours that attendees will sign up for
during the arrival dinner:
        • North Shore Bike Tours
        • Snorkeling at Salt Pond Beach Park
        • Catamaran Tour on Na Pali Coast
        • Surfing at Hanalei Bay
        • Kehaha Beach Luau
Sincerely,


Jose Ramirez
Universal Corporate Events
```

Save the File in PDF

Bill is on assignment out of the country. To be sure the letter reaches him, you will send it as a PDF email attachment.

7. Save the file in PDF format and close the PDF if it automatically opens.

The .docx file is still open.

8. Use the **View** tab on the Ribbon to view the document in **Read Mode** and then use the button on the status bar to switch back to **Print Layout** view.

9. Save and close the file and then exit Word.

Project Grader

This chapter does not include Project Grader exercises. Project Grader content is based on the learning objectives for a chapter, and sometimes those learning objectives cannot be accurately graded by the system. Objectives from this chapter that can be accurately graded may be included in later chapters, if applicable.

◢ Extend Your Skills

These exercises challenge you to think critically and apply your new skills in a real-world setting. You will be evaluated on your ability to follow directions, completeness, creativity, and the use of proper grammar and mechanics. Save files to your chapter folder. Submit assignments as directed.

W1-E1   That's the Way I See It

You have decided to start your own landscaping business, and you are going to conduct online research to see what's involved. Your friend is studying for his MBA. You will send him a letter containing the results of your research and ask him what he thinks of your idea.

Create a business letter, including a list of five landscaping tools that your research shows you will need to purchase. Then research what is involved in becoming a certified landscape professional and explain how you plan to earn your certification. Finally, list three tips for running a successful landscaping business. The letter should include at least three paragraphs (one to give an overview of the business, one or more to discuss certification, and one for the conclusion) and a list of three tips. Save the file in the older version .doc format, naming it: **W1-E1-NewBusiness**

W1-E2   Be Your Own Boss

You own Blue Jean Landscaping, a service that helps customers be their own landscapers. You provide the plans and directions and then the customer helps with the labor. A customer would like you to help her landscape her front yard. Use your imagination to decide on your business's location and climate. Conduct online research to determine what plants work well for the climate you envision. Send the client a business letter to propose four plant options that would work well for the location and climate. The letter should contain both an introductory and concluding paragraph, as well as a list of four plant options. Each option should be associated with a sentence or two explaining why it is a good choice. Save the file in PDF format as: **W1-E2-NewClient**

W1-E3   Demonstrate Proficiency

Stormy BBQ is a local BBQ restaurant featuring fresh, locally grown vegetables and local grass-fed pork and beef. As the marketing manager of Stormy BBQ, you've decided to hold a chili cook-off to attract new clients. Use online research to learn how to have a successful cook-off and also research rules for the chefs to ensure that they are competing on a level playing field.

Create a correctly formatted business letter to send to prospective chili chefs listing three important guidelines for a successful cook-off and three competition rules for your chefs. The letter should include both an introductory and concluding paragraph, as well as the rules that have been established. Make up the name and address for the first chef you want to invite. Save your letter in PDF as: **W1-E3-ChiliChef**

2 | Creating a Résumé in a Table

In the information age, it can be difficult to sort through and process vast amounts of content. With so much information to digest, it's often difficult for employers to find the right job candidates, so a résumé that stands out is the single best way to secure your dream job. Tables provide a flexible, easy, and effective tool for displaying organized information and making sure you're noticed. In this chapter, you will merge and split table cells; align table text; apply table styles; and insert, delete, and resize rows and columns.

LEARNING OBJECTIVES

▸ Create a table

▸ Build an effective résumé in a table

▸ Select data in a table

▸ Format tables

▸ Apply table styles

▸ Print documents

📁 Project: Landing the Perfect Job

Your cover letter is complete, and now it's time for your résumé. You need to summarize your qualifications and experience, focusing on skills that target the position you are applying for. You also need to demonstrate that your skills fit the needs the employer has expressed. You decide to use a table for your résumé since it will make your résumé easy for a hiring manager to quickly read.

You also intend to make as many professional contacts as possible in the next few months, and using a table to track those contacts will be very helpful. You'll take advantage of the table's Sort feature to organize the data and apply formatting that will make it attractive and, more important, easy to read.

📖 What's Important in a Résumé?

The purpose of a résumé is to win an interview. Many hiring managers will take less than a minute to review a résumé; therefore, your résumé needs to immediately capture the reader. It needs to be dynamic, targeted, and designed to emphasize your experience, qualifications, and skills, particularly those that transfer to the job. Like the cover letter, one page is generally preferred.

There are three primary types of résumé: *chronological*, *functional*, and *combination*. A chronological résumé assumes you are continuing along a career path, listing your most recent position first. It is good for showing your growth within a profession. A functional résumé is skill and accomplishment based. It can be used by those just out of school, career changers, or those with gaps in their employment history. A combination résumé is a combination of chronological and functional, listing your skills and experience first, followed by your employment history.

Introducing Tables

Tables provide a convenient method for organizing and aligning data in an easy-to-read format, and they afford a nice way to break up a text-heavy document. Formatting with table styles adds flair to your documents, and tables draw your reader's attention to key items.

Just as with most actions on a computer, there are multiple ways to insert a table. All of them are located in the Insert tab of the Ribbon, under the Tables group. You can use the Table button, the Insert Table dialog box, and the Quick Tables gallery. You can even convert tabular columns to a table.

Contextual tabs appear in context with the task you are performing. A lot of features use contextual tabs. With tables, contextual tabs appear on the Ribbon when the insertion point is in a table.

Creating New Tables

Tables are organized in columns and rows. Where columns and rows intersect, they form a rectangle known as a cell.

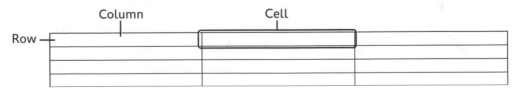

When you create a new table, you can select how many rows and columns you'd like it to have. You can always add or remove rows and columns later if you end up changing your mind.

 View the video "Creating Tables."

Navigating and Selecting Data in a Table

You can move the insertion point by clicking in a cell, or you can use keystrokes for navigating. Here are the keystrokes you are likely to use most often:

▶ `Tab` for moving to the next cell

▶ `Shift`+`Tab` for moving to the previous cell

▶ Arrow keys for moving to adjacent cells

Just as in a regular text document, if you want to format or modify something in a table, you select it first. The mouse pointer changes shape depending on whether you're selecting a cell, row, column, or the entire table. For example, to move a table, you can click the move tool that appears at the top left of inserted tables.

View the video "Selecting Data with the Mouse."

DEVELOP YOUR SKILLS: W2-D1

In this exercise, you will insert a table into a document and use selection and navigation techniques. Then you will enter data into your table.

1. Start Word and create a new document using the **Blank Document** template.
2. Navigate to your **Word Chapter 2** folder and save the document as: `W2-D1-StellaResume`
3. Choose **Home→Paragraph→Show/Hide** ¶ to display formatting marks.
4. Follow these steps to insert a **2×4** table from the Ribbon:

Ⓐ Click the **Insert** tab.

Ⓑ Click the **Table** button.

Ⓒ Drag in the grid and click the fourth cell in the second column.

Notice that the insertion point is in the table and that the contextual Table Tools' Design and Layout tabs appear on the Ribbon.

Select Table Elements and Navigate in a Table

Remember, the Mini toolbar appears when you select table data, just as when you select regular text. It contains frequently used commands. You can choose a command or ignore the toolbar, and it will fade away.

5. Apply the following selection techniques:
   - Hover the mouse over the left margin and use the **selection arrow** to select a row.
   - Click the **move handle** ⊞ in the upper-left corner of the table to select the entire table. (The insertion point or the mouse pointer must be in the table for the move handle to appear.)
   - Hover the mouse pointer just above the top border of the table and use the **down-pointing, black mouse pointer** to select a column.

6. Deselect by clicking anywhere in the table and then use the following notes to navigate in a table:
   - Use `Tab` and `Shift`+`Tab` to move forward and back one cell at a time.
   - Position the insertion point at the end of a row (not the last row) and tap `Tab` to move to the beginning of the next row.
   - Press `Alt`+`Page Up` to move to the top of the column.
   - Press `Alt`+`Page Down` to move to the end of the column.

Enter Data in a Table

7. Enter the following information:

Stella·Martin¶ 127·Stevens·Street¶ Cleveland,·OH··44113¶ 216-555-1212¶ SSMartin5@yahoo.com¤	¤
OBJECTIVE¤	¤
QUALIFICATIONS¤	¤
EXPERIENCE¤	¤

8. Save the document.

Modifying a Table

Whenever you click in a table or select cells, rows, or columns, the contextual Layout tab appears. All the features you'll need to modify your table's structure are located here. Also, some of these features are available in the pop-up menu when you right-click in a table.

Inserting Rows and Columns

You can insert new columns and rows into an existing table. If you want to insert multiple rows or columns, you must first select the same number of existing rows or columns as you want to insert. For example, to insert two new rows, select two existing rows first. You can also add a row to the bottom of a table with a tap of the `Tab` key when the insertion point is in the last table cell.

A quick and easy way to insert a single row or column is with the insert control that appears when the mouse pointer is hovered just above or to the left of the table, and between rows or columns.

216-555-1212¶
SSMartin5@yahoo.com¤
OBJECTIVE¤
QUALIFICATIONS¤
EXPERIENCE¤

≡ Table Tools→Layout→Rows & Columns | Right-click in the table and choose Insert

Merging/Splitting Cells and Aligning Data

You can merge two or more adjacent cells in the same row or column into a single cell. The merge option is often used to create a heading row that spans the width of the table. You can also split a single cell into multiple cells.

You can split the entire table, if desired. The first step is to position the insertion point anywhere in the row that you want to become the first row of the second table. Then, execute the Split Table command. When formatting marks are visible, you will see a paragraph between the two tables. To rejoin the table, delete the paragraph symbol.

≡ Table Tools→Layout→Merge→Merge Cells *or* Split Cells | Right-click in the table and choose Merge Cells *or* Split Cells

≡ Table Tools→Layout→Merge→Split Table

Aligning Table Data

You can align data horizontally or vertically, and you can change the direction of text. You can also modify the cell margins thereby customizing the spacing between cells.

≡ Table Tools→Layout→Alignment

DEVELOP YOUR SKILLS: W2-D2

In this exercise, you will use several techniques to insert and delete rows. You will also merge cells and align data within cells.

1. Choose **File→Save As** and navigate to your **Word Chapter 2** folder.
2. Name the file: **W2-D2-StellaResume**

Insert and Delete Rows

3. Make sure the insertion point is in the table.

4. Move the mouse pointer to the left edge of the table between the first and second rows until the insert control appears as shown.

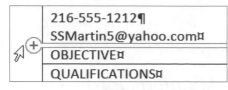

5. Click the **insert control** to add a row to the table.

   You will leave this row blank to add white space between the heading row and the rest of the table.

6. Position the insertion point in the last table cell (last column, last row) and then tap Tab to generate a new row.

   If you want to add several columns or rows at once, you must select the number of columns or rows that you want to add.

7. Use the selection arrow in the left margin to select the **QUALIFICATIONS** and **EXPERIENCE** rows.

8. Follow these steps to insert two rows in the table:

   Ⓐ Position the mouse pointer within the selected rows and right-click to display the menu.

   Ⓑ Choose **Insert**.

   Ⓒ Choose **Insert Rows Above** from the submenu.

   Two rows are inserted because two rows were selected. Now you will delete one of the rows.

9. Select the second blank row, position the mouse pointer in the gray selected area, and right-click to display the menu.

10. Choose **Delete Rows** from the menu.

    Now you will insert another blank row.

11. Use the selection arrow to select the **EXPERIENCE** row and then right-click in the selected row.

12. Choose **Insert** from the menu and then choose **Insert Rows Above** from the submenu. Click anywhere in the table to deselect the row.

13. Use the **insert control** to insert another row at the bottom of the table.

Merge Cells and Align Data

14. Position the selection arrow to the left of the first row and click to select the row.

15. Choose **Table Tools→Layout→Merge→Merge Cells** ▦.

    Row 1 is now one cell that spans the width of the table.

16. Choose **Table Tools→Layout→Alignment**.

    The alignment options on the left of the Alignment group offer several ways of aligning data within the cells.

17. Follow these steps to center the heading data:

Ⓐ Hover the mouse pointer over the buttons in the group on the left and notice the ToolTips that describe the alignment options.

Ⓑ Choose the **Align Center** option.

Ⓒ Hover the mouse pointer over the two buttons on the right and read the ToolTips.

18. Save the file.

Sizing Columns and Rows

There are a number of techniques for resizing columns and rows. The adjust pointer, which is a double-headed arrow, appears whenever you position the mouse pointer on a row or column gridline. You can adjust the column width or row height by using the adjust pointer to drag the gridline. The Cell Size group in the contextual Table Tools' Layout tab provides handy tools for precise sizing.

≡ Table Tools→Layout→Cell Size

DEVELOP YOUR SKILLS: W2-D3

In this exercise, you will continue modifying the table by resizing columns and rows. Then you will finish entering data in the résumé.

1. Save your file as: **W2-D3-StellaResume**

   The left column is wider than it needs to be.

2. Choose **View→Show→Ruler**.

3. Follow these steps to narrow the left column:

	Stella Martin
	127 Stevens Street
	Cleveland, OH 44113
	216-555-1212
	SSMartin5@yahoo.com
OBJECTIVE	← - - - - - - - - - - - - - - - -+ ⬤**A**
	⬤**B**
QUALIFICATIONS	

    A Position the mouse pointer on the center vertical gridline; it changes to the adjust pointer (a double-headed arrow).

    B Drag left until the column is approximately 1½" wide. You can use the ruler at the top of the page as a guide.

4. Position the mouse pointer on the bottom border of the *OBJECTIVE* row and notice the adjust pointer is a double-headed arrow pointing up and down.

5. Drag down a bit to increase the row height and then position the insertion point in the *OBJECTIVE* row.

6. Choose **Table Tools→Layout→Cell Size** and hover the mouse pointer over the buttons to observe their purpose.

These buttons offer more precise sizing options. Notice the height of the OBJECTIVE *row in the Table Row Height field. (Your measurement may differ.)*

ew	Design	Layout	🔘 T
	0.36" ⬍	⊟ Distribute	

7. Position the insertion point in the next row and notice the default row height is 0.19".

Now you will resize the OBJECTIVE *row to the same size as the other rows.*

8. Position the insertion point in the *OBJECTIVE* row, then click in the **Table Row Height** field, type **0.19**, and tap ⌨Enter⌨.

Enter Data

9. Position the mouse pointer in the second cell of the *OBJECTIVE* row and type: **Retail Computer Sales**

10. Position the insertion point in the second cell of the *QUALIFICATIONS* row.

Now you will type a bulleted list of Stella's qualifications.

11. Choose **Home→Paragraph→Bullets** ☰, type **Hardware/Software**, and tap ⌨Enter⌨.

The next bullet will need to be demoted one level; however, inside a table, you cannot use the ⌨Tab⌨ *key to demote. Remember, using* ⌨Tab⌨ *in a table moves the insertion point to the next cell.*

12. Choose **Home→Paragraph→Increase Indent** 📄.

13. Complete the list, including the last bullet:

- **Hardware/Software**
    - **In-depth knowledge of computer hardware and peripherals**
    - **Understanding of computer operating systems and end-user applications, including Windows and Microsoft Office Suite**
    - **Maintain hardware and software knowledge via blogs, newsletters, and conventions**
    -

Now you need to promote the last bullet. This time you will decrease the indent.

14. Choose **Home→Paragraph→Decrease Indent** ⬒.

15. Type the following list, remembering to use the **Increase Indent** ⬒ button to demote:

- **Sales**
    - **Ability to build good customer relations**
    - **Good presentation skills**
    - **Familiar with sales-proven strategies**
    - **Ability to close the sale**

16. Position the insertion point in the second cell of the *EXPERIENCE* row; type **Sales Intern, Best Computers (Summers, 2013–2016)** and tap ⎡Enter⎤.

17. Type the remaining lists, remembering to use **Increase Indent** ⬒ and **Decrease Indent** ⬒ to demote and promote bullet points:

Sales Intern, Best Computers (Summers, 2013–2016)

- **Presales**
    - **Prepared demonstrations describing hardware and software features and benefits**
    - **Prepared proposals and sales contracts**
- **Sales**
    - **Sold various brands of PCs, tablets, and notebooks, including IBM, Hewlett Packard, Compaq, and Macintosh**
    - **Recommended software based on customer needs**
    - **Performed follow-up activities necessary to close sales**
    - **Closed difficult deals and exceeded sales goals**
    - **Assisted in promotional events**
    - **Recognized as Intern of the Month on three occasions**
- **Post Sales**
    - **Scheduled delivery and installation and implemented training schedules**
    - **Followed up with customers to ensure satisfaction**

18. Position the insertion point in the first cell of the last row and type: **EDUCATION**

19. In the second cell of the *EDUCATION* row, type: **Computer Science Graduate, Case Western University**

20. Choose **File→Print** to view your document in the Print screen.

Notice that the résumé is too high on the page.

21. Click **Back** ⬅ to return to the Word screen.

22. Choose **Layout→Page Setup dialog box launcher** ⌐, click the **Layout** tab, choose **Center** from the Vertical Alignment field, and click **OK**.

23. Save and close the file.

Formatting with Borders, Shading, and Styles

Borders, shading, and styles can enhance the readability of a table, and they add pizzazz. Whenever you click in a table or select cells, rows, or columns, the contextual Design tab appears. The features you need to modify your table's formatting are located here. Among other things, the Layout tab allows you to convert an entire table to text, or you can select specific parts of a table to convert to text.

The Borders and Shading buttons have memory, meaning they reflect the last option chosen in the current session. This is handy if you want to apply the same effect multiple times. You can also remove borders from a table to provide a nice aesthetic effect. Often, gridlines will remain as a guide for you to build out your table, but these gridlines will not show up on a printed page.

Just like regular text, you can also use the formatting tools on the Home tab to format tables. Or, use the Mini toolbar, which provides convenient formatting tools right at your mouse pointer when you select data. When selecting styles, you can hover your mouse over the various options to see a Live Preview of how the table will look should you decide to apply that style.

DEVELOP YOUR SKILLS: W2-D4

In this exercise, you will open a document and convert the existing text into a table. Then, you'll apply formatting using borders, shading, and styles. Finally, you will convert part of the table to text. Stella has started a list of hiring managers she plans to contact. Because she intends to make many contacts, a table is the perfect tool for staying organized.

1. Navigate to your **Word Chapter 2** folder, open **W2-D4-JobContacts**, and save it as:
   `W2-D4-JobContactsRevised`

   The text in this document looks disorganized. You can convert it into a table to give the content more structure.

2. Use Ctrl + A to select the entire document and then choose **Insert→Tables→Table→ Convert Text to Table**.

3. In the dialog box that appears, leave all default settings and click **OK**.

   Word uses existing tabs and paragraphs from the original text to organize the information.

4. If necessary, click the **move handle** ⊞ in the upper-left corner of the table to select the entire table.

   Remember, the insertion point has to be in the table, or you have to hover the mouse pointer over the table for the move handle to appear.

5. Choose **Table Tools→Design→Borders→Borders** ⊞ **menu button** ▾ and choose **No Border**.

   You may see gridlines within the table, but they won't print; they are there just to guide you. The Borders menu button ▾ on the Design tab provides the option to turn gridlines on or off.

6. Select the first table row, choose **Table Tools→Design→Borders→Borders** ⊞ **menu button** ▾, and then choose **Outside Borders**.

7. Keep the first row selected and choose **Table Tools→Design→Table Styles→Shading** ◱ **menu button** ▾.

8. Choose **Gray, Accent 3, Darker 25%** and click anywhere else in the table to deselect the first row.

Use Table Styles

9. Make sure the insertion point is in the table, navigate to **Table Tools→Design→Table Styles**, and then hover the mouse pointer over the styles shown.

   Live Preview displays the various styles as they would look on your table, so you can see what will change before you commit.

10. Click the **More** button to display the full gallery of styles.

11. Choose **Grid Table 5 Dark – Accent 1**.

    The style overrides your cell margin spacing, borders, and shading. In turn, you can override Table Styles formatting by applying direct formatting.

12. Select the first row of the table; choose **Home→Font→Font menu button** ▾→ **Century Gothic**. Click anywhere in the table to deselect the row.

13. Save the file but leave it open.

Convert Table to Text

Now you will separate the header information on the résumé from the rest of the table without changing the way it looks.

14. Open **W2-D3-StellaResume** and save it as: **W2-D4-StellaResume**

15. Select the entire top row of the table, where the contact information appears.

16. Choose **Table Tools→Layout→Data→Convert to Text** ▦.

17. In the dialogue box that appears, leave the default *Paragraph Marks* option selected and click **OK** to convert the header row to text. Doing so removes it from the table.

Remove Table Borders

Now that you know about table borders, you can remove the default borders on the résumé to give it a sleeker look.

18. Click the **move handle** to select the entire table.

19. Choose **Table Tools→Design→Borders→Borders** ⊞ **menu button** ▾.

20. Choose **No Border** from the menu and then click anywhere inside the table to deselect.

21. Save and close the résumé.

Sorting Data in a Table

When sorting a table, you can choose to sort one or more columns in ascending or descending order and specify whether the first row of the table is a header row. The header row will not be sorted with the rest of the data.

You can sort a table by up to three levels. For example, say you have a table containing column headings for city, state, and zip. You can sort the table first by state, then by city within state, and then by zip code within city.

		Second sort level (City)	First sort level (State)	Third sort level (Zip)
Name	**Address**	**City**	**State**	**Zip**
Laurie Chu	61 Granger Road	Flagstaff	Arizona	86002
Martin Hernandez	45 Priscilla Court	Holbrook	Arizona	86025
Maria Valera	254 Part Street	Colorado Springs	Colorado	80840
Ella Goodspeed	32 Ash Lane	Denver	Colorado	80215
Adam Chaffee	51 Stony Lane	Denver	Colorado	80226

DEVELOP YOUR SKILLS: W2-D5

In this exercise, you will sort data in the Job Contacts file so you can easily locate information as the contacts table continues to grow. In this example, the table will be sorted by city and by company name within the city. You could also sort the table by company name if you're looking for a particular company, or by contact date if you want to locate a company you contacted on a certain date.

Before You Begin: *The W2-D4-JobContactsRevised file should still be open on the screen.*

1. Save the file as: **W2-D5-JobContactsRevised**

2. With the insertion point in the table, choose **Table Tools→Layout→Data→Sort** ⊞ to open the Sort dialog box.

As the list grows longer, it will be convenient to have the cities sorted together so you can focus on one geographic area at a time.

3. In the Sort By field, click the **menu button** ▾ and choose **City** from the menu.

Notice the Ascending and Descending option buttons on the right. Because you won't change that option, the cities will be sorted in Ascending (A to Z) order.

4. In the Then By field, choose **Co Name**.

This will sort the company names alphabetically within each city.

My list has
⦿ Header <u>r</u>ow   ○ No header ro<u>w</u>

Notice the Header Row button in the bottom-left corner of the dialog box. This option indicates that the table has a header row, which prevents the header row from being sorted in with the rest of the data.

5. Click **OK** and observe the sorted table.

 As new rows are added to the bottom of the table, simply execute the sort again to re-establish the sort order.

6. Save the file and leave it open.

Working with Print and Print Preview

The Print command and Print Preview features are available in Backstage view. Here you can choose various ways to print your document, and you can use the Print Preview feature to see how your document will look when printed. You can also use the printer selection menu to export the document as a PDF file.

≡ File→Print │ Ctrl + P

DEVELOP YOUR SKILLS: W2-D6

In this exercise, you will work with the Print screen in Backstage view. You will explore printing options, and you will preview the document to see how it will look when it prints.

1. Choose **File→Print**.

A number of options in the Settings area help you control printing.

2. Take a moment to explore the options by clicking them to see what choices are available.

Notice the top portion of the Print panel. You can choose the number of copies and any printer properties you want to modify.

You can choose a printer here, which includes an option to print to PDF.

3. If directed, click the **Print** button. If you want to conserve paper and ink and not print a page, you might print to PDF using the Microsoft Print to PDF option under the Printer selection menu button ▾, or simply click the **Back** ⬅ button.

Note! *If you printed to PDF, be sure to change back to your default printer the next time you print.*

4. Exit Word.

 What to Do Before a Job Interview

Many job search sites, such as Monster.com and Careerbuilder.com, offer career advice including interviewing tips. A web search of *interview tips* will also lead you to lots of tips to steer you in the right direction. Here are a few things to keep in mind:

▶ Anticipate the interviewer's questions and prepare your answers. You can even search for interview questions that are typical for a specific career, such as *interview questions for electrical engineers*.

▶ Practice, practice, practice. Get a friend or colleague to role play interviews with you. The more you practice, the more confident you will be during the interview.

▶ Think of questions you would like to ask the interviewer, especially those that demonstrate your interest in the job and company.

▶ Decide on your wardrobe. Conduct an Internet search for *how to dress for an interview*. Also, it's fine to ask the person scheduling the interview what the company dress code is. When in doubt, err on the side of conservatism.

▶ What to take with you: driving directions and contact information, folder/briefcase, paper copies of your résumé, pen, and notepad.

▶ What to not take with you: ear buds, cell phone that is not turned off, baseball cap, chewing gum, food or drink, distracting jewelry.

Self-Assessment

Check your knowledge of this chapter's key concepts and skills using the Self-Assessment in your ebook or online (eLab course or Student Resource Center).

Reinforce Your Skills

REINFORCE YOUR SKILLS: W2-R1

Insert Tables and Format Table Elements

Kids for Change is partnering with the local Center for Environmental Health to identify products in the home that present a risk to babies. In this exercise, you will create and enter data in a table. You will resize columns, rows, and cell margins, and you will change alignment. You will use a Quick Table, convert a tabular document to a table, and split and merge cells.

1. Start Word and create a document using the **Blank Document** template saved as:
   W2-R1-RiskToBabies
2. Choose the **Insert→Tables→Table** 🖩 button and create a **3×6** table.
3. Enter the data shown here; then select the first row and choose **Home→Font→Bold** B :

Tip! *Remember, you can add rows to the bottom of a table by tapping ⌷Tab⌷ when you reach the last table cell.*

Member Name	School	Research Assignment
Stacey	Highland	Harmful chemicals
Jacob	Lincoln	Cribs
Noah	Tri-way	Baby slings
Emma	Blue Ridge	Bath seats
Olivia	Springville	Highchairs
Nanda	Arlington	Infant swings

Now you will resize the columns.

4. Position the mouse pointer on the border between *Member Name* and *School*.
5. When the mouse pointer changes to the adjust pointer, drag to the left about ¾".
6. Resize the second and third columns to be just as wide as they need to be to fit the data without allowing any text to wrap within the cell.
7. Position the adjust pointer on the bottom border of the top row and drag down until the row is about twice its original height.
8. Select the first row and choose **Table Tools→Layout→Alignment→Align Center** 🔲.

   Next you will insert a calendar Quick Table so you can keep track of meetings with the Center for Environmental Health.

9. Position the insertion point at the end of the document and tap ⌷Enter⌷ twice.
10. Choose **Insert→Tables→Table** 🖩, slide the mouse pointer down to **Quick Tables**, and insert **Calendar 2**.

    Now you will copy a tabular table from another file and paste it into your document.

Convert a Tabular Document to a Table

11. Open **W2-R1-FoodRisk** and then select the entire document.
12. Choose **Home→Clipboard→Copy** 📋 and then close the file.

13. Position the insertion point at the end of the **Risk to Babies** document and tap Enter .

14. Choose **Home→Clipboard→Paste** 📋 and, if necessary, display formatting marks.

    Notice that the columns in this tabular table are separated by a single tab. Remember, there must be only one tab between columns for the conversion to work properly.

15. Select the entire tabular table and choose **Insert→Tables→Table** ▦ **→Convert Text to Table**.

16. Accept the defaults in the dialog box and click **OK**.

17. Use the mouse pointer to select the **Food** and **Risk Factor** columns.

18. Choose **Table Tools→Layout→Alignment→Align Center**.

19. Choose **Table Tools→Layout→Alignment→Cell Margins** ⊞ .

20. In the Table Options dialog box, change the top and bottom margins to **0.04** and click **OK**.

    This increases the vertical space between cells.

21. Click in the first table row.

22. Choose **Table Tools→Layout→Rows & Columns→Insert Above** ⊞ and then position the insertion point in the first cell of the new row.

23. Choose **Table Tools→Layout→Merge→Split Cells** ⊞ .

24. In the Split Cells dialog box, change the number of columns to **4**; click **OK**.

25. Select the first row.

26. Choose **Table Tools→Layout→Merge→Merge Cells** ⊞ .

27. Click in the new row and type: **Food Risk**

28. Save and close the file.

REINFORCE YOUR SKILLS: W2-R2

Format and Sort a Table

Kids for Change members are planning a demonstration of safe cleaning products at the Community Center. They plan to distribute a table document that lists safe products you can use in the kitchen. In this exercise, you will use table formats to design a professional-looking table that is engaging and easy to read.

1. Open **W2-R2-SafeClean** and save it as: **W2-R2-SafeCleanRevised**

2. Make sure the insertion point is in the table.

3. Choose **Table Tools→Design→Table Styles**, open the **Table Styles** gallery, and choose **Grid Table 4 – Accent 6**.

    Hint: It's a green style.

4. Select the table and choose **Table Tools→Design→Borders→Borders** ⊞ **menu button ▾→Outside Borders**.

5. Select the first row and choose **Table Tools→Design→Borders→Borders** ⊞ **menu button ▾→Bottom Border**.

6. With the first row still selected, choose **Table Tools→Design→Table Styles→Shading** 🎨 **menu button ▾**.

7. Choose **Green, Accent 6, Darker 50%** (last green color in the right column).

8. Select the entire table and choose **Home→Font→Font menu button** ▼→**Comic Sans MS**.

9. Select in the first column starting at **Clean coffee pot** through the end of the column.

10. Choose **Home→Font→Italic** I.

11. Save and close the file.

Sort a Data Table

Dylan, a Kids for Change member, volunteers at a green cleaning supply company so he can become familiar with safe cleaning products. He has been asked to take inventory this month, which is a good way to get to know the products. Dylan plans to sort the inventory list by Category and then by Sub-Category. This will make it easier to locate the items in the warehouse.

12. Open **W2-R2-Inventory** and save it as: `W2-R2-InventoryRevised`

13. Select the entire table and choose **Table Tools→Layout→Data→Sort** ; if necessary, choose the **Header Row** option in the bottom-left corner of the Sort dialog box.

14. Choose **Sort By menu button** ▼→**Category** and then choose **Then By→Sub-Category**; click **OK**.

    It will now be easier for Dylan to inventory the cleaning supplies.

Use Print and Print Preview

15. Choose **File→Print** to display the Print options in the Backstage view.

16. Choose the **Printer menu** button ▼ to see the list of available printers and select **Microsoft Print to PDF**. Leave all other settings as they are.

17. Click the **Print** button and, in the save dialog box that appears, navigate to your student exercise files folder.

18. Save the PDF print as: `W2-R2-InventoryPrint`

    If the PDF file is automatically opened, close it.

19. Save and close the file.

REINFORCE YOUR SKILLS: W2-R3

Insert and Format Tables

This holiday season Kids for Change members are working with the local fire department to collect toys for needy kids. The members will be assigned to different neighborhoods for collecting toys. In this exercise, you will format a table that tracks how many toys each member collects. In preparation for sending out mailing lists and tracking additional donations, you will sort a table, insert a Quick Table, and convert text to a table.

1. Open **W2-R3-Toys** and save it as: `W2-R3-ToysRevised`

2. Select the second and third columns of the first table.

3. Choose **Table Tools→Layout→Alignment→Align Center** .

4. Select the entire table and choose **Table Tools→Layout→Alignment→Cell Margins** .

5. Change the top and bottom margins to **0.06** and then click **OK**.

Merge Cells, Format the Table, and Sort Data

6. Select the four **Sycamore** cells in the third column.

7. Choose **Table Tools→Layout→Merge→Merge Cells** ⊞ and then delete three of the *Sycamore* entries.

8. Use the same technique to merge the *Homestead Valley* and *Middle Ridge* cells, and then delete three *Homestead Valley* and three *Middle Ridge* entries.

9. Select the entire table.

10. Choose **Table Tools→Design→Borders→Borders** ⊞ **menu button ▼→No Border**.

    Only the gridlines, which do not print, are visible—unless they were turned off. (Remember, you can turn gridlines on and off via the Table Tools' Design tab and the Borders menu button ▼.)

11. Choose **Table Tools→Design→Table Styles→More** ▼ **→Grid Table 4 – Accent 5 style**.

    Hint: It's a blue style.

    Several Kids for Change regional directors plan to meet after the toy collection to discuss plans for next year's collection. They compiled a mailing list of directors who will be notified of the meeting. Now you will sort the mail, as presorted mail results in lower postage rates.

12. Scroll to the table on page 3 and position the insertion point in the table.

13. Choose **Table Tools→Layout→Data→Sort** ⧩.

14. Ensure that **Header Row** in the Sort dialog box is chosen and then choose to sort first by **State**, then by **City**, and finally by **Zip**. Click **OK**.

    The California cities are sorted in ascending alphabetic order within State, and the Dallas Zip codes are sorted in ascending numeric order within City.

Insert Rows and Resize Columns

15. Scroll to the table on page 4 and click to place the insertion point anywhere inside the table.

    Region 5 was accidentally omitted.

16. Position the mouse pointer to the left of, and between, the last two rows until the insert control appears.

Region
1
2
3
4
6

17. Click the **insert control** to insert a blank row between the last two rows and then enter the following data in the new row:

5	1,951	2,543

18. Select the entire table and choose **Table Tools→Layout→Cell Size→AutoFit** ⊞ **→AutoFit Contents**.

Insert a Quick Table and Convert Text to a Table

Kids for Change members decided to take up a collection from friends and family to purchase additional toys. You will insert a Quick Table for tracking the donations.

19. If necessary, display formatting marks and then position the insertion point next to the last paragraph symbol on page 4.

20. Choose **Insert→Tables→Table** ▦**→Quick Tables→Tabular List**.

21. Select the **ITEM** heading and type **MEMBER** in its place; select the **NEEDED** heading and type **AMOUNT** in its place.

22. Select the remaining rows, tap Delete , and then enter the new data as shown:

MEMBER	AMOUNT
Ella	$20
Tom	$17
Roger	$32
Stella	$15
Jennifer	$22
Max	$29
Jose	$35
Albert	$40

23. Scroll to page 2 and select the rows in the tabular table.

24. Choose **Insert→Tables→Table** ▦**→Convert Text to Table**.

25. When the Convert Text to Table dialog box appears, click **OK** and then save and close the file.

Apply Your Skills

Insert and Modify a Table

Universal Corporate Events is finalizing its schedule for the autumn cruises. You have been asked to complete the September cruise schedule for the Bahamas. In this exercise, you will insert a new table, align data, and resize columns and cell margins.

1. Start Word, open **W2-A1-CorpEvents**, and save it as: **W2-A1-CorpEventsRevised**
2. If needed, display formatting marks and then position the insertion point on the first blank line below *Oceanic Cruise Lines*.
3. Insert a **4×4** table and enter the data shown:

Date	Itinerary	Ship	From
09/02/25	4-night Bahamas Cruise from Miami	Oceanic Star	$560
09/09/25	3-night Bahamas Cruise from Miami	Oceanic Jewel	$600
09/30/25	7-night Bahamas Cruise from New York	Oceanic Odyssey	$1159

You accidentally overlooked the September 22 cruise, so you'll add that now.

4. Use the **insert control** to add a row between the last two rows and then enter this information:

09/22/25	7-night Bahamas Cruise from New York	Oceanic Star	$1120

5. Select the last two columns and then center-align the text.
6. Use the adjust pointer to resize the columns to the approximate width shown in the following figure:

Date	Itinerary	Ship	From
09/02/25	4-night Bahamas Cruise from Miami	Oceanic Star	$560
09/09/25	3-night Bahamas Cruise from Miami	Oceanic Jewel	$600
09/22/25	7-night Bahamas Cruise from New York	Oceanic Star	$1120
09/30/25	7-night Bahamas Cruise from New York	Oceanic Odyssey	$1159

7. Set the top/bottom margins of all cells to: **0.08"**
8. Insert a new row at the top of the table.
9. Merge the cells in the new row and type **Travel Special** as the table heading.

   Next, you will convert a table to text.

10. Scroll to page 2 and select the entire table.
11. Choose **Table Tools→Layout→Data→Convert to Text** 🖼 and then click **OK**.
12. Save and close the file.

Format and Sort Tables

A Universal Corporate Events sales rep has asked you to prepare two tables of travel packages that he will present to two different clients. In this exercise, you will format the tables with borders, shading, and table styles, and then you will sort the data.

1. Open **W2-A2-Universal** from your **Word Chapter 2** folder and save it as: **W2-A2-UniversalRevised**

2. Remove the borders from the table on page 1.

3. Select the first row and use the **Borders** ⊞ **menu** button ▼ to apply a bottom border.

4. Apply a bottom border to the last row of the table.

5. Select the first row and then choose **Table Tools→Design→Table Styles→ Shading** 🖌 **menu button ▼→Gold, Accent 4, Darker 25%**.

6. Select the third row and apply: **Gold, Accent 4, Lighter 60%**

7. Apply the same color you used in the third row to the fifth row.

8. Scroll to page 2, position the insertion point in the table, choose **Table Tools→Design→ Table Styles**, and open the Table Styles gallery.

9. Choose **Grid Table 6 Colorful – Accent 4**; it's a yellow style.

Sort Data and Insert a Row

10. Using the page 2 table, specify that the table has a header row and sort by the **Travel Package** column in ascending order.

11. Using the page 1 table, insert a blank row at the top of the table, merge the cells in the first row, and type: **Universal Corporate Events**

12. Use **Align Center** ▣ to center the heading and then apply shading, **Gold, Accent 4, Lighter 40%**.

    The black print in the second row is a bit hard to read.

13. Change the font color to white.

Print the File

14. Open the Print window in the Backstage view.

15. Use the **Printer menu** button ▼ to select your printer and print the file.

    If you'd rather stay green and print a digital version of the file, select Microsoft Print to PDF and save the file as a PDF print.

16. Save and close the file.

Create and Format Tables

The Universal Corporate Events marketing manager has asked you to create a list of the day tours from Paris. She also asked that you reformat the list of African trips and modify and reformat the Asian tour table. In this exercise, you will create a table, convert a table to text, and sort and reformat a table.

1. Open **W2-A3-Travel** from your **Word Chapter 2** folder; save it as **W2-A3-TravelRevised** and, if necessary, display formatting marks.

2. Position the insertion point next to the first paragraph symbol at the top of the page.

3. Insert a **4×5** table and enter the data as shown:

Day Tours	From	When	Duration
Versailles	$70	Daily except Mon	4 hrs.
Eiffel Tower	$75	Daily	3 hrs.
Louvre Museum	$65	Daily except Tue	2.5 hrs.
Moulin Rouge Show	$153	Daily	4.5 hrs.

4. Scroll to page 3 and select the table.

5. Convert the table to text; ensure that the Tabs option is chosen in the dialog box.

Sort a Table

6. Scroll to page 2 and position the insertion point in the table.

7. Open the Sort dialog box, indicate that the table has a header row, and sort by the **Destination** column in ascending order.

8. Delete the Discount column and use the **insert control** to add a column between *Dates* and *Duration*.

9. Enter the information as shown:

Departure
San Francisco
Los Angeles
Los Angeles
San Diego
San Francisco

10. Select **columns 2–5** and position the mouse between two of the selected columns until you see the column adjust pointer.

11. Double-click to autofit the columns to the width of the longest entry in each of the selected columns.

12. Insert a row at the top of the table and merge all cells in the row.

13. Type **Universal Corporate Events** in the row and center-align the text.

14. Select the entire table and remove all borders.

15. Select the first row, apply outside borders, and apply the shading color **Blue, Accent 1, Lighter 60%**.

16. Save and close the file; exit Word.

🗒️ Project Grader

If your class is using eLab (labyrinthelab.com), you may upload your completed Project Grader assignments for automatic grading. You may complete these projects even if your class doesn't use eLab, though you will not be able to upload your work.

PROJECT GRADER: W2-P1

Formatting a Business Letter

Global Games International has been providing products to Taylor Games for many years. In this exercise, you will create a well-formatted letter to send to customers that introduces some new items they may want to add to their product line.

1. Download and open your Project Grader starting file.
   - *Using eLab:* Download **W2_P1_eStart** from the Assignments page. You *must* start with this file or your work cannot be automatically graded.
   - *Not using eLab:* Open **W2_P1_Start** from your **Word Chapter 2** folder.

2. Replace the word *collection* at the end of the first main paragraph with: `product line`

3. Insert an empty paragraph above the complimentary close, *Sincerely.*

4. Apply **Bullets** formatting to these lines:
   - *Net 30 terms*
   - *90 day returns policy*
   - *No minimum orders*
   - *Free shipping on orders over $50.00*

5. In the Catan table row, change the number *51.00* to: `55.00`

6. Add the following new rows to the table:
   - Add this header row to the top of the table:

Item Name	Category	Your Cost	Suggested Retail

   - Add these rows to the bottom of the table:

History of Board Games	Books	9.50	15.00
Monopoly Deluxe	Board Games	10.50	18.50

7. In table **columns 3** and **4**, apply **Align Right** paragraph formatting to all cells.

8. Sort the table using these settings:

Setting	Value
Sort by	**Category** in **Ascending** order
Then by	**Item Name** in **Ascending** order
My list has	**Header row**

9. Apply the table style **Grid Table 4 – Accent 1** to the table.

10. Set these table column widths:

Column	Width
Column 1	**2"**
Column 3	**0.9"**
Column 4	**1.5"**

11. Save your document.
    - *Using eLab:* Save it to your **Word Chapter 2** folder as: `W2_P1_eSubmission` and attach the file to your eLab assignment for grading.
    - *Not using eLab:* Save it to your **Word Chapter 2** folder as: `W2_P1_Submission`

PROJECT GRADER: W2-P2

Enhancing a Welcome Letter for New Members

In this exercise, you will enhance a welcome letter for new Classic Cars Club members. The letter needs a table and formatting to organize and present the information in a professional manner.

1. Download and open your Project Grader starting file.
   - *Using eLab:* Download **W2_P2_eStart** from the Assignments page. You *must* start with this file or your work cannot be automatically graded.
   - *Not using eLab:* Open **W2_P2_Start** from your **Word Chapter 2** folder.

2. On the empty paragraph above *Today's Date*, insert a **2 column** by **1 row** table.

3. Enter this text in the new table:

Classic Cars Club	PO Box 6987 Ferndale, WA 98248

4. In **cell 1**, apply **14 pt** and **Bold** formatting to the *Classic Cars Club* text.

5. Apply these table cell alignments:

Cell	Alignment
Cell 1	**Align Center Left**
Cell 2	**Align Center Right**

6. Remove all table borders.

7. Insert two more empty paragraphs above *Today's Date*. Feel free to replace the *Today's Date* text with the current date in the format you desire.

> **Classic·Cars·Club¤**
> ¶
> ¶
> ¶
> Today's·Date¶

8. Apply **Bullets** formatting to these paragraphs:
- Free entry to local and regional shows
- A 30% entry discount on the national show
- A 25% discount on merchandise purchases
- A free Classic Cars Club plaque
- A free Classic Cars Club license plate frame

9. Set these column widths for the three-column table in the center of the document:

Column	Width
Column 1	**1.5"**
Column 2	**2.25"**
Column 3	**1"**

10. Sort the table using these settings:
- Sort by: **Locations** in **Ascending** order
- My list has: **Header row**

11. Insert a new row at the top of the table.

12. Merge all cells in the new row.

13. Enter text in and apply formatting to the merged cell as follows:
- Enter the text: `Available Partner Discounts`
- Apply **14 pt** and **Bold** formatting to the text you just entered
- Apply **Center** paragraph alignment

14. Select all table cells starting with **row 2** (don't include the **row 1** merged cell) and apply these border settings to the selection:

Setting	Value
Line Style	**Solid, single line**
Line Weight	**½ pt**
Borders	**Outside Borders**

> ──────────── ▾
> ½ pt ────── ▾

15. Apply **White, Background 1, Darker 15%** shading to all cells in **row 2**.

16. Apply these border settings to all cells in **row 2**:

Setting	Value
Border Line Style	**Solid, single line**
Border Line Weight	**1½ pt**
Borders	**Bottom Border**

17. Apply **Bold** font formatting to all text in **row 2**.

18. Save your document.

- *Using eLab:* Save it to your **Word Chapter 2** folder as `W2_P2_eSubmission` and attach the file to your eLab assignment for grading.

- *Not using eLab:* Save it to your **Word Chapter 2** folder as: `W2_P2_Submission`

◢ Extend Your Skills

These exercises challenge you to think critically and apply your new skills in a real-world setting. You will be evaluated on your ability to follow directions, completeness, creativity, and the use of proper grammar and mechanics. Save files to your chapter folder. Submit assignments as directed.

W2-E1 That's the Way I See It

You own a hardware store, and a few building contractors order from you in large quantities. Track their contact information in a ten-row table with column heads for Name, Address, City, State, and Zip. Your business covers four states: Utah, Arizona, New Mexico, and Colorado. Include each state and sort by State, then by City, then by Zip. Add a column at the end of the table for Phone and enter the new data. Add a header row, centering your company name. Apply a table style and then save the file as: **W2-E1-Contractors**

W2-E2 Be Your Own Boss

Business is "blooming" at Blue Jean Landscaping; you need to get control of inventory. Decide how many landscapers work for you and the number of items needed to keep them supplied. Create a six-row table listing tools, such as spades and hoes. Note how many you have and how many you need to add. Include headings for Item, Location, Units Needed, Units in Stock, Units to Add, and Price. Add five rows of data, sort by Item, and resize the columns as needed. Add a header row centering the company name. Add borders and shading for readability. Print the file or use Microsoft Print to PDF to create a PDF version. Save the file as: **W2-E2-Inventory**

W2-E3 Demonstrate Proficiency

The chef at Stormy BBQ will introduce a new dish. Decide on the dish and then create a document named: **W2-E3-Order**.

Set up a table for the food order; include item, price, quantity, and cost and then enter five food items. Sort the table in an order you think most useful. Add a heading row and center the restaurant name. Size the table so it's easy to read and apply a table style of your choice.

3 | Creating Reports

In this chapter, you will create a simple report. Reports are important documents often used in business and education to distribute information, communicate ideas, and share viewpoints and plans on a variety of topics. You will format your report using tabs, indents, margin changes, and headers and footers. You will also learn about research papers, a requirement for nearly every college student as well as professionally employed individuals. Your paper will include footnotes, citations, a bibliography, and a table of figures. Finally, you will explore Track Changes, a feature that allows for collaborative editing of a document.

LEARNING OBJECTIVES

▸ Work with columns and set margins

▸ Format text and apply styles

▸ Insert headers and footers

▸ Add footnotes and endnotes

▸ Insert citations and a bibliography

▸ Incorporate captions and a table of figures

▸ Insert comments and use Track Changes

📂 Project: Researching Social Media and Internet Commerce

My Virtual Campus is a social networking technology company. It sells web applications to colleges and universities. Your marketing manager, José Morales, has asked you to look into the latest trends in social media in schools. It is important to understand how the "always connected" generation is using technology in the pursuit of education. Your manager also wants you to download an online article regarding social media in education that he can distribute in the next staff meeting. And he wants you to make the article's dense text more readable by using heading styles, headers and footers, and white space.

You are also working on your masters in marketing, and your professor wants you to write a research paper about the origins and evolution of Internet commerce. You will use many sophisticated features, such as headers and footers, footnotes, citations, and bibliographies in creating this research paper.

Creating a Business Report

When writing a business report, you want it to be easy to read. Dense blocks of text are difficult to read, so break up your report with lists, headings/subheadings, and white space. Use a clear, easy-to-read font, such as Calibri (Word's default font), Arial, or Times New Roman. Here are some principles of communication you may want to keep in mind when writing a report:

- ▶ Plan before you write.
- ▶ Know your audience.
- ▶ Use active voice.
- ▶ Avoid wordiness.
- ▶ Use plain language; avoid overblown words.
- ▶ Don't use clichés.
- ▶ Use parallel structure.
- ▶ Edit out anything that doesn't add to your meaning.
- ▶ Organize your writing into short sections.

Setting Margins

Margins determine the amount of white space around the edges of the page. You can set margins for the entire document, a section, or selected text. The default margins in the Blank Document and Single Spaced (Blank) templates, as well as many others, are one inch all around. You can choose from a gallery of preset margins, or you can set your own custom margins.

≡ Layout→Page Setup→Margins ▢

Indenting Text

Indents offset text from the margins. You can set indents by using the buttons on the Ribbon or by adjusting the indent markers on the ruler. The Increase and Decrease Indent buttons adjust the indent of an entire paragraph (or one or more selected paragraphs) and affect the left indent only. They adjust the indent based on the default tab stops, which are set at every half inch.

View the video "Indent Markers."

≡ Home→Paragraph→Increase Indent 📑 or Decrease Indent 📑

DEVELOP YOUR SKILLS: W3-D1

In this exercise, you will increase the margins in a report to provide a little more white space. You will use the Increase Indent button on the Ribbon to offset quotes in the report, and you will create your own custom indents using the indent markers on the ruler.

1. Open **W3-D1-SocMediaRpt** from your **Word Chapter 3** folder and save it as:
   `W3-D1-SocMediaRptRevised`
2. If necessary, choose **View→Show→Ruler**.

   Now you will increase the margin width to add more white space to the report.
3. Choose **Layout→Page Setup→Margins** ⊞ and notice the preset margin settings.

   You want a 1.5" left and right margin, and that is not available in the preset list, so you will customize your own settings.
4. Choose **Custom Margins** at the bottom of the menu.
5. On the Margins tab of the Page Setup dialog box, change the left and right margins to **1.5"** and then click **OK**.

Margins			
Top:	1"	Bottom:	1"
Left:	1.5"	Right:	1.5"

   Notice the gray margin areas at the ends of the ruler; they have increased to 1.5".

   Now you will use the Increase Indent button to offset quotes in the report.
6. Below *The Net Generation* heading, select the second and third paragraphs, which are inside quotation marks.

7. Choose **Home→Paragraph→Increase Indent** .

The paragraphs indent from the left a half inch based on the default tab settings; however, you want to indent the paragraphs from both the right and the left. So, now you will use the indent markers on the ruler to complete the job.

8. Follow these steps to adjust the left and right indents:

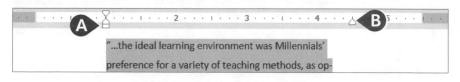

"...the ideal learning environment was Millennials' preference for a variety of teaching methods, as op-

Ⓐ Position the mouse pointer on the **Left Indent** marker (bottom rectangle) and drag to the **1"** mark.

Ⓑ Drag the **Right Indent** marker to the **4½"** mark.

9. Save the report.

Setting Custom Tab Stops

Default tab stops are set every half inch, so the insertion point moves a half inch whenever you tap Tab. You can customize tab stops if you want other settings.

Warning! *Never use the Spacebar key to line up columns. Even if it looks right on the screen, it most likely will not print correctly.*

Using the Ruler to Set Custom Tabs

Word has four types of custom tab stops: left, right, center, and decimal. You can set all four types using the horizontal ruler. It is critical that you position the insertion point in the line where you plan to set tabs. Tab settings are carried inside the paragraph symbol to the next paragraph when you tap Enter.

Use the Tabs box to choose the tab type. (ToolTips describe the symbols.)

You indicate the tab placement by clicking in the desired location on the ruler.

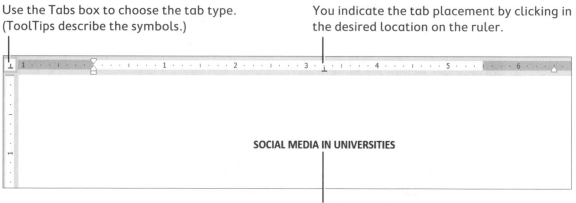

SOCIAL MEDIA IN UNIVERSITIES

This heading is centered by a center tab.

Tip! *You can delete a custom tab by dragging it off the ruler with your mouse. When you release the mouse button, the tab disappears.*

Using the Tabs Dialog Box to Set Custom Tabs

You can also set custom tab stops in the Tabs dialog box. You can specify precise positions for tabs, choose the type of tab (alignment), clear custom tab stops, and set dot leader tabs. A leader tab generates a row of dots when you tap Tab. You often see dot leaders in a table of contents separating a topic from its page number.

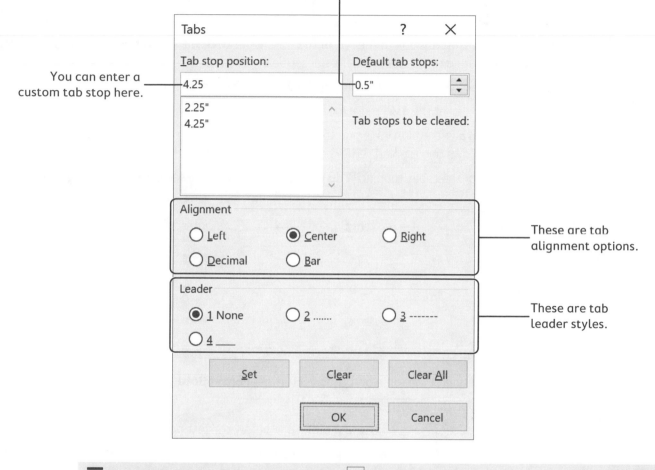

You can change the default tab stops here.

You can enter a custom tab stop here.

These are tab alignment options.

These are tab leader styles.

≡ Home→Paragraph dialog box launcher 🔲 →Tabs...

DEVELOP YOUR SKILLS: W3-D2

In this exercise, you will set custom tabs and create two tabbed tables.

1. Save your report as: **W3-D2-SocMediaRptRevised**

2. If necessary, display formatting marks.

3. Position the insertion point on the blank line below the section titled *Rapid Increase in the Use of Social Media*.

4. Follow these steps to set tabs for the first table:

 Tip! *If you accidentally click the tab in the wrong place, you can drag it to a new location with the mouse pointer, or you can drag it off the ruler and try again.*

Ⓐ Verify that the Tabs box at the left of the ruler is set to a Left Tab. If not, click the box until it rotates around to Left Tab. (ToolTips describe the tab type.)

Ⓑ Click the bottom edge of the ruler at the **2¼"** mark to set a tab.

Ⓒ Click the ruler at the **4¼"** mark for the second tab.

Ⓓ Type **Media** in the blank line and then type the next two entries, tapping [Tab] where you see the arrows and tapping [Enter] at the end of the line.

5. Type the rest of the table, tapping [Tab] and [Enter] where you see the arrows and paragraph symbols:

Media	→	2013	→	2015¶
Facebook	→	79%	→	84%¶
Twitter	→	35%	→	40%¶
Instagram	→	30%	→	36%¶
Snapchat	→	16%	→	23%¶

6. Select the first line of the table and choose **Home→Font→Bold** B .

Now you will type the second table.

7. Position the insertion point on the first blank line below the last paragraph of the document.

Look at the ruler and notice that the tabs you set for the first table have disappeared. The tab settings for the first table are carried in the paragraph symbols for that table only.

8. Follow these steps to set the tabs for and type the second table:

Media	→	Launched	→	2015·Users¶
Facebook	→	2004	→	1.5·billion·monthly·active·users¶
Twitter	→	2006	→	1.5·billion·monthly·active·users¶
Instagram	→	2010	→	300·million·active·users¶
LinkedIn	→	2003	→	380·million·users·worldwide¶

Ⓐ Set left tabs at the **2¼"** mark and the **3½"** mark.

Ⓑ Type the table as shown, applying bold formatting to the first line of the table.

9. Save the file and close it.

Formatting Text and Using Styles

A style is one of the most powerful formatting tools. It is a *group of formats* enabling you to apply multiple formats to a block of text all at once. Styles are based on the current template's theme, which is a set of colors, fonts, and graphic effects. There are styles for document elements, such as headings, titles, and special character formats, providing consistent formatting throughout a document.

Spacing in Letters

The default line spacing in Word 2019 is 1.08 rather than the traditional 1.0 single spacing. It adds an extra 8% more space between lines than regular single spacing. It also adds 8 points of space after paragraphs. Therefore, rather than tapping ⎡Enter⎤ twice at the end of a paragraph, you just tap ⎡Enter⎤ once, and Word adds the extra spacing.

When you choose the Blank Document template on the Start screen or on the New screen in Backstage view, you are using the default spacing. Some documents, however, typically require single spacing, such as business letters, reports, and proposals. These methods are available for applying single spacing:

▸ Single Spaced (Blank) template

▸ Line and Paragraph Spacing button

Applying Traditional Spacing Using the Single Spaced (Blank) Template

Choosing the Single Spaced (Blank) template from the Start screen or from the New screen opens a single-spaced document. This is a good choice if the majority of your document will be single spaced. If you use single spacing in only part of your document, the Line and Paragraph Spacing button is a good choice.

Changing Spacing Using the Line and Paragraph Spacing Button

If you start a new document using 1.08 spacing and then decide to apply single spacing to a portion of the document, you can choose the 1.0 option in the Line and Paragraph Spacing button menu. You must select (highlight) the text to be single spaced or, at a minimum, position the insertion point in the paragraph before changing the spacing. If you wish to use other spacing such as double or triple spacing, the Line and Paragraph Spacing button is the place to go.

≡ Home→Paragraph→Line and Paragraph Spacing 🔲 | Right-click in the text→Paragraph→ Line Spacing

---

DEVELOP YOUR SKILLS: W3-D3

In this exercise, you will use the Single Spaced (Blank) template, and you will modify spacing in your cover letter.

1. Choose **File→New** to display the templates.
2. Click the **Single Spaced (Blank)** template to start a single-spaced document.

   A window appears describing the template.
3. Click the **Create** 🗋 button to start the document.

Tip! *If you double-click the template, the document will open immediately.*

4. Choose **File→Save As**, navigate to your **Word Chapter 3** folder, and save the file as: `W3-D3-CoverLtr`

5. Type **Nove** but stop typing when AutoComplete displays a pop-up tip.

6. Tap [Enter] to automatically insert *November* in the letter.

   Word recognizes certain words and phrases, such as names of the months and days, and offers to complete them for you.

7. Finish typing the date as: **November 24, 2021**

8. Tap [Enter] three times to provide space between the date and the inside address.

9. If necessary, choose **Home→Paragraph→Show/Hide** [¶] to display formatting marks.

10. Type the inside address and salutation as shown.

    If you catch a typo, you can [Backspace] *enough times to remove the error and then continue typing.*

    `Mr. Blake Carter, Hiring Manager`[Enter]

    `Global Computer Sales and Service`[Enter]

    `347 Wellington Street`[Enter]

    `San Francisco, CA  94123`[Enter]

    [Enter]

    `Dear Mr. Carter:`[Enter]

    [Enter]

    [Enter]

11. Type the following body paragraphs.

    Remember, you are using the single-spaced template now and there is no additional spacing when you tap [Enter] *at the end of the paragraphs. You have to tap* [Enter] *twice to create white space between paragraphs.*

    `I am applying for the position of Retail Computer Sales advertised on your website. I am a recent Computer Science graduate from Case Western University, where I attained a 3.9 GPA. During the summers, I worked as an intern in the sales department at Best Computers in Cleveland. I am extremely interested in discussing your sales position, which aligns well with my education and sales experience.`[Enter]

    [Enter]

    `I am impressed with your excellent products and reputation. I am confident that I am a strong candidate, and I will contact you in the near future to arrange an interview.`[Enter]

    [Enter]

    [Enter]

Change Line Spacing

12. Position the insertion point anywhere in the first main paragraph.

13. Choose **Home→Paragraph→Line and Paragraph Spacing** [⇳≡].

14. Slide the mouse pointer over the menu options and notice that Live Preview shows how the selected paragraph will look if the formatting is applied.

Notice the Add Space Before Paragraph and Add Space After Paragraph options. These options add an extra 12 points of space before or after a paragraph.

15. Choose **3.0** (triple space).

Remembering that single spacing is appropriate for a business letter, you decide to change back to single spacing.

16. Choose **Home→Paragraph→Line and Paragraph Spacing** 📳 and choose **1.0**.

17. Save your letter.

Aligning Text Horizontally and Vertically

You can control how text aligns horizontally on the page using the paragraph alignment buttons in the Paragraph group on the Home tab. You can determine vertical alignment of text on a page using the Vertical Alignment feature in Page Setup.

TEXT ALIGNMENT OPTIONS	
Horizontal Alignment	**Vertical Alignment**
• Align Left (default) • Center • Align Right • Justify (text distributed evenly between left/right margins)	• Top (default) • Center • Justified (text distributed evenly between top/bottom margins) • Bottom
☰ Home→Paragraph→choose the desired alignment	☰ Layout→Page Setup ⌐ dialog box launcher→Layout tab→Page→Vertical Alignment

DEVELOP YOUR SKILLS: W3-D4

In this exercise, you will change the horizontal and vertical alignment in your letter.

1. Choose **File→Save As** and save your file as: `W3-D4-CoverLtr`

2. Position the insertion point anywhere in the date line.

3. Choose **Home→Paragraph→Center** ≡ to center the date between the margins.

Notice that the Center button on the Ribbon is highlighted, indicating that center alignment is in effect at the insertion point.

4. Choose **Home→Paragraph→Align Right** ≡ to place the date at the right-hand margin.

You've decided you prefer to have the date left-aligned.

5. Choose **Home→Paragraph→Align Left** ≡.

Now you will type the close, the signature, and an enclosures notification.

6. Position the insertion point next to the last paragraph symbol in the document.

7. Type the end of the letter as shown, tapping [Enter] wherever you see a paragraph symbol.

7. Type the end of the letter as shown:

Sincerely, Enter

Enter

Enter

Enter

Stella Martin Enter

Enter

Enclosure Enter

Center the Letter Vertically

8. Scroll down to the end of the page.

There is too much white space at the bottom of the letter, so now you will center the letter vertically on the page.

9. Click the **Layout** tab on the Ribbon.

10. Click the **dialog box launcher** ⬚ in the bottom-right corner of the Page Setup group to open the Page Setup dialog box.

11. Follow these steps to center the letter vertically on the page:

Ⓐ Click the **Layout** tab.

Ⓑ Click the **Vertical Alignment** field to display the menu.

Ⓒ Choose **Center** from the menu.

Ⓓ Click **OK** at the bottom of the dialog box to close it.

Now you will use the zoom controls to zoom out so you can see the entire page.

12. Click the **Zoom Out** button (at the bottom-right corner of the screen) enough times to see the entire page.

The letter is centered vertically on the page.

13. Click the **Zoom In** button enough times to return to 100%.

14. Save and close the letter.

Types of Styles

There are many built-in styles, and you are always working within a style. There are two basic types of styles: character and paragraph. You can use the Styles gallery and Styles task pane to apply styles.

▶ Character styles: Character styles are applied to the word the insertion point is in or a selected group of words. Character styles contain only character formats, not paragraph formats. You can apply character styles *within* a paragraph that is formatted with a paragraph style.

▶ Paragraph styles: Paragraph styles are applied to all text in selected paragraphs or to the paragraph containing the insertion point. You can use any character or paragraph format in a paragraph style. For example, you may want to format a heading with a large, bold font (character formatting) and apply paragraph spacing before and after the heading (paragraph formatting).

View the video "Using the Styles Gallery and the Styles Task Pane."

≡ Home→Styles→Styles Gallery | Home→Styles dialog box launcher ⬚

Collapsing Heading Topics

When you apply a heading style and the insertion point is in the heading, a small triangle marker appears at the left (whether formatting marks are displayed or not). You can click the marker to collapse and expand the text below it. In the following illustration, the text below *The Net Generation* is collapsed, allowing you to focus on certain parts of a document.

> ◁ ▷ ▪ The·Net·Generation¶
>
> ▪ Rapid·Increase·in·the·Use·of·Social·Media¶
> A·study·conducted·by·Harvard's·Institute·of·Politics·(iop.harvard.edu)·reports·use·of·

In this illustration, *The Net Generation* content is expanded.

> ▪ The·Net·Generation¶
> In·her·article·appearing·in·The·Teaching·Professor,·August/September·2009,·Dalton·State·
> College·psychology·professor·Christy·Price·makes·the·following·observations:¶
>
>> "...the·ideal·learning·environment·was·Millennials'·
>> preference·for·a·variety·of·teaching·methods,·as·
>> opposed·to·a·"lecture·only"·format."¶
>
>> "Respondents·thought·professors·who·involved·them·in·
>> class·with·a·variety·of·methods·(not·just·lecture)·as·
>> more·connected·to·millennial·culture."¶
>
> ▪ Rapid·Increase·in·the·Use·of·Social·Media¶
> A·study·conducted·by·Harvard's·Institute·of·Politics·(iop.harvard.edu/use-social-

In this exercise, you will use Live Preview in the Styles gallery to find styles that will give your report a professional, polished look. You will apply the Title style to the report's main heading and the Heading 1 style to the headings within the report.

1. Open **W3-D5-SocMediaRpt** from your **Word Chapter 3** folder and save it as: **W3-D5-SocMediaRptRevised**

2. Click anywhere in the report's main heading, **SOCIAL MEDIA IN UNIVERSITIES**, at the top of page 1.

3. Choose the **Home→Styles→More** ⊡ **button** to open the Styles gallery.

4. Hover the mouse pointer over the Title style to see its effect on the heading and then click to apply the style.

   Now you'll open the Styles task pane. It includes all the styles that are in the Styles gallery.

5. Click the **dialog box launcher** ⊡ in the bottom-right corner of the Styles group.

   Next you'll apply the Heading 1 style to the headings in the body of the report.

6. Position the insertion point in **The Net Generation** heading and then click the **Heading 1** style in the task pane to apply that style to the heading.

7. Use the same technique to apply the Heading 1 style to the remaining headings: **Rapid Increase in the Use of Social Media** and **University Recruiting Through Social Networking**.

8. Close the Styles task pane.

   Now you will collapse and expand the text below The Net Generation heading.

9. Scroll up and position the insertion point in **The Net Generation** heading to display the triangle marker to the left of the heading.

10. Click the **marker** to collapse the text below the heading.

    Collapsing parts of a document allows you to focus on the remaining parts.

11. Click the **marker** again to expand the text.

12. Save the report.

Inserting Headers/Footers, Comments, and Page Breaks

Headers and footers appear at the top and bottom of every page in a document, respectively, above and below the margins. You can place text, page numbers, dates, and other items in the header and footer areas. When you enter information in these areas, it is repeated on every page of the document. There is a variety of built-in header and footer formatting styles, or you can create your own.

The Comment feature is a great collaboration tool. It allows reviewers and originators to communicate about a document by posting comments to each other.

> **Lab Student** A few seconds ago
> Jose, please let me know if you need additional information regarding social media in education.
>
> ⤷ Reply   ⤷ Resolve

Clicking the reply button in the comments balloon allows threaded conversations between the originator and reviewers.

At times, you may wish to break up portions of your document by adding a page break. For example, you may want a report conclusion, appendix, or bibliography to each appear on separate pages. Word allows you to enter these page breaks with a simple Ribbon command, or by tapping `Ctrl`+`Enter`.

≡ Insert→Header & Footer→Header 🖹 or Footer 🖹 or Page Number ⧉

≡ Insert→Comments→Comment ⧉

≡ Layout→Page Setup→Breaks→Page ⧉

DEVELOP YOUR SKILLS: W3-D6

In this exercise, you will add headers and page numbers to the report using the built-in formats. Then you will insert a page break and add a comment to your report.

1. Save your file as: **W3-D6-SocMediaRptRevised**
2. Choose **Insert→Header & Footer→Header** 🖹 and choose the **Sideline** format from the gallery.
3. Click **Document Title** and type **My Virtual Campus** in its place.
4. Double-click in the document to close the header.
5. Choose **Insert→Header & Footer→Page Number** ⧉ and select **Bottom of Page**.
6. Scroll down in the gallery and choose **Large Color 3**.
7. Double-click in the document to close the page number footer.

   You can open the header/footer area by double-clicking anywhere in either the header or footer area.

8. Double-click the footer area to open it and then double-click in the document again to close it.
9. Scroll through the report and observe the headers and page numbers.

   It would look better to have at least two lines of the first table at the top of the second page.

10. Position the insertion point in front of *Instagram* in the first table and press `Ctrl`+`Enter` to insert a page break.

Add a Comment

Now you will add a comment for your marketing manager. He will see it when he reads your report.

11. Scroll to the top of the document and select the word **Universities** (the anchor point for the comment) in the title.

12. Choose **Insert→Comments→Comment** and type the following in the comment balloon on the right:

   Jose, please let me know if you need additional information regarding social media in education.

13. Save and then close the report.

Arranging Text in Multiple Columns

You can use newspaper-style columns (also known as newsletter-style columns) to arrange text in multiple columns. In newspaper layout, text flows down one column and wraps to the top of the next column, as in a newspaper or magazine. Newspaper columns can enhance readability, as the eye doesn't have to travel far across the page before reading the next line, and they break up dense text with random gaps. Columns are automatically reformatted as you add or delete text during editing cycles.

You can quickly set your text in columns with the Columns button on the Ribbon, or you can open the Columns dialog box where you can set up more sophisticated column layouts. For example, you can insert a line between columns and specify the width of each column.

These are commonly used column styles.

You can check this option if you want a line between columns.

You can preview your column setup here.

You can customize column widths and between-column spacing here.

≡ Layout→Page Setup→Columns

≡ Layout→Page Setup→Columns →More Columns

Column Breaks and Section Breaks

You can manually force a column to end by inserting a column break, thus moving the text at the break point to the top of the next column. This technique is often used to place headings at the top of columns and to balance columns on the last page of a multicolumn document.

Whenever you make a document-level formatting change that doesn't apply to the entire document, you need one or more section breaks to define the portion of the document affected by the change. For example, in a columnar magazine article, you may see a title line that extends across the page and then the body of the article is formatted in two columns. You need a section break to separate the one-column title from the two-column body of the article.

TYPES OF SECTION BREAKS

Section Break	Purpose
Next Page	Inserts a section break and starts the new section on the next page
Continuous	Inserts a section break and starts the new section on the same page
Odd Page	Inserts a section break and starts the new section on the next odd-numbered page; a blank page may be inserted to force the odd-page section break
Even Page	Inserts a section break and starts the new section on the next even-numbered page; a blank page may be inserted to force the even-page section break

The following illustration shows the use of continuous section breaks that are sectioning off the two-column portion of a document:

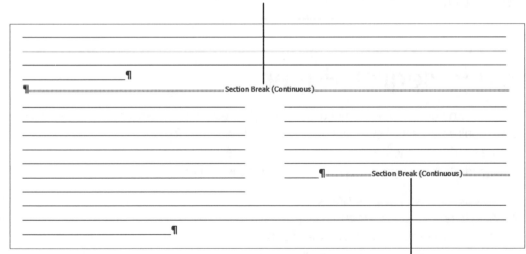

The section above this break has one-column formatting, and the section below it has two-column formatting.

Section Break (Continuous)

Section Break (Continuous)

This section break ends the two-column section.

≡ Layout→Page Setup→Breaks ⊟→Page Breaks→Column

≡ Layout→Page Setup→Breaks ⊟→Page Breaks and then choose a Section Break type

Because the article your marketing manager wants to distribute at the next staff meeting consists of dense text, he wants you to set the article in newspaper columns to enhance readability. In this exercise, you will insert a section break after the introduction, and then you will lay out the second section of the document in two columns.

1. Open **W3-D7-SocMedForStaff** from your **Word Chapter 3** folder and save it as:
   `W3-D7-SocMedForStaffRevised`

2. If necessary, display the formatting marks.

   You want the introductory paragraph to span the page, so you will insert a section break before the social media article and then set the rest of the article in columns.

3. Position the insertion point in the second blank line following the first paragraph.

4. Choose **Layout→Page Setup→Breaks** ⊟ **→Continuous**.

   This starts a new section on the same page.

5. Delete the blank line at the top of the second section.

6. Position the insertion point in the second section.

7. Choose **Layout→Page Setup→Columns** ⊞ **→Two**.

8. Scroll to page 2, and you'll see that the columns are not well-balanced.

9. Position the insertion point at the beginning of the last paragraph in the left column beginning with *In the real world*.

10. Choose **Layout→Page Setup→Breaks** ⊟ **→Column**.

11. Save and close the file.

Writing a Research Paper

There are a number of documentation styles for research papers, each with its own specific formatting requirements. For example, IEEE standards are used for research in computers and electronics; APA is used in psychology research; Turabian style is used for research in literature, history, and the arts; and MLA is primarily used for research in the humanities.

The Modern Language Association publishes the *MLA Handbook for Writers of Research Papers*. The MLA style has specific formatting requirements, *some* of which are already defaults within Word. For example, the default margins of one inch comply with the MLA requirement. However, Word does not comply with *all* MLA guidelines by default.

Warning! *This chapter does not presume to be a resource for MLA guidelines. Refer to the MLA handbook or the MLA website (mla.org) for guidance in complying with MLA requirements.*

Working with Footnotes, Endnotes, and Citations

Footnotes, endnotes, and citations are important elements of most research papers. You use them to comment on, or cite a reference to, a designated part of the text. Footnotes appear at the bottom of pages on which they are inserted; endnotes, as the name implies, appear at the end of a document or section; and citations appear on a separate Works Cited page at the end of the document. Works

Cited is another name for a bibliography. You can enter the source information when you create the citation or insert a placeholder and add the source data later. To help you enter the information correctly, example text appears for each of the various fields in the Create Source dialog box.

Create Source

Type of Source	Web site ▾

Bibliography Fields for MLA

Author	
	☐ Corporate Author
Name of Web Page	
Year	
Month	
Day	
Year Accessed	
Month Accessed	
Day Accessed	
Medium	

☐ Show All Bibliography Fields

Tag name   Example: Kramer, James D; Chen, Jacky

Placeholder1

☁ **View the video "Inserting Footnotes."**

☁ **View the video "Inserting Citations."**

☰ References→Footnotes→Insert Footnote AB¹ *or* Insert Endnote 📑

☰ References→Citations & Bibliography→Insert Citation 🗗

DEVELOP YOUR SKILLS: W3-D8

In this exercise, you will begin the research paper that your marketing professor requested. You will use footnotes and endnotes to clarify information and citations to support your premise.

1. Open **W3-D8-Internet** from your **Word Chapter 3** folder and save it as:
   `W3-D8-InternetRevised`

2. If necessary, choose **View→Views→Print Layout** 📄.

   Footnotes may differ in appearance depending on the view you are using.

3. Position the insertion point at the top of the document and type the following four lines of text above the title:

Brian Simpson`Enter`

Professor Williams`Enter`

Marketing 222`Enter`

May 10, 2021

Notice the paragraph text is double-spaced and the extra space after the paragraphs has been removed per MLA requirements. Now you will insert footnotes.

4. Position the insertion point to the right of the period at the end of the first paragraph.

5. Choose **References→Footnotes→Insert Footnote** `AB¹`.

The footnote reference mark appears at the insertion point, and a corresponding footnote appears at the bottom of the page.

6. Follow these steps to complete the footnote:

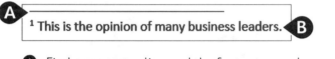

Ⓐ Find a separator line and the footnote number.

Ⓑ Type this text in the footnote area.

7. Use the same process to insert the footnote reference marks and the associated footnotes shown here:

> The commercial potential of the Internet stems from the fact that it is a global network with
>
> inexpensive access.² The Internet is also available 24x7. The multimedia capability to the Internet is
>
> important for marketing and advertising. Quick product delivery, automated order-taking, and low
>
> overhead are several more factors that are driving Internet commerce.³

> ¹ This is the opinion of many business leaders.
> ² Some nations still have high rates due to limited competition among Internet service providers.
> ³ These factors depend upon the capabilities of individual companies.

The default formatting of footnotes in Word does not adhere to MLA requirements. The text should use the same formatting as the body of the document (double-spaced, first line indented). You will format the footnotes later.

Now you will convert your footnotes to endnotes.

8. Choose **References→Footnotes dialog box launcher** `⌐` and click **Convert**.

Footnote and Endnote	? ✕
Location	
⦿ Footnotes:	Bottom of page ⌄
○ Endnotes:	End of document ⌄
	Convert...

9. When the Convert Notes dialog box opens, click **OK** and then close the Footnote and Endnote dialog box.

10. Scroll through the document and notice that the footnotes are no longer at the bottom of page 1; they now appear as endnotes on the last page.

    You decide that you prefer having the notes on the same page as the material they refer to, so you will convert the endnotes back to footnotes.

11. Choose **References→Footnotes dialog box launcher** 🔲 and click **Convert**.

12. Click **OK** in the Convert Notes dialog box and then close the Footnote and Endnote dialog box.

    Now you will choose the bibliography style for your paper and insert a citation.

13. Choose **References→Citations & Bibliography→Style menu button ▼→MLA Seventh Edition**.

    A citation should be placed inside the period at the end of a sentence.

14. At the end of the first paragraph on page 2, position the insertion point between the word *online* and the period and then tap [Spacebar].

15. Choose **References→Citations & Bibliography→Insert Citation** 🔲 and then choose **Add New Source**.

16. Follow these steps to create the new source to insert as the citation:

Create Source	
Type of Source	Web site ◀A
Bibliography Fields for MLA	
B▶Author	Swaney, Chriss
	☐ Corporate Author
Name of Web Page	Carnegie Mellon Study Finds Shopping Online Results in Less Environmental Impact
Year	2009
Month	March
Day	3
Year Accessed	2021
Month Accessed	March
Day Accessed	10
Medium	https://www.cmu.edu/news/archive/2009/March/march3_onlineshopping.shtml

☐ Show All Bibliography Fields

Tag name   Example: Document   C

Swa09 ◀D   E

Ⓐ If necessary, choose **Web site**.

Ⓑ Type the author's name as shown.

Ⓒ Enter the remaining information.

Ⓓ The system uses tags internally to uniquely identify a source. The Tag Name you see may vary from this one.

Ⓔ Click **OK**.

Note! *Remember, Word does not follow all MLA guidelines. Refer to the* MLA Handbook *or website when writing academic papers.*

Insert Citation Placeholders

17. On page 2, position the insertion point at the end of the third bullet point between *themselves* and the period and tap Spacebar.

18. Choose **References→Citations & Bibliography→Insert Citation** and then choose **Add New Placeholder**.

19. Type **Fowler** in the Placeholder Name box and then click **OK**.

20. Position the insertion point at the end of the document between *years* and the period and tap Spacebar.

21. Choose **References→Citations & Bibliography→Insert Citation** and then choose **Add New Placeholder**.

22. Type **Mogg** in the Placeholder Name box and then click **OK**.

23. Save the file.

Editing and Formatting Footnotes and Citations

You can edit footnote text directly in the footnote area. In addition to editing the text of a footnote, you can also:

▶ Reposition: You can change the position of a footnote reference mark by dragging it to another location in the document.

▶ Format: You can change various formatting features of footnotes. For example, you can change the numbering scheme, change the starting number, or even replace a footnote number with a special character.

▶ Delete: You can delete a footnote and its reference number by selecting and deleting the entire footnote, including the number, at the bottom of the page. You can also delete the footnote by deleting the superscript footnote number in the text itself.

You can add source information to a citation placeholder by clicking the placeholder menu button ▼ and choosing the option to edit the source.

View the video "Editing Footnotes and Citations."

DEVELOP YOUR SKILLS: W3-D9

In this exercise, you will format, edit, and delete footnotes and edit citation placeholders and sources.

1. Save your file as: **W3-D9-InternetRevised**

2. Position the insertion point at the beginning of the second paragraph on page 1 and scroll, if necessary, to see the three footnote reference marks and the footnotes at the bottom of the page.

3. Choose **References→Footnotes dialog box launcher** to display the Footnote and Endnote dialog box.

4. If necessary, at the top of the dialog box, choose **Footnotes**.

5. In the Number Format field, click the **menu** button ▼ and choose **A, B, C ...**, and then click **Apply**.

The footnote numbers change to alphabetic characters. You use the same technique to change the format of endnotes.

6. Choose **References→Footnotes dialog box launcher** ⬚; change the Number Format back to the first option, numbers; and then click **Apply**.

7. If necessary, choose **View→Show→Ruler**.

8. Select the three footnotes at the bottom of the page and then follow these steps to format them:
   - Change line spacing to: **double-space**
   - Change the font size to: **11 pt**
   - On the ruler, drag the **First Line Indent** marker (top triangle) to the **½"** mark.

Delete and Edit Footnotes and Edit Citation Placeholders

9. Select the reference mark following *marketplace* in the body of the document and tap ⬚Delete⬚.

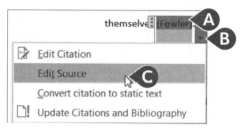

The reference mark and the footnote are removed, and the remaining footnotes renumber.

10. Click **Undo** ⬚ to reinsert the footnote.

11. Position the insertion point between the last word and the period of the first footnote, tap ⬚Spacebar⬚, and type: **and economists**

12. Scroll to the *Fowler* citation at the end of the third bullet on page 2.

13. Follow these steps to open the Edit Source dialog box:

   themselve⬚ (Fowler) **A**
   B

   - ⬚ Edit Citation
   - Edit Source **C**
   - Convert citation to static text
   - ⬚ Update Citations and Bibliography

   A Click the **Fowler** citation placeholder.

   B Click this **menu** button ▼.

   C Choose **Edit Source**.

14. Enter the following information in the Edit Source dialog box in the order shown:
   - Type of Source: **Web Site**
   - Author: **Fowler, Geoffrey**
   - Name of Web Page: **The Green Side of Online Shopping**
   - Year: **2009**
   - Month: **March**
   - Day: **3**
   - Year Accessed: **2021**
   - Month Accessed: **March**
   - Day Accessed: **14**
   - Medium: **blogs.wsj.com/digits/2009/03/03/the-green-side-of-online -shopping/tab/article**

15. Click **OK**.

16. Click **Yes** if a message appears asking if you want to update the master list and current document.

   The citation may have picked up the name of the web page (title). If so, continue with step 17; otherwise, skip to step 18.

17. If necessary, click the **menu** button ▾ to the right of the Fowler citation and choose **Edit Citation**; then, check the **Title** box to suppress the title and click **OK**.

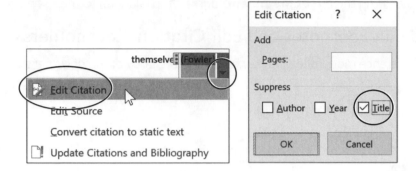

   Now you will edit the Mogg placeholder.

18. Click the **Mogg** citation placeholder at the end of the document.

19. Click the **menu** button ▾ and choose **Edit Source**.

20. Enter the following information in the dialog box in the order shown:
   - Type of Source: **Web Site**
   - Author: **Mogg, Trevor**
   - Name of Web Page: **Google says its drone delivery service could take flight in 2017**
   - Year: **2015**
   - Month: **November**
   - Day: **3**
   - Year accessed: **2021**
   - Month Accessed: **March**
   - Day Accessed: **14**
   - Medium: **digitaltrends.com/cool-tech/google-aiming-to-launch -drone-delivery-service-in-2017**

21. Click **OK** and then save the file.

Working with Bibliographies

A bibliography is a list of the sources cited in the preparation of a document. Bibliographies are auto-matically generated based on the source information that you provide in the Create Source dialog box. The bibliography picks up the correct punctuation; however, certain formatting requirements are not defaults and must be addressed separately.

 The bibliography options may not format references as needed. Use the Insert Bibliography command to create citations more precisely.

 View the video "Bibliography Options."

☰ References→Citations & Bibliography→Bibliography 📑

DEVELOP YOUR SKILLS: W3-D10

In this exercise, you will create a bibliography for the citations in your paper. You will title the page as Works Cited, as this chapter is following the MLA documentation style. Finally, you will edit an existing citation, update the bibliography, and format the paragraphs with double spacing.

1. Save your file as: **W3-D10-InternetRevised**
2. Position the insertion point at the end of the document and then press Ctrl+Enter to insert a new page for the bibliography.
3. Choose **Home→Paragraph→Center** ≡, type **Works Cited**, and tap Enter.

Insert and Update the Bibliography

4. Choose **References→Citations & Bibliography→Bibliography** 📑.
5. Choose **Insert Bibliography** at the bottom of the menu.
6. Scroll up to the second page, click the **Fowler** citation, and then click the **menu** button ▼.
7. Choose **Edit Source** to open the dialog box.
8. Change the Day Accessed to **10** and click **OK**.
9. If the citation picked up the name of the web page, click the **menu** button ▼, choose **Edit Citation**, check the **Title** checkbox, and click **OK**.
10. Scroll down to the *Works Cited* page and notice the date has not changed yet in the list.
11. Right-click anywhere in the list and choose **Update Field** from the menu that appears.

green-side-of-online-shop...
, Trevor. *Google says its dron...*
http://www.channelseller...
...could-take-flight-in-2017/
ey, Chriss. *Carnegie Mellon St...*
https://www.cmu.edu/ne...

✂	Cut
📋	Copy
📋	**Paste Options:**

Update Field
Edit Field...
Toggle Field Codes
A Font...
¶ Paragraph...

Notice the date accessed for the Fowler citation changed to 10 March 2021. Now you will format the list.

12. Select the bibliography list but not the *Works Cited* title.

 Note! *If you click the list, it highlights in light gray. You must drag with the mouse to select the list, which then highlights in a darker gray.*

13. Choose **Home→Paragraph→Line and Paragraph Spacing** 📊 and then choose **2.0**.

14. Save the file.

Inserting Captions and a Table of Figures

You use captions to insert text associated with images in a paper. The captions then become entries in the table of figures. You can edit captions after you place them by making the changes directly in the caption and then updating the table of figures to reflect the edits. Bibliographies and tables of figures do not update automatically when changes are made to the citation or caption entries. To update these fields, simply right-click inside the field and choose Update Field.

⚠️ **View the video "Inserting Captions."**

≡ References→Captions→Insert Caption 🖼️

DEVELOP YOUR SKILLS: W3-D11

In this exercise, you will insert a file that contains PowerPoint slides from a presentation. You will add captions to the slides in preparation for creating a table of figures.

1. Save your file as: **W3-D11-InternetRevised**

2. Position the insertion point after the third footnote reference mark in the body of the document (not the footnote area) toward the bottom of the first page.

> overhead are several more factors that are driving Internet commerce.[3]
>
> Internet commerce will be a driving force in the global economy of the twenty-first century.

3. Tap [Enter] and then press [Ctrl]+[Enter] to insert a page break.

4. Choose **Insert→Text→Object** 🖼️ **menu button** ▾ →**Text from File**.

5. In the Insert File dialog box, navigate to your **Word Chapter 3** folder, choose **W3-D11-Evolution**, and click **Insert**.

6. If necessary, display formatting marks and then position the insertion point in the first blank line below the first slide.

7. Choose **References→Captions→Insert Caption** 🖼️.

The Caption dialog box should match the left image in the following step.

8. If *Figure 1* does not appear in the Caption text box, follow these steps; otherwise, go to the next step.

Ⓐ Click the **Label menu** button ▾ and choose **Figure**.

Ⓑ Click **Numbering** to open the Caption Numbering dialog box.

Ⓒ Click the **Format menu** button ▾ and then choose the **1,2,3, …** format.

Ⓓ Click **OK**.

9. If necessary, position the insertion point to the right of *Figure 1* in the Caption text box.

10. Tap [Spacebar], type **DOD and ARPANET**, and click **OK** to insert the caption.

The caption is placed at the left margin.

11. Choose **Home→Paragraph→Center** ☰.

12. Position the insertion point in the first blank line below the second slide.

13. Choose **References→Captions→Insert Caption** 🖼.

14. Tap [Spacebar], type **NSF**, and click **OK**.

15. **Center** ☰ the caption.

16. Add these captions and center them:

Slide Number	Caption Text
3	MILNET and TCP/IP
4	First Graphical Browser
5	Netscape
6	Fourteen Years of Evolution
7	Delivery Drones?

Now you will edit a caption.

17. Return to **slide 2**, select **NSF**, and type **National Science Foundation** in its place.

18. Save the file.

WORD

Inserting a Table of Figures

Academic papers often include a table of figures at the front, which guides the reader to illustrations, charts, tables, and other figures. This is particularly helpful in long documents. The table entries conveniently function as hyperlinks if you are reading the document online.

≡ References→Captions→Insert Table of Figures 📄

DEVELOP YOUR SKILLS: W3-D12

In this exercise, you will generate a table of figures from the captions you inserted earlier.

1. Save your file as: **W3-D12-InternetRevised**

2. Move the insertion point to the top of the document, before the word *Brian*, and press
   Ctrl + Enter to insert a page break.

3. Press Ctrl + Home to position the insertion point at the top of the new page, type
   Table of Figures, and tap Enter twice.

4. **Center** ≡ the heading, add **Bold** B , and set the font size to **16** points.

5. Place the insertion point in the blank line below the heading.

6. Choose **References→Captions→Insert Table of Figures** 📄.

7. Follow these steps to complete the table:

General	
Formats:	Distinctive ∨ — Ⓐ
Caption label:	Figure ∨ — Ⓑ
☑ Include label and number	
	Ⓒ

   Ⓐ Choose **Distinctive** as the format.

   Ⓑ If necessary, choose **Figure** as the caption label.

   Ⓒ Click **OK**.

8. Save and then close the file.

Using Track Changes

The Track Changes feature is a useful tool when working with team members to collaborate on a report or other documents. You can electronically distribute copies to different members, and, with Track Changes, the changes they make are marked. You can merge the changes from all copies into a single document, and then you can review each change and accept or reject it.

Turn Track Changes on or off.

Choose how you want changes to appear in the document.

Choose the types of revisions you want to see, such as formatting and insertions and deletions.

View all changes in a list.

Reviewing Tracked Changes

It's easy to find and review changes to a document. When you review changes, you can jump from one change to the next, giving you the opportunity to accept or reject each change in order. You can also accept or reject all changes at once. After you accept or reject a change, the revision marks are removed.

This button accepts the currently selected change.

This button rejects the currently selected change.

These buttons navigate to the next or previous tracked change.

These options appear when you click the Accept menu button ▼. Similar choices are available on the Reject button.

Self-Assessment

Check your knowledge of this chapter's key concepts and skills using the Self-Assessment in your ebook or online (eLab course or Student Resource Center).

Reinforce Your Skills

Format a Recycling Report

Kids for Change is planning a recycling fair, and you are creating a recycling report to be distributed during the fair. In this exercise, you will work with margins, indents, tabs, styles, and footers, and then you will format the body of the report into two columns. Finally, you will add a comment to the report.

1. Open **W3-R1-Recyc** from your **Word Chapter 3** folder and save it as:

   W3-R1-RecycRevised

   The document could use a little more white space in the left and right margins.

2. Choose **Layout→Page Setup→Margins** ⊞ **→Normal**.

   This widens the left and right margins to 1". Now you'll indent the quote from the EPA to make it stand out on the page.

3. If necessary, choose **View→Show→Ruler**.

4. Position the insertion point in the third paragraph.

5. Place the mouse pointer on the **Left Indent** marker (the rectangle) and drag it to the **½"** mark and then place the mouse pointer on the **Right Indent** marker and drag it to the **6"** mark.

"Electronic products are made from valuable resources and materials, including metals, plastics, and glass, all of which require energy to mine and manufacture. Donating or recycling consumer electronics conserves our natural resources and avoids air and water pollution, as well as greenhouse gas emissions that are caused by manufacturing virgin materials."

   Now you will set tabs for a table indicating where people can drop off electronics they want to recycle.

6. Position the insertion point at the bottom of the document.

7. Type the following heading line using the default tab grid, tapping ⃞Tab⃞ where you see the arrows and tapping ⃞Enter⃞ at the end of the line:

Ellsworth·Electronics →   →   Arlington·Electronics →   →   →   Wilson·Appliances¶   ¶

8. Select the heading line and choose **Home→Font→Bold** ⃞B⃞.

9. Position the insertion point in the blank line below the heading line where you will set custom tabs.

10. Click the **Tabs** box as many times as necessary to display the Center Tab. (It looks like an upside-down T.)

11. Perform these actions to set the following tab stops:
    - Click the ruler one tick mark to the right of **½"**.
    - Click one tick mark to the right of the **3"** mark.
    - Click at the **5½"** mark.

The center tab will cause the text to center around the tabs.

12. Type the following table, tapping ⎡Tab⎤ where you see the arrows and ⎡Enter⎤ where you see paragraph symbols:

Ellsworth·Electronics →	→	→	Arlington·Electronics →	→	→	Wilson·Appliances¶
→ Audio	→		Mobile·phones		→	Stoves¶
→ Car·&·GPS	→		Computers	→		Refrigerators¶
→ Mobile·phones	→		Digital·cameras	→		Freezers¶
→ Video·games	→		MP3·players	→		Washing·machines¶

Now you will adjust the last tab stop so it is better centered.

13. Select all lines to which the tab stop applies and drag the tab one tick mark to the right of **5½"**.

Ellsworth·Electronics →	→	→	Arlington·Electronics →	→	→	Wilson·Appliances¶
→ Audio	→		Mobile·phones		→	Stoves¶
→ Car·&·GPS	→		Computers	→		Refrigerators¶
→ Mobile·phones	→		Digital·cameras	→		Freezers¶
→ Video·games	→		MP3·players	→		Washing·machines¶

Now you will apply a style to the Report heading.

14. Position the insertion point in the heading line at the top of the page.

15. Choose **Home→Styles** and then click the **More** ⎡▼⎤ button to open the Styles gallery.

16. Choose **Title** from the gallery.

17. Place the insertion point anywhere in the line of text above the three columns you've created and choose **Home→Paragraph→Center** ⎡≡⎤.

The line is now centered on the page over the columns.

Add a Footer and a Comment

18. Choose **Insert→Header & Footer→Footer** ⎡□⎤ and choose **Edit Footer** at the bottom of the menu.

19. Type **Kids for Change** at the left side of the footer.

Look at the ruler and notice that there are two custom tab stops: a center tab at 3¼" and a right tab at 6½".

20. Tap ⎡Tab⎤ twice.

The insertion point is now aligned at a Right Tab.

21. Type **January, 2021** and then double-click in the body of the document to close the footer area.

Set the Document in Two Columns and Add a Comment

22. Select the body of the document from the first paragraph through the last bullet point.

23. Choose **Layout→Page Setup→Columns** 🖿 **→Two**.

It might look better to keep the EPA quote together.

24. Position the insertion point in front of the line starting *The EPA provides*.

25. Choose **Layout→Page Setup→Breaks** 🖿 **→Column**.

26. Choose **Layout→Page Setup dialog box launcher** ⟍ and change the vertical alignment to **Center** under the Layout tab.

27. Click **OK** to close the dialog box.

Now you will insert a comment.

28. Move to the top of the document and select **Recycling** in the heading.

29. Choose **Insert→Comments→Comment** 🗐 and type the following in the comment balloon:

Jordan, please review and add any comments. I'll start on the Plastics Recycling section next.

30. Save and close the file.

REINFORCE YOUR SKILLS: W3-R2

Create a Research Report

A Kids for Change volunteer has asked you to create another handout for the fair with an emphasis on acting locally. In this exercise, you will prepare the handout by inserting endnotes, footnotes, citations, a bibliography, and a table of figures.

1. Open **W3-R2-GlobalLocal** from your **Word Chapter 3** folder and save it as:
W3-R2-GlobalLocalRevised

2. Position the insertion point after the period following *sales* in the second paragraph.

> Kids for Change is a non-profit organization that helps minors in their
>
> social/community service within the mindset of "Think Globally, Act Locally."
>
> fundraisers, such as car washes, bake sales, and rain barrel sales. The kids are

3. Choose **References→Footnotes→Insert Endnote** 🖸.

The insertion point jumps to the end of the document.

4. Type the following endnote text:

Proceeds go to organizations such as the local pantry.

5. Position the insertion point after the comma following *construction* in the second to last line of the second paragraph.

> fundraisers, such as car washes, bake sales, and rain barrel sales.
>
> community recycling drives, researching green construction, and
>
> garden program.

6. Choose **References→Footnotes→Insert Endnote** ⬚ and type the following endnote text:

Kids for Change successfully encouraged a local businessman to use green construction in a building addition.

You noticed a word is missing in the first endnote, so you will make that change now.

7. In the first endnote, position the insertion point to the left of *pantry*, type **food**, and tap Spacebar.

You've decided to convert the endnotes to footnotes so they will appear on the same page as the text they refer to.

8. Choose **References→Footnotes dialog box launcher** ⬚ and then click the **Convert** button.

9. When the Convert Notes message appears, click **OK**; close the Footnote and Endnote dialog box.

Insert Citations

10. Choose **References→Citations & Bibliography** and then, if necessary, choose **MLA Seventh Edition** from the Style menu.

11. At the end of the fourth paragraph that begins with *The slogan*, position the insertion point between the word *activists* and the period, and then tap Spacebar.

> practices – like environmental stewardship –
>
> of reference for some far-thinking activists|

12. Choose **References→Citations & Bibliography→Insert Citation** ⬚ and then choose **Add New Source**.

13. Enter the following information in the Create Source dialog box and then click **OK**:
    - Type of Source: **Web Site**
    - Author: **Sathian, Sanjena**
    - Name of Page: **Think Locally, Act Globally**
    - Year: **2011**
    - Month: **July**
    - Day: **11**
    - Year Accessed: **2021**
    - Month Accessed: **September**
    - Day: **15**
    - Medium: **tyglobalist.org/onlinecontent/blogs/ think-locally-act-globally**

14. Position the insertion point following *Fluids* at the end of the fourth bullet point in the Jennifer King quote and then tap Spacebar.

> • Vehicle Fluids|

15. Choose **References→Citations & Bibliography→Insert Citation** ⬚ and then choose **Add New Source**.

16. Enter the following information in the Create Source dialog box and then click **OK**:
    - Type of Source: **Web Site**
    - Author: `King, Jennifer`
    - Name of Page: `How Does Car Pollution Affect the Environment & Ozone Layer?`
    - Year: (Leave blank.)
    - Month: (Leave blank.)
    - Day: (Leave blank.)
    - Year Accessed: `2021`
    - Month Accessed: `September`
    - Day: `15`
    - Medium: `homeguides.sfgate.com/car-pollution-affect-environment-ozone-layer-79358.html`

17. Position the insertion point at the end of the document between *Nations* and the period, and then tap [Spacebar].

> ...ns (CFCs). And a treaty banning
>
> United Nations .

18. Choose **References→Citations & Bibliography→Insert Citation** 🔽 and then choose **Add New Source**.

19. Enter the following information in the Create Source dialog box and then click **OK**:
    - Type of Source: **Web Site**
    - Author: `Trex, Ethan`
    - Name of Page: `Whatever Happened to the Hole in the Ozone Layer?`
    - Year: `2012`
    - Month: `May`
    - Day: `23`
    - Year Accessed: `2021`
    - Month Accessed: `September`
    - Day: `15`
    - Medium: `mentalfloss.com/article/30733/whatever-happened-hole-ozone-layer`

20. Position the insertion point at the end of the document, tap [Enter] twice, and then press [Ctrl]+[Enter] to insert a new page for the bibliography.

21. Choose **Home→Paragraph→Center** ≡, type `Works Cited`, and then tap [Enter].

22. Choose **References→Citations & Bibliography→Bibliography** 📖.

23. Choose **Insert Bibliography** at the bottom of the menu.

24. Select all eight lines of the bibliography and choose **Home→Paragraph→Line and Paragraph Spacing** ‡≡ **menu button** ▾ **2.0** to double-space the bibliography.

Insert Captions

Now you will insert a document that contains slides from a PowerPoint presentation, and you will add captions to the slides.

25. If necessary, display the formatting marks, and then position the insertion point on the blank line before the page break at the end of page 2 and tap Enter.

26. Choose **Insert→Text→Object** 🔲 **menu button** ▾**→Text from File**.

27. In the Insert File dialog box, navigate to your **Word Chapter 3** folder and double-click **W3-R2-YouCanHelp** to insert the file in your document.

28. Position the insertion point in the first blank line below the first slide.

29. Choose **References→Captions→Insert Caption** 📄.

30. If *Figure 1* does not appear in the Caption text box, follow these steps; otherwise, go to the next step:

- Click the **Label menu** button ▾ and choose **Figure**.
- Click the **Numbering** button to open the Caption Numbering dialog box.
- Click the **Format menu** button ▾ and choose the **1,2,3, ...** format.
- Click **OK**.

31. If necessary, position the insertion point to the right of *Figure 1* in the Caption text box. Then tap Spacebar, type **Conduct a Home Survey**, and then click **OK**.

Now you will center the caption.

32. Choose **Home→Paragraph→Center** ≡ and then position the insertion point in the first blank line below the second slide.

33. Choose **References→Captions→Insert Caption** 📄.

34. Tap Spacebar, type **Reduce Car Use**, and click **OK**.

35. **Center** ≡ the caption.

36. Add the following captions and center them:

Slide	Caption
Slide 3	**Use Used**
Slide 4	**Think Before You Toss**

Insert a Table of Figures

37. Move the insertion point to the top of the document and insert a page break.

38. Move the insertion point to the top of the new page, type **Table of Figures**, and tap Enter twice.

39. Center the heading, apply bold, and set the font size as 16 pt.

40. Place the insertion point in the blank line below the heading.

41. Choose **References→Captions→Insert Table of Figures** 📄.

42. In the bottom-left of the Table of Figures dialog box, if necessary, change the format to **Distinctive**, ensure that the Caption Label says **Figure**, and then click **OK**.

43. Save and close the file.

Create an Organic Gardening Report

Kids for Change will host an organic gardening exhibition in the spring, and the planning is underway. You have already started a report about organic gardening for the exhibition. In this exercise, you will format the layout; apply styles; add a footer; and insert footnotes, endnotes, and citations. Then you will assign gardening duties to volunteers who will work in the Kids' garden starting in the spring. You will also create tabular columns and insert a comment.

1. Open **W3-R3-OrganicFood** from your **Word Chapter 3** folder and save it as: **W3-R3-OrganicFoodRevised**

   The left and right margins are a bit too wide in this document.

2. Choose **Layout→Page Setup→Margins** ▢ **→Normal**.

   Now you will apply Styles to the title and report headings.

3. Choose **Home→Styles dialog box launcher** ▢ to open the Styles task pane.

4. Apply the **Title** style to the document title and then apply the **Heading 1** style to the other two headings: *Plant Production* and *Support Organic Food*.

5. Close the Styles task pane.

   Next, you will format the first two main paragraphs in columns.

6. Select the text from the first paragraph through the *Plant Production* heading and its following paragraph.

7. If necessary, display the formatting marks.

8. Choose **Layout→Page Setup→Columns** ▢ **→Two**.

   When you select text and then apply columns, the section breaks are inserted automatically.

Insert Captions and a Table of Figures

9. Position the insertion point on the first blank line below the first picture.

10. Choose **References→Captions→Insert Caption** ▢.

11. Make sure *Figure* is in the Label field and the numbering format is 1,2,3, ...

12. If necessary, position the insertion point to the right of *Figure 1* in the Caption text box.

13. Tap [Spacebar], type **Build Healthy Soil**, click **OK**, and then center the caption.

14. Position the insertion point in the first blank line below the second picture.

15. Choose **References→Captions→Insert Caption** ▢.

16. Tap [Spacebar], type **Keep Chemicals Out of the Air, Water, Soil, and Our Bodies**, click **OK**, and then center the caption.

17. Follow the same process to place a centered caption titled **Taste Better and Truer Flavor** below the third picture.

18. Position the insertion point at the top of the document, press [Ctrl]+[Enter] to insert a page break, and then position the insertion point at the top of the new first page.

19. Type **Table of Figures** and tap Enter twice; then center the heading, add bold formatting, and set the font size to 16 points.

20. Position the insertion point in the blank line below the heading.

21. Choose **References→Captions→Insert Table of Figures** 📄.

22. In the dialog box, make sure Distinctive is the format style, ensure that the caption label is Figure, and click **OK**.

Add Footnotes and Citations

23. Position the insertion point to the right of the colon at the end of the first line below the *Support Organic Food* heading.

24. Choose **References→Footnotes→Insert Footnote** AB¹ and type the following text in the footnote area:

See Sustainable Plant Agriculture for details on growing organic plants.

Now you will choose the style for citations.

25. Choose **References→Citations & Bibliography→Style menu button** ▾ and, if necessary, choose **MLA Seventh Edition**.

26. Position the insertion point between the period and the word *bay* at the end of the second paragraph following the *Plant Production* heading, and tap Spacebar.

> may conduct more sophisticated crop rotations and spread mulch or manure to keep weeds at bay.

27. Choose **References→Citations & Bibliography→Insert Citation** 📝 and then choose **Add New Source**.

28. Enter the following information and then click **OK**:
    - Type of Source: **Web Site**
    - Author: **Mayo Clinic, Staff**
    - Name of Web Page: **Nutrition and healthy eating**
    - Year: (Leave blank.)
    - Month: (Leave blank.)
    - Day: (Leave blank.)
    - Year accessed: **2021**
    - Month Accessed: **October**
    - Day Accessed: **15**
    - Medium: **mayoclinic.org/healthy-lifestyle/nutrition-and-healthy -eating/in-depth/organic-food/art-20043880**

29. Position the insertion point at the end of the third bullet point below the *Support Organic Food* heading and tap Spacebar.

30. Choose **References→Citations & Bibliography→Insert Citation** 📝 and then choose **Add New Source**.

31. Enter the following information and then click **OK**:

- Type of Source: **Web Site**
- Author: `Greene, Alan, Scowcroft, Bob, Tawse, Sylvia`
- Name of Web Page: `Top 10 Reasons to Support Organic in the 21st Century`
- Year: (Leave blank.)
- Month: (Leave blank.)
- Day: (Leave blank.)
- Year Accessed: `2021`
- Month Accessed: `October`
- Day Accessed: `15`
- Medium: `organic.org/articles/showarticle/article-206`

Insert a Bibliography and Add a Footer

32. Position the insertion point at the end of the document and press ⌷Ctrl⌷+⌷Enter⌷ to insert a page break.

33. Choose **Home→Paragraph→Center** ≣, type `Works Cited`, and tap ⌷Enter⌷.

34. Choose **References→Citations & Bibliography→Bibliography** and then choose **Insert Bibliography**.

35. Choose **Insert→Header & Footer→Footer** and then scroll down and choose **Retrospect**.

36. Type `Kids for Change` in the author object (you may have to delete default text; print is automatically set in all caps) and notice that the page number appears on the right side of the footer.

37. Double-click in the document to close the footer area.

38. Save and close the file.

Now you will finish creating the document for assigning gardening project duties.

39. Open **W3-R3-GardenProj** from your **Word Chapter 3** folder and save it as:
`W3-R3-GardenProjRevised`

40. Position the insertion point at the end of the document and type the following heading line, tapping ⌷Tab⌷ wherever you see an arrow and tapping ⌷Enter⌷ at the end of the line:

Volunteer →	→ **Vegetable** →	→ **Assigned·Space·in·Feet¶**
¶		

41. Add bold formatting to the heading line.

Now you will set center tabs for the body of the table.

42. If necessary, position the insertion point on the blank line below the heading line.

43. Click the **Tabs** box to display the Center Tab, if necessary.

44. Place tabs in the following locations:

- Between the second and third tick marks from the left margin
- Between the second and third tick marks to the right of 1½"
- The first tick mark to the right of 3½"

| Volunteer | Vegetable | Assigned Space in Feet |

Remember, if you click a tab in the wrong position, you can drag it to the correct position or drag it down and off the ruler and try again.

45. Type the body of the table as shown, tapping ⌐Tab¬ wherever you see an arrow and tapping ⌐Enter¬ at the end of each line:

Volunteer →	→	Vegetable →	→	Assigned·Space·in·Feet¶
→ Kirk	→	corn	→	10·x·8¶
→Rachael	→	peas	→	8·x·4¶
→ Lena	→	green·beans	→	8·x·3¶
→ Bly	→	tomatoes	→	10·x·8¶
→Trevor	→	cauliflower	→	8·x·4¶
→ Neil	→	carrots	→	6·x·4¶

Now you will accept a suggested change and insert a comment.

46. Right-click on the word **gardening** at the end of the second full paragraph and choose **Accept Insertion** from the menu.

47. Select the word **Change** in the heading, choose **Insert→Comments→Comment**, and type the following in the comment balloon: `Jeremy, please check the assigned spaces and make sure they are accurate.`

48. Save and close the file.

Apply Your Skills

APPLY YOUR SKILLS W3-A1

Complete a Trip Report on Belize

You went on a familiarization trip to Belize for Universal Corporate Events and have written a trip report about the country. In this exercise, you will format the layout of the document, apply styles to headings, and insert footers and a comment.

1. Open **W3-A1-Belize** from your **Word Chapter 3** folder and save it as:

   W3-A1-BelizeRevised

   The text is pretty dense on this page. It needs to be lightened up and better organized to make it more readable. You will start by widening the margin areas.

2. Choose **Layout→Page Setup→Margins** ▦ **→Normal**.

   Headings will allow the reader to scan the document for high-level concepts, adding to the document's readability. You will apply styles to the document's headings.

3. Apply the **Heading 2** style to the heading at the top of the document and then apply the **Intense Reference** style to the remaining headings: *Overview, Diving and Snorkeling, Ruins,* and *Artists.*

   Offsetting the text from the headings will also add to the document's readability.

4. Position the insertion point in the paragraph following the *Overview* heading.

5. Choose **Home→Paragraph→Increase Indent** ▤.

6. Use the same technique to indent all the remaining paragraphs except the *Artists* paragraph. (If you select all the paragraphs following the *Ruins* heading, you can indent them all at once.)

   Next you will set the document in columns.

7. Select the text starting with the *Overview* heading through the last paragraph following the *Ruins* heading. (Do not include the *Artists* paragraph.)

8. Format the selected text in a two-column layout.

   The Ruins *heading is at the bottom of the left-hand column. It would look better at the top of the right-hand column.*

9. Position the insertion point in front of the *Ruins* heading and insert a column break to move the heading to the top of the next column.

Insert a Footer

10. Add a footer using the **Ion (Dark)** option.

    You will use the objects in the footer for a different purpose than the labels specify.

11. Type **Universal Corporate Events** in the Document Title object and delete the Author Name object.

12. Close the footer area.

Set Custom Tabs

Now you will add information about some of the talented local artists.

13. If necessary, turn on the ruler and display the formatting marks.

14. Position the insertion point in the second blank line at the end of the document.

15. Type the following heading row, using the formatting marks as a guide; be sure to tap Enter at the end of the heading line:

16. Add bold formatting to the heading row.

17. Position the insertion point in the line below the heading row and, if necessary, set custom Center Tabs.

18. Type the rest of the table, using the formatting marks as a guide:

→	→	→	**Artist**→	→	→	→	→	**Media**¶
	→		Amy·Brown		→			Ceramic·sculpture·and·oils¶
	→		Pamela·Braun		→			Oil·and·watercolor¶
	→		Walter·Castello		→			Acrylic·on·canvas¶
	→		Savanna·Redman		→			Oil·and·watercolor¶
	→		Alissa·Reid		→			Acrylics·and·oils¶

Now you'll add a comment to the document.

19. Place the insertion point anywhere inside the document heading and center it.

20. Select **Belize** in the document heading, insert a comment, and add the following text to the comment balloon:

`Arrielle, since this is my first trip report, would you please check it out and add any comments you may have?`

21. Save and close the file.

APPLY YOUR SKILLS W3-A2

Report on Italian Tourist Sites

Because you used to live in Italy, Universal Corporate Events has asked you to create a report detailing some Italian tourist sites and providing tips on train travel in Italy. In this exercise, you will insert footnotes and citations and generate a bibliography for your report. Then you will add captions to pictures and create a table of figures.

1. Open **W3-A2-Italy** from your **Word Chapter 3** folder and save it as: `W3-A2-ItalyRevised`

2. Position the insertion point at the end of the first paragraph, after the period following *each*.

3. Insert this footnote: `Other major attractions are listed on this website`.

4. In the paragraph beginning *In the article*, position the insertion point after the period following the word *choices*.

5. Insert this footnote: `This article also offers advice on train schedules, buying tickets, and boarding your train.`

Enter Citations and a Bibliography

6. Set the report style to **MLA Seventh Edition**, if necessary. (Hint: Go to the References tab.)

7. Position the insertion point after *Colosseum* in the fourth bullet point at the top of the document.

8. Tap Spacebar and insert a citation with the following source information. Be sure to check the Corporate Author box before entering the Author information.

   - Type of Source: **Web Site**
   - Corporate Author: `Rome Travel Guide`
   - Name of Web Page: `Rome, Italy travel guide`
   - Year: (Leave blank.)
   - Month: (Leave blank.)
   - Day: (Leave blank.)
   - Year Accessed: `2021`
   - Month Accessed: `May`
   - Day Accessed: `23`
   - Medium: `rome.info`

9. Position the insertion point after *Pompeii* at the end of the fourth bullet point under the *Day Trips* heading.

10. Tap Spacebar and insert a citation with the following source information:

    - Type of Source: **Web Site**
    - Author: `Casura, Lily`
    - Name of Web Page: `Daytrips from Rome`
    - Year: (Leave blank.)
    - Month: (Leave blank.)
    - Day: (Leave blank.)
    - Year Accessed: `2021`
    - Month Accessed: `May`
    - Day Accessed: `23`
    - Medium: `tripadvisor.com.au/Guide-g187791-1296-Rome_Lazio.html`

11. Position the insertion point between *more* and the period at the end of the last paragraph.

12. Tap Spacebar and insert a citation with the following source information:

    - Type of Source: **Web Site**
    - Author: `Bakerjian, Martha`
    - Name of Web Page: `Italy Train Travel`
    - Year: (Leave blank.)
    - Month: (Leave blank.)
    - Day: (Leave blank.)
    - Year Accessed: `2021`
    - Month Accessed: `May`
    - Day Accessed: `23`
    - Medium: `goitaly.about.com/od/italytransportation/a/trains.htm`

13. Position the insertion point at the end of the document, tap Enter twice, and insert a page break.

14. Type **Works Cited** as the heading and tap ⌷Enter⌷ twice.

15. Center the heading and then position the insertion point on the second blank line below the heading.

16. Insert a bibliography on the new page using the **Insert Bibliography** command.

17. Select all five lines of the bibliography and choose **Home→Paragraph→Line and Paragraph Spacing** ⌷≣⌷ **menu button ▾→2.0**.

18. Scroll to the top of the document, position the insertion point at the end of the *Colosseum* bullet point, and then tap ⌷Enter⌷ twice.

    Next, you will insert pictures of Rome's major attractions.

19. Choose **Insert→Text→Object** ⌷◰⌷ **menu button ▾→Text from File**.

20. Navigate to your **Word Chapter 3** folder and insert: **W3-A2-RomePics**

21. Positioning the insertion point on the first blank line below each picture, insert and center the following captions using the **1,2,3, …** number format and the **Figure** label:

Picture	Caption
Picture 1	**Trevi Fountain**
Picture 2	**St. Peter's Square**
Picture 3	**Spanish Steps**
Picture 4	**Colosseum**

22. Insert a page break at the top of the document; at the top of the new page, type **Table of Figures** and tap ⌷Enter⌷ twice.

23. Center the heading, apply bold formatting, and change the font size to 16 pt.

24. Position the insertion point on the blank line below the heading and generate the table of figures using the **Formal** format and **Figure** as the caption label.

25. Save and close the file.

APPLY YOUR SKILLS: W3-A3

Create Travel Reports

Universal Corporate Events is planning a Bangkok getaway for one of its clients, and you've been asked to research travel within Bangkok and interesting sites to see. In this exercise, you will format the layout of your report and add footnotes, citations, a bibliography, captions, and a table of figures. You have also been asked to write a sales report listing Universal Corporate Events' pending deals. You will work with margins and custom tabs, add header text, and insert a comment.

1. Open **W3-A3-Bangkok** from your **Word Chapter 3** folder and save it as:
   W3-A3-BangkokRevised

   The document needs some formatting to make it more readable. First you will add some styles to the document.

2. Select the title at the top of the document and apply the **Heading 1** style.

3. At the bottom of the page, apply the **Subtle Reference** style to the bulleted items.

4. If necessary, display the ruler, and then position the insertion point in the second paragraph.

5. Position the mouse pointer on the **Left Indent** marker (the rectangle) on the ruler and drag it to the ½" mark.

6. Drag the **Right Indent** marker to the **6"** mark.

7. Select text beginning with **Bangkok's Chao Praya Express Boats** down through **Myanmar** and then set the text in two columns.

   Next, you will insert pictures, add captions, and generate a table of figures.

8. Insert the **W3-A3-BNKPics** file at the end of the document.

9. Position the insertion point on the blank line below each picture and then insert and center the following captions using the **1,2,3, ...** number format and the **Figure** caption label:

Picture	Caption
Picture 1	Chatuchak Market
Picture 2	Pak Klong Talat
Picture 3	Bangkok Farmers Market
Picture 4	Pratunam Market

10. Insert a page break at the top of the document, and at the top of the new page, type **Table of Figures** and tap Enter twice.

11. Center and apply bold formatting to the heading and then generate the table of figures on the blank line below the heading using the **Formal** format and **Figure** as the caption label.

Insert Footnotes and Citations

12. Position the insertion point in the first line of the first paragraph on page 2, to the right of *markets,* and insert this footnote:

   ---
   [1] **Floating markets piled high with tropical fruits and vegetables provide an exciting shopping adventure.**

13. Position the insertion point in the same line, this time to the right of *temples,* and insert this footnote:

   [2] **Don't miss Wat Traimit's Golden Buddha or Wat Po's famous Reclining Buddha.**

14. If necessary, choose the **MLA Seventh Edition** style for citations.

15. Insert a citation at the end of the indented paragraph at the top of the document and add the following source information:
    - Type of Source: **Web Site**
    - Author: **Thyberg, David**
    - Name of Web Page: **Bangkok Travel Tips**
    - Year: (Leave blank.)
    - Month: (Leave blank.)
    - Day: (Leave blank.)
    - Year Accessed: **2021**
    - Month Accessed: **September**
    - Day Accessed: **20**
    - Medium: **getawaytips.azcentral.com/bangkok-travel-tips-1945.html**

16. Insert a citation at the end of the second column next to *Myanmar* and add the following source information:
    - Type of Source: **Web Site**
    - Author: **Rowthorn, Chris**

- Name of Web Page: **Take the boat out of Bangkok**
- Year: **2012**
- Month: **April**
- Day: **13**
- Year Accessed: **2021**
- Month Accessed: **September**
- Day Accessed: **20**
- Medium: **bbc.com/travel/story/20120413-take-the-boat-out-of-bangkok**

17. Insert a citation at the end of the fourth bullet point at the end of page 2, and add the following source information:

- Type of Source: **Web Site**
- Author: **Hauglann, Maria Wulff**
- Name of Web Page: **6 Markets in Bangkok You Should Not Miss**
- Year: **2014**
- Month: **July**
- Day: **15**
- Year Accessed: **2021**
- Month Accessed: **September**
- Day Accessed: **20**
- Medium: **nerdnomads.com/6-markets-in-bangkok-you-should-not-miss**

Now you will generate a bibliography.

18. Insert a page break at the end of the document, type the title, **Works Cited**, center it on the page, and then tap ⌈Enter⌋ twice.

19. Generate the bibliography on the first blank line below the title using the **Insert Bibliography** command.

20. Save and close the file.

Create a Sales Report

21. Open **W3-A3-SalesRpt** from your **Word Chapter 3** folder and save it as:
W3-A3-SalesRptRevised

22. Change the margins to the preset **Normal** style.

23. Apply the **Title** style to the **Sales Report** heading.

24. Position the insertion point on the second blank line at the end of the text, type **Pending Deals**, and format it with the **Heading 1** style.

25. Position the insertion point on the blank line below the *Pending Deals* heading and tap ⌈Enter⌋.

26. Use the ruler to set Left tabs at **2½"** and **4½"** and then type the following table, bolding the heading line:

Company		Destination		Dates¶
Rogers·Electronics	→	Hawaii	→	Oct·2·through·7¶
Wilson·Construction	→	Miami	→	Oct·11·through·17¶
Milltown·Mortgage	→	New·York·City	→	Oct·20·through·27¶

27. Select the entire table and move the 2½" tab to **2¼"** and the 4½" tab to **4¾"**.

Insert a Header and a Comment

28. Insert a header using the **Blank** style and type `Universal Corporate Events` as the header.

29. Select **Report** in the heading line and insert the following comment: `Emma, do you have any prospects to add to the list?`

30. Save and close the file.

Project Grader

If your class is using eLab (labyrinthelab.com), you may upload your completed Project Grader assignments for automatic grading. You may complete these projects even if your class doesn't use eLab, though you will not be able to upload your work.

PROJECT GRADER: W3-P1

The History of Board Games Research Paper

The Taylor Games management team wants a research paper on the history of board games to use for various promotional activities. In this exercise, you will use appropriate research-paper tools and professional formatting to prepare the research paper.

1. Download and open your Project Grader starting file.
   - *Using eLab:* Download **W3_P1_eStart** from the Assignments page. You *must* start with this file or your work cannot be automatically graded.
   - *Not using eLab:* Open **W3_P1_Start** from your **Word Chapter 3** folder.

2. Set the document's margins to **Normal** (all four margins are 1").

3. On page 1, apply these styles:

Style	Apply To
Title style	**The History of Board Games** title
Heading 1 style	**Introduction** and **History** headings
Heading 2 style	**Ancient Board Games** and **United States** headings
Heading 3 style	**The Mansion of Happiness** heading

4. Apply these formats to the text paragraph that's below the Introduction heading:

Format	Value
First Line Indent	**0.5"**
Line Spacing	**Single**

5. Near the bottom of page 1, insert a page break in front of *The Mansion of Happiness* heading.

6. At the bottom of page 1, apply 0.5" left and right indents to the large text paragraph (the Thomas Jefferson quotation).

7. On **page 2**, apply a two-column layout from the start of *The Mansion of Happiness* heading to the end of the second large *Mansion of Happiness* text paragraph. Include the paragraph mark at the end of the second text paragraph in the columns.

The Mansion of Happiness

The earliest board games published in the United States were based upon Christian morality. The Mansion of Happiness (1843), for example, sent players along a path of virtues and vices that led to the Mansion of Happiness. The Game of Pope and Pagan, or The Siege of the Stronghold of Satan by the Christian Army (1844) pitted an image on its board of a Hindu woman committing suttee against missionaries landing on a foreign shore. The missionaries are cast in white as "the symbol of innocence, temperance, and hope" while the pope and pagan are cast in black, the color of "gloom of error, and ... grief at the daily loss of empire".

American Protestants believed a virtuous life led to success, but the belief was challenged mid-century when the country embraced materialism and capitalism. In 1860, The Checkered Game of Life rewarded players for mundane activities such as attending college, marrying, and getting rich. Daily life rather than eternal life became the focus of board games. The game was the first to focus on secular virtues rather than religious virtues and sold 40,000 copies its first year.

The District Messenger Boy

8. Follow these guidelines to insert a new comment on page 2 below the two-column layout:
   - Insert the new comment to the right of *The District Messenger Boy* heading.
   - Enter this comment text: **My columns are a work in progress.**

9. On **page 3**, collapse the *Luck, Strategy, and Diplomacy* heading.

10. Follow these guidelines to insert a footnote on **page 1** in the text paragraph below the *Ancient Board Games* heading:
    - Insert the footnote at the end of the text paragraph to the right of the period.

Ancient Board Games
Board games have been played in important historical sites, artifacts, and do civilization gameboards in Iran.
United States
In 17th and 18th century colonial

    - Use this footnote text: **The earliest known board game was from Egypt.**

11. On **page 2**, insert a new citation source at the end of the first paragraph in the second column:
    - Type of Source: **Article in a Periodical**
    - Author: **Fessenden, Tracy**
    - Title: **"Culture and Redemption: Religion, the Secular, and American Literature"**
    - Periodical Title: **Princeton University Press**
    - Year: **2007**
    - Pages: **271**

The Mansion of Happiness

on a foreign shore. The missionaries are cast in white as "the symbol of innocence, temperance, and hope" while the pope and pagan are cast in black, the color of "gloom of error, and ... grief at the daily loss of empire".

12. On page 2, insert a new citation source at the end of the second paragraph in the second column:
    - Type of Source: **Article in a Periodical**
    - Author: **Hofer, Margaret K.**
    - Title: **"The Games We Played: The Golden Age of Board & Table Games"**
    - Periodical Title: **Princeton Architectural Press**
    - Year: **2003**

board of a Hindu woman committing suttee against missionaries landing	on secular virtues rather than religious virtues and sold 40,000 copies its first year. ◄───────
The District Messenger Boy	

13. Use these guidelines to insert two captions on page 2:
    - For both captions, set the label to **Figure** and include the label in the caption.
    - Caption 1: Insert the caption in the empty paragraph below the Mansion of Happiness picture using this caption text: **The Mansion of Happiness (1843)**
    - Caption 2: Insert the caption in the empty paragraph below the Game of the District Messenger Boy picture using this caption text: **Game of the District Messenger Boy (1886)**

14. Use these guidelines to insert a bibliography on **page 5**:
    - Insert it in the empty paragraph below the *Bibliography* heading.
    - Use the **Built-In, Works Cited** format.
    - Delete the *Bibliography* heading paragraph.

15. Use these guidelines to insert a Table of Figures on **page 6**:
    - Insert it in the empty paragraph below the *Table of Figures* heading.
    - Accept all default table of figures settings.

16. Insert a footer using the **Built-in, Banded** style to place a page number at the center of the bottom of each page.

17. Save your document.
    - *Using eLab:* Save it to your **Word Chapter 3** folder as: **W3_P1_eSubmission** and attach the file to your eLab assignment for grading.
    - *Not using eLab:* Save it to your **Word Chapter 3** folder as: **W3_P1_Submission**

PROJECT GRADER: W3-P2

The History of the Chevrolet Corvette

The Classic Cars Club is hosting a Chevrolet Corvette exhibit at an upcoming show. In this exercise, you will put the finishing touches on a Corvette history report that will be distributed to attendees. You'll make the document shine by adding a cover page and applying formatting.

1. Download and open your Project Grader starting file.
   - *Using eLab:* Download **W3_P2_eStart** from the Assignments page. You *must* start with this file or your work cannot be automatically graded.
   - *Not using eLab:* Open **W3_P2_Start** from your **Word Chapter 3** folder.
2. In the *Eight Generations of Corvettes* heading, accept the tracked insertion and deletion.

3. Apply the **Heading 1** style to these paragraphs:
   - **Eight Generations of Corvettes**
   - **Introduction**
   - **First Generation (C1; 1953-1962)**

4. Set the document's margins to **Normal** (all four margins are 1").

5. Use these guidelines to create custom tab stops on the empty paragraph below the *Eight Generations of Corvettes* heading:

Tab Stop 1

Property	Value
Tab Stop Position	`0.5"`
Alignment	**Left**
Leader	**1 None**

Tab Stop 2

Property	Value
Tab Stop Position	`3.25"`
Alignment	**Center**
Leader	2

Tab Stop 3

Property	Value
Tab Stop Position	`6"`
Alignment	**Right**
Leader	2

6. Use your custom tab stops and these guidelines to enter the following text paragraphs.
   - Tab before each column entry so you're using all three of your custom tab stops in each paragraph. So start with a Tab before typing: **First Generation**
   - You should see leader dots between columns.

```
First Generation      1953-1962        2
Second Generation     1963-1967        3
Third Generation      1968-1982        4
```

7. Insert this new comment to the right of the page 4 entry: **I should use the Table of Contents feature.**

8. Insert a page break before the *Introduction* heading.

9. Set page 1's vertical alignment to **Center**.

10. Insert the **Built-in, Banded** footer so it displays page numbers on all pages except for page 1.

11. Insert the **Built-in, Blank** header, displaying it on all pages except page 1, and use this text: **History of the Chevrolet Corvette**

12. Save your document.
   - *Using eLab:* Save it to your **Word Chapter 3** folder as **W3_P2_eSubmission** and attach the file to your eLab assignment for grading.
   - *Not using eLab:* Save it to your **Word Chapter 3** folder as: **W3_P2_Submission**

✈ Extend Your Skills

These exercises challenge you to think critically and apply your new skills in a real-world setting. You will be evaluated on your ability to follow directions, completeness, creativity, and the use of proper grammar and mechanics. Save files to your chapter folder. Submit assignments as directed.

W3-E1 That's the Way I See It

You are an intern working in the corporate offices of a major grocery store chain. Your manager has asked you to research the pros and cons of reusable shopping bags compared to plastic bags. Start a new document and name it: **W3-E1-ShopBags**

Type a creative title and an original introductory paragraph for the paper and include two footnote comments in the paragraph. Using an Internet search, find two sources who favor reusable shopping bags and two sources who do not. Pull information from these sources and compare the two sides of the issue using a two-column tabular table listing the pros and cons. Insert citations at the end of each source and generate a bibliography from the citations. Add a page number in the footer area. Insert two pictures you find on the Internet representing reusable bags and plastic bags. Add captions to the pictures and create a table of figures. Use styles and indenting, and widen the left and right margins to make your report more readable. Save the file.

W3-E2 Be Your Own Boss

As the owner of Blue Jean Landscaping, you plan to hold a rose-pruning seminar for your customers. Research pruning techniques and create a report of your research results to hand out to customers at the event. Start a new document and name it: **W3-E2-RoseSeminar**

Type a creative title and an original introductory paragraph and include a footnote comment in the paragraph. Cite three different sources in your report and generate a double-spaced bibliography of your citations. Insert a header that includes your company name. Use styles and indents, and increase the margin width to add to the paper's readability. Set the body of the report in a two-column format and insert a column break, if necessary, to balance the columns. Include a comment at the top of the document asking your partner to review the document and make any suggestions she likes. Save the file.

W3-E3 Demonstrate Proficiency

The owner of Stormy BBQ is proud to serve free-range beef. He wants his employees to understand the benefits of using natural, grass-fed beef so they can discuss the idea with customers. He has asked you to prepare a report that he can distribute to all employees. Start a new document and name it: **W3-E3-GrassFed**

Conduct online research on the benefits of using free-range, natural beef. Type a creative title and center it horizontally. Type an original introductory paragraph that includes two commentary footnotes. Cite three sources who favor free-range beef. Generate a bibliography for the citations. Use indents and styles, and adjust the margins to make your paper more readable. Add a footer that includes the company name and page numbers.

Insert **W3-E3-Cattle** as a Text from File object into your report. Insert creative captions for the pictures and generate a table of figures. Create a two-column tabular table listing the disadvantages of feedlot cattle (fossil fuel–intensive, for example) versus the advantages of grass-fed cattle (higher in omega-3 fatty acids, for example). Include at least five rows in the table. Insert a comment at the top of the document asking your admin to look it over for spelling and grammar errors. Save the file.

4 Creating a Promotional Brochure

A picture is worth *at least* a thousand words. If you need to communicate information quickly and vividly, graphics are the best tool in your toolbox. In this chapter, you will add graphic elements, such as WordArt, to a brochure. SmartArt graphics provide a gallery of predesigned diagrams such as lists, processes, cycles, hierarchies, and relationships that help you communicate your ideas. Borders and page color add a polished look to your brochure. Live preview galleries allow you to quickly test many choices while deciding what looks best for your brochure. All these and more help you create materials that are both dynamic and informative.

LEARNING OBJECTIVES

- ▸ Create an eye-catching brochure
- ▸ Insert shapes in a document
- ▸ Add pictures, text boxes, WordArt, and special effects to a document
- ▸ Choose page setup features
- ▸ Communicate information with SmartArt
- ▸ Format the page background
- ▸ Wrap text around a document
- ▸ Print part of a document

📁 Project: Promoting an Ergonomics Seminar

As the owner of Ergonomic Office Solutions, you have decided to create a presentation about the benefits of an ergonomic office. Your friend, Tommy Choi, owner of Green Clean, has provided you with his customer database. Knowing Tommy's customers are already interested in the environment, you believe they would be interested in your products. You decide to create a brochure to mail to local businesses promoting a seminar. You will use product pictures as well as shapes, WordArt, and SmartArt to create a brochure that is both informative and visually appealing.

Working with Shapes

There is a large gallery of graphic shapes available to you, including lines, text boxes, rectangles, ovals, and many others. They can add interest to documents, such as flyers and brochures, and you can type text in most shapes. You can also rotate, resize, and move shapes.

Inserting, Resizing, and Moving Shapes

You insert shapes from the Shapes gallery. When a shape is selected (displays round handles), the contextual Drawing Tools and Format tabs appear, where you can choose many styles and designs for your shape.

To select the shape for moving or resizing, you must click along the border of the shape. If you've inserted text, clicking inside the text will not select the shape; it will place the cursor inside the text.

Resizing shapes with the resizing handles does not constrain the proportions by default. If you wish to keep the length and width proportional to the shape as it was originally inserted, hold the [Shift] key and use the corner handles to resize. The [Shift] key can also be used to select multiple shapes at once.

⚠️ **View the video "Using Shapes."**

≡ Insert→Illustrations→Shapes ⬙ | Drawing Tools→Format→Insert Shapes

In this exercise, you will draw, size, and move shapes. You'll maintain a shape's proportions with the Shift *key when resizing, and you'll see how the mouse pointer changes appearance based on various ways you work with shapes.*

1. Open **W4-D1-Brochure** and save it in your **Word Chapter 4** folder as: `W4-D1-BrochureRevised`

2. If necessary, turn on formatting marks.

   Notice that a number of paragraph symbols are already in the document. It can be easier to work with graphics if some spacing is already set up.

3. Choose **Insert→Illustrations→Shapes** ⬡ to display the Shapes gallery.

4. Choose **Rectangle: Rounded Corners** from the Rectangles category.

   Rectangles

   Basic Shapes

   Rectangle: Rounded Corners

   After you choose a shape, the mouse pointer changes to a crosshair icon resembling a plus sign (+), which you click and drag in the document to create the shape.

5. Click and drag anywhere in the document to draw a rounded rectangle.

6. Choose **Insert→Illustrations→Shapes** ⬡ and then choose **Rectangle: Rounded Corners** again.

7. Hold the Shift key and drag to draw another rounded rectangle.

   This time you drew a perfect square with rounded corners instead of an elongated rectangle, even though you started with the same shape. Holding down the Shift *key while drawing maintains the proportional relationship between the shape's width and height.*

Resize and Rotate Shapes

8. With the square shape selected (displaying round handles), follow these steps to resize the shape:

  Ⓐ Position the mouse pointer on the top-right corner sizing handle.

  Ⓑ Hold Shift and drag diagonally toward the center of the shape to resize while maintaining proportions.

  Ⓒ Drag from a side handle to change only the height or width of the object.

9. Follow these steps to rotate the shape:

Ⓐ Position the mouse pointer on the rotation handle; the mouse pointer appears as a circular arrow.

Ⓑ Click and drag to the right about 45 degrees; the mouse pointer appears as four small arrows when rotating.

Tip! *Holding* ⌈Shift⌉ *allows you to select multiple shapes at once. Then you can delete, move, or format them all at once.*

10. If necessary, click one of the shapes to display the handles and then hold ⌈Shift⌉ and click the other shape.

11. Tap ⌈Delete⌉ to remove both shapes.

You can use the ruler to help align and size shapes and other graphic images. It may or may not be visible on your screen.

12. If necessary, choose **View→Show→Ruler**.

Notice that there are two rulers: one at the top and one at the side of the screen. The margin areas (1" by default) are the gray areas at the left, right, top, or bottom ends of the rulers. The typing areas are white.

Margin area   Typing area

13. Choose **Insert→Illustrations→Shapes** ⬡ and choose **Rectangle: Rounded Corners** again.

14. Starting about 1" from the top of the page and about 2" from the left of the page (or 1" from the left-hand margin), draw a **1" tall** rectangle that spans the page but remains within the margins.

15. Position the mouse pointer on the shape until the pointer appears as a four-headed arrow.

16. Practice dragging the shape to move it and then return it to its original position.

17. Save the file.

Adding Text and Formatting Shapes

You can add text to shapes you draw. This is handy if, for example, you want to create a flyer announcing an event. Just select the shape and begin typing the announcement. Text is automatically centered horizontally and vertically, and it wraps within a shape as you type.

The contextual Format tab contains many tools you can use to add pizzazz to a shape, including Shape Styles, Shadow effects, and 3-D effects. The contextual Format tab also has its own Shapes gallery in the Insert Shapes group. It contains the same shapes as the Shapes gallery located in the Illustrations group on the Insert tab.

View the video "Adding Text to and Formatting Shapes."

≡ Drawing Tools→Format→Shape Styles

DEVELOP YOUR SKILLS: W4-D2

In this exercise, you will add text to a shape and format the text. Then you will format the shape using the Shape Styles gallery.

1. Save your file as: **W4-D2-BrochureRevised**
2. If necessary, select the rectangle shape at the top of the page by clicking anywhere on it.
3. Tap Caps Lock , type **ERGONOMIC OFFICE SOLUTIONS**, tap Enter , and type **PRESENTS**. Tap Caps Lock once more to turn it off.

   Notice that the text is automatically centered in the shape.
4. Click the border of the shape, taking care not to drag.

Tip! *Selecting a shape by clicking the border selects everything inside the shape. Thus, the text in the shape is selected, although it is not highlighted.*

5. Choose **Home→Font→Font menu button ▾ →Tahoma**.
6. Keep the shape selected, click **Bold**, and make the font **22 pt**.
7. If your shape is not big enough for the larger text, drag a **sizing handle** to enlarge it.

   Next, you will use the Shape Styles gallery to format the shape.
8. Make sure the object is selected so the contextual Format tab is available and then choose **Drawing Tools→Format→Shape Styles→More ▾** to open the gallery.

9. Choose **Subtle Effect — Blue, Accent 1**.
10. Save the file.

Using WordArt and Inserting Pictures

WordArt is great for creating smart-looking text objects and special effects, such as logos and headings in newsletters, flyers, and brochures. You can create WordArt by adding your own text to a WordArt object, or you can apply a WordArt object to existing text. You can use the built-in designs as they are, or you can customize them.

You can browse through your computer, or other computers, to locate pictures and other images for your document, or you can search online.

Search for pictures saved as files on a computer.

Search online for pictures and other images.

 Word now allows users to insert icons and 3D models. Icons provide simple black-and-white images of various items, while 3D models are dynamic objects that can be rotated in three dimensions.

≡ Insert→Text→WordArt 🄰

≡ Insert→Illustrations→Pictures 🖼 *or* Online Pictures 🖼

≡ Insert→Illustrations→Icons 🔖 *or* Insert→Illustrations→3D Models ⬡

Cropping and Enhancing Pictures

WordArt and pictures can be rotated, resized, and moved like other objects. The cropping tool can be used to remove any unwanted parts of a picture. The Set Transparent Color tool makes portions of the image transparent, allowing anything under it to show through WordArt.

 View the video "Enhancing Pictures."

Aligning Objects

You can manually drag and drop objects to align them, but using the Align feature on the contextual Format tab is more precise. Select the objects you want to align and then choose the desired alignment.

 The terms object and image are both used when referring to graphical elements such as shapes, WordArt, and pictures.

 Depending on your screen size and resolution, you may see a slightly different icon for the Align button.

≡ Drawing Tools→Format→Arrange→Align 🔲

DEVELOP YOUR SKILLS: W4-D3

In this exercise, you will add a WordArt object and align it with a shape. You will insert and resize a picture and make its background transparent. Then you will format and move the table.

1. Save your file as: **W4-D3-BrochureRevised**
2. Click in the document below the rectangle.
3. Choose **Insert→Text→WordArt** [A].
4. Choose **Fill: Black, Text color 1; Outline: White, Background color 1; Hard Shadow: Aqua, Accent color 5** from the menu that appears and then type: **The Ergonomically Challenged Office**

5. Place the mouse pointer on the border of the WordArt object and then drag to position it about 1" below the rectangle.

   Don't worry about centering it below the shape; you will center align the objects in the next steps.

6. With the WordArt object still selected, hold down [Shift] and click the rounded rectangle above it that you created earlier.

   Both objects should be selected—handles appear on both.

7. Choose **Drawing Tools→Format→Arrange→Align** [⬚]→**Align Center**.

   This center-aligns the objects with each other.

8. If necessary, drag the selected objects so they are centered on the page between the margins.

Insert a Picture

9. Scroll down and position the insertion point in the left cell of the table.
10. Choose **Insert→Illustrations→Pictures** [⬚].
11. Navigate to your **Word Chapter 4** folder and double-click **ErgoChair.jpg** to insert it.
12. Hold down [Shift] and resize the picture using a corner handle until it matches the height of the text on the right.

    This picture has a white background. Later, you will add background color to your brochure and the picture's white background won't blend with the background color. Therefore, you will make it transparent, allowing the brochure's background color to show through.

13. With the chair image selected, choose **Picture Tools→Format→Adjust→Color** [⬚].
14. Choose **Set Transparent Color** at the bottom of the menu.

15. Click in the white background of the image.

This makes the white background transparent, so when you add the page color to the brochure, the color will show through the picture's transparent background.

16. Click anywhere to deselect the image. Then position the mouse pointer on the line between the two cells and double-click to resize the cell.

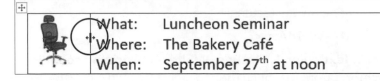

17. Select the table using the **move handle** and then choose **Home→Paragraph→Center** ▤.

18. With the table still selected, choose **Home→Paragraph→Borders** ⊞ **menu button ▾**.

19. Choose **No Border** to complete the page.

20. If gridlines appear in the table (although they won't print), follow these steps to remove them:
- Make sure the table is selected.
- Choose **Table Tools→Layout→Table→View Gridlines** ⊞.

21. Save your file.

Using Text Boxes and Page Setup Options

A text box is a special type of shape designed for inserting text or graphics. You may wonder how inserting a text box is different from drawing a shape and adding text inside it. It's because of the formatting. All documents are based on a theme, which contains a set of theme colors and theme fonts. The default theme for a new blank document is Office. When you originally created the rounded rectangles, a blue fill color was the default fill color for *shapes*. Text boxes do not contain those formatting characteristics. You can format all of the text by selecting the text box itself or format only a portion of the text by selecting the part you want to change. The techniques for rotating, sizing, and moving are the same for text boxes as for other graphics.

 View the video "Creating a Text Box."

☰ Insert→Illustrations→Shapes ▨→Text Box │ Insert→Text→Text Box ▣

Page Setup Options

Commonly used page setup options include page breaks, margins, page orientation, and paper size. All of these are located in the Page Setup group on the Layout tab. Some page setup options also appear in the Print screen in Backstage view.

 You can use Ctrl + Enter *to quickly insert a manual page break.*

 View the video "Page Setup Options."

☰ Layout→Page Setup

In this exercise, you will insert a text box, align it with other objects, and format the text box border and the text within it. Then you will insert a page break to create a second page for your brochure.

1. Save your file as: **W4-D4-BrochureRevised**
2. Choose **Insert→Illustrations→Shapes** and then choose **Text Box** from the Basic Shapes category in the Shapes gallery.
3. Position the mouse pointer below the WordArt object you created previously and drag to draw a text box about **2" wide** and **½" tall**.
4. Type this text and size the box so the text wrapping is the same as shown:

> Email EOS@Yahoo.com or call
> 712-555-0123 to register.

5. If the email address appears as a hyperlink, right-click it and choose **Remove Hyperlink**.
6. Make sure the text box is selected and then choose **Home→Paragraph→Center**.
7. Choose the **Drawing Tools→Format→Shape Styles→Shape Outline** menu button ▼ and choose **Blue, Accent 1, Lighter 40%**.
8. With the text box still selected, hold down [Shift] and select the two objects above it.
9. Choose **Drawing Tools→Format→Arrange→Align** and then choose **Align Center**.
10. Click to deselect. If necessary, move the text box so it is well-balanced on the page.

    You will now insert a page break to create a second page.

11. Position the insertion point at the bottom of the page.
12. Choose **Layout→Page Setup→Breaks**→**Page**.

    Notice the other Page Setup options, including Margins, Orientation, and Size.

13. If necessary, display formatting marks and notice the page break symbol and the new second page.

    Now you will delete the page break and use keystrokes to re-insert a page break.

14. Position the insertion point in front of the page break symbol and tap [Delete].
15. Press [Ctrl]+[Enter] to insert another page break.
16. Save your file and leave it open.

Linking Text Boxes

Sometimes you need a selection of text to begin in one text box and end in another. Making such a change manually can be difficult; any other changes you make to the formatting, layout, or content of the document can move and change your text boxes. It's far easier to have Word do the work for you.

Once you've created the boxes you want to use, you link them together with the Create Link command under the Format contextual tab. When you choose this command, the mouse pointer turns into a pitcher, and you can "pour" the contents from the first text box to the next. Once the text boxes are linked in this way, resizing either box will cause the text to automatically adjust: If one box can no longer fit a line of text, the additional text will automatically move into the linked box.

≡ Drawing Tools→Format→Text→Create Link

In this exercise, you will insert a text box into which you will "pour" the text from another box that has already been created. You will then resize the first box.

1. Open **W4-D5-Linking** and save it in your **Word Chapter 4** folder as: `W4-D5-LinkingRevised`

2. Place the insertion point in the line below the green callout quote in the middle column.

3. Choose **Insert→Text→Text Box menu button ▾→Simple Text Box**.

    Word inserts the text box at the location of your insertion point, but the box is too wide, so you will resize it.

4. Drag the handles at the left and right sides of the text box so the sides line up with the rest of the content in the middle column.

5. Click anywhere inside the text box to select the placeholder content and tap **Delete** to remove it.

    Word automatically resizes the text box vertically to a single line. This height will change when you "pour" the linked text.

6. Click anywhere inside the text box at the top of the middle column and choose **Drawing Tools→Format→Text→Create Link** 🔗.

    Note that the cursor changes into an upright pitcher.

7. Hover the cursor over the empty text box below.

    The cursor now changes into a pouring pitcher.

8. Click inside the empty text box to "pour" the contents and link the boxes.

The linked content between both text boxes is six lines total. You decide that each box should contain three lines.

9. Drag the center-bottom handle of the top text box up to resize it and remove the bottom line.

   The linked content automatically adjusts; the fourth line of the first text box is now the first line of the second text box.

10. Save and close the file.

Working with SmartArt

It is often easier to grasp concepts if information is presented graphically rather than textually. The SmartArt gallery provides a large variety of graphics that you can add to documents. The gallery makes it easy to combine predesigned graphics with text to create sophisticated figures. SmartArt images are divided into the following categories.

Category	Purpose
List	Shows nonsequential data
Process	Shows a progression, a timeline, or sequential steps in a task, process, or workflow
Cycle	Shows a continual process
Hierarchy	Creates a hierarchical structure or shows a decision tree
Relationship	Illustrates associations
Matrix	Shows how parts relate to a whole
Pyramid	Shows proportional relationships
Picture	Used to convey a message with or without explanatory text, or to use pictures to complement a list or process

≡ Insert→Illustrations→SmartArt

Inserting SmartArt Text and Modifying an Image

You can use the SmartArt text pane to add text to your image. You open the pane by clicking the tab that appears on the left side of the image. Text placeholders in the image are replaced with text that you enter in the SmartArt text pane. The font size adjusts based on the amount of information you type. If you prefer, you can type directly in the text placeholders in the image.

If you cannot find the exact image you want, you can modify, add, and delete shapes within the graphic. SmartArt objects are formatted the same way as other graphic shapes.

(!) **View the video "SmartArt Text and Bullets."**

(!) **View the video "Modifying SmartArt."**

In this exercise, you will create a SmartArt graphic. Then, you will customize and resize the graphic.

1. Your brochure file should still be open. Save it as: **W4-D6-BrochureRevised**
2. If necessary, move the insertion point to the top of page 2.
3. Choose **Home→Paragraph→Center** ≣.

   This will center the SmartArt image that will be inserted next on the page.
4. Choose **Insert→Illustrations→SmartArt** .
5. Follow these steps to insert a SmartArt graphic:

  Ⓐ Choose the **List** category.

  Ⓑ Scroll down and choose **Vertical Block List**.

6. Read the description in the bottom-right corner of the dialog box and then click **OK**.
7. If the text pane is not visible, click the **tab**.

Customize the Image

This image has three major text objects, but you will use only one.

8. Position the mouse pointer to the left of the first major bullet and drag down to select the first six bullets.

9. Tap `Delete` to remove the bullets.

10. Follow these steps to begin entering the seminar topics:

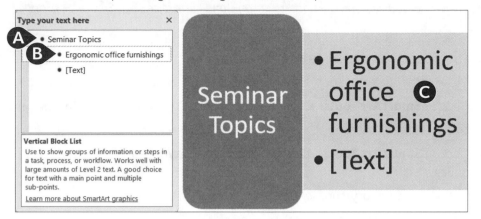

Ⓐ Position the insertion point to the right of the first bullet and type: **Seminar Topics**

Ⓑ Tap `↓` and type: **Ergonomic office furnishings**

Ⓒ Notice that the text appears in the graphic as you type.

11. Tap `↓` to go to the next line and type: **Mobile workstations**

12. Tap `Enter` to generate the next bullet and then type: **Technology support**

13. Tap `Enter` as needed and then type the following items to complete the list:
- **Personal lighting options**
- **Q&A**

14. Click **Close** `×` in the upper-right corner of the text pane.

15. Click the outside border frame to make sure the *entire* SmartArt image is selected.

You will resize the SmartArt object next. If an object within the main frame is selected, you could accidentally resize only a part of the SmartArt object. Clicking the outside border frame prevents that.

16. Drag the bottom-center sizing handle up until the image is approximately half as tall as the original image.

17. Save your file.

Changing a SmartArt Style

The SmartArt Styles gallery allows you to apply interesting variations of the original graphic. Live Preview lets you sample the effects of the various styles without actually applying them.

≡ SmartArt Tools→Design→SmartArt Styles

In this exercise, you will add a SmartArt graphic and customize both SmartArt graphics by applying colors and styles.

1. Save your file as: **W4-D7-BrochureRevised**
2. Make sure the outside border of the seminar topics image is selected.
3. Choose **SmartArt Tools→Design→SmartArt Styles→Change Colors** .
4. In the Accent 1 category, choose: **Gradient Loop – Accent 1**
5. Choose **SmartArt Tools→Design→SmartArt Styles→More** ⌄ to display the SmartArt Styles gallery.
6. In the 3-D category, choose: **Metallic Scene**

    Next, you will add another SmartArt image.

7. Press Ctrl + End to move to the end of the document and then tap Enter twice.
8. Choose **Insert→Illustrations→SmartArt** 📊.
9. Choose the **Process** category, choose **Basic Chevron Process**, and then click **OK**.

    You can type directly in the image without opening the text pane.

10. Click the **[Text]** placeholder in the first arrow on the left and type: **Our Products**
11. Click in each **[Text]** placeholder and enter the text as shown:

12. Click the outside border of the image and follow these steps to add an arrow to the graphic:

    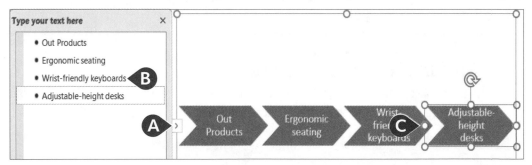

    Ⓐ Click the **tab** to open the text pane.

    Ⓑ Position the insertion point after the word *keyboards* and tap Enter.

    Ⓒ Type **Adjustable-height desks** in the new arrow.

13. **Close** ✕ the text pane.

Format the Image

14. Click the outside border of the shape.

15. Choose **SmartArt Tools→Design→SmartArt Styles→Change Colors** ⬚.

16. Choose the fourth item in the Accent 1 category: **Gradient Loop — Accent 1**

17. Click the **More** button on the SmartArt Styles gallery and in the 3-D category choose **Cartoon**.

18. Save your file.

Formatting the Page Background

Page background formats add color and visual variety to your documents. Page colors and borders provide the finishing touches that add professional polish. For example, you can add colors from the Page Colors gallery that are specifically designed to blend with a document's theme. Border colors are also designed to tastefully complement page colors.

Adding Page Colors and Page Borders

The Page Colors gallery is similar to other galleries you have worked with. The colors that appear in the Theme Colors section of the gallery, as the name implies, are based on the theme currently in effect in the document.

Page borders surround the outer edges of the entire page. You can adjust the color (again, based on the current theme), line thickness, and other features of the border.

≡ Design→Page Background→Page Color 🖼 *or* Page Borders 🗋

DEVELOP YOUR SKILLS: W4-D8

In this exercise, you will use Live Preview to sample background colors. Then you will add a background color to your brochure and a border around the pages.

1. Save your file as: **W4-D8-BrochureRevised**

2. Choose **Design→Page Background→Page Color** 🖼.

3. Hover the mouse pointer over several colors in the Theme Colors area of the gallery.

Live Preview displays the effects of the different colors.

4. Choose **Dark Blue, Text 2, Lighter 40%**.

Now you'll add a page border.

5. Choose **Design→Page Background→Page Borders** 🗋.

6. Choose **Box** from the Setting area in the left-hand panel.

7. Follow these steps to format the page border:

Style:

Color:

Width:

3 pt

Art:

(none)

Ⓐ Choose the **double-line** style.

Ⓑ Choose **Blue, Accent 1, Lighter 40%**.

Ⓒ Choose a width of **3 pt** and then click **OK**.

8. Save and then close your file.

Adding Special Effects to Text

To add interest and dimension to brochures, you can use graphic effects. For example, you can add WordArt for flair. There is a full array of WordArt formatting tools available on the contextual Drawing Tools Format tab.

Various special effects are available for standard fonts as well. Options include strikethrough, superscript/subscript, small caps, and all caps.

≡ Insert→Text→WordArt 🄰

≡ Home→Font dialog box launcher ⬚

In this exercise, you'll familiarize yourself with special text effects while creating a short newsletter for Raritan Clinic East. You will start with a WordArt heading, which you will format with a new fill color, font color, and text effects. Then you will use the Font dialog box to adjust the font style and size, and then you will add font effects.

1. Open a new, blank document and save it to your **Word Chapter 4** folder as:
W4-D9-RaritanNewsltr

2. Display formatting marks and then type these heading lines at the top of the document:

Raritan Clinic East

The Children's Clinic

November, 2021

3. Tap Enter three times.

4. Select **Raritan Clinic East** but do not select the paragraph mark at the end of the line.

5. Choose **Insert→Text→WordArt** and then choose **Fill: Blue, Accent color 1; Shadow**.

6. With the WordArt object selected, follow these steps to place it in line with the text:

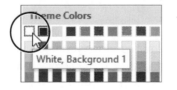

    Ⓐ Click the **Layout Options** smart tag.

    Ⓑ Choose **In Line with Text** and then click in the document to close the gallery.

7. Click the border of the WordArt to select the entire object.

8. Choose **Drawing Tools→Format→Shape Styles→Shape Fill menu button** ▼ and then choose **Blue, Accent 5, Lighter 40%** from the gallery.

9. Choose **Drawing Tools→Format→WordArt Styles→Text Fill menu button** ▼ and then choose **White, Background 1**.

10. With the object selected, choose **Drawing Tools→Format→WordArt Styles→ Text Effects** Ⓐ.

11. Drag the mouse pointer down to the Transform category and choose **Chevron: Down**.

Now you will center all headings and format one of the headings.

12. Position the mouse pointer in the left margin area next to the WordArt object and then click and drag down to select the WordArt and the other two headings.

13. Choose **Home→Paragraph→Center** ≡.

14. Select **The Children's Clinic** and then choose **Home→Font dialog box launcher** to display the Font dialog box.

Ⓐ Choose **Calibri**, **Bold**, **18 pt**.

Ⓑ In the Effects area, check **Small Caps**.

Ⓒ Click **OK**.

15. Save the file.

Using Picture Effects

We've already briefly explored adding pictures into your documents. Once your pictures have been inserted, you'll be able to apply great picture effects, such as shadows, reflections, glows, soft edges, bevels, and 3-D rotations. These effects can help make an otherwise ordinary image *pop* with unique flair.

≡ Insert→Illustrations→Pictures 🖼️

≡ Picture Tools→Format→Picture Styles→Picture Effects 🔘

DEVELOP YOUR SKILLS: W4-D10

In this exercise, you will insert and crop an image. Then you will add a picture effect to the image.

1. Save your file as: **W4-D10-RaritanNewsltr**
2. Position the insertion point on the blank line below the date.
3. Choose **Insert→Illustrations→Pictures** 🖼.
4. Navigate to your **Word Chapter 4** folder and double-click the **RaritanClinic.png** graphics file to insert it.

   Next you will crop the words off of the image.

5. With the picture selected, choose **Picture Tools→Format→Size→Crop** 📐.
6. Position the mouse pointer on the right-center cropping handle and drag left to crop off the words *Raritan Clinic East*.
7. Position the mouse pointer on the bottom-center cropping handle and drag up to remove the words at the bottom of the image; click in the document to finish cropping.
8. If necessary, choose **View→Show→Ruler**, and then resize the image using one of the corner sizing handles, making it approximately **1½" wide**.
9. With the image selected, choose **Picture Tools→Format→Picture Styles→Picture Effects** 🔲.
10. Drag the mouse pointer to the **Shadow** category and in the Outer category choose **Offset: Bottom Right**.
11. Choose **Home→Paragraph→Center** ☰.
12. Save the file.

Setting Up Columns

When working with images and pictures, you may need extra flexibility in creating your columns. With the Columns dialog box, you can specify column and spacing width or have Word put a vertical line between columns.

DEVELOP YOUR SKILLS: W4-D11

In this exercise, you will insert a section break and lay out the newsletter in columns. Then you will customize the column layout.

1. Save your file as: **W4-D11-RaritanNewsltr**
2. Position the insertion point on the second blank line below the picture object and choose **Layout→Page Setup→Breaks** ⊟ **→Continuous**.
3. Position the insertion point anywhere above the section break and choose **Layout→Page Setup→Columns** 🔲.

   Notice that one column is highlighted. Whenever text or images span the width of the page between the margins, it is considered one column.

4. Position the insertion point below the section break.

5. Choose **Insert→Text→Object** [icon] **menu button** ▼→**Text from File**.

6. Navigate to your **Word Chapter 4** folder and double-click **NewsltrTxt**.

7. Choose **Layout→Page Setup→Columns** [icon] and then choose **More Columns** to open the Columns dialog box.

8. Follow these steps to customize the columns :

- Ⓐ Use the **spin box** to change the number of columns to **2**.

- Ⓑ Remove the checkmark from this checkbox.

- Ⓒ Use the **spin box** to change the width of column 1 to **3.5"** and notice that column 2 resizes automatically. If necessary, set the spacing to **0.5"** as well.

- Ⓓ Place a checkmark in the **Line Between** box to add a line between your columns.

9. Click **OK** and then scroll through the document to see the effect.

   The columns don't really look good this way. While you could click Undo if you were to change your mind at a later time, there is still a quick way to return the columns back to equal size.

10. Choose **Layout→Page Setup→Columns** [icon]→**More Columns**.

11. Click the **Equal Column Width** checkbox and click **OK**.

12. Scroll through the document to see how it looks.

13. Save the file.

Artistic Effects and Wrapping Text Around a Picture

There are many tools on the contextual Format tab that allow you to customize images. Artistic effects can take your image styling to the next level. Some effects represent the image in pencil, paint, and various textures. In addition, you can set Wrapping controls that will force your document text to wrap around any images you've inserted. To do this, use the Layout Options smart tag that appears to the top right of an image whenever that image is selected.

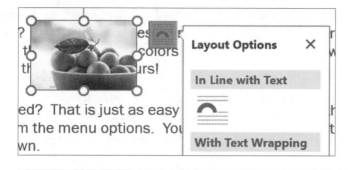

≡ Picture Tools→Format→Adjust→Artistic Effects 🖼

DEVELOP YOUR SKILLS: W4-D12

In this exercise, you will insert a picture and apply an artistic effect as well as a picture style to it. Next, you will use the Layout Options smart tag to wrap text around the picture. Then you will balance the columns at the end of the newsletter.

1. Save your file as: **W4-D12-RaritanNewsltr**
2. Position the insertion point on page 2 to the left of the heading *The New Vaccine*.
3. Choose **Insert→Illustrations→Pictures** 🖼.
4. Navigate to your **Word Chapter 4** folder and double-click **VaccinePic.jpg** to insert the picture in the newsletter.
5. Resize the picture using a corner handle until it is about **1½" wide**.

Apply an Artistic Effect and a Picture Style

6. With the picture selected, choose **Picture Tools→Format→Adjust→Artistic Effects** 🖼 and then choose **Crisscross Etching**.
7. Choose **Picture Tools→Format→Picture Styles→More** ⊡ on the Picture Styles gallery.
8. Use Live Preview to sample various styles and then choose **Simple Frame, Black**.

Wrap Text Around a Picture

9. With the picture selected, click the **Layout Options** smart tag and choose the **Tight** text wrapping option.

10. Click in the document to close the Layout Options gallery.

   Now you will balance the columns on page 2.

   You don't have to insert column breaks and move text around to balance columns. Inserting a Continuous section break at the end of the columns you want to balance is a quick trick for accomplishing the task.

11. Position the insertion point after the period following *disease* at the end of page 2.

12. Choose **Layout→Page Setup→Breaks** ⊟ **→Continuous**.

13. Save the file.

Printing Part of a Document

Sometimes you may want to print only part of a longer document—maybe a page or two, or even just a couple of paragraphs. This can save both time and supplies. Several techniques make this an easy task; they are found in the Print screen in Backstage view.

Custom Print options allow you to specify which pages to print.

CUSTOM PRINT OPTIONS	
Print Consecutive Pages	Enter the page number of the first page to print, type a hyphen, and then type the page number of the last page to print.
Print Nonconsecutive Pages and Ranges	Enter the page numbers you want to print separated by commas (for example: 3,5,7,10-15).
Print a Block of Text	Select the text to print. Navigate to the Print screen in Backstage view. Choose Print Selection from the drop-down list.

≡ File→Print

DEVELOP YOUR SKILLS: W4-D13

In this exercise, you will explore options for printing part of a document. You will see how to print consecutive and nonconsecutive pages as well as a block of selected text.

1. Choose **File→Print** to display the Print screen in Backstage view.

   In the Settings part of the screen, notice that Print All Pages is the default.

2. Click the **menu button** ▼ next to *Print All Pages*.

3. Follow these steps to review the printing options:

Ⓐ This option is available only when you select text prior to accessing the Print screen.

Ⓑ This choice prints the page where the insertion point is located.

Ⓒ This option allows you to specify printing only certain pages.

4. Click the **menu** button ▾ to close the menu.

Tip! *You can specify which custom pages to print in the Pages field without opening the menu. When you begin entering page numbers, the setting automatically switches to Custom Print.*

5. If you want to conserve resources and not print, click the **Back** ⊖ button or print to PDF (you can make that choice in the Printer drop-down list).

6. Save the file and exit Word.

Self-Assessment

Check your knowledge of this chapter's key concepts and skills using the Self-Assessment in your ebook or online (eLab course or Student Resource Center).

Reinforce Your Skills

Create a Flyer Recognizing an Outstanding Volunteer

Kids for Change has a volunteer program, and the person who volunteers the most hours in a quarter is recognized for his or her service. In this exercise, you will create a flyer announcing Janisha Robinson as the winner for this quarter. You will work with shapes, WordArt, pictures, and text boxes.

1. Start Word and create a new file based on the **Blank Document** template. Save it as: **W4-R1-JanishaFlyer**

2. Display formatting marks and tap [Enter] 20 times.

   It can be easier to work with graphics if some spacing is already set up.

3. If necessary, choose **View→Show→Ruler** to display the ruler.

4. Choose **Insert→Illustrations→Shapes** , and in the Stars and Banners category, choose **Ribbon: Tilted Down**.

5. Position the crosshair mouse pointer next to the paragraph symbol at the top of the page.

6. Press and hold the mouse button and drag until the image is about **6½" wide** and **1½" tall**.

7. Type **Outstanding Member** in the image and then click the border to select the entire shape.

8. Choose **Home→Font→Font menu button** ▾ →**Comic Sans MS** and then apply boldface and make the font size 28 pt.

9. Choose **Home→Font→Font Color** [A] **menu button** ▾ and choose **Red** in the Standard Colors category.

Insert and Crop a Picture

10. Position the insertion point a little below the graphic.

11. Choose **Insert→Illustrations→Pictures**, navigate to your **Word Chapter 4** folder, and double-click **Janisha.jpg**.

    Now you will resize the picture.

12. Press and hold [Shift] and then position the mouse pointer on the handle in the upper-right corner of the picture.

13. Drag diagonally toward the center until the picture is about **3" wide**.

    Next you will crop off the left side of the picture.

14. Make sure the picture is selected and then choose **Picture Tools→Format→Size→Crop** .

15. Follow these steps to crop the picture:

Ⓐ Position the mouse pointer on the left-center cropping handle.

Ⓑ Drag to the right to Janisha's right hand and then click in the document to deselect.

Next you will place a border on the picture to give it a finished look.

16. Select the picture and then choose **Picture Tools→Format→Picture Styles→ Picture Border ⬜ menu button** ▾ and pick a shade of blue that you think will blend well.

Now you will choose a layout option that will allow you to freely move the picture on the page.

17. Click the **Layout Options** smart tag at the upper-right side of the picture and choose **In Front of Text** (bottom-right in the *With Text Wrapping* section).

18. Drag the picture to the center of the page.

Use WordArt

19. Position the insertion point a little below the picture.

20. Choose **Insert→Text→WordArt** ⒜ and choose **Fill: Black, Text color 1; Outline: White, Background color 1; Hard Shadow: Blue, Accent color 5**.

21. Type **Janisha Robinson** in the image and then click the **outside border** to select the entire image.

22. Choose **Drawing Tools→Format→WordArt Styles→Text Effects** ⒜ **→Transform**.

23. In the Warp category, choose **Chevron: Down**.

24. Center the WordArt on the page.

Add a Text Box

25. Choose **Insert→Illustrations→Shapes** ⬦**→Text Box**.

26. Below Janisha's name, draw a text box that is approximately **4" wide** and **2½" tall** and then type the following text:

```
Kids Helping Communities
• After-school tutor
• Schoolyard cleanup
• Meals for shut-ins
• Emergency relief food collection
```

27. Click the border of the text box, choose **Home→Font→Font menu button** ▾ → **Comic Sans MS**, and apply 20 pt font size; resize the text box if needed.

28. Hold down ⎢Shift⎥ and select all the images.

29. Choose **Drawing Tools→Format→Arrange→Align** ⬚→**Align Center**.

This center-aligns the images with each other.

30. Use the **zoom slider** in the bottom-right corner of the screen to zoom out until you see the entire page.

31. If necessary, adjust the position of the images so they are well-balanced on the page, and then zoom back to **100%**.

32. Save and close the file.

REINFORCE YOUR SKILLS: W4-R2

Create a Flyer for Charity

Kids for Change is partnering with a local charity to collect clothing and household products for people with developmental disabilities. You have been asked to create a flyer to help in the collection process. In this exercise, you will change page orientation, work with graphic images, and add page color and a page border to the flyer.

1. Start a new, blank document and save it as: **W4-R2-DonationsFlyer**

2. If necessary, choose **View→Show→Ruler**.

3. Choose **Layout→Page Setup→Orientation** ⬚→**Landscape**.

4. Tap ⎢Enter⎥ 15 times to set up some spacing in advance and then position the insertion point at the top of the page.

5. Choose **Insert→Illustrations→Pictures** ⬚, navigate to your **Word Chapter 4** folder, and double-click **Donations.png**.

Now you will use a text-wrapping layout option so you can easily move the image.

6. Make sure the image is selected and then click the **Layout Options** smart tag at the upper-right corner of the image and choose **In Front of Text** (bottom-right).

7. Drag the image to center it between the margins.

8. Position the insertion point below the picture.

Add WordArt and SmartArt

9. Choose **Insert→Text→WordArt** 🄰 and choose **Fill: Gray, Accent color 3; Sharp Bevel**.

10. Type the following text in the WordArt image:

    `We need clothing, furniture, appliances, and household items.`

11. Click outside the image to deselect.

12. Position the insertion point below the WordArt image.

13. Choose **Insert→Illustrations→SmartArt** 🖼; then click the **List** category, choose **Vertical Box List**, and click **OK**.

Now you will resize the SmartArt image so it fits on the first page.

14. Press and hold ⎡Shift⎤ and then position the mouse pointer on the handle in the upper-right corner of the image.

15. Drag diagonally toward the center of the image until it is about **3" wide**.

    It should now be positioned on the first page.

16. Click the **Layout Options** smart tag to the right of the image and choose **In Front of Text**.

    Now you can move the image freely on the page.

17. Center the image between the margins.

Recolor the Image

18. Click the outside border to select the entire image.

19. Choose **SmartArt Tools→Design→Change Colors** ⬡ and choose **Colored Fill — Accent 3**.

20. Type the following in the three *[Text]* areas:

    `Place boxes or bags by 8 a.m.`

    `Donations will be picked up by dark`

    `Thank you for your contributions!`

21. Click outside the image to deselect.

Change the Page Color and Add a Page Border

22. Choose **Design→Page Background→Page Color** 🎨 and then choose **White, Background 1, Darker 25%**.

    Instead of using lines for the border, you will use an art border.

23. Choose **Design→Page Background→Page Borders** 🗔.

24. Click the drop-down arrow in the Art field at the bottom of the dialog box and choose the **hot air balloons**.

The hot air balloons option is the 12th in the list; you may need to scroll down to find it.

25. Click **OK** and then turn off formatting marks.

26. Use the **zoom controls** at the bottom right of the screen to zoom out and see the entire page.

27. If necessary, adjust the position of the images so they are well-balanced on the page, and then zoom back to 100%.

28. Save and close the file.

REINFORCE YOUR SKILLS: W4-R3

Create a Recycling Flyer

Kids for Change held a recycling campaign last month. Your cousin, Ingrid, is enjoying a semester studying at the Sorbonne in Paris. She saw the flyer you created, and she would like to implement a recycling program at the university. She asks that you create a copy of your flyer on standard European-size paper, A4. In this exercise, you will recreate the flyer using graphic images, a picture, a text box, a page background, and a border.

1. Start a new document using the **Blank Document** template and save it as: **W4-R3-RecycleFlyer**

2. Choose **Layout→Page Setup→Size** 📄**→A4**.

3. Display the formatting marks and ruler, if necessary.

4. Tap Enter about 25 times to set up spacing in your flyer and then position the insertion point at the top of the page.

5. Choose **Insert→Text→WordArt** 🔲 and choose **Fill: Light Gray, Background color 2; Inner Shadow**.

6. Type **Reduce, Reuse, Recycle** in the WordArt image and then click the outside border.

7. Choose **Drawing Tools→Format→WordArt Styles→Text Fill** 🔲 menu button ▾→ **Green, Accent 6**.

8. Choose **Drawing Tools→Format→Shape Styles→Shape Effects** 🔲**→Shadow**.

9. In the Outer category, choose **Offset: Top Left**.

10. Choose **Drawing Tools→Format→WordArt Styles→Text Effects** 🔲**→Transform**.

11. In the Warp category, choose **Chevron: Up**.

12. If necessary, drag the WordArt to center it between the margins, and then position the insertion point a little below it.

Add a Picture to the Flyer

13. Choose **Insert→Illustrations→Pictures** 🖼, navigate to your **Word Chapter 4** folder, and double-click **World.jpg**.

14. Hold down ⎵Shift⎵ and resize the picture until it's about **3" wide**.

15. Click the **Layout Options** smart tag, choose **In Front of Text**, and then drag the picture to center it on the page.

    Now you will place a border on the picture.

16. With the picture selected, choose **Picture Tools→Format→Picture Styles→ Picture Border** 🖉 **menu button** ▾→**Weight→3 pt**.

17. Choose **Picture Tools→Format→Picture Styles→Picture Border menu button** ▾→ **Green, Accent 6, Darker 25%**.

Add a Text Box

18. Choose **Insert→Illustrations→Shapes** ⬡→**Text Box**.

19. Draw a text box a little below the picture about **3½" wide** and **2" tall** and then type the following bulleted list in the text box:

    - **Separate your trash**
    - **Always look for recycle bins**
    - **Reuse shopping bags**
    - **If it's broken, fix it**
    - **Buy recycled products**

20. Click the border of the text box and choose **Home→Font→18 pt**.

21. Resize your text box, if needed; don't allow the text to wrap.

22. Click the border to select the object.

23. Choose **Drawing Tools→Format→Shape Styles→Shape Outline** 🖉 **menu button** ▾→ **No Outline**.

24. Choose **Drawing Tools→Format→Shape Styles→Shape Fill** 🖾 **menu button** ▾ and choose **Green, Accent 6, Lighter 60%**.

Use a Shape

25. Choose **Insert→Illustrations→Shapes** ⬡, and in the Stars and Banners category, choose **Star: 6 points**.

26. While holding down ⎵Shift⎵, draw a star about **2½" wide** below the text box and on the left side of the page.

27. Choose **Drawing Tools→Format→Shape Styles** and from the Shape Styles gallery choose **Colored Fill – Green, Accent 6**.

28. Type the following in the star:

    Be a star!

    Do your part!

Insert SmartArt

29. Position the insertion point a little below the text box.

30. Choose **Insert→Illustrations→SmartArt** ; then click the **Cycle** category, choose **Text Cycle**, and click **OK**.

31. Type the following items in the *[Text]* boxes in any order:

`Paper`

`Metal`

`Plastic`

`Hazardous Waste`

`Glass`

32. Hold down [Shift], resize the image until it's about **3½" wide**, click the **Layout Options** smart tag, and choose **In Front of Text**.

33. Arrange the star and SmartArt, as needed, so the star is on the left below the text box and the SmartArt is on the right below the text box.

34. Click the outside border of the SmartArt.

This image has an inside frame and an outside frame.

35. Click one of the arrows in the image, and you'll see both frames.

36. With both frames selected, choose **SmartArt Tools→Format→Shape Styles**; in the Shape Styles gallery, choose **Colored Fill – Green, Accent 6**.

This recolors the arrow that you originally clicked to display both frames. Also, notice that the Shape Styles gallery is now displaying the color you chose.

37. Click the next arrow (you won't see handles on the arrow) and click the green color that's visible in the gallery.

38. Continue until all arrows are recolored and then deselect the image.

39. Use the **zoom controls** to zoom out until you see the entire page.

40. If needed, rearrange the objects so they are balanced on the page to your satisfaction and zoom back to 100%.

Add Page Color and a Page Border

41. Choose **Design→Page Background→Page Color** ▨ **→Green, Accent 6, Lighter 60%**.

42. Choose **Design→Page Background→Page Borders** ▯ and then choose a line style, color, and width of your choice; click **OK**.

43. Save and close the file.

Apply Your Skills

Create a Services Flyer

The Universal Corporate Events marketing manager asked you to create a flyer highlighting services that Universal Corporate Events offers. In this exercise, you will use a picture and graphics to add zing to your flyer.

1. Start a new, blank document and save it as: **W4-A1-Services**
2. Tap Enter enough times to position the insertion point close to the bottom margin and then move the insertion point to the top of the page.
3. Select the **Scroll: Horizontal** shape from the Stars and Banners category to insert it.
4. Drag in the document until the scroll is about **6½" wide** and **1" tall**.
5. Type **Take Off with Universal Corporate Events** and then change the font size to 24 pt.
6. Resize the shape, if necessary, and then position the insertion point a bit below the shape.
7. Insert the **Plane.jpg** picture located in your **Word Chapter 4** folder.
8. Click the **Layout Options** smart tag and choose **In Front of Text**.
9. While maintaining the height/width proportions, resize the picture to about **3" wide**, and then position the picture just below the Shapes image and center it between the margins.

   Now you'll add a border to the picture.

10. Choose **Picture Tools→Format→Picture Styles→Picture Border menu button ▾→ Weight→3 pt**
11. Change the picture border color to **Blue, Accent 1, Darker 25%**.

Add WordArt and a Text Box

12. Position the insertion point below the picture, insert a WordArt graphic, and apply **Fill: Blue, Accent color 1; Shadow**.
13. Type **Services We Offer**; center the graphic on the page.
14. Format the WordArt image by choosing the **Text Effects, Bevel** category and choosing **Round**.
15. Then in the Text Effects, Transform category, choose **Arch** (first form in the Follow Path category).
16. Insert a text box shape below the WordArt image that is about **4" wide** and **1½" tall**.
17. Enter the following in the text box, including the bullet points:
    - **Online itinerary**
    - **Online flight tracking**
    - **Travel insurance**
    - **Visa and passport services**
18. Remove the outline border from the text box.
19. Change the text to 22 pt and then resize the text box, if needed.

Align Images

20. Hold the [Shift] key and select all four objects.

21. Use the Align feature to center-align the objects with each other.

22. If necessary, drag the selected objects to center them between the margins.

23. Zoom out to Full Page View and adjust the placement of the images as you deem necessary for the flyer to appear well-balanced; then zoom back to 100%.

24. Save and close the file.

APPLY YOUR SKILLS: W4-A2

Create a European Tours Flyer

A Universal Corporate Events sales rep has asked you to create a flyer for a corporate client who is planning an employee rewards plan. The client will be choosing among three options for the reward tour. In this exercise, you will change the page orientation, format the page background, and use SmartArt to highlight the details of the recommended tours.

1. Start a new, blank file and save it as: **W4-A2-CorpTours**

2. Use landscape orientation for the flyer, tap [Enter] until the insertion point is close to the bottom margin, and then position the insertion point at the top of the page.

3. Choose the Page Color **Gold, Accent 4, Lighter 60%**.

4. Add a page border, making the formatting choices as shown (color is Gold, Accent 4, Darker 25%):

5. Use a WordArt image of your choice to add a **Universal Corporate Events** heading to the flyer; use a Text Fill color that blends well with the background color and a Text Effect of your choice.

6. Position the insertion point about **1"** below the heading and click the SmartArt graphic **Vertical Chevron List**, which is in the Process category, to insert it.

7. Resize the graphic to about **3" wide** and **3½" tall**.

8. Click the **Layout Options** smart tag and choose **In Front of Text**.

9. In the first blue *[Text]* box, type **London**; type **Berlin** and **Rome** in the next two blue *[Text]* boxes.

10. In the bulleted list to the right of *London*, enter **Stonehenge**, **Windsor Castle**, and **Tate Gallery**.

11. Enter **Dresden**, **Potsdam**, and **Rothenburg** for *Berlin* and **Pompeii**, **Tuscany**, and **Capri** for *Rome*.

Format the WordArt Graphic

12. Change the SmartArt color using the first color option in the Colorful category.

13. Select the white rectangle next to *London* and change the Shape Fill color to a color that you feel complements the London object.

14. Use the same technique to color the *Berlin* and *Rome* rectangles.

15. Arrange and size the objects in a balanced manner on the page.

16. Save and close the file.

APPLY YOUR SKILLS: W4-A3

Create a Mileage Awards Flyer

Universal Corporate Events provides car rentals for travelers, and the company is currently offering mileage awards. In this exercise, you will create a flyer highlighting the award offerings. You will use graphics for interest and format the flyer background for a polished, professional look.

1. Start a new, blank document and save it as: **W4-A3-CarRental**

2. Tap Enter until the insertion point is close to the bottom margin and then move the insertion point to the top of the page.

   Next you will use WordArt to create a heading for the flyer.

3. Insert a new WordArt image, using the design in the third row, fifth column.

4. Enter the following text: **Universal Corporate Events**

Add a Text Box and a Picture

5. Insert a text box below the WordArt about **3½" wide** and **1" tall** and then type the following lines in the text box:

   Get behind the wheel!

   Get more reward travel!

6. Change the font size to 22 pt; resize the text box, if necessary.

7. Change the font color to **Light Gray, Background 2, Darker 50%**.

   Later you will add page color, and removing the text box's white fill background and its outline will make the text box blend in better.

8. Change the Shape Fill to **No Fill** and change the Shape Outline to **No Outline**.

9. Position the insertion point a bit below the text box; then, insert **Driver.jpg** from your **Word Chapter 4** folder.

10. While maintaining the picture's proportions, resize the picture to about **2½" wide**.

11. Click the **Layout Options** smart tag and choose **In Front of Text**. Then center the picture between the margins.

12. With the picture selected, click **Center Shadow Rectangle** in the Picture Styles gallery.

13. Position the insertion point just below the picture and click **Wave** in the Stars and Banners category of the Shapes gallery.

14. Draw the shape about **4½" wide** and **1" tall**, type `Book Now!` in the shape, and change the font size to 36 pt.

15. With the shape selected, choose **Drawing Tools→Format→Shape Styles→Shape Fill→ Gray, Accent 3**.

16. Change the shape outline to **White, Background 1**.

17. Position the insertion point a bit below the shape.

18. Choose **Insert→Illustrations→SmartArt**, and in the List category, choose **Vertical Box List**.

19. While maintaining its proportions, resize the shape to about **3" wide**.

20. Click the **Layout Options** smart tag, choose **In Front of Text**, and then select all three blue shapes.

21. Choose **SmartArt Tools→Format→Shape Styles→Shape Fill** and then choose **Gray, Accent 3**.

22. Select all three white rectangles and choose the same color for the **Shape Outline** ✐.

23. Center the SmartArt between the margins at the bottom of the page and then type the following in the three *[Text]* areas:

    `100 award miles per day`

    `125 bonus miles per day`

    `150 miles for booking with us`

24. Click elsewhere to deselect, then zoom out to a full page view and, if needed, arrange the objects so they are well-balanced and centered on the page, and then zoom back to 100%.

Add a Page Color and a Page Border

25. Choose the page color **Light Gray, Background 2, Darker 10%**.

26. Choose **Design→Page Background→Page Borders** and choose a line style that you prefer; then apply the **White, Background 1** color and **3 pt** width.

    There is more white in the bottom half of the flyer. It may look better if the SmartArt heading were white.

27. Change the SmartArt Text Fill to **White, Background 1**.

28. Save and close the file; exit Word.

Project Grader

If your class is using eLab (labyrinthelab.com), you may upload your completed Project Grader assignments for automatic grading. You may complete these projects even if your class doesn't use eLab, though you will not be able to upload your work.

PROJECT GRADER: W4-P1

Creating a Holiday Celebration Flyer

It's been a great year for Taylor Games, so the management team is organizing an end-of-year holiday celebration. In this exercise, you will prepare a flyer to announce the event.

1. Download and open your Project Grader starting file.
   - *Using eLab:* Download **W4_P1_eStart** from the Assignments page. You *must* start with this file or your work cannot be automatically graded.
   - *Not using eLab:* Open **W4_P1_Start** from your **Word Chapter 4** folder.

2. Insert the **Taylor Games Logo.png** picture from your **Word Chapter 4** folder.

3. Apply a page border using these settings:

Setting	Value
Setting	**Box**
Style	**Solid line** (first option on the list)
Width	**3 pt**
Color	**Blue, Accent 1**

4. Apply the page color **Blue, Accent 1, Lighter 80%**.

5. Insert a **Rectangle: Rounded Corners** shape below the Taylor Games Logo.

Rectangles

6. Set the shape height to **8"** and the shape width to **2.6"**.

7. Use these guidelines to position the rectangle:
   - Move it vertically until the spacing below the Taylor Games logo is about the same as the spacing above the bottom page border.
   - Move it horizontally until the left edge closely aligns with the left edge of the Taylor Games logo.

8. Enter this text in the rectangle using a font size of **22**. Make sure you underline the heading as shown here:

<u>Fun Activities</u>

Face Painting

Drawing Contest

Magic Show

Board Games

Card Games

Darts

And more...

9. Insert a new text box shape above the text box that's on the right side of the page.

10. Set the Shape Height to **2.2"** and the Shape Width to **4.4"**.

11. Align the new text box using these guidelines:

- Use **Align Top** to align the top edges of the rounded corners rectangle and text box. Make sure the text box moves and the rounded corners rectangle remains stationary.
- Use **Align Left** or **Align Right** to align the vertical edges of the two text boxes. Make sure the new text box moves and the other text box remains stationary.

12. Enter this text in your new text box using a font size of **18** and **Bold** formatting:

Date: December 9th

Time: 5:00-9:30 PM

Where: Mission Hills Restaurant

Why: Celebrating the holidays and a great year at Taylor Games

13. Use these guidelines to insert **WordArt** to the right of the Taylor Games logo:

- WordArt Style: **Fill: Blue, Accent color 1; Shadow**
- Move the WordArt so it's to the right of the Taylor Games logo and above the *December 9th* text box.
- Enter the text: **Holiday Celebration**

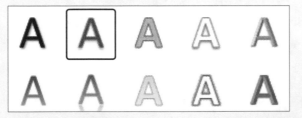

14. Set the shape height to **0.8"** and the shape width to **4.4"**.

15. Use these guidelines to position the WordArt:

- Move it up or down so it's roughly centered with the Taylor Games logo.
- Use **Align Left** or **Align Right** to align the edges of the WordArt with the *December 9th* text box. Make sure the WordArt moves and the *December 9th* text box remains stationary.

16. Make these formatting changes to the *December 9th* text box and the text box below it:

Property	Value
Shape Fill	**Blue, Accent 1, Lighter 80%**
Shape Outline	**No Outline**

17. Insert a **Star: 5 Points** shape in the open space at the bottom of the page.

18. Set the shape height to **3 "** and the shape width to **3 "**.

19. Use these guidelines to position the star:

- Move the star up so its bottom edge is higher than the bottom edge of the rounded-corners rectangle.
- Move the star horizontally so it is nearly centered below the text box above it.
- Use **Align Bottom** to align the bottom edge of the star with the bottom edge of the rounded-corners rectangle. Make sure the star moves down and the rounded-corners rectangle remains stationary.

20. Enter this text in the star using a font size of **22 pt: What a Year!**

21. Apply this shape effect to the star: **Glow: 5 point; Gold, Accent color 4**

Glow Variations

22. Save your document.

- *Using eLab:* Save it to your **Word Chapter 4** folder as **W4_P1_eSubmission** and attach the file to your eLab assignment for grading.
- *Not using eLab:* Save it to your **Word Chapter 4** folder as: **W4_P1_Submission**

A Promotional Flyer to Attract New Gold Members

The Classic Cars Club needs a membership benefits flyer to be posted at various locations in the upcoming national show. In this exercise, you will turn a text-only informational document into an attractive flyer.

1. Download and open your Project Grader starting file.
   - *Using eLab:* Download **W4_P2_eStart** from the Assignments page. You *must* start with this file or your work cannot be automatically graded.
   - *Not using eLab:* Open **W4_P2_Start** from your **Word Chapter 4** folder.

2. Apply these Page Border settings:

Setting	Value
Setting	**Box**
Style	**Dashed line** (third option on the list)
Color	**Automatic**
Width	**3 pt**

3. Apply the page color **Blue, Accent 1, Lighter 80%**.

4. Use the **Columns, Line Between** setting to display a line between the columns.

5. Insert the **Classic Cars 2.jpg** picture from your **Word Chapter 4** folder in front of the word *The* in the first paragraph.

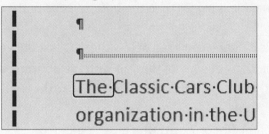

6. Set the picture's shape height to: **1.4"**

7. Apply the **Pencil Grayscale** artistic effect.

8. Set the picture's wrap text option to **Square**.

9. Apply a **Black, Text 1** picture border.

10. Insert a **WordArt** text box using these guidelines:
    - WordArt Style: **Fill: Gold, Accent color 4; Soft Bevel**
    - Move the WordArt so it's in the empty space above the columns.
    - Enter the text: `Classic Cars Club Gold Membership!`

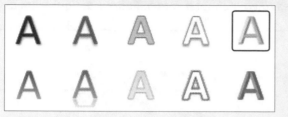

11. Set the shape height to `0.9"` and the shape width to `8"`.

12. Use these guidelines to position the WordArt:
    - Move it up or down so it's roughly centered between the top page border and the tops of the columns.
    - Move it horizontally so the center of the WordArt object is aligned with the line between the columns.

13. Insert the **Wave** shape in the blank space below the columns.

14. Set the shape height to `1.5"` and the shape width to `9"`.

15. Use these guidelines to position the shape:
    - Move it horizontally so the center of the shape is aligned with the line between the columns.
    - Move it up or down so it's roughly centered between the bottom page border and the bottoms of the columns.

16. Enter this text in the shape using a font size of **22 pt**: `Join before April 30 and receive a 25% new-member discount!`

17. Apply the **All Caps** font effect to the Gold Member Benefits heading at the top of the right column.

18. Save your document.
    - *Using eLab:* Save it to your **Word Chapter 4** folder as `W4_P2_eSubmission` and attach the file to your eLab assignment for grading.
    - *Not using eLab:* Save it to your **Word Chapter 4** folder as: `W4_P2_Submission`

◢ Extend Your Skills

These exercises challenge you to think critically and apply your new skills in a real-world setting. You will be evaluated on your ability to follow directions, completeness, creativity, and the use of proper grammar and mechanics. Save files to your chapter folder. Submit assignments as directed.

W4-E1 That's the Way I See It

You just completed your training as a dietician, and now you are ready to advertise your services by distributing a brochure throughout the area. Start a new document and save it as: **W4-E1-GoodDiet**

Design a brochure using WordArt, a picture, and a text box and use page color and a page border to give your brochure a polished look. Create a tagline for your business and explain the services you offer and the benefits of eating well. Also include a suggestion that the reader schedule an appointment today.

W4-E2 Be Your Own Boss

As the owner of Blue Jean Landscaping, a Georgia company, you hope to increase sales as your customers get ready to spruce up their gardens with spring plants. Start a new document and save it as: **W4-E2-Spring**

Create a flyer using landscape orientation and include graphics of your choice and a picture. Describe the services you provide and use upbeat verbiage about spring gardening in Georgia. Suggest plants that are appropriate for Georgia's climate. If needed, conduct an Internet search for information about plants that grow well in Georgia in the spring. Give your flyer a finished look by adding page color and a page border.

W4-E3 Demonstrate Proficiency

Stormy BBQ is expanding to include a catering department! You have been asked to create a brochure announcing this new venture. Start a new document and save it as: **W4-E3-Catering**

Include pictures of food that would normally be found in a BBQ restaurant, formatting and cropping them as necessary. Use a SmartArt graphic to list the types of events that you provide catering for and format the image to blend well with the pictures you have chosen. Use one or more text boxes containing testimonials from test customers who have already enjoyed your catering services. Add page color and a page border to your brochure.

5 | Using Mail Merge

I n this chapter, you will use the Mail Merge feature to turn boilerplate letters into personalized correspondence. The data source (list of variable information, such as the recipients' addresses) and the main document (form letter) need to be set up and proofed only once. Then you can generate hundreds of letters without checking each one. And you can use Mail Merge for more than letters. You can generate envelopes, labels, legal documents, or just about any fixed-text document that requires variable information. A data source can be a Word document, an Excel worksheet, an Access database, or an Outlook contact list.

LEARNING OBJECTIVES

▸ Build data sources

▸ Create main documents

▸ Perform a mail merge

▸ Deal with merge problems

▸ Generate envelopes and labels

📂 Project: Promoting Exercise Classes

Raritan Clinic East is a pediatric medical practice. The practice serves patients ranging in age from newborn to eighteen years. As the administrator who oversees the STAYFIT exercise classes at the clinic, once a week you receive the contact information for all new patients who would benefit from these classes. You will send a letter to the patients explaining the program. Once you set up the main document, you will be able to use it over and over for new patients. And once you design a flexible data source, you can use that same source layout for the exercise letters as well as other communications.

Introducing Mail Merge

Mail Merge is most often used for generating personalized documents, such as Word letters, mailing labels, and envelopes. But Mail Merge is a versatile tool that can be used with any type of document that combines boilerplate text with variable information, such as email, standard contracts, and legal verbiage. Mail Merge can be a big time-saver and is valuable for managing large mailings.

Components of Mail Merge

Merging creates a document that combines information from two files. They are known as the main document and the data source.

▸ **Main document:** This document controls the merge. It is a Word document that contains the fixed information and merge codes into which the variable information is merged. A typical form letter, for instance, has a different inside address and greeting line in each letter, while the rest of the text is the same for everyone receiving the letter.

▸ **Data source:** The data source can be another Word document, a spreadsheet, a database file, or contact list in Outlook. The data source contains field names that correspond with the merge codes in the main document.

▸ **Merged document:** This document is the result of the merge. It is basically multiple "copies" of your letter, with each copy replacing the merge codes with a different recipient's name and information.

You can merge an existing main document with an existing data source, or you can create the main document and data source while stepping through the merge process.

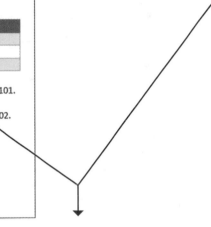

«AddressBlock»

«GreetingLine»

«First_Name», welcome to Raritan Clinic East, one of the finest clinics in the field of pediatric medicine. As part of our ongoing effort to provide the best patient care, we offer an extensive STAYFIT program. Being active helps you be healthier and stronger—and feel your best. And «Your_Doctor» wants the best for you!

In designing your fitness program, choose from the following offerings:

Aerobic Exercise	Flexibility Training	Strength Training
Dance and Movement	Qi Gong	Calisthenics
Water Aerobics	Tai Chi	Free Weights
Zumba	Yoga	Pilates

Having trouble finding the right exercise program for you? Contact a health coach. Call 1-800-555-0101.

Classes are every evening from 7:00–8:00 p.m. Advanced registration is required. Call 1-800-555-0102.

Sincerely,

Molly Lincoln
STAYFIT Coordinator

The data source can be Mail Merge recipient list, a Word table, an Excel spreadsheet, or an Access database.

The main document contains standard text and merge codes where variables from the data source will be merged.

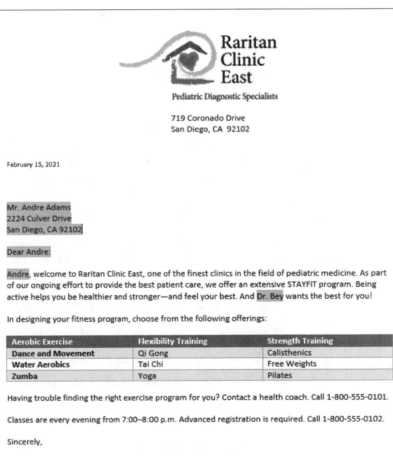

Here is a completed merge document with the variables from the data source.

The Benefits of Mail Merge

Mail Merge saves a lot of time. Imagine you want to send a letter to 100 customers. Without Mail Merge, you would have to type the same text in all 100 letters (or copy and paste 100 times). However, with Mail Merge, you create one main document with the standard text and one data source containing customer names and addresses.

You will also really appreciate Mail Merge when you later decide you want to make a change. Using Mail Merge, you can edit the main document once and remerge it with the data source to produce a new merged document. Without Mail Merge, you would need to edit each letter individually.

The Mailings Tab

The Mailings tab provides guidance in setting up the main document and data source, and it helps you conduct the merge. The Start Mail Merge group is the beginning point. Alternatively, you can use the Step-by-Step Mail Merge Wizard from the Start Mail Merge menu to walk you through the process.

Here you identify an existing
data source or create a new one.

You specify the type of document
(letters, envelopes, or labels) here.

Start Mail
Merge ▾

Select
Recipients ▾

Edit
Recipient List

Start Mail Merge

Working with the Data Source

Data sources typically contain names, addresses, telephone numbers, and other contact information. However, you can include any information in a data source. For example, you could include part numbers and prices to create a parts catalog. You can create a data source in Word, or you can use an external data source, such as an Access database or Excel spreadsheet. Once a data source is created, it can be merged with many different main documents.

 View the video "Creating a Data Source."

DEVELOP YOUR SKILLS: W5-D1

In this exercise, you will use the Start Mail Merge group on the Ribbon to specify a letter as your main document. Then you will customize the data source columns and enter data.

1. Open **W5-D1-ExerciseLtr** from your **Word Chapter 5** folder and save it as:
   W5-D1-ExerciseLtrRevised

2. Choose **Mailings→Start Mail Merge→Start Mail Merge** ▭ **→Letters**.

   You are indicating that the letter you just opened will be the main document. Now you will create your mailing list.

3. Choose **Mailings→Start Mail Merge→Select Recipients** ▭ **→Type a New List**.

   The New Address List dialog box opens. Now you will remove unnecessary fields and add a new field.

4. Click **Customize Columns** to open the Customize Address List dialog box.

5. Choose **Company Name** and click **Delete**; click **Yes** to verify the deletion.

6. Delete **Address Line 2**, **Country or Region**, **Home Phone**, **Work Phone**, and **E-mail Address**.

7. Follow these steps to add a field:

Customize Address List	? ✕
Field Names	
Title	Add... —Ⓐ
First Name	
Last Name	Delete
Address Line 1	
City	Rename...
State	
ZIP Code	

Add Field ? ✕

Type a name for your field

Your Doctor	—Ⓑ	Ⓒ
OK	Cancel	Move Up
		Move Down

Ⓐ Click **Add**.

Ⓑ Type **Your Doctor** and click **OK**.

Ⓒ Click **OK** to close the Customize Address List dialog box.

Enter Records

8. Follow these steps to begin the first record:

    The insertion point should be in the Title field.

New Address List ? ✕

Type recipient information in the table. To add more entries, click New Entry.

Title	First Name	Last Name	Address Line 1	City
Mr. Ⓐ	Ⓑ			

Ⓐ Type **Mr.** in the Title field.

Ⓑ Tap [Tab] to move to the next field.

 Tip! *Don't type spaces after entering information in a field; Word will take care of it. You can click a field and make editing changes if necessary.*

9. Type **Talos** and tap [Tab] to move to the next field.

10. Finish entering the Talos Bouras data shown, tapping [Tab] between fields. The list of fields will scroll as you [Tab] and type:

Mr. Talos Bouras	Ms. Nicole Romero	Mr. Michael Chowdrey
854 Whitmore Drive	132 Lake Street	900 C Street
San Diego CA 92101	San Diego CA 92102	La Jolla CA 92103
Dr. Gonzalez	Dr. Mansee	Dr. Kelly

11. When you complete the first record, click **New Entry** or tap [Tab] to generate a new row for the next record; then enter the two remaining records shown.

Tip! *If you accidentally tap [Tab] after the last record, just click Delete Entry to remove the blank record.*

12. Leave the New Address List dialog box open.

Reviewing Your Records

It's a good idea to review your records for accuracy before saving the data source. However, if you miss an error, you can always edit it later.

New Address List				?	✕
Type recipient information in the table. To add more entries, click New Entry.					
Title ▼	First Name ▼	Last Name ▼	Address Line 1	✛City ▼	
▷ Mr.	Talos	Bouras	854 Whitmore ...	San Diego	

If an entry is wider than the field, position the mouse pointer between column headers and drag to widen (or use the arrow keys to scroll through the entry).

DEVELOP YOUR SKILLS: W5-D2

In this exercise, you will examine your records for accuracy and save your data source.

1. Position the mouse pointer on the scroll bar at the bottom of the dialog box and drag right and left to view all the fields.

2. Follow these steps to review your records:

New Address List				Ⓑ ?	✕
Type recipient information in the table. To add more entries, click New Entry.					
Title ▼	First Name ▼	Last Name ▼	Address Lin...	✛City ▼	S
▷ Mr.	Talos	Bouras Ⓐ	854 Whitmore D	San Diego	C
Ms.	Nicole	Romero	132 Lake Street	San Diego	C
Mr.	Michael	Chowdrey	900 C Street	La Jolla	C

Ⓐ Position the insertion point here and use the **arrow keys** to move through the entry.

Ⓑ Position the mouse pointer here and drag to the right to display the entire entry.

3. Review your entry and correct any typos, and then click **OK** to open the Save Address List dialog box.

4. Save the data source file in your **Word Chapter 5** folder as: `W5-D2-ExerciseLtrData`

   Your data source is now connected to the main document.

Managing the Address List

The Mail Merge Recipients dialog box lets you sort and filter address lists, choose records to include in the mail merge, and edit the data source. If you used a Word table, Excel spreadsheet, or other file for your data source, you can edit directly in that data source file. You can also use the New Address List dialog box to create, edit, or delete records and customize columns.

 View the video "Working with the Address List."

In this exercise, you will work with the Mail Merge Recipients dialog box, where you can sort, filter, and edit your mailing list.

1. Choose **Mailings→Start Mail Merge→Select Recipients** ▣ **→Use an Existing List**.
2. Navigate to your **Word Chapter 5** folder and double-click **W5-D2-ExerciseLtrData**.
3. Choose **Mailings→Start Mail Merge→Edit Recipient List** ▣.
4. Follow these steps to sort and filter the list and open the Edit Source dialog box:

Ⓐ Click this **field header** to sort the list in ascending order by Last Name.

Ⓑ Click the drop-down arrow and choose **Chowdrey** to filter out other entries. Click the arrow again and choose **(All)** to redisplay all records.

Ⓒ Click the **data source** to activate the Edit button.

Ⓓ Click **Edit** to open the Edit Data Source dialog box.

The Edit Data Source dialog box looks and operates like the New Address List dialog box. The entries appear in the order in which they were originally entered.

5. Follow these steps to edit a record:

Title	First Name	Last Name	Address Line 1	City
Mr.	Talos	Bouras	854 Whitmore …	San Diego
Ms.	Nicole	Romero	132 Lake Street	San Diego
▷ Mr.	Michael	Chowdrey	900 C Street	La Jolla

Edit Data Source

To edit items in your data source, type your changes in the table below. Column headings display fields from your data source and any recipient list fields to which they have been matched (in parentheses).

Data source being edited: W5-D2-ExerciseLtrData.mdb

Ⓐ Click this address to select it.

Ⓑ Type **146 Meadow Lane** in its place.

6. Follow these guidelines to enter the three records in the following illustration:
- Click the **New Entry** button or tap [Tab] at the end of the row for each new record.
- Tap [Tab] to move from one field to the next.
- If you accidentally tap [Tab] after the last record, use **Delete Entry** to remove the blank record.

Ms. Mary Wright	Mr. Derek Navarro	Mr. Andre Adams
1240 Potrero Avenue	3300 Maple Drive	2224 Culver Drive
San Diego CA 92101	La Jolla CA 92103	San Diego CA 92102
Dr. Gonzalez	Dr. Storm	Dr. Bey

7. Review the entries for accuracy and then click **OK** to close the dialog box.

8. Click **Yes** when the message appears verifying your update.

9. Click **OK** to close the Mail Merge Recipients dialog box.

Working with the Main Document

You accomplish a merge by combining a main document with a data source. Merge fields in a main document correspond to fields in the data source. Some merge codes, such as the Address Block code, are composite codes consisting of a number of grouped fields. For example, the Address Block code includes Title, First Name, Last Name, Address, City, State, and Zip.

Merge fields are replaced with the corresponding data from your data source. They appear exactly as you typed them into your data source and exactly where you placed them in your main document.

«Title» «First_Name» «Last_Name» can be contacted at «Home_Phone».

becomes

Ms. Alexia Lopez can be contacted at 831-555-0132.

View the video "Inserting Merge Fields in the Main Document."

DEVELOP YOUR SKILLS: W5-D4

In this exercise, you will set up a form letter. The exercise letter main document should still be open.

1. If necessary, choose **Home→Paragraph→Show/Hide** [¶] to display formatting characters.

2. Select the **Today's Date** line and tap [Delete].

3. Choose **Insert→Text→Date & Time** [icon].

4. Choose the third date format, check **Update Automatically**, if necessary, and click **OK**.

Checking the Update Automatically option means the date in your letter will always be the current date, which is a convenient option for form letters that you want to use again.

5. Tap [Enter] four times after inserting the date.

Now you will insert the Address Block code.

6. Choose **Mailings→Write & Insert Fields→Address Block** [icon].

The Insert Address Block dialog box allows you to choose a format for the address block.

7. Follow these steps to insert an Address Block code:

Ⓐ Choose different formats and view the preview on the right; then choose **Mr. Joshua Randall Jr.**

Ⓑ Leave the remaining options as shown and click **OK**.

The <<AddressBlock>> code appears in the letter. During the merge, the information from the data source will be inserted at the Address Block code location.

8. Tap [Enter] twice.

Now you will insert the Greeting Line code.

9. Choose **Mailings→Write & Insert Fields→Greeting Line** 📄.

10. Follow these steps to modify and insert the Greeting Line code:

Ⓐ Change this option to a colon (:).

Ⓑ Note the generic greeting that will be used for data records if they are missing last names.

Ⓒ Choose **Joshua** from the list and then click **OK**.

11. Tap [Enter] twice.

12. Follow these steps to insert the First Name code into the letter:

Ⓐ If necessary, position the insertion point to the left of *Welcome*.

Ⓑ Click the **Insert Merge Field menu** button ▼.

Ⓒ Choose **First_Name**.

13. Type a comma and tap ⌷Spacebar⌷, then delete the uppercase *W* and replace it with a lowercase *w*.

14. Position the insertion point to the left of *wants* as shown:

> «First_Name», welcome to Raritan Clinic East, one of the finest clinics in the field of pediatric medicine. As part of our ongoing effort to provide the best patient care, we offer an extensive STAYFIT program. Being active helps you be healthier and stronger—and feel your best. And wants the best for you!¶

15. Choose **Mailings→Write & Insert Fields→Insert Merge Field** 📋 **menu button** ▼, choose **Your_Doctor**, and then tap ⌷Spacebar⌷.

16. Take time to review your letter, making sure the merge fields match this example. In particular, make sure you use the proper punctuation between fields and the text.

The merge fields are highlighted in this figure to help you locate them; your merge fields do not need to be highlighted. (The Highlight Merge Fields button is in the Write & Insert Fields group.)

> «AddressBlock»
>
> «GreetingLine»
>
> «First_Name», welcome to Raritan Clinic East, one of the finest clinics in the field of pediatric medicine. As part of our ongoing effort to provide the best patient care, we offer an extensive STAYFIT program. Being active helps you be healthier and stronger—and feel your best. And «Your_Doctor» wants the best for you!

Note! *Any punctuation or spacing errors that occur in your main document will appear in every merged letter.*

17. Choose **Home→Paragraph→Show/Hide** ¶ to turn off formatting marks.

18. Save your file.

Conducting a Merge

Merging combines a main document with a data source document. If you are merging a form letter with a data source, Word produces a personalized copy of the form letter for each record in the data source.

It's always a good idea to preview the merge results before you complete the merge so you can make any corrections. If you notice an error that needs to be fixed in the main document, simply click Preview Results again to return to the main document.

Use this button to display the first record from your data source in the letter.

Navigate through the letters with these buttons.

You can click here to have Word check for errors, such as an invalid field code.

When you feel confident that your letter and data source are accurate, you are ready to complete the merge.

This option merges letters on the screen so you can edit individual letters, if desired.

This choice merges directly to the printer.

You can also merge to email messages.

To Save or Not to Save?

Merged documents are rarely saved because they can easily be reconstructed by merging the main document with the data source. Instead, merged documents are usually previewed, printed, and closed without saving. But you can certainly save the merged document if you wish to have a record of it. If a merged document contains errors, you can close it without saving, edit the main document or data source, and conduct the merge again.

DEVELOP YOUR SKILLS: W5-D5

In this exercise, you will use the Preview Results command to review your letters; then you will complete the merge on the screen.

1. If necessary, switch to the **Mailings** tab.

2. Follow these steps to preview the merge:

Ⓐ Click **Preview Results** to display the first inside address.

Ⓑ Use the navigation buttons to scroll through all your merged documents.

3. Choose **Mailings→Finish→Finish & Merge** 📄**→Edit Individual Documents**.

4. Click **OK** to merge all records.

5. Scroll through the letters and scan their contents.

   Notice that there is one letter for each record in the data source.

6. Close the merged document without saving.

7. Choose **Mailings→Preview Results→Preview Results** 🔍 again to display the main document instead of the previews.

Working with Merge Problems

Several common errors can cause a merge to produce incorrect results. The merged document (or preview) will usually provide clues as to why a merge fails to produce the intended results. Once you identify an error in the merged document, such as leaving out a comma or space before or after a merge field, you can then conduct the merge again to determine whether the error was fixed. Repeat this process until the merge works as intended.

COMMON MERGE PROBLEMS

Problem	Solution
The same error appears in every merge letter.	The problem is in the main document. Correct the error and perform the merge again.
Some letters are missing data.	Some records in the data source are missing data. Add data and perform the merge again.
Some letters have incorrect data.	Some records in the data source are incorrect. Correct the errors and perform the merge again.

DEVELOP YOUR SKILLS: W5-D6

In this exercise, you will examine your document for merge problems. This exercise does not address all possible merge problems; it does, however, address one specific error that you will make intentionally. You will insert a colon after the Greeting Line code.

1. Position the insertion point after <<*GreetingLine*>> and type a colon (**:**).

2. Choose **Mailings→Finish→Finish & Merge** 📄**→Edit Individual Documents**.

3. Click **OK** to merge all records.

4. Browse through the merged document and notice there are two colons following the greeting line in every letter.

   Because the error occurs in every letter, you know the error is in the main document.

5. Locate any other errors and notice how often the errors occur (in every merged letter or just one).

   Next you will correct the double colon error and any other errors you discovered that occurred in all letters.

6. Close the merged document without saving; then remove the colon following *<<GreetingLine>>* and save the main document.

7. Follow these guidelines if you find a data error in just one letter:
   - Choose **Mailings→Start Mail Merge→Edit Recipient List** .
   - In the Mail Merge Recipients dialog box, highlight the **data source** in the bottom-left corner and click **Edit**.
   - Fix any errors and click **OK**; click **Yes** to update the data.
   - Click **OK** to close the dialog box.

8. When you have corrected any errors, execute the merge again.

9. Close the merged document without saving it and then save and close the exercise letter main document.

Merging Envelopes and Labels

When you begin a mail merge, you are presented with options for the type of main document you can create. In addition to form letters, you can choose envelopes, labels, and other types of documents. You can use the same data source for various main documents. For example, you can use the same data source for envelopes and mailing labels that you used for the form letter.

Generating Envelopes with Mail Merge

Mail Merge lets you choose the envelope size and formats. The standard business (Size 10) envelope is the default. Check your printer manual for instructions on loading envelopes.

Various envelope sizes are available.

Here you can choose the font and positions of the delivery and return addresses.

DEVELOP YOUR SKILLS: W5-D7

In this exercise, you will choose an envelope as the main document and connect the exercise letter data file to the envelope.

1. Start a new, blank document.

2. Choose **Mailings→Start Mail Merge→Start Mail Merge ⬚→Envelopes**.

3. In the Envelope Options dialog box, if necessary, choose **Size 10** as the envelope size and click **OK**.

   Now you will attach the same data source that you used for your letter.

4. Choose **Mailings→Start Mail Merge→Select Recipients** 🖼️ **→Use an Existing List**.

5. In the Select Data Source dialog box, navigate to your **Word Chapter 5** folder and open **W5-D2-ExerciseLtrData**.

Arranging the Envelope

You can insert an Address Block code in the envelope main document just as you do for form letter main documents. If you are not using envelopes with preprinted return addresses, you can type your return address. You save an envelope main document like any other main document.

DEVELOP YOUR SKILLS: W5-D8

In this exercise, you will place the return address and the Address Block code on the envelope. Then you will merge the envelope main document with the data source.

1. If necessary, display formatting marks.

2. Type this return address, starting at the first paragraph symbol in the upper-left corner of the envelope:

   Raritan Clinic East

   719 Coronado Drive

   San Diego, CA 92102

3. Position the insertion point next to the paragraph symbol toward the center of the envelope.

4. Choose **Mailings→Write & Insert Fields→Address Block** 📄.

5. Click **OK** to accept the default address block settings.

   The address information from the data source will appear in this location. Now you will preview the merge.

6. Choose **Mailings→Preview Results→Preview Results** 🔍 to display a record from the data source in the envelope.

7. Use the navigation buttons in the Preview Results group to scroll through all of your merged envelopes.

8. Choose **Mailings→Finish→Finish & Merge** 📄 **→Edit Individual Documents** and click **OK** to merge all records.

9. Turn off formatting marks and then scroll through the envelopes and notice that there is one envelope for each record in the data source.

   You could use the envelopes for mailing the letters created in the previous exercises. Each letter would have a corresponding envelope because they are generated from the same data source.

10. If necessary, fix any problems with the mail merge and merge the envelopes again.

11. Close the merged document without saving it.

12. Choose **Mailings→Preview Results→Preview Results** 🔍 to turn off the preview.

13. Save the main document envelope in your **Word Chapter 5** folder as **W5-D8-ExerciseLtrEnv** and then close it.

Generating Labels with Mail Merge

You can use Mail Merge to generate mailing labels for each record in a data source. Mail Merge lets you choose the label format, sheet size, and other specifications. It also lets you insert an Address Block code and other codes in the main document. Like other main documents, a label main document can be saved for future use.

View the video "Using Label Options."

DEVELOP YOUR SKILLS: W5-D9

In this exercise, you will set up a labels main document and merge it with the data source used in the previous exercises.

1. Start a new, blank document and, if necessary, display formatting marks; also, if necessary, set the zoom back to 100%.

2. Choose **Mailings→Start Mail Merge→Start Mail Merge** ⬚**→Labels**.

3. Follow these steps to choose a printer option and a label:

Label Options	? ✕
Printer information	
○ <u>C</u>ontinuous-feed printers **Ⓐ**	
◉ P<u>a</u>ge printers <u>T</u>ray: Default tray ▾	
Label information	
Label <u>v</u>endors: Avery US Letter **Ⓑ** ▾	
<u>Find updates on Office.com</u>	
Product n<u>u</u>mber:	Label information
5160 Address Labels	Type: Address Labels
5161 Address Labels	Height: 1"
5162 Address Labels	Width: 2.63"
5163 Shipping Labels **Ⓒ**	Page size: 8.5" × 11"
5164 Shipping Labels	
5165 Full-Sheet Shipping Labels	
<u>D</u>etails... <u>N</u>ew Label... Delete	OK Cancel

Ⓐ Choose **Default Tray**. The text in parentheses may vary based on the printer model.

Ⓑ Choose **Avery US Letter**.

Ⓒ Choose **5160 Address Labels** and click **OK**.

The labels main document appears in the window. Labels are contained in a Word table, but don't worry. You don't have to be a table expert to create labels.

Connect the Data Source

4. Choose **Mailings→Start Mail Merge→Select Recipients** ⬚**→Use an Existing List**.

5. In the Select Data Source dialog box, navigate to your **Word Chapter 5** folder and open **W5-D2-ExerciseLtrData**.

6. Make sure the insertion point is next to the paragraph symbol in the first address label.

   Notice that the space for the first label is blank and all the rest have a Next Record code in them. Now you will add the Address Block code.

7. Choose **Mailings→Write & Insert Fields→Address Block** 🗎 and click **OK**.

8. Choose **Mailings→Write & Insert Fields→Update Labels** 🗘 to place the Address Block code in all labels.

   Your address will fit the labels better if you remove the additional spacing.

9. Select the table and choose **Layout→Paragraph**; then type **0** in the Before field and tap [Enter].

10. Choose **Mailings→Preview Results→Preview Results** 🔍 to see how the labels will look when you print them.

11. Turn off Preview Results when you are finished.

Conduct the Merge

12. Choose **Mailings→Finish→Finish & Merge** 🗎→**Edit Individual Documents**.

13. Click **OK** to merge all the records.

14. Close your merged document without saving it.

15. Save the labels main document in your **Word Chapter 5** folder as: `W5-D9-MergeLabels`

16. Close the document and then exit Word.

Self-Assessment

Check your knowledge of this chapter's key concepts and skills using the Self-Assessment in your ebook or online (eLab course or Student Resource Center).

Reinforce Your Skills

REINFORCE YOUR SKILLS: W5-R1

Create a Data Source and Main Document

In this exercise, you will create a data source and main document for a Kids for Change mailing. The kids are holding a fundraiser for a microlending project that focuses on providing economic opportunities for entrepreneurs in India. They will conduct a mailing to announce the upcoming project and canvass their neighborhoods for donations.

1. Start Word, open **W5-R1-Fundraiser** from your **Word Chapter 5** folder, and save it as:
   `W5-R1-FundraiserRevised`
2. Choose **Mailings→Start Mail Merge→Start Mail Merge** 📄**→Letters** to identify the fundraising letter as the main document.
3. Choose **Mailings→Start Mail Merge→Select Recipients→Type a New List**.
4. Click **Customize Columns**.
5. Click **Address Line 2** and click **Delete**; click **Yes** to confirm the deletion.
6. Also delete the following fields:
   - Country or Region
   - Home Phone
   - Work Phone
   - E-mail Address
7. Click **Add**, type **Member First Name**, and then click **OK**.
8. Also add a field called **Member Last Name** and then click **OK** twice.
9. With the insertion point in the Title field, type **Ms.** and tap [Tab].
10. Follow these guidelines to complete the data source list:
    - Continue typing and tabbing to complete the first record shown.
    - Be sure to include the member first name, *Eric*, and last name, *Speck*, in the first record.
    - Tap [Tab] to begin a new record and then continue typing and tabbing to enter the next three records.
    - Note that there is no company information for the third record; [Tab] through that field.
    - If you accidentally tap [Tab] following the last record, use the **Delete Entry** button to remove the blank record.

Ms. Loretta Morales	Mr. Tony D'Agusto
Morales Super Market	Tony's Trattoria
311 Ocean Street	675 Miller Ave.
Miami FL 33130	Miami FL 33129
Member: Eric Speck	Member: Wendy Chang

Mr. Allan Morgan	Ms. Margarita Elizondo
951 4th Street	Elan Fashions
Miami FL 33136	307 Dolphin Way
	Miami FL 33136
Member: Stella Hopkins	Member: Diego Cantero

11. Review your records for accuracy; click **OK** when you are satisfied with your work.

12. Save the data source in your **Word Chapter 5** folder as: `W5-R1-FundraiserData`

Set Up the Main Document

13. In the fundraiser letter, select **[Inside Address]** (but not the paragraph symbol at the end of the line) and tap `Delete`.

14. Choose **Mailings→Write & Insert Fields→Address Block** ▤ and then click **OK** to accept the default address block settings.

15. Delete **[Name]** in the greeting line but not the paragraph symbol at the end of the line.

16. Choose **Mailings→Write & Insert Fields→Greeting Line**.

17. Choose **Joshua** and **colon** in the Greeting Line Format area as shown and click **OK**.

18. In the last sentence of the first paragraph, delete **[Member Name]**.

19. Choose **Mailings→Write & Insert Fields→Insert Merge Field menu button** ▼→ **Member_First_Name**.

20. Tap `Spacebar` and insert the **Member_Last_Name** field.

21. Save and close the letter.

REINFORCE YOUR SKILLS: W5-R2

Merge a Letter, Envelopes, and Labels

Kids for Change is starting an after-school tutoring program. The tutoring supervisor will send form letters to parents announcing the program. In this exercise, you will merge a data source with a letter. You will also merge the data source with envelopes and labels.

1. Open **W5-R2-ParentLtr** from your **Word Chapter 5** folder and save it as: `W5-R2-ParentLtrRevised`

   Notice the merge fields in the letter, including four merge fields in the body of the letter, and that <<Child_Name>> appears twice.

2. Choose **Mailings→Start Mail Merge→Start Mail Merge** ▤→**Letters**.

3. Choose **Mailings→Start Mail Merge→Select Recipients→Use an Existing List**.

4. Navigate to your **Word Chapter 5** folder and open **W5-R2-ParentData**.

5. Choose **Mailings→Preview Results→Preview Results**.

6. Navigate through the records and then turn off Preview Results.

7. Choose **Mailings→Finish→Finish & Merge** ▤→**Edit Individual Documents** and then click **OK** to merge all records.

8. Scroll through the merged letters; close the file without saving it.

9. Save and close the parent letter main document.

Generate Envelopes

10. Start a new, blank document.

11. Choose **Mailings→Start Mail Merge→Start Mail Merge→Envelopes**.

12. Click **OK** to accept the envelope defaults.

13. Choose **Mailings→Start Mail Merge→Select Recipients→Use an Existing List**.

14. Navigate to your **Word Chapter 5** folder and open **W5-R2-ParentData** to attach the data source to the envelope.

15. If necessary, display formatting marks; then type this return address at the first paragraph symbol in the upper-left corner of the envelope:

```
Kids for Change
726 Throckmorton Ave.
Sacramento, CA  95613
```

16. Position the insertion point next to the paragraph symbol toward the center of the envelope.

17. Choose **Mailings→Write & Insert Fields→Address Block**; click **OK** to accept the address block defaults.

18. Choose **Mailings→Preview Results→Preview Results**.

19. Navigate through the records and then turn off Preview Results.

20. Save the envelope as **W5-R2-ParentEnv** and close the envelope file.

Generate Mailing Labels

21. Start a new, blank document.

22. Choose **Mailings→Start Mail Merge→Start Mail Merge→Labels**.

23. If necessary, choose **Avery US Letter** as the Label Vendor and **5160 Easy Peel Address Labels** as the Product Number, and then click **OK**.

24. Choose **Mailings→Start Mail Merge→Select Recipients→Use an Existing List**.

25. Navigate to your **Word Chapter 5** folder and open **W5-R2-Parent Data**.

26. Display formatting marks, if necessary, and then make sure the insertion point is next to the paragraph symbol in the first label.

27. Choose **Mailings→Write & Insert Fields→Address Block**; click **OK** to accept the address block defaults.

28. Choose **Mailings→Write & Insert Fields→Update Labels** to insert the Address Block code on all labels.

29. Choose **Mailings→Preview Results→Preview Results** to verify all labels will print correctly.

Because the addresses are three lines, they fit on the Avery 5160 labels without removing extra spacing.

30. Turn off Preview Results to return to the labels main document.

31. Save the labels file in your **Word Chapter 5** folder as: **W5-R2-ParentLabels**

32. Close the file.

Merge Letters and Envelopes

Kids for Change is sponsoring a walkathon fundraiser to buy musical instruments for the local elementary school. The walkathon supervisor will be contacting Kids for Change members and encouraging their participation. In this exercise, you will designate a letter as the main document and create a data source. Then you will preview the results and correct any merge problems before conducting the merge. Finally, you will generate envelopes for the letters.

1. Open **W5-R3-Walkers** from your **Word Chapter 5** folder and save it as:
   W5-R3-WalkersRevised

2. Choose **Mailings→Start Mail Merge→Start Mail Merge→Letters** to designate the Walkers letter as the main document.

3. Choose **Mailings→Start Mail Merge→Select Recipients→Type a New List**.

   Now you will customize the data source columns.

4. Click **Customize Columns** to display the Customize Address List dialog box.

5. Click **Company Name** and click **Delete**; click **Yes** to confirm the deletion.

6. Delete the following fields and then click **OK**:
   - **Address Line 2**
   - **Country or Region**
   - **Work Phone**
   - **E-mail Address**

7. In the Title field, type **Mr.** and tap Tab to move to the next field.

8. Type **Sean** in the First Name field, tap Tab, and type **Corn** in the Last Name field.

9. Continue tabbing and typing to complete the *Sean Corn* record as shown, tap Tab to begin the next record, and then enter the remaining records:

Mr. Sean Corn 308 Alhambra Avenue Monterey CA 93940 831-555-0134	Mr. Craig Dostie 31200 Erwin Street Monterey CA 93940 831-555-0167	Ms. Alexia Lopez 2134 Harbor Blvd. Monterey CA 93942 831-555-0132
Ms. Margaret Wong 1308 West Ramona Blvd. Monterey CA 93940 831-555-0198	Ms. Phyllis Coen 4745 Buffin Avenue Monterey CA 93943 831-555-0178	Mr. Winston Boey 263 East Howard Street Monterey CA 93944 831-555-0196

10. Review your records for accuracy and make any necessary corrections.

    Now you will sort your list by Last Name.

11. Click the **Last Name** column header to sort the list alphabetically in ascending order and then click **OK**.

12. Navigate to your **Word Chapter 5** folder and save the file as: **W5-R3-WalkersData**

Set Up the Main Document and Correct Merge Problems

13. Follow these guidelines to insert the merge codes:
   - Replace *INSIDE ADDRESS* with the **Address Block** code using the default formats.
   - Replace *GREETING LINE* with the **Greeting Line** code, changing the Greeting Line Format name to **Joshua**.
   - In the last paragraph, replace *HOME PHONE* with the **Home_Phone** code.

14. Use the Preview Results feature to review your letters, correct any errors in the main document, and then turn off Preview Results.

Phyllis Cohen's name is misspelled in the data source. You will make that correction now.

15. Choose **Mailings→Start Mail Merge→Edit Recipient List** .

16. Click the **data source** in the bottom-left corner and click **Edit**.

17. Change the spelling from *Coen* to **Cohen** and then click **OK**.

18. Click **Yes** to verify the update and then click **OK** to close the Mail Merge Recipients dialog box.

19. Turn on Preview Results and use the navigation buttons to verify the change to the data source and any changes you made to the main document; then turn off Preview Results.

20. Choose **Mailings→Finish→Finish & Merge** →**Edit Individual Documents** and then click **OK**.

21. Scroll through your letters and then close the merged document without saving it; save and close the main document letter.

Merge Envelopes

22. Start a new, blank document.

23. Choose **Mailings→Start Mail Merge→Start Mail Merge→Envelopes**.

24. Make sure the envelope is **Size 10** and click **OK**.

Now you will attach the data source to your envelope.

25. Choose **Mailings→Start Mail Merge→Select Recipients** →**Use an Existing List**.

26. Navigate to your **Word Chapter 5** folder and open **W5-R3-WalkersData**.

27. If necessary, turn on formatting marks; then type this return address at the top paragraph symbol in the upper-left corner of the envelope:

```
Kids for Change
456 Bayside Road
Monterey, CA  93943
```

28. Position the insertion point next to the paragraph symbol toward the middle of the envelope.

29. Choose **Mailings→Write & Insert Fields→Address Block** and then click **OK**.

30. Choose **Mailings→Preview Results→Preview Results**.

31. Use the navigation buttons to view all envelopes and then turn off the preview.

32. Choose **Mailings→Finish→Finish & Merge→Edit Individual Documents** and then click **OK**.

33. Scroll through the envelopes and then close the file without saving it.

34. Save the envelope main document in your **Word Chapter 5** folder as **W5-R3-WalkersEnv** and close the document.

✏ Apply Your Skills

Create a Data Source and Main Document

Universal Corporate Events is announcing a new affordable and flexible program for its small-business clients. In this exercise, you will create a small-business client data source, and you will review the records and sort the list. Then you will specify a letter as a main document and insert merge fields in the letter.

1. Open **W5-A1-SmallBiz** from your **Word Chapter 5** folder and save it as: **W5-A1-SmallBizRevised**

2. Specify the Small Biz letter as the main document.

   Now you will customize the columns for your new data source.

3. Delete and add columns as needed to create the following fields in your data source:
   - Title
   - First Name
   - Last Name
   - Company Name
   - Address Line 1
   - City
   - State
   - Zip Code
   - Agent Name

4. Add these records to your data source:

Mr. Tony Simpson	Mr. Jason Jones	Ms. Debbie Thomas
Bigger Time Video Distributors	Move It Distribution	Barker Books
312 York Lane	2233 Crystal Street	497 Tennessee Street
Richmond CA 94804	San Mateo CA 94403	Richmond CA 94804
Agent Name: **David Roth**	Agent Name: **Tammy Nelson**	Agent Name: **Jacob Williams**

5. Sort the data source in ascending alphabetic order by **Company Name**.

6. Save the data source in your **Word Chapter 5** folder as: **W5-A1-SmallBizData**

7. Delete the *Today's Date* placeholder, choose **Insert→Text→Date & Time** 📅, choose the third date format, and make sure **Update Automatically** is checked.

8. Follow these guidelines for inserting merge codes in the main document:
   - Replace *INSIDE ADDRESS* with the **Address Block** code using the default formats.
   - Replace *GREETING LINE* with the **Greeting Line** code and change the ending punctuation to a colon.
   - In the last paragraph, replace *AGENT NAME* with the **Agent_Name** code.

9. Preview the letters and check that the spacing is correct, and then turn off the preview and make any needed changes.

10. Save and close the letter.

Complete a Merge

Universal Corporate Events is conducting a seminar on visa requirements for United States citizens. It is sending a form letter invitation to its clients' in-house travel agents. In this exercise, you will merge letters, envelopes, and labels. You will also correct merge problems.

1. Open **W5-A2-VisaLtr** from your **Word Chapter 5** folder and save it as: **W5-A2-VisaLtrRevised**

2. Designate the letter as the main document and **W5-A2-VisaData** from your **Word Chapter 5** folder as the data source.

3. Preview the merge and notice that there is an error in the greeting line.

4. Close the preview and then edit the main document and preview the letters again, checking that the greeting line is correct.

5. Close the preview; save and close the main document.

Merge Envelopes and Labels

6. Start a new, blank document and create a **Size 10** envelope as the main document with this return address:

   Suzanne Frost, Sales Manager

   Universal Corporate Events

   129 Potter Road

   Middlefield, CT 06455

7. Attach **W5-A2-VisaData** as the data source for the envelopes.

8. Insert an **Address Block** code in the middle of the envelope using the default formats.

9. Preview the envelopes.

10. Save the envelope main document in your **Word Chapter 5** folder as **W5-A2-VisaEnv** and then close it.

11. Start a new, blank document and create a label main document using **Avery US Letter** as the Label Vendor and **5160 Address Labels** as the Product Number.

12. Attach **W5-A2-VisaData** as the data source.

13. Insert the **Address Block** code in the first label using the default formats and use the **Update Labels** command to replicate the Address Block code on all labels.

14. Preview the results and notice that the addresses don't fit well on the labels.

15. Close the preview, select the labels table, and remove Word's extra spacing by entering **0** in the Before field.

   Hint: The Before field is at Layout→Paragraph.

16. Preview the results again to ensure that the labels fit correctly.

17. Close the preview and save the labels main document in your **Word Chapter 5** folder as: **W5-A2-VisaLabels**

18. Close the labels main document.

Create a Mail Merge for Trip Winners

A Universal Corporate Events client is rewarding its top sales performers with a trip to Tokyo. It will send an itinerary letter to the company's winners. In this exercise, you will create a data source using customized columns and add merge codes to main documents. You will preview and merge the main documents with the data source, make an editing change to a record, and sort the data source.

1. Open **W5-A3-TokyoLtr** from your **Word Chapter 5** folder and save it as: **W5-A3-TokyoLtrRevised**

2. Specify the letter as the main document and then start a new data source list.

3. Customize the columns by deleting some fields and keeping the fields shown here:
   - Title
   - First Name
   - Last Name
   - Company Name
   - Address Line 1
   - City
   - State
   - Zip Code

4. Create the data source using these three records and save it as: **W5-A3-TokyoData**

Ms. Jasleen Mahal	Mr. George Iverson	Mr. Anthony Waldek
Superior Storage Devices	Superior Storage Devices	Superior Storage Devices
951 Industrial Way	951 Industrial Way	951 Industrial Way
Trenton NJ 08601	Trenton NJ 08601	Trenton NJ 08601

5. Follow these guidelines to insert merge codes in the letter:
   - Replace *INSIDE ADDRESS* with **Address Block** code using the default formats.
   - Replace *GREETING LINE* with **Greeting Line** code using the default formats.
   - In the first paragraph, replace *COMPANY NAME* with the **Company_Name** code.
   - In the last paragraph, replace *FIRST NAME* with the **First_Name** code.

Preview the Merge Results

6. Preview the merge, make sure the spacing is correct, and then close the preview.

7. Modify the spacing in the main document, if necessary.

   You want the greeting line to be less formal, so you will change the format to the recipient's first name.

8. Right-click the **Greeting Line** code and choose **Edit Greeting Line** from the menu.

9. In the Greeting Line Format area, click the drop-down arrow next to *Mr. Randall*, choose **Joshua** from the list, and click **OK**.

10. Preview the letters again to ensure the change was made and then turn off the preview.

11. Merge the letter with the data source, choosing **Edit Individual Documents**, and then scroll through the letters.

12. Close the merged document without saving it; save and close the main document.

Merge Envelopes and Labels

13. Start a new, blank document, designate it as a mail merge envelope, and use a **Size 10** envelope.

14. Insert this return address on the envelope:

    ```
    Ms. Tasha Reynolds
    Universal Corporate Events
    456 Riverview Road
    Trenton, NJ  08601
    ```

15. Attach the Tokyo data source to the envelope and insert the **Address Block** code using defaults.

16. Merge the envelopes and check them for accuracy; if necessary, correct any errors and conduct the merge again.

17. Close the merge document without saving it.

18. Save the envelope main document as **W5-A3-TokyoEnv** and then close it.

19. Start a new, blank document and designate it as **Labels**.

20. Choose **Avery US Letter** as the Label Vendor and **5160 Address Labels** as the Product Number.

21. Attach the Tokyo data source, insert the **Address Block** code with default settings in the first label, and update the labels to replicate the **Address Block** code in all labels.

22. Preview the labels and notice the addresses don't fit well because of Word's extra spacing.

23. Close the preview, select the labels table, and remove the extra spacing.

24. Preview the labels again to verify the change in spacing and then close the preview.

25. Save the labels main document as **W5-A3-TokyoLabels** and then close it.

Project Grader

If your class is using eLab (labyrinthelab.com), you may upload your completed Project Grader assignments for automatic grading. You may complete these projects even if your class doesn't use eLab, though you will not be able to upload your work.

PROJECT GRADER: W5-P1

Taylor Games New Items Letter

Taylor Games wants to track customer purchases, storing that information in a data source. In this exercise, you will set up a prototype data source and a letter that will be sent to existing customers promoting new items.

1. Download and open your Project Grader starting file.
   - *Using eLab:* Download **W5_P1_eStart** from the Assignments page. You *must* start with this file or your work cannot be automatically graded.
   - *Not using eLab:* Open **W5_P1_Start** from your **Word Chapter 5** folder.

   You'll now set up a mail merge using W5_P1_eStart as your mail merge main document.

2. Create a new Address List for your main document using these guidelines:
   - Delete these field names from the Field Names list: **Title**, **Company Name**, **Address Line 2**, **Country or Region**, **Home Phone**, **Work Phone**, and **E-mail Address**.
   - Add a field named **Item Type** to the end of the Field Names list.

3. Add these three customer entries to your Address List:

First Name	Last Name	Address Line 1	City	State	ZIP Code	Item Type
Curt	Smith	555 Rock Lane	Danville	CA	94506	Dice
Fred	Parker	664 Park Road	Scottsdale	AZ	85258	Games
Kim	Price	1775 Pine Place	Elmira	NY	14901	Books

4. Save your address list to your **Word Chapter 5** folder as: `W5_P1 Address List.mdb`

5. In the main document on the second empty paragraph below *Today's Date*, insert an **Address Block** using the **Joshua Randall Jr.** format.

6. Replace the FIRSTNAME and ITEMTYPE placeholder text with merge fields as follows. Make sure the spacing between the merge fields and surrounding text is the same as the current spacing between the placeholders and text.
   - Replace the two occurrences of *FIRSTNAME* with the **First_Name** merge field.
   - Replace *ITEMTYPE* in the first body paragraph with the **Item _Type** merge field.

7. Replace the *Today's Date* text by typing the current date in whatever format you like best. Maintain the current one empty paragraph spacing between the date and address block.

8. Finish & merge all records, creating editable individual documents. If necessary, review your merge results, make corrections in your source document, and remerge.

9. Save the merged letters to your **Word Chapter 5** folder as `W5_P1 Merged Letters` and then close the document.

10. Save your main document.
    - *Using eLab:* Save it to your **Word Chapter 5** folder as `W5_P1_eSubmission` and attach the file to your eLab assignment for grading.
    - *Not using eLab:* Save it to your **Word Chapter 5** folder as: `W5_P1_Submission`

PROJECT GRADER: W5-P2

Generating Mail Merge Envelopes

You've been asked to generate envelopes from an existing Classic Cars Club database. In this exercise, you will set up the necessary main document and conduct a merge to produce the desired envelopes.

1. Download and open your Project Grader starting file.
   - *Using eLab:* Download **W5_P2_eStart** from the Assignments page. You *must* start with this file or your work cannot be automatically graded.
   - *Not using eLab:* Open **W5_P2_Start** from your **Word Chapter 5** folder.

   You'll now set up a mail merge using the empty W5_P2_eStart as your mail merge main document.

2. Start your mail merge by changing the document type to **Envelope, Size 10**.

3. Enter the following return address in the top-left corner:

   `Lisa Rowling`
   `Classic Cars Club`
   `356 Maple Lane`
   `Renton, WA 98056`

4. Use the existing list **W5_P2 Addresses** from your **Word Chapter 5** folder as your data source and use the table **Sheet1$**.

5. Insert an **Address Block** in the rectangular box near the bottom-center of the envelope using the **Joshua Randall Jr.** format.

6. Finish and merge all records, creating editable individual envelopes. If necessary, review your merge results, make corrections in your source document, and remerge.

7. Save the merged envelopes to your **Word Chapter 5** folder as `W5_P2 Merged Envelopes` and then close the document.

8. Save your main document.
   - *Using eLab:* Save it to your **Word Chapter 5** folder as `W5_P2_eSubmission` and attach the file to your eLab assignment for grading.
   - *Not using eLab:* Save it to your **Word Chapter 5** folder as: `W5_P2_Submission`

◢ Extend Your Skills

These exercises challenge you to think critically and apply your new skills in a real-world setting. You will be evaluated on your ability to follow directions, completeness, creativity, and the use of proper grammar and mechanics. Save files to your chapter folder. Submit assignments as directed.

W5-E1 That's the Way I See It

You are planning a field trip for the fifth-grade class you teach. Create a permission letter informing parents of the trip and how it relates to students' school work (e.g., visiting an aquarium after studying about ocean life). Include a request for parents to sign and return the letter. Save the letter as: **W5-E1-FieldTripLtr**

Create a three-record data source of parent names and addresses and any other variables you choose. Customize the data source with only the column headings you need. Save the data source as **W5-E1-FieldTripData** and insert merge codes in the form letter. Merge the main document and data source. Save the merged document as: **W5-E1-FieldTripLtrMerged**

Create an envelope main document with your return address, merge it with your data file, and save it as: **W5-E1-FieldTripEnvMerged**

W5-E2 Be Your Own Boss

You are introducing a rewards program for Blue Jean Landscaping customers. Create a form letter of two to three paragraphs describing how customers can accumulate points toward purchases. Mention three other benefits (make them up) for program members. Save the letter as: **W5-E2-RewardsLtr**

Create a data source of three customers' names and addresses and any other fields you want to use. Customize the data source for only those columns needed. Save it as **W5-E2-RewardsData** and insert merge field codes in the letter. Conduct the merge, saving the merged document as: **W5-E2-RewardsLtrMerged**

Finally, create a labels document named **W5-E2-RewardsLabels** and merge it with the data source. Save the merged labels as: **W5-E2-RewardsLabelsMerged**

W5-E3 Demonstrate Proficiency

Stormy BBQ has added brisket of beef to its menu! It offered a free beef brisket meal and a $20 gift certificate to the first five customers who visited its restaurant on New Year's Day. It plans to mail the certificates to the qualifying customers. As a Stormy BBQ employee, you have been asked to compose a congratulatory letter to go with the certificates. Compose an appropriate letter of two or three paragraphs saved as: **W5-E3-CertLtr**

Create a name and address data source for five winners. Customize the data source by adding any fields you want to use in your letter; delete any fields you don't intend to use. Save the data source as **W5-E3-CertData** and merge the letter and the data source. Save the merge document as: **W5-E3-CertLtrMerged**

Finally, create an envelope main document to go with the mailing and include Stormy BBQ's return address and the Address Block code on a Size 10 envelope. Save the envelope main document as **W5-E3-CertEnv** and preview the envelopes to verify that they will print correctly. Make corrections if necessary, merge the envelope with your data source, and then save the merged document as: **W5-E3-CertEnvMerged**

6 | Using Themes

Themes are the most efficient way to apply formatting. They allow you to create and customize personal aesthetic choices, keep documents consistent, and apply mass formatting changes with a single click. Other tools, such as Quick Parts and Building Blocks, or your own custom templates, allow you to take this efficient personalization approach to a whole new level. In this chapter, you will build a customized theme. You will also use built-in and custom Quick Parts and Building Blocks. Finally, you will use all these tools to create custom templates.

LEARNING OBJECTIVES

▸ Customize a theme

▸ Create personalized color and font sets

▸ Add Quick Parts and Building Blocks to a document

▸ Insert cover pages

▸ Apply custom Building Blocks across documents

▸ Create and use personal Templates

▸ Customize the default font

📁 Project: Creating a Client Newsletter

As a leading pediatric facility, Raritan Clinic East stays ahead of the curve by updating its protocols with the latest discoveries. It stays in regular contact with its patient population through a monthly newsletter. As an administrator for the clinic, you have been tasked with finding ways to make the newsletter creation process more efficient. Now that you've wrapped up the content for November's newsletter on meningitis, you will use the document to create and save custom themes, Quick Parts, and Building Blocks into a final template, which can be used for future newsletters.

📖 Six Tips for an Effective Newsletter

A newsletter is an effective way to keep in touch with clients. It adds a personal touch that can create a bond between your organization and the reader. Follow these guidelines when composing a newsletter:

▸ Know your audience.

▸ Have a compelling opening line.

▸ Use a clean, simple layout with plenty of white space.

▸ Be informative and educational, and provide true value.

▸ Use graphics, but don't overdo it.

▸ Insert headings and subheadings to organize your information into easy-to-read segments.

Using Themes and Style Sets

Themes and style sets are document-level formatting features that can instantly add color and visual variety to your entire document. A theme is a combination of colors, fonts, and graphic elements that you can apply to any document. Style sets change font and paragraph properties. Themes and style sets create the biggest impact when you use built-in styles.

≡ Design→Document Formatting→Themes 🅰️

≡ Design→Document Formatting→Style Sets gallery

Customizing a Theme

You can customize any theme to match your creative side. Changing a theme font changes any text formatted with fonts that have (Headings) or (Body) next to their names in the font list. Calibri Light (Headings) and Calibri (Body) are the theme fonts for the default Office theme. When you change the theme, the associated theme fonts change. You can also customize the theme color.

 Any customizations you make to themes are not document specific; they will be applied to your copy of Microsoft Word. These custom themes can be deleted simply by right-clicking on the custom theme thumbnail and choosing Delete.

In this exercise, you will use a Childhood Diseases Seminar handout, which uses Word's built-in styles, to try out some theme options. A cover page has been added for you. You will use Live Preview to examine a variety of themes and style sets, and you will also apply a new theme and style set to your report.

Before You Begin: *Download the student exercise files from your eLab course or the Student Resource Center (labyrinthelab.com/office19) and determine your file storage location before beginning this exercise.*

1. Open **W6-D1-SickKids** from your **Word Chapter 6** folder and save it as:
   W6-D1-SickKidsRevised

2. Scroll to page 1 of the main document (not the cover page) and position the insertion point in the *Raritan Clinic East* heading.

   Notice that the built-in Title style is highlighted in the Styles task pane. You may have to click More ▼ *to see it.*

3. Position the insertion point in the *Childhood Diseases Seminar* subheading and see that the built-in Heading 1 style is active in the Styles task pane.

4. Examine the other headings, and you can see that built-in styles have been applied.

   Remember, themes and style sets are most effective when using the built-in styles.

5. Scroll up to the cover page and choose **Design→Document Formatting→Themes** 🅰 **menu button** ▼ to display the Themes gallery.

6. Hover the mouse pointer over several different themes and observe the changes in your document.

7. Choose the **Frame** theme.

8. Scroll through the document to see the impact of the new theme.

   The built-in headings in the body of the document respond to the change in theme.

Change the Theme Color and Font

9. Scroll so that the bottom of the cover page and the top of page 1 are both visible.

10. Choose **Design→Document Formatting→Colors** 🔲 **menu button** ▼.

    Note! *As you change theme colors, the colors on the menu button change as well. The theme and font buttons also change as you customize their features.*

11. Use **Live Preview** to examine the different color schemes to see their effects and then choose **Blue Warm**.

12. Choose **Design→Document Formatting→Fonts** 🄰 **menu button** ▼.

13. Use **Live Preview** to examine the font options and then choose **Franklin Gothic**.

Change the Style Set

14. Choose **Design→Document Formatting** and then click **More** ▼ to open the Style Sets gallery.

15. Use **Live Preview** to examine the different Style Sets and then choose **Centered**.

16. Scroll through the document to see the changes.

17. Save the file.

Note! *Always leave your file open at the end of an exercise unless instructed to close it.*

Create Custom Color and Font Sets

Besides using Word's built-in style sets, you can also create your own customized color and font sets from scratch. These fully customized color sets and font sets can make your documents shine with your personal flair. To create customized colors, you enter Red, Green, and Blue values that together create a final color, the digital equivalent of a painter mixing colors on a palette. Once you've made all these changes to the original theme, you can then save them as your own customized theme in the default Document Themes folder. Doing so causes your theme to appear in the Themes menu. Once saved, you can apply your personal themes to documents in the same way you apply built-in themes.

≡ Design→Document Formatting→Colors→Customize Colors

≡ Design→Document Formatting→Fonts→Customize Fonts

≡ Design→Document Formatting→Themes→Save Current Theme

DEVELOP YOUR SKILLS: W6-D2

In this exercise, you will use the Childhood Diseases Seminar handout to create customized color and font sets for Raritan Clinic. For the color set, you'll use the same colors you see in the company logo. You will apply your custom sets to your document and save these choices in a new theme. Finally, you'll apply your custom theme to the monthly newsletter.

1. Save your file as: **W6-D2-SickKidsRevised**

2. If necessary, scroll so the bottom of the cover page and the top of page 1 are both visible.

   You will begin by creating a custom color set.

3. Choose **Design→Document Formatting→Colors ▣ menu button ▾→Customize Colors**.

   In the Create New Theme Colors dialog box, the various boxes correspond to the colors used throughout the theme, including title text, graphics like the horizontal lines above and below the title, shapes, and more.

4. In the Create New Theme Colors dialog box, select the **Text/Background – Light 1 menu button ▾** and choose **More Colors**.

5. In the Colors box, choose the **Custom** tab, if necessary, and enter these numbers into the boxes for Red, Green, and Blue to get a lavender color:

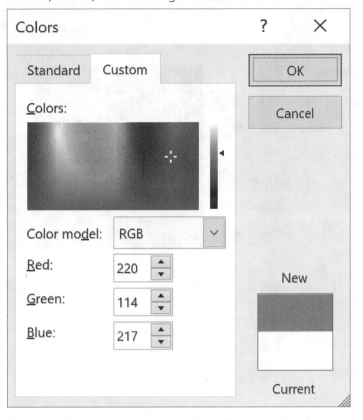

These numbers correspond to a value of how much red, green, and blue make up this lavender color, seen as the outline of the heart shape in the Raritan logo. The color values range from 0 to 255. In this color, there's a lot of red and blue, but only about half as much green. Most companies will have the RGB values of their company colors, such as this color set, on hand for branding needs.

6. Click **OK** to close the Colors box.

7. Click the **Text/Background – Dark 2 menu button** ▼, choose **More Colors**, and enter **32** for Red, **94** for Green, and **200** for Blue to get the dark blue color seen in the Raritan logo; click **OK**.

8. For **Accent 1**, enter **112** for Red, **202** for Green, and **255** for Blue to get the light blue color; click **OK**.

9. For **Accent 3**, enter **218** for Red, **98** for Green, and **114** for Blue to get the burnt red color seen in the heart on the Raritan logo; click **OK**.

10. Review the settings:

Create New Theme Colors   ?   ✕

Theme colors		Sample
Text/Background – Dark 1	▣ ▾	
Text/Background – Light 1	▣ ▾ Ⓐ	
Text/Background – Dark 2	▣ ▾ Ⓑ	
Text/Background – Light 2	▣ ▾	
Accent 1	▣ ▾ Ⓒ	
Accent 2	▣ ▾	
Accent 3	▣ ▾ Ⓓ	
Accent 4	▣ ▾	
Accent 5	▣ ▾	
Accent 6	▣ ▾	
Hyperlink	▣ ▾	
Followed Hyperlink	▣ ▾	

Name: Raritan Color Set

Reset   Save   Cancel

Ⓐ Text/Background – Light 1 affects the font colors on the cover page and should be lavender.

Ⓑ Text/Background – Dark 2 affects the Title style and the box on the right side of the cover page and should be blue.

Ⓒ Accent 1 affects the Heading 1 style and the box on the left side of the cover page and should be light blue.

Ⓓ Accent 3 affects the horizontal lines above and below the Title style and should be a burnt red.

11. Enter `Raritan Color Set` in the Name box and click **Save** to close the Create New Theme Colors dialog box; then scroll through the cover page and page 1 to see the applied colors.

Create a Custom Font Set

12. Choose **Design→Document Formatting→Fonts** A **menu button** ▾ **→Customize Fonts**.

13. Change the **Heading** font to **Cambria** and the **Body** font to **Times New Roman**.

Create New Theme Fonts	? ✕
Heading font: Cambria ⌄ **Body font:** Times New Roman ⌄ **Name:** Raritan Font Set	**Sample** **Heading** Body text body text body text. Body t⸍ Save Cancel

14. Enter `Raritan Font Set` in the Name box, click **Save**, and then scroll through the document to see the applied fonts.

Note! *You can now see your custom color and font sets in their respective menus under the Design tab. These sets will appear as available choices for all documents from now on, just like the built-in color sets.*

Create and Apply a Custom Theme

Now you will use these customizations to create a new theme, which you will then apply to another Raritan document.

15. Choose **Design→Document Formatting→Themes** 🅰 **menu button ▾→Save Current Theme**.

16. In the dialog box that appears, enter `Raritan Theme` as the File Name and click **Save**.

17. Save and close the file.

18. Open **W6-D2-RaritanNewsltr** from your **Word Chapter 6** folder and scroll through the document to see how it looks.

19. Choose **Design→Document Formatting→Themes** 🅰 **menu button ▾→Raritan Theme** and then scroll through the document to see the color and font changes.

20. Save the file as: `W6-D2-RaritanNewsltrRevised`

Working with Quick Parts and Building Blocks

Quick Parts are text and/or graphic elements you can use over and over again to save time. Like any other element in your document, Quick Parts adopt the themes you apply, including the color, font, and style sets. There are many different types of Quick Parts. Document Property Quick Parts and Auto Text Quick Parts are the most common; they are created by the user. Document Property Quick Parts allow you to input fields into your document that are filled in from a different source, similar to Mail Merge; however, unlike Mail Merge, this tool pulls information from the document properties you specify in the Backstage view. AutoText Quick Parts allow you to save pieces of text that you use repeatedly, so you don't have to type the same material multiple times.

Building Blocks is another term for Quick Parts, but it usually refers to Quick Parts that provide a traditional part of a newsletter or article, such as pull quotes and side bars. There are prebuilt Building Blocks available for your immediate use, but you can also create your own custom Building Blocks.

 Quick Parts and Building Blocks that you customize and create are not document specific; they will be applied to your copy of Microsoft Word.

View the video "Inserting Quick Parts and Building Blocks."

≡ Insert→Text→Explore Quick Parts 🔲

≡ Insert→Text→Explore Quick Parts 🔲→Building Blocks Organizer

---

DEVELOP YOUR SKILLS: W6-D3

In this exercise, you will insert Document Property fields into the Raritan Newsletter and fix a field that isn't working properly. Then, you'll insert a new sidebar for the second page. Finally, you'll create new AutoText Quick Parts from the company's master marketing document and insert one of these into the newsletter's new sidebar.

1. Save your file as: **W6-D3-RaritanNewsltrRevised**
2. Click the **File** tab to check the document properties and then click **Show All Properties** at the bottom right of the screen to see more fields.

   Notice that the word Newsletter *has been entered as the document's Title property.*
3. Click **Back** ⬅ to return to the document.

Insert Document Property Quick Parts

4. Place the insertion point in the blank line below the company logo and choose **Insert→Text→Explore Quick Parts 🔲 menu button ▾→Document Property→Title**.

   Notice that the field was automatically populated with Newsletter, *from the Title property box you saw in the Backstage view.*
5. Place your insertion point at the end of the Subject line (after the colon), tap [Spacebar], and choose **Insert→Text→Explore Quick Parts 🔲 menu button ▾→Document Property→Subject**.

   This time just the field placeholder appears, meaning the Subject property is blank for this document. You'll fix that now.
6. Click the **File** tab and then click **Show All Properties**.
7. In the Subject box, enter: **Meningitis**

Status	Add text
Categories	Add a category
Subject	Meningitis
Hyperlink Base	Add text
Company	Raritan Clinic East

8. Click **Back** ⬅ to return to the document.

The Subject field has now been replaced with the word Meningitis.

9. Place your insertion point at the end of the next line (after the colon), tap `Spacebar`, and choose **Insert→Text→Explore Quick Parts** 🖼 **menu button** ▾**→Document Property→Comments**.

Insert Building Blocks

10. Scroll to the second page and place the insertion point anywhere inside the text.

11. Choose **Insert→Text→Explore Quick Parts** 🖼 **menu button** ▾**→Building Blocks Organizer**.

In the Building Blocks Organizer dialog box, the options are sorted by the second column: Gallery. You may need to expand the column sizes to see the entries in the Name and Gallery columns.

Name	Gallery	Cate...	Te
Lab Student	AutoText	Gene	N
LS	AutoText	Gene	N
Works Cited	Bibliographies	Built-	Bi
References	Bibliographies	Built-	Bi
Bibliography	Bibliographies	Built	B

12. Scroll down to the Text Boxes section, select **Whisp Sidebar**, and click **Insert**.

Name	Gallery	Cate..
Slice Sidebar (Lig	Text Boxes	Built-
Slice Sidebar (Dar	Text Boxes	Built-
Slice Quote	Text Boxes	Built-
ViewMaster Side	Text Boxes	Built-
ViewMaster Quot...	Text Boxes	Built-
ViewMaster Quot...	Text Boxes	Built-
Whisp Sidebar	Text Boxes	Built-
Whisp Quote	Text Boxes	Built-
URGENT 2	Watermarks	Urger
DO NOT COPY 1	Watermarks	Confi.

Whisp Sidebar

Left-aligned sidebar with Whisp accent gradient fill

13. Remove the **[Sidebar Title]** field and type **Location** in its place.

Create and Insert AutoText Quick Parts

14. Open **Raritan Marketing** from your **Word Chapter 6** folder.

15. Select both paragraphs under the Staff heading and choose **Insert→Text→Explore Quick Parts** 📑 **menu button** ▾ **→AutoText→Save Selection to AutoText Gallery**.

16. In the dialog box, enter **Staff** into the Name box, leave all other settings as they are, and click **OK**.

Create New Building Block	?	✕
Name:	Staff	
Gallery:	AutoText	⌄
Category:	General	⌄
Description:		
Save in:	Normal	⌄
Options:	Insert content only	⌄

17. Select the paragraph under the Location heading and add it to the AutoText Gallery using the name: **Location**

18. Add the *Hours of Operation* and *Policy* paragraphs to the AutoText Gallery as well, and then close the Raritan Marketing file.

Now that these paragraphs have been added as AutoText Quick Parts, you can insert them over and over again, without needing to refer back to the original source document.

19. In the Newsletter, remove the Sidebar body placeholder text (beginning with [Sidebars are great...) in the field below the Title and choose **Insert→Text→Explore Quick Parts** 📑 **menu button** ▾ **→AutoText→Location**.

20. Save the file.

Inserting Cover Pages

A cover page catches a reader's eye as the first dynamic part of your document. You can easily add professional polish to a document by using a built-in cover page. There are a number of predesigned (that is, built-in) cover pages to choose from. Cover pages automatically adopt the colors and fonts of your chosen theme, but if desired, you can modify the color and other design elements to achieve a cover page that best suits your needs.

≡ Insert→Pages→Cover Page 📄 menu button ▾

DEVELOP YOUR SKILLS: W6-D4

In this exercise, you will add a cover page to your newsletter and remove some of the unnecessary Document Property Quick Parts fields automatically entered in the cover page.

1. Save your file as: **W6-D4-RaritanNewsltrRevised**
2. Choose **Insert→Pages→Cover Page** 📄 **menu button** ▾, scroll through the gallery of available options, and choose **Banded**.

   The title at the top of the page, as well as the author and company at the bottom of the page, were automatically inserted based on the document properties.

3. Scroll to the bottom of the cover page and click anywhere inside the **Author** field, which currently displays the text *Raritan Employee*.

   Now that you've clicked inside the field, the bounding box appears, as well as a tab that shows the field name.

4. Click the **Author** tab to select the entire field and then tap [Delete].

5. Use the same technique to delete the **Company Address** field.
6. Save the file.

Using Building Blocks Across Documents

In addition to using the built-in Quick Parts and Building Blocks, you can also create your own by simply selecting the block you want to use and adding it to the Quick Part Gallery. Once you've created your custom building block, you can apply it to other documents as needed. Like their built-in counterparts, these custom building blocks will adapt the look of whatever theme has been applied to the target document.

☰ Insert→Text→Explore Quick Parts 🔲 →Save Selection to Quick Part Gallery

In this exercise, you'll add the first several lines of your newsletter to the Quick Part Gallery for use in later documents. You'll also add the company logo as a Quick Part.

1. Scroll to the top of the first page in the main document. In the second line beneath the company logo, delete the word **November** and replace it with: **(Enter Month)**

2. Select the entire heading of the first page, from the WordArt down through the Chief Development Officer's name.

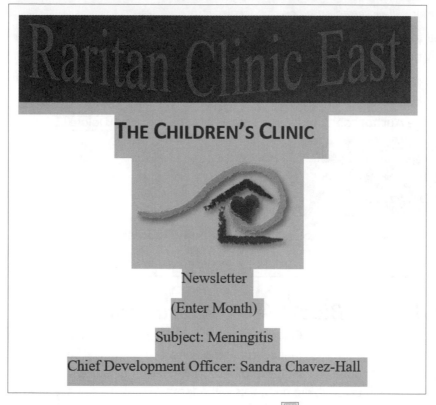

3. Choose **Insert→Text→Explore Quick Parts** 📄 **menu button ▾→Save Selection to Quick Part Gallery**.

4. In the dialog box, enter **Newsletter Opener** in the Name box and click **OK**.

5. Click the Raritan Clinic East logo to select it and choose **Insert→Text→Explore Quick Parts** 📄 **menu button ▾→Save Selection to Quick Part Gallery**.

6. Enter **Raritan Logo** as the Quick Part name and click **OK**.

7. Choose **Insert→Text→Explore Quick Parts** 🔲 **menu button** ▼ to see your custom Quick Parts.

These Quick Parts are now permanently available for your use.

8. Close the file; click **Don't Save** if Word prompts you.

Using Templates

All documents are based on a template that can include text, formatting, graphics, and other objects, as well as themes with custom color, font, and style sets. The default template is Blank document. The benefit of templates is that they do not change when documents *based on them* change. When you start a new document, you are opening a *copy* of the template. This lets you use templates repeatedly as the basis for new documents. Word provides a variety of ready-to-use templates, or you can create your own personal templates.

Templates are located in the Start screen or in Backstage view when you are starting a new file. Basing a new document on a template can save you a lot of time, as much of the work is already included.

≡ File→New

In this exercise, you will search for a newsletter template and use it as the basis for a new newsletter style that Raritan will adopt in the future. You will then apply your custom theme, ensuring that future Raritan newsletters have a consistent look and style.

1. Choose **File→New** and then follow these steps to locate a newsletter template:

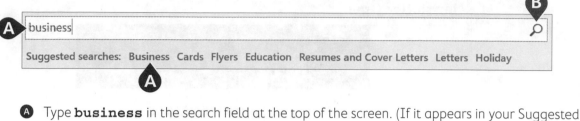

Ⓐ Type **business** in the search field at the top of the screen. (If it appears in your Suggested Searches, click it to start the search instantly.)

Ⓑ If necessary, click the **Start Searching** button.

The options that appear for Suggested Searches may vary.

2. Scroll through the templates and double-click **Blue Curve Letterhead**.

3. To apply your customized theme choices to this prebuilt template, choose **Design→Document Formatting→Themes** menu button ▾ →**Raritan Theme**.

4. Save the file as: **W6-D6-FutureNewsltr**

Saving Personal Templates

When you create a document containing specific formatting, text, themes, and graphics, you can save it as a template in the Custom Office Templates folder. When you save a personal template, the Personal category appears on the templates screen, with your templates inside.

This Personal category refers to Word-supplied templates such as personal letterhead.

Search for online templates	
Suggested searches: Business Personal Industry	
FEATURED PERSONAL	

This PERSONAL category refers to templates you create yourself.

In this exercise, you will prepare the open document for use in future newsletters. You will remove several unnecessary fields, add document properties, and insert a few company-specific elements. When the document is ready, you'll save it as a template.

1. Click anywhere inside the **Company Name** field at the top of the document, click the Select Table's **move handle** ⊞ button, and tap [Backspace].

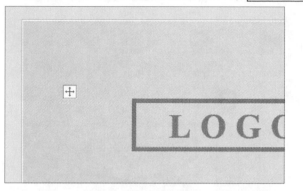

In some instances, the table may not be completely deleted. If the move handle button is still displayed, click it again and tap [Backspace] again to ensure the table is fully deleted.

2. Choose **Home→Paragraph→Center Alignment** ☰.

3. Choose **Insert→Text→Explore Quick Parts** 🗐 **menu button** ▾→**Newsletter Opener**.

Your custom Quick Part has been inserted into the new template. The previous entries for the Title, Subject, and Comments have been replaced with fields, as you have not yet entered any properties into this document.

4. Click the **File** tab to enter the Backstage view and then click **Show All Properties**.

5. Enter **Newsletter** in the Title box and **Sandra Chavez-Hall** in the Comments box.

6. Click **Back** ⊕ to return to the document.

The Title and Comments fields have been replaced. The subject will change for each newsletter, so you've left that field to be filled in manually later.

7. If necessary, place the insertion point in the blank line below the Chief Development Officer line and then choose **Layout→Page Setup→Breaks** ⊟ **menu button** ▾→**Continuous** to insert a Continuous break above where the document will be split into two columns.

8. Delete the greeting line and the two lines above it.

[]
[Street Address, City, ST ZIP Code]

Dear ,

9. Delete the three closing lines at the bottom of the page, labeled *Warm Regards*, *Name Here*, and *Your Title*.

10. Click anywhere inside the body text to select it and tap $\boxed{\text{Delete}}$.

11. Choose **Layout→Page Setup→Columns** ▦ **menu button** ▼**→More Columns**.

12. In the Columns dialog box, change the settings as follows:

Columns		?	×

Presets

One Two Three Left Right

Number of columns: 2 ⬥A   B⬥ ☑ Line **b**etween

Width and spacing

Col #:	Width:	Spacing:
1:	3.5"	0.5"
2:	3.5"	

☑ **E**qual column width

Apply to: This section

☐ Start new column

C⬥ OK   Cancel

Ⓐ Change the number of columns to **2**.

Ⓑ Check the **Line Between** box.

Ⓒ Click **OK**.

The line between columns will not appear until enough text is entered to complete a column.

13. Save your file as: `W6-D7-FutureNewsltr`

Now that the template is ready to be reused for future Raritan newsletters, you'll save it as a template.

14. Choose **File→Save As→Browse** and change the Save as Type menu to **Word Template**.

15. Navigate to your **Word Chapter 6** folder, type `W6-D7-NewsltrTemplate` into the Name box, and click **Save**.

16. Close the file.

17. In Windows File Explorer, navigate to your **Word Chapter 6** folder and double-click the **W6-D7-NewsltrTemplate**.

A new document has been created from your template, with all your text theme choices and Quick Parts immediately included. The new document is ready for use as a newsletter.

18. Save the file to your **Word Chapter 6** folder as `W6-D7-DecemberNewsltr` and then close it.

Customizing the Default Font

The main default template in Microsoft Word is the Blank document template, which uses the Office theme, complete with the Office color and font sets. The default font for this theme, and therefore for Microsoft Word at large, is Calibri, 11-point size. This is often shown in available font lists as Body, a term referring to the built-in default text. If you prefer another font to be automatically selected whenever you create a new document with the Blank document template, you can change it in the Font dialog box using the Set As Default button.

Font		?	X

Font   Advanced

Font:
Arial

- Algerian
- **Arial**
- Arial Black
- Arial Narrow
- Arial Rounded MT Bold

Font style:
Regular

- Regular
- Italic
- Bold
- Bold Italic

Size:
14

- 10
- 11
- 12
- **14**
- 16

Font color: **Automatic**   Underline style: **(none)**   Underline color: **Automatic**

Effects

- ☐ Strikethrough
- ☐ Double strikethrough
- ☐ Superscript
- ☐ Subscript
- ☐ Small caps
- ☐ All caps
- ☐ Hidden

Preview

Arial

This is a TrueType font. This font will be used on both printer and screen.

[Set As Default]   [Text Effects...]   [OK]   [Cancel]

≡ Home→Font→dialog box launcher ⊡

DEVELOP YOUR SKILLS: W6-D8

In this exercise, you will change the default Word font to Times New Roman, 12-point font, and open a new document to test the settings. Then, you'll change the default font back to its original settings.

1. Create a new document with the default **Blank document** template.
2. Choose **Home→Font→dialog box launcher** ⊡.

3. In the Font dialog box, change the font to **Times New Roman** and the size to **12**.

Font:	Font style:	Size:
Times New Roman	Regular	12
Times New Roman	**Regular**	10
Trebuchet MS	Italic	11
Tw Cen MT	Bold	**12**
Tw Cen MT Condensed	Bold Italic	14
Tw Cen MT Condensed Extra Bold		16

Now that you've changed the font settings, you can make these changes the new default.

4. Click the **Set as Default** button.

5. In the window that appears, select **All documents based on the Normal template?** and click **OK**.

Microsoft Word   ?   ✕

Do you want to set the default font to Times New Roman, 12 pt for:

   ◯ This document only?

   ◉ All documents based on the Normal template?

          [OK]   [Cancel]

Your changes have now become the new default font. Let's test it.

6. Close the file without saving and open a new file based on the **Blank document** template.

   The Font box now shows Times New Roman, and the Size box shows 12.

7. Type a few words to see the new default.

8. Choose **Home→Font→dialog box launcher** 🔲 , change the Font to **+Body** at the top of the font list, and change the size to **11**.

9. Click **Set as Default**, choose **All documents based on the Normal template?**, and click **OK**.

10. Close the file, choosing not to save if prompted.

Self-Assessment

Check your knowledge of this chapter's key concepts and skills using the Self-Assessment in your ebook or online (eLab course or Student Resource Center).

Reinforce Your Skills

REINFORCE YOUR SKILLS: W6-R1

Create a Consistent Newsletter Theme

Leaders at Kids for Change want to create consistency across all publications the organization creates. In this exercise, you will modify an existing newsletter's theme and save it for future use. Then, you'll save the file as a template.

1. Open **W6-R1-SchoolHabitat** from your **Word Chapter 6** folder.

2. Choose **Design→Document Formatting→Themes menu button** ▼ and choose **Organic** from the Themes gallery.

3. Choose **Design→Document Formatting→Colors menu button** ▼ and select **Blue** from the Colors gallery.

4. Choose **Design→Document Formatting→Fonts menu button** ▼, scroll down if necessary, and select **Georgia** from the Font gallery.

5. Choose **Design→Document Formatting** and then click **More** ▼ to open the Style Sets gallery.

6. Choose **Basic (Elegant)**, the first option in the first row under Built-In. Scroll through the document to see the changes you've made.

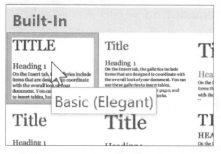

Customize and Save the Theme

7. Choose **Design→Document Formatting→Colors menu button** ▼→**Customize Colors**.

8. In the Create New Theme Colors dialog box, select the **Text/Background - Dark 1 menu button** ▼ and choose **More Colors**.

9. In the Colors box, choose the **Custom** tab, if necessary, and enter **5** for Red, **104** for Green, and **57** for Blue; click **OK**.

10. Select the **Accent 1 menu button** ▼ and choose **Blue, Accent 1, Lighter 60%** in the fifth column, third row, under Theme Colors.

11. Enter **Kids for Change Color Set** in the **Name** box and click **OK**.

12. Choose **Design→Document Formatting→Fonts menu button** ▼→**Customize Fonts**.

13. Change the **Heading** font to **Cambria**; leave the Body font as Georgia.

14. Enter **Kids for Change Font Set** in the **Name** box and click **Save**.

15. Choose **Design→Document Formatting→Themes menu button** ▼→**Save Current Theme**.

16. In the dialog box, enter **Kids for Change Theme** as the filename and then click **Save**.

Save a Personal Template

17. Scroll to the top of the cover page and delete the word **March** below the *Newsletter* heading.

18. Scroll to the top of the main document and replace the WordArt text, currently showing *Schoolyard Habitat*, with the word: `Title`

19. Select all the text in the two columns and tap Delete . Leave the butterfly image as a place-holder for future images.

20. Choose **File→Save As→Browse** and change the Save as Type menu to **Word Template**.

21. Save the file to your **Word Chapter 6** folder as: `W6-R1-KidsforChangeTemplate`

22. Close the file.

REINFORCE YOUR SKILLS: W6-R2

Add Pizazz to a Wetlands Protection Newsletter

Kids for Change is starting a wetlands protection project. It's issuing a press release discussing the importance of wetlands and asking for volunteers to become part of the project. In this exercise, you will add a cover page, create a custom Quick Part, and place a Building Block at the end of the document.

1. Open **W6-R2-Wetlands** from your **Word Chapter 6** folder and save it as: `W6-R2-WetlandsRevised`

2. Choose **Insert→Pages→Cover Page menu button** ▼ and select the **Ion (Light)** option.

3. Click anywhere inside the Year field at the top right of the screen, click the **Year** tab that appears above and then tap Delete .

4. Repeat this process to delete the **Author Name** field beneath the title and subtitle.

5. Choose **Insert→Text→Explore Quick Parts menu button** ▼ →**Document Property**→ **Comments**.

Now that you've entered the field, you'll need to fill in the document property so your name appears.

6. Click the **File** tab to enter the Backstage view and then type your name into the Comments box.

7. Click **Back** to return to the document.

Use a Custom Quick Part

8. Open **Kids for Change header** from your **Word Chapter 6** folder.

9. Press Ctrl + A to select the entire document.

10. Choose **Insert→Text→Explore Quick Parts menu button** ▼ →**Save Selection to Quick Part Gallery**.

11. In the dialog box, enter `Kids for Change opener` in the Name box and click **OK**.

12. Close the file to return to the newsletter.

13. Scroll to the bottom of the newsletter and place the insertion point in the blank line below the last paragraph in the second column.

14. Choose **Insert→Text→Explore Quick Parts menu button** ▼ and choose the **Kids for Change opener** you created.

Add a Closing Building Block

15. Choose **Insert→Text→Explore Quick Parts menu button ▾→Building Blocks Organizer**.

16. In the dialog box, scroll down to the Text Boxes section, select **Filigree Sidebar**, and click **Insert**.

17. Click anywhere inside the **Sidebar Title** field and tap [Delete].

18. Type **Volunteer for this project!** as the new title.

Note that the new title is capitalized automatically.

19. Click anywhere inside the text below the Quick Part title, tap [Delete], and type: **Reach out to us on Facebook to volunteer for this or other Kids for Change projects!**

20. Save and close your document.

REINFORCE YOUR SKILLS: W6-R3

Create a Newsletter to Fight Water Pollution

Kids for Change is starting a Protect Our Waterways project to fight water pollution. The supervisor for the project is using a newsletter as a means of getting the word out. In this exercise, you will set up the newsletter with a theme, cover page, custom Quick Part, and Building Block.

1. Open **W6-R3-WaterPollution** from your **Word Chapter 6** folder and save it as: **W6-R3-WaterPollutionRevised**

2. Choose **Design→Document Formatting→Themes menu button ▾** and then choose **Basis** from the Themes gallery.

3. Choose **Design→Document Formatting→Colors menu button ▾** and then select **Blue II** from the Colors gallery.

Add a Custom Quick Part to a Cover Page

4. Open the **Kids for Change contact** file from your **Word Chapter 6** folder.

5. Press [Ctrl]+[A] to select the entire document.

6. Choose **Insert→Text→Explore Quick Parts menu button ▾→Save Selection to Quick Part Gallery**.

7. In the dialog box that appears, enter **Kids for Change contact** in the Name box and click **OK**.

8. Close the file to return to the newsletter.

9. Choose **Insert→Pages→Cover Page menu button ▾** and select the **Grid** option.

10. Click anywhere inside the **Abstract** field just below the title on the cover page, click the **Abstract** tab that appears above, and tap [Delete].

11. Repeat the process to delete the **Document subtitle** field on the right side of the page.

12. Choose **Insert→Text→Explore Quick Parts menu button ▾** and choose the **Kids for Change contact** you created.

Add a Centered Building Block

13. Scroll down to the main document and place the insertion point anywhere inside the two-column text.

14. Choose **Insert→Text→Explore Quick Parts menu button ▾→Building Blocks Organizer**.

15. In the dialog box, scroll down to the Text Boxes section, select **Simple Quote**, and then click **Insert**.

16. Tap [Delete] to remove the placeholder text and type: `Kids Empowering Communities`

17. Save and close the file.

📎 Apply Your Skills

APPLY YOUR SKILLS: W6-A1

Create a Travel Newsletter Theme

Universal Corporate Events keeps its clients informed about the latest travel industry news by publishing a monthly newsletter. In this exercise, you will modify an existing newsletter's theme and save the file as a template to be used in future publications.

1. Open **W6-A1-CorpTravel** from your **Word Chapter 6** folder.
2. Apply the **Organic** theme.
3. Apply the **Blue Warm** color set.
4. Apply the **Corbel** font set.
5. Apply the **Lines (Simple)** style set.
6. Change the **Text/Background – Dark 1** color to an orange custom color, with **249** for Red, **166** for Green, and **26** for Blue.
7. Change Accent 2 to **Blue-Gray, Accent 1**.
8. Name the color set: **Universal Events Color Set**
9. Change the Body font to **Calibri**; leave the Heading font as Corbel.
10. Name the font set: **Universal Events Font Set**
11. Save the current theme as: **Universal Events Theme**

Save a Personal Template

12. Scroll to the top of the cover page and delete the word **July** below the *Newsletter* heading.
13. Delete the paragraph under the *Abstract* heading on the right side of the cover page. Replace it with: **Enter Summary Here**
14. Leaving the graphic as a placeholder, select all of the text in both columns, from the *Four Hidden Benefits...* header through the end of the second page, and tap ⬚Backspace⬚.
15. Save the file as a template to your **Word Chapter 6** folder, giving it the name: **W6-A1-UniversalEventsTemplate**
16. Save and close the file.

APPLY YOUR SKILLS: W6-A2

Add Zest to a Bleisure Newsletter

This month's Universal Corporate Events newsletter focuses on the latest "bleisure" (a blend of business and leisure) travel trend. In this exercise, you will add a cover page, custom Quick Part, and Building Block to the newsletter, which is designed to keep clients' travel agents updated with the latest developments in the travel industry.

1. Open **W6-A2-BleisureTravel** from your **Word Chapter 6** folder and save it as: **W6-A2-BleisureTravelRevised**
2. Insert the **Motion** cover page from the cover page gallery.

3. Delete the **Year** field at the top of the page and the **Author** and **Date** fields at the bottom of the page.

4. Change the file's Company property to: **Universal Corporate Events**

5. Scroll down to the main document and place the insertion point after the colon at the end of the Company line.

6. Tap $\boxed{\text{Spacebar}}$ and choose **Insert→Text→Explore Quick Parts menu button** ▾→ **Document Property→Company**.

7. Place the insertion point after the colon at the end of the Contact line, tap $\boxed{\text{Spacebar}}$, and choose **Insert→Text→Explore Quick Parts menu button** ▾→**Document Property→ Comments**.

Add a Custom Quick Part to a Building Block

8. Place the insertion point anywhere inside the body text in the left column of the main document.

9. Use the Building Blocks Organizer dialog box to insert a **Banded Sidebar** from the Text Boxes section.

10. Replace the Title placeholder at the top of the sidebar with: **Bleisure Stats**

11. Open **Bleisure Survey Statistics** from your **Word Chapter 6** folder.

12. Select the entire document and use the selection to create a custom Quick Part with the name **Statistics**; close the file.

13. Click anywhere inside the sidebar body text placeholder and tap $\boxed{\text{Delete}}$ to remove it.

14. Insert the **Statistics** custom Quick Part as the new sidebar body text.

15. Save and close your document.

APPLY YOUR SKILLS: W6-A3

Create a Travel Tips Newsletter

Universal Corporate Events shares travel tips with its clients' travel agents in this month's newsletter. In this exercise, you will set up the travel tips newsletter to incorporate a theme, cover page, custom Quick Part, and Building Block.

1. Open **W6-A3-TravelTips** from your **Word Chapter 6** folder and save it as: **W6-A3-TravelTipsRevised**

2. Apply the **Integral** theme.

3. Apply the **Blue Green** color set.

4. Open the **Universal Corp contact** file from your **Word Chapter 6** folder.

5. Select the entire document; add it as a custom Quick Part with the name **UCE contact** and then close the file.

6. Insert a **Grid** cover page from the cover page gallery.

7. Delete the **Abstract** and **Subtitle** fields from the cover page.

8. Place the **UCE contact** custom Quick Part inside the darker box on the right side of the page.

9. Scroll down to the main document and place the insertion point anywhere inside the two-column text.

10. Using the Building Blocks Organizer dialog box, insert the **Simple Quote** Quick Part from the Text Boxes gallery section.

11. Remove the placeholder text and type **Use Yelp for the best source of local cuisine** into the Simple Quote Quick Part box.

12. Save and close the file.

📄📋 Project Grader

This chapter does not include Project Grader exercises. Project Grader content is based on the learning objectives for a chapter, and sometimes those learning objectives cannot be accurately graded by the system. Objectives from this chapter that can be accurately graded may be included in later chapters, if applicable.

◢ Extend Your Skills

These exercises challenge you to think critically and apply your new skills in a real-world setting. You will be evaluated on your ability to follow directions, completeness, creativity, and the use of proper grammar and mechanics. Save files to your chapter folder. Submit assignments as directed.

W6-E1 That's the Way I See It

As a small-business owner, you want to keep your customers interested in what you're doing, so you decide to send out monthly newsletters. Determine the type of business you own and then draft the beginnings of a newsletter, with a title placeholder and a placeholder paragraph split into two columns. Insert a cover page and remove any fields you don't want to use, leaving at least one. Create a custom theme consisting of a custom color and font set. Save the color set, font set, and theme with unique names related to your business. Save your newsletter as a template with the name: **W6-E1-MyBiz**

W6-E2 Be Your Own Boss

As the owner of Blue Jean Landscaping, you decide to keep in touch with customers by distributing a newsletter. Start a new document and save it as: **W6-E2-Landscape**

Draft a newsletter with a title, two blank lines below the title, and a few paragraphs of body text split into two columns. Insert a cover page of your choice and delete any fields you don't want to use. Use the Backstage view to change the document properties for the fields you keep. In the two blank lines below the title, place two more document property fields and change those document properties in the Backstage view. Using another blank document, insert a shape or graphic and then insert two lines of contact information. Save what you've created as a custom Quick Part and insert it into your main document. Insert and fill in another Building Block of your choice.

W6-E3 Demonstrate Proficiency

Stormy BBQ keeps its customers engaged through a monthly newsletter. This month's newsletter will describe the benefits of local farm-raised pork and beef. Conduct online research to gather the primary content for your newsletter, ensuring you cite your sources. Create a newsletter with a title and a few paragraphs of body text split into two columns. Insert a cover page of your choice, removing or replacing fields as you choose. Apply a custom theme with a unique name. Use another blank document to create a short custom Quick Part and place it inside your main document. Add a Building Block of your choice from the Building Blocks Organizer dialog box. Save your file as: **W6-E3-FarmRaised**

7 | Working with Long Documents

L ong documents are important in both academia and business. They range in type from dissertations to research reports. In this chapter, you will use styles to provide consistent heading formatting, which leads the reader's eye through the document. You will customize styles and other features to suit your needs, and you will use several techniques to quickly navigate long documents. Finally, you will work with long tables to make them easy to read and to find information.

LEARNING OBJECTIVES

▸ Format with styles

▸ Create and manage custom styles

▸ Customize bullets and numbering

▸ Navigate long documents

▸ Format long tables

▸ Add captions

⌒ Project: Reporting on Common Childhood Illnesses

Raritan Clinic East periodically hosts seminars for parents of young children to discuss common childhood illnesses. As a certified nursing assistant, you have been asked to research these illnesses and compile a report that the clinic will use as a handout for the seminars. You will use styles and other formatting features to make your report engaging to the reader. Then you will create a table to keep track of the attendees.

Formatting Text with Styles

A style is a collection of formats that you can apply to text. When you type a document, you are automatically using a style. This is typically the Normal style, which includes Calibri font, 11 pt, left-justified, and so forth. Or you might be using a custom template that is set up with a different default style. Styles are based on the current template's theme. Styles help you provide consistent formatting throughout a document.

The Styles gallery on the Ribbon is limited to frequently used styles. For a more in-depth approach and access to more styles, you must open the Styles task pane.

⚠ **View the video "The Styles Gallery and the Styles Task Pane."**

≡ Home→Styles dialog box launcher ⌐⌐

Custom Styles

Thus far, you've used Word's built-in styles. However, there may be situations in which the built-in styles don't meet your needs; for example, Raritan Clinic East has formatting standards set for different types of documents, and you can create custom styles to meet those standards. When creating these custom styles, you can also define the *level* in which you want them to be listed, which will determine how these headings are placed in a table of contents or your document's Headings list.

There are two approaches to creating custom styles. The method you choose is a matter of personal preference; both are equally effective and are described below:

▸ **Style by definition:** Choose all formats from the Create New Style from Formatting dialog box.

▸ **Style by example:** Format a block of text with the formats you wish to include in your style. The Create New Style from Formatting dialog box can copy the formats from your formatted text.

⚠ **View the video "Create a Style by Definition and a Style by Example."**

DEVELOP YOUR SKILLS: W7-D1

In this exercise, you will create custom styles. You'll begin by opening the Styles task pane and creating a new style by example for the document heading. Then you will create a style by definition.

1. Open **W7-D1-SickKids** from your **Word Chapter 7** folder and save it as:
   W7-D1-SickKidsRevised

2. Select the **Raritan Clinic East** heading at the top of the document.

   Now you will apply the example formatting.

3. Choose **Home→Font→Font menu button** ▼ and then choose **Tahoma** from the menu.

4. Click the **Font Size menu button** ▼ and choose **24 pt**.

5. Choose **Home→Paragraph→Center** ≣.

6. Choose **Home→Styles dialog box launcher** ⌐ to display the Styles task pane.

7. At the bottom of the task pane, click the **New Style** ⚉ button to open the Create New Style from Formatting dialog box.

8. Follow these steps to complete the new style:

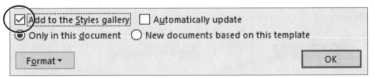

Ⓐ The example formatting you applied earlier shows here.

Ⓑ Name the style: **Doc Head**

Ⓒ Make sure the Style type is **Paragraph**.

Ⓓ If necessary, set the new style to be based on the **Normal** style and set the formatting for the following paragraph to **Normal**.

9. At the bottom of the dialog box, make sure the **Add to the Styles gallery** box is checked and then click **OK**.

When the text that has the style applied is selected or the insertion point is in the text, your new style is highlighted in the Styles gallery on the Ribbon and in the Styles task pane.

WORD

Create Styles by Definition

Now you'll create a style by definition for the subheading at the top of the document.

10. Click in the **Childhood Diseases Seminar** subheading.

11. Click the **New Style** button at the bottom of the Styles task pane.

12. Set up the top portion of the dialog box as shown:

Properties	
Name:	Subhead 1
Style type:	Paragraph
Style based on:	¶ Normal
Style for following paragraph:	¶ Normal

You could do some font formatting in this dialog box, but you will choose the Format button instead because it provides more font options.

13. Click the **Format** button at the bottom of the dialog box, choose **Font** to open the Font dialog box, and choose **Tahoma** from the Font list.

Tip! *If you type a t in the field at the top of the font list, the list automatically scrolls to the Ts.*

14. Choose **14 pt** as the font size, check the **Small Caps** checkbox, and click **OK**.

Your font choices appear in the dialog box, and the preview screen displays the effect of your choices. Next, you will change the level of this subhead.

15. Click the **Format** button and choose **Paragraph**.

16. Click the **Outline Level menu button** ▾ and choose **Level 1**.

Paragraph	? ✕

Indents and Spacing | Line and Page Breaks

General

Alignment: Left ▾

Outline level: Level 1 ▾ ☐ Collapsed by default

Notice that there are nine possible levels. Level 1 will be farthest left, Level 2 will be indented, Level 3 will be further indented, and so on.

17. Click **OK**.

Next you will center the subheading.

18. Click the **Center** button in the paragraph alignment group and click **OK**.

The new style appears in the Styles gallery on the Ribbon and in the Styles task pane.

Formatting

Tahoma ▾

Now you will create styles for the subheadings in the body of the document. You will have two levels of subheadings, and you will create styles by example for these subheadings.

19. In the next line, select **WebMD** and format it with **Arial**, **14 pt**.

20. Click the **New Style** 🖾 button and follow these guidelines to finish creating the style:
    • Name: `Subhead 2`
    • Style Type: **Paragraph**
    • Style Based On: **Normal**
    • Style for Following Paragraph: **Normal**

21. Notice the example font formatting you applied in the Formatting area of the dialog box and then click **OK**.

    You will apply the Subhead 2 style to another subheading in the document.

22. Scroll to page 3, position the insertion point in the subheading **Parents.com**, and choose **Subhead 2** from the Styles gallery.

23. Scroll back up to page 1, position the insertion point in the **RSV** subheading, and choose **Home→Font→Font menu button** ▼.

24. Choose the **Arial** font and the **12 pt** font size.

25. Click the **New Style** 🖾 button and follow these guidelines to finish creating the style:
    • Name: `Subhead 3`
    • Style Type: **Paragraph**
    • Style Based On: **Normal**
    • Style for Following Paragraph: **Normal**

26. Notice the example settings in the Formatting area and then click **OK**.

    Now you will apply Subhead 3 to the rest of the subheadings in the document.

27. Click in the **Ear Infection** subheading and choose **Subhead 3** from the Styles task pane.

28. Use the same technique to apply Subhead 3 to the remaining subheadings:
    • **Glue Ear**
    • **Croup**
    • **Hand-Foot-and-Mouth Disease**
    • **Pinkeye**
    • **Fifth Disease**
    • **Common Cold**
    • **Strep Throat**
    • **Influenza**
    • **Symptoms You Should Never Ignore**

29. Save the file.

Modifying Styles and Clearing All Formatting

You can modify a built-in style as well as styles that you create. Modifying styles can help you maintain consistency when you make formatting changes and can speed up that process. You can make global formatting changes by modifying a style. When you change a style, the change is applied to all the text in the current document that is formatted with the style. This eliminates the need to modify each text block individually—a big time saver.

Sometimes it is easier to reformat text from the beginning instead of trying to figure out which formats were used. This can be particularly helpful if you've inherited a heavily formatted document. The Clear All Formatting command in the Styles task pane is a quick way to remove styles and all other unwanted formatting from a document or a selected block of text.

≣ Home→Font→Clear All Formatting 🗛

Using Styles Across Documents

By default, custom styles you create are available only for the document in which you created them. However, you may want your custom styles to be available in other documents as well. You can do this by specifying that you want the style to be available in all *New documents based on this template*. Doing this in a document created from the default Blank document template will make the style available in all new blank documents you create from that point on.

☑ Add to the Styles gallery   ☐ Automatically update
○ Only in this document   ◉ New documents based on this template

Format ▾

Warning! *Adding styles to the template this way is a permanent change. The only way to remove these custom styles from the template is through the Organizer on the Developer tab (activated through the Customize Ribbon tab on the Options screen) under Document Template.*

DEVELOP YOUR SKILLS: W7-D2

In this exercise, you will modify the Subhead 3 style. When you do, you will see how it impacts all text formatted with that style. Then you will use the Clear All Formatting feature to remove formatting from a heading.

1. Save your file as: **W7-D2-SickKidsRevised**
2. Hover the mouse pointer over *Subhead 3* in the Styles task pane and click the **menu** button ▼ that appears.
3. Choose **Modify** from the menu to open the Modify Style dialog box.

   This dialog box contains the same elements as the Create New Style from Formatting dialog box.
4. Click **Italic** $\boxed{I}$ and then click **OK**.
5. Scroll through the document and see that all subheadings with the Subhead 3 style are now italicized.

   You've decided to reformat the heading at the top of the document. Because this style is used only once in the document, it's easier to clear all the formatting and apply direct formatting to the heading.
6. Select the **Raritan Clinic East** heading at the top of the document, scroll to the top of the Styles task pane, and choose **Clear All**.
7. Click the **Home→Font dialog box launcher** ⌐ and choose **Tahoma**, **22 pt**, **Small Caps**; click **OK**.
8. Choose **Home→Paragraph→Center** ≡.

   The Normal style is highlighted in the task pane. You applied direct formatting to text that is formatted with the Normal style.
9. Save the file.

Removing and Deleting Styles

You can remove a style from the Styles gallery on the Ribbon without removing it from the Styles task pane. Because the Styles gallery on the Ribbon is a quick way to get to styles, you should save it for just the styles you use frequently. You can leave the style in the task pane for future use, or, if you prefer, you can delete it from the task pane. Completely deleting a style removes its formatting from the document.

DEVELOP YOUR SKILLS: W7-D3

In this exercise, you will remove the Doc Head style from the Styles gallery and then delete it from the task pane.

1. Save your file as: **W7-D3-SickKidsRevised**
2. If the Doc Head style is not visible in the Styles gallery on the Ribbon, click **More** ⏷ to open the gallery and then locate the Doc Head style.
3. Right-click the style name and choose **Remove from Style Gallery**.

   Doc Head is still visible in the Styles task pane. You'll delete it next.
4. Hover the mouse pointer over *Doc Head* in the Styles task pane, click the **menu** button ▼ that appears, and choose **Delete Doc Head**.
5. When the message appears verifying the deletion, click **Yes**.

   The style is deleted from the task pane.
6. Save and close the file.

Customizing Bullet and Number Formats

The Bullets and Numbering libraries enable you to choose a different style for your bulleted or numbered list. You can also define your own custom formats. When working with long documents, you may want to adjust the formatting for certain lists as a visual cue that certain lists go together or should be considered separately.

Bullet Library   Numbering Library

You can customize bullet styles by defining a symbol, picture, font, or alignment. You can customize numbering by defining style, font, format, and alignment.

Define New Bullet

Bullet character

[Symbol...] [Picture...] [Font...]

Alignment:

[Left ▾]

Customize Bullet Format

Define New Number Format

Number format

Number style:

[1, 2, 3, ... ▾] [Font...]

Number format:

[1.]

Alignment:

[Left ▾]

Customize Number Format

≡ Home→Paragraph→Bullets

≡ Home→Paragraph→Numbering

DEVELOP YOUR SKILLS: W7-D4

In this exercise, you will choose a different bullet style from the Bullet Library. Then you will create a custom bullet using a symbol as the new bullet style.

1. Open **W7-D4-SickKids** from your **Word Chapter 7** folder and save it as:
   W7-D4-SickKidsRevised
2. Scroll to page 4 and position the insertion point in the **Symptom #1** line.
3. Choose **Home→Paragraph→Bullets** 🔳 **menu button** ▾ and choose the square bullet (location may vary).

   Bullet Library

   | None | ● | ○ | ■ |

   All the bullets in the list are updated. Next you will create a custom bullet.

4. Choose **Home→Paragraph→Bullets** 🔳 **menu button** ▾ and choose **Define New Bullet**.

5. Follow these steps to define a symbol as a new bullet:

A Click the **Symbol** button to open the Symbol dialog box.

B If necessary, choose the **Wingdings** font.

C Make sure the scroll box is at the top of the scroll bar, choose this symbol (location may vary), and click **OK** twice.

Again, all of the bullets have changed to the custom bullet.

6. Choose **Home→Paragraph→Bullets** ☷ **menu button** ▾.

The new bullet was added to the library. Now you'll remove the bullet so the next student who uses your computer will have the same experience.

7. Right-click the new bullet in the Bullet Library area and choose **Remove**.

8. Display the Bullet Library again and notice the new bullet is removed from the Bullet Library area but remains under Recently Used Bullets; close the menu.

9. Save your file.

Using Special Characters

Special characters appear in the Symbol dialog box. There are a variety of special characters, including nonbreaking hyphens or spaces. Nonbreaking characters allow you to keep terms together that should remain together on one line, such as dates, phone numbers, and names.

≡ Insert→Symbols→Symbol Ω →Special Characters

In this exercise, you will insert nonbreaking spaces in doctors' names that appear in the document. This will correct doctors' names that split across two lines, and it's also a safety measure in the event that future edits would cause the name to split across two lines.

1. Save your file as: **W7-D5-SickKidsRevised**

2. Scroll to page 3, locate the fifth line in the *Common Cold* paragraph, and position the insertion point after *Fred*.

> might lead to an overdose," says pediatrician Fred Hirschenfang, M.D.,

3. Tap Delete to remove the space.

4. Choose **Insert→Symbols→Symbol** Ω and then choose **More Symbols** from the menu.

5. Click the **Special Characters** tab in the Symbol dialog box and choose **Nonbreaking Space**.

6. Click the **Insert** button at the bottom of the dialog box and then click **Close**.

7. If necessary, display the formatting marks to see the character that represents a nonbreaking space.

8. Position the insertion point after the comma following the last name and Delete the space.

9. Choose **Insert→Symbols→Symbol** Ω **→More Symbols**, click the **Special Characters** tab, and choose **Nonbreaking Space**.

   Notice the shortcut keystrokes for a nonbreaking space: Ctrl + Shift + Space . *You can use the keystrokes for the remaining two names.*

10. Click the **Insert** button and then click **Close**.

11. Scroll to the sixth line in the next paragraph and notice the doctor's name that starts at the end of the line.

12. Position the insertion point after the *y* in *Jay* and tap Delete .

13. Press Ctrl + Shift + Space to insert a nonbreaking space.

14. Use the same technique to replace the space following the comma after the last name with a nonbreaking space.

15. Locate Dr. Hirschenfang's name starting at the end of the sixth line in the *Influenza* paragraph and replace the space between *Dr.* and his last name with a nonbreaking space.

16. Save the file.

Navigating Long Documents

A number of helpful tools make it easier to navigate long, complex documents. The Navigation pane provides several ways to move around a document, while Advanced Find and wildcard characters enable specialized searches. Bookmarks are useful if you frequently need to return to the same location in a document. If you want to compare two separate parts of the same document, using the Split Window feature is a great way to do so.

The Navigation Pane

The Navigation pane provides three primary methods for locating a search term in a document: headings, pages, and results.

Search terms are entered here. →

> **Navigation** ▼ ✕
>
> cold   ✕ ▾
>
> Result 1 of 6   ▲ ▼
>
> Headings   Pages   **Results**
>
> to the throat, and they may get blocked when a **cold** causes inflammation. This traps fluid inside
>
> Often caused by the same viruses as the common **cold**, pinkeye spreads rapidly in schools and day

The arrows allow you to search up and down the document.

▸ Headings: The Headings option will list any heading styles in your document. If the search term appears within a heading, it will be highlighted. Click a heading to jump to that part of the document.

▸ Pages: The Pages option displays thumbnails of pages where the search term appears; clicking a thumbnail jumps the document to that page.

▸ Results: The Results option displays the search term in context; clicking one of the results jumps the document to that page.

≡ View→Show→Navigation Pane │ Ctrl + F

Advanced Find and Wildcard Characters

Word can conduct specialized searches. By default, the Find tool does not filter results based on capitalization or whole words only. To filter results based on capitalization or whole words, you can use Advanced Find. In addition, you can use wildcard characters when you're not sure exactly what you're looking for. For example, if you don't know exactly how a name in your document is spelled, but you know parts of it, you can search for it using wildcard characters in place of the parts you don't know. The most common wildcard characters are the question mark (?) and the asterisk (*). The question mark can be used in place of a single unknown character, while the asterisk can be used in place of any number of characters.

≡ Home→Editing→Find menu button ▾→Advanced Find 🔍

Bookmarks

You can assign a bookmark name to text or other objects in a document. Once a bookmark is set up, you can easily navigate to it by choosing the desired bookmark name from the Bookmark dialog box. A bookmark name can be up to 40 characters, including letters and numbers, but it must begin with a letter and cannot contain spaces or symbols.

≡ Insert→Links→Bookmark 🔖

The Split Window

Imagine you want to check whether the executive summary of a report accurately reflects the report's content. Splitting the window is the answer. You can view the executive summary in one window and scroll through the rest of the document in the other window. Once you've applied the split, you can click and drag the split bar to adjust the height of each window.

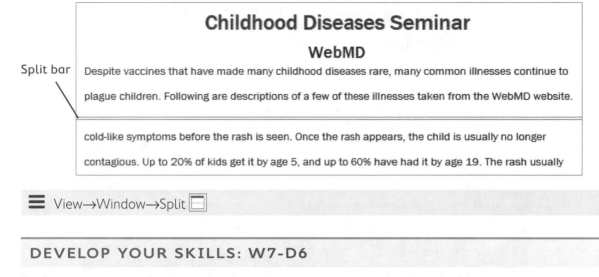

Split bar

Childhood Diseases Seminar

WebMD

Despite vaccines that have made many childhood diseases rare, many common illnesses continue to plague children. Following are descriptions of a few of these illnesses taken from the WebMD website.

cold-like symptoms before the rash is seen. Once the rash appears, the child is usually no longer contagious. Up to 20% of kids get it by age 5, and up to 60% have had it by age 19. The rash usually

☰ View→Window→Split 🔲

DEVELOP YOUR SKILLS: W7-D6

In this exercise, you will navigate in a long document using several techniques: Navigation pane, bookmarks, and split window.

1. Save your file as: **W7-D6-SickKidsRevised**
2. Choose **View→Show→Navigation Pane** and enter **cold** as your search term.

Tip! *You can also open the Navigation pane by pressing* Ctrl + F *.*

3. Choose the **Results** option at the top of the Navigation pane and click the fourth result, **Common Cold**.

   The document jumps to that location. Notice that the term is highlighted in yellow wherever it appears.

4. Click the **Headings** option at the top of the Navigation pane.

   If the document contains heading styles, they are listed here. The headings where the search term appears are highlighted in yellow.

5. Click the **Ear Infection** heading to jump to that part of the document and notice again that the search term is highlighted in yellow.

6. Click the **Pages** option at the top of the pane to see thumbnails of the pages that contain the search term.

7. Click the second thumbnail to jump to that page.

8. Click the up and down arrows in the upper-right corner of the Navigation pane to scroll through all occurrences of the term.

9. Close the Navigation pane.

Use Bookmarks

10. Scroll to page 4 and select **Symptoms** in the heading titled *Symptoms You Should Never Ignore*.

11. Choose **Insert→Links→Bookmark** 🔖, type **Symptoms** in the Bookmark Name field, and click **Add**.

12. Press ⌈Ctrl⌉+⌈Home⌉ or scroll up to move to the top of the document.

13. Choose **Insert→Links→Bookmark** 🔖.

14. *Symptoms* is already selected, so click **Go To** to jump to the bookmarked text and then click **Close**.

Split the Window

15. Choose **View→Window→Split** ▭.

    A split bar appears across the window. On the right-hand side of the screen are two scroll bars, one for the top window and one for the bottom window.

16. In the top window, scroll to the top of page 1; in the bottom window, scroll to the top of page 3.

    You can also split the window into different proportions, allowing more text to show on one side.

17. Position the mouse pointer on the split bar; when it changes to a double-headed arrow, drag the **split bar** up about an inch.

18. Double-click the **split bar** to return to one window.

19. Save and close the file.

Working with Large Tables

If you're working with large tables, making them user-friendly is important. It should be easy for the reader to scan a table and get information. If possible, columns should be wide enough to prevent text from wrapping within the cells. Adding white space within the table makes the text appear less dense. Repeating column headers from one page to the next is essential for the reader to understand the meaning of the data. Sizing a table to best fit the page adds to its readability. Adding a caption helps clarify the table topic.

≡ Table Tools→Layout→Cell Size dialog box launcher ⌐

≡ Table Tools→Layout→Alignment→Cell Margins ⊞

DEVELOP YOUR SKILLS: W7-D7

In this exercise, you will modify a large table, making it easier to read by widening columns where text is wrapping, adding white space within cells, and repeating column headers from page to page. You'll also add a caption to the table.

1. Open **W7-D7-SeminarAttendees** from your **Word Chapter 7** folder and save it as:
   W7-D7-SeminarAttendeesRevised

   The text is wrapping in several columns, making it difficult to read. At the same time, the table already spans the width of the page. Rotating this document to landscape (horizontal) orientation and changing the table width should solve the problem.

2. Choose **Layout→Page Setup→Orientation** 📄 and then choose **Landscape**.

3. Choose **Table Tools→Layout→Cell Size dialog box launcher** ⌐.

4. In the Table Properties dialog box, click the **Table** tab, if necessary.

5. Change Preferred Width to **9"** and click **OK**.

   Adding white space within the cells will add to the table's readability.

6. Choose **Table Tools→Layout→Alignment→Cell Margins** ▣.

7. In the Table Options dialog box, change the top and bottom cell margins to **0.05** and click **OK**.

8. If necessary, position the insertion point in the first row of the table.

   This is the row that will repeat at the top of each page.

9. Choose **Table Tools→Layout→Cell Size dialog box launcher** ▣ and click the **Row** tab.

10. Place a checkmark in the **Repeat as header row at the top of each page** checkbox and click **OK**.

11. Scroll down to see the header row at the top of page 2.

    Now you will add a caption to the table.

12. Choose **References→Captions→Insert Caption** ▣ and then click the **New Label** button toward the bottom of the dialog box.

13. In the New Label dialog box, type **Childhood Diseases Seminar Attendees** and click **OK**; click **OK** again to close the Caption dialog box.

14. Scroll to the bottom of the document to see the caption.

    Captions are typically numbered, but because this is the only table in the document, numbering is not necessary.

15. If necessary, position the insertion point at the end of the caption and then tap ⌷Backspace⌷ twice to delete the number.

16. Save and close the file; exit Word.

Self-Assessment

Check your knowledge of this chapter's key concepts and skills using the Self-Assessment in your ebook or online (eLab course or Student Resource Center).

Reinforce Your Skills

Create a New Members Handout

Kids for Change wants new members to understand the importance of its motto, Think Globally, Act Locally. One of the members researched the origins of the phrase, and now you've been asked to format the document to make it more engaging. In this exercise, you will use styles to add appeal. You will begin by testing several different styles to see what you like best.

1. Start Word, open **W7-R1-GlobalLocal** from your **Word Chapter 7** folder, and save it as: **W7-R1-GlobalLocalRevised**

2. Position the insertion point in **Introduction** at the top of page 1.

   You will apply a built-in style first.

3. Choose **Home→Styles** and in the Styles gallery, choose **Heading 1**.

   Now you will create a style by example.

4. Select the **Definition** heading for the next paragraph.

5. Choose **Home→Font dialog box launcher** .

6. In the Font dialog box, choose **Arial Black**, **14 pt**, and **Small Caps**, and then click **OK**.

7. Choose **Home→Font→Font Color menu button** ▾ and choose **Brown, Accent 1, Darker 25%** from the color pallet.

8. Choose **Home→Styles dialog box launcher**.

9. Click the **New Style** button at the bottom of the task pane.

10. Complete the information at the top of the dialog box:
    - Name: **MyStyle1**
    - Style Type: **Paragraph**
    - Style Based On: **Normal**
    - Style for Following Paragraph: **Normal**

    Your formatting has been copied into the Formatting area of the dialog box.

11. If necessary, click the **Add to the Styles gallery** checkbox and click **OK**.

    The style name now appears in the Styles gallery on the Ribbon and in the Styles task pane. Next, you will create a style by definition.

12. Scroll down and position the insertion point in the heading, **Origin in Town Planning**.

13. Click the **New Style** button at the bottom of the task pane.

14. Complete the information at the top of the dialog box:
    - Name: **MyStyle2**
    - Style Type: **Paragraph**
    - Style Based On: **Normal**
    - Style for Following Paragraph: **Normal**

15. In the Formatting area, choose **Century Schoolbook**, **14 pt**, and center alignment, and then click **OK**.

16. Scroll down and position the insertion point in the heading for the last paragraph, *Origins of the Phrase*, and apply the built-in **Heading 2** style.

Modify a Style

After scanning the different styles, you've decided to modify the Heading 1 style.

17. Position the insertion point in the **Introduction** heading at the top of page 1.

18. Hover the mouse pointer over the *Heading 1* style in the Styles task pane, click the **menu** button ▾, and choose **Modify**.

19. Click the **Format** button at the bottom of the dialog box and choose **Font**.

20. Choose **Bold** in the Font Style field, click the **menu** button ▾ in the **Font Color** field, and choose **Brown, Accent 1, Darker 25%**.

21. Check the **Small Caps** checkbox and click **OK**.

22. Click **OK** in the Modify Style dialog box as well.

Notice that the modifications you made are reflected in the style name in the Styles gallery. Now you need to decide on a style for the subheadings. You will modify the Heading 2 style.

23. Scroll to the last page and click in the heading **Origins of the Phrase**. Hover the mouse pointer over *Heading 2* in the Styles task pane, click the **menu** button ▾, and choose **Modify**.

24. In the Formatting area, click the **Bold** button, click the **menu** button ▾ in the color field, and choose **Brown, Accent 1, Darker 25%**, and then click **OK**.

You are happy with the Heading 2 style, so now you'll apply it to the other subheadings.

25. Scroll up, position the insertion point in the heading **Origin in Town Planning**, and then click the **Heading 2** style in the Styles task pane.

26. Scroll up, position the insertion point in the **Definition** heading, and then apply the **Heading 2** style.

Because you won't be using MyStyle1 and MyStyle2, you will delete them from the Styles task pane.

27. Hover the mouse pointer over *MyStyle1* in the task pane, click the **menu** button ▾, and choose **Delete MyStyle1**.

28. When the message appears confirming the deletion, click **Yes**.

The style was also removed from the Styles gallery on the Ribbon.

29. Use the same technique to delete MyStyle2.

30. Close the Styles task pane and then save and close the file.

Help Kids Cultivate Social and Emotional Skills

Many educational organizations have developed training programs to help teachers work with children in developing social and emotional skills. Kids for Change members are evaluating various programs to determine which program they would like to see implemented in their local schools. In this exercise, you will customize bullet and number formats, use navigation techniques to quickly move around long documents, and format a large table to enhance its readability.

1. Open **W7-R2-SocLearningforKids** from your **Word Chapter 7** folder and save it as: **W7-R2-SocLearningforKidsRevised**

2. Scroll down and position the insertion point in the first bulleted list on page 1.

3. Choose **Home→Paragraph→Bullets menu button** ▼ and choose **Define New Bullet**.

4. Click the **Symbol** button.

5. Choose the **Webdings** font; scroll to the top of the gallery, if necessary; choose the character shown (location may vary); and click **OK** twice.

6. Position the insertion point in the next bulleted list that starts at the bottom of page 1.

7. Choose **Home→Paragraph→Bullets menu button** ▼ and choose the same bullet, which appears in the Recently Used Bullets, Bullet Library, and Document Bullets categories.

8. Use the same technique to change the bullets in the last bulleted list at the bottom of page 3.

   Now you will remove the new bullet so the next student who uses your computer will have the same experience.

9. Choose **Home→Paragraph→Bullets menu button** ▼, right-click the new bullet in the Bullet Library area, and choose **Remove**.

Apply Numbers to a List

10. Scroll up, select the list that appears below the heading *The 12 Tools* at the top of page 3, and choose **Home→Paragraph→Numbering**.

    Now you'll choose a different number format for the list.

11. Choose **Home→Paragraph→Numbering menu button** ▼ and then choose the **Number Alignment: Left** format with parentheses under Numbering Library (location may vary).

    Notice that the last three numbers are left-aligned with the numbers above. They should be right-aligned.

12. Choose **Home→Paragraph→Numbering menu button** ▼ and then choose **Define New Number Format**.

13. Click the **menu** button ▼ in the Alignment field, choose **Right**, and click **OK**.

    Notice how the numbers are now aligned.

Navigate in a Document

You know that you'll often have to navigate through this document as team members have questions about its contents, so you want to take some time to practice quick navigation techniques.

14. Press ⌐Ctrl⌐+⌐F⌐ to open the Navigation pane and then type **toolbox** in the search field.

15. Click the down-pointing arrow at the top of the Navigation pane several times to jump to the term.

16. Make sure the **Results** category at the top of the pane is active; scroll down and click the last result in the list to jump to that location.

17. Click the **Headings** category at the top of the pane and click **Dovetail Learning** to jump to that location.

18. Close the Navigation pane.

Insert a Bookmark

If there is a section of the document that you will return to frequently, using a bookmark provides a way to locate it easily.

19. Double-click **Dovetail** in the heading line.

20. Choose **Insert→Links→Bookmark**, type **Dovetail** in the Bookmark Name field, and click **Add**.

21. Press ⌐Ctrl⌐+⌐Home⌐ or scroll up to move to the top of the document.

22. Choose **Insert→Links→Bookmark**.

23. Click **Go To** in the Bookmark dialog box to jump to the bookmark and then click Close.

Split the Window

Now you will compare the mission statements for Wings for Kids and Dovetail Learning.

24. Choose **View→Window→Split** ⊟ and in the top window scroll to the top of page 1 until the mission statement is visible.

25. In the bottom window, scroll until the mission statement for Dovetail Learning is visible.

    This is an easy way to compare two different parts of a document.

26. Double-click the split bar in the middle of the window to return to one window.

27. Save and close the file.

Work with a Large Table

You will use the Members mailing list to send members the document about social learning. In preparation for that, you will now enhance the table by making it more readable.

28. Open **W7-R2-Members** and save it as: **W7-R2-MembersRevised**

29. Choose **Table Tools→Layout→Alignment→Cell Margins**, change the top and bottom cell margins to **0.08**, and click **OK**.

    The table is now spilling over to the next page. You will repeat the header row so it will also appear at the top of the next page.

30. If necessary, position the insertion point in the header row of the table.

31. Choose **Table Tools→Layout→Cell Size dialog box launcher**.

32. Click the **Row** tab, check **Repeat as header row at the top of each page**, and click **OK**.

33. Scroll down to see the header row at the top of the second page.

34. Save and close the file.

REINFORCE YOUR SKILLS: W7-R3

Format a Report on Childhood Obesity

Kids for Change is sponsoring a seminar on childhood obesity, presented by representatives from the World Health Organization and the Centers for Disease Control and Prevention. The organizations have already submitted background reading for the seminar. In this exercise, you will format the document to make the paragraphs and tables more engaging. You will also use techniques for navigating a long document.

1. Open **W7-R3-Obesity** from your **Word Chapter 7** folder and save it as: **W7-R3-ObesityRevised**

2. If the Styles task pane is not open, choose **Home→Styles dialog box launcher** to open it.

3. If necessary, position the insertion point in the heading at the top of the document, and then choose the **Title** style from the task pane.

4. Scroll down to page 2, position the insertion point in the heading **CDC Introduction**, and apply the **Title** style.

5. Scroll back to the top of page 1 and position the insertion point in the first subtitle, which begins with *What can be done*.

6. Apply the **Subtitle** style from the Styles task pane and then apply **Subtitle** to the remaining headings:
    - **General recommendations**
    - **Societal recommendations**
    - **What Needs to Be Done?**
    - **What Can Parents Do?**

    You decide that the subtitles are not very appealing, so you will modify the Subtitle style.

7. Position the insertion point in the first subtitle at the top of page 1.

8. Hover the mouse pointer over **Subtitle** in the Styles task pane, click the **menu** button ▼, and choose **Modify** from the menu.

9. In the Formatting area of the dialog box, click the **Italic** button and change the font size to **16 pt**, and then click **OK**.

10. Scroll through the document and notice the subtitles are updated throughout the document.

11. Scroll to the bottom of page 2 and notice the subtitle at the bottom of the page.

    It should be moved to the top of the next page.

12. Position the insertion point in front of the subtitle and press Ctrl + Enter to insert a page break and move the subtitle to the top of the next page.

13. Close the Styles task pane.

Customize Bullet Formats

14. Place the insertion point in the first item of the bulleted list on page 1, choose **Home→Paragraph→Bullets menu button** ▼, and choose **Define New Bullet**.

15. Click the **Symbol** button in the Define New Bullet dialog box.

16. In the Symbol dialog box, choose the **Wingdings 2** font, scroll to about the middle of the list and choose the symbol shown, and then click **OK** twice.

17. Scroll down to the next bulleted list and click the first item.

18. Choose **Home→Paragraph→Bullets menu button** ▼ and choose the same button style.

19. Use the same technique to reformat the last bulleted list.

Navigate in a Long Document

20. Scroll to the top of page 2 and select **CDC** in the heading.

21. Choose **Insert→Links→Bookmark**, type **CDC** in the Bookmark Name field, and click **Add**.

22. Press Ctrl + Home or scroll up to move to the top of the document.

23. Choose **Insert→Links→Bookmark**, click the **Go To** button to jump to the bookmark, and then close the dialog box.

24. Press Ctrl + F to open the Navigation pane and then type **WHO** in the search field.

    The document scrolls to the first occurrence of WHO.

25. Click the insertion point in the page and then close the Navigation pane.

26. Choose **View→Window→Split** and scroll in the bottom pane until the *CDC Introduction* heading appears.

    This is a great way to compare different parts of the same document without opening a separate window.

27. Double-click the **split bar** to return to a single window.

28. Save and close the file.

Work with a Long Table

Kids for Change has scheduled its programs and seminar topics well in advance, so it has plenty of time to coordinate the events. However, the table is not easy to read, and it's difficult to locate data. You will format the table to make it easier to work with.

29. Open **W7-R3-Programs** from your **Word Chapter 7** folder and save it as: **W7-R3-ProgramsRevised**

30. Position the insertion point in the table and choose **Table Tools→Layout→Alignment→Cell Margins**.

31. Change the top and bottom margins to **0.08** and click **OK**.

    The increased margins caused the table to flow to the next page. Next, you will set up the header row to repeat on every page.

32. If necessary, position the insertion point in the header row at the top of the table.

33. Choose **Table Tools→Layout→Cell Size dialog box launcher**.

34. If necessary, click the **Row** tab, and then check **Repeat as header row at the top of each page** and click **OK**.

35. Scroll to page 2 to see the repeating header row.

36. Save and close the file.

Apply Your Skills

APPLY YOUR SKILLS: W7-A1

Multitask with Styles

When planning a corporate event for a client, Universal Corporate Events representatives are often challenged with juggling details ranging from managing hundreds of hotel reservations and travel accommodations to organizing meals and side trips. Your manager has asked you to research the concept of multitasking and prepare a report on your findings. Your content has been approved, and it is now time to format the document to make it appealing to the reader. In this exercise, you will enhance the document by formatting with styles.

1. Open **W7-A1-Multitasking** from your **Word Chapter 7** folder and save it as:
   `W7-A1-MultitaskingRevised`

   You will start by creating a style by example.

2. Select the **Introduction** heading at the top of the document, apply the **Stencil** font, **16 pt**, and center the heading.

3. Open the Styles task pane and click the **New Style** button.

4. Follow these guidelines to complete the top part of the dialog box:
   • Name: `IntroStyle`
   • Style Type: **Paragraph**
   • Style Base On: **Normal**
   • Style for Following Paragraph: **Normal**

5. If necessary, check the **Add to the Styles gallery** checkbox at the bottom of the dialog box and click **OK**.

   Notice that the new style appears in the Styles gallery on the Ribbon and in the Styles task pane. Next, you will apply a built-in style and then modify it.

6. Position the insertion point in the next heading, **The multitasking myth**, and apply the **Heading 2** style.

7. Hover the mouse pointer over the *Heading 2* style in the Styles task pane, click the **menu** button ▾, and choose **Modify**.

8. Click the **Format** button at the bottom of the dialog box and choose **Font**.

9. In the Font dialog box, set the font to **Bold**, **14 pt**, and the color to **Black, Text 1**.

10. Check the **Small Caps** checkbox and then click **OK** twice.

11. Apply the modified Heading 2 style to the rest of the subtitles in the document:
    • **You're not really multitasking**
    • **It's slowing you down**
    • **You're making mistakes**
    • **You're not actually good at it**

    You decide to change the Introduction *heading so it blends better with the subheadings.*

12. Position the insertion point in the **Introduction** heading and choose the **Title** style from the Styles task pane.

13. You don't plan to use the IntroStyle anymore, so using the Styles task pane, delete the style and then close the task pane.

14. Click the **Home** tab and notice that the IntroStyle has been removed from the Styles gallery on the Ribbon.

15. Save and close the file.

APPLY YOUR SKILLS: W7-A2

Plan a Bicycle Trip in the Loire Valley

A client of Universal Corporate Events is planning a bicycling trip in the Loire Valley of France as a reward for Employee of the Year winners in each of its branch offices. Universal Corporate Events is providing a sample itinerary for the client to review. In this exercise, you will polish the sample itinerary for the trip. The client has also requested a list of châteaux in the Loire Valley, so you will prepare that in a table and format it.

1. Open **W7-A2-LoireTour** from your **Word Chapter 7** folder and save it as: **W7-A2-LoireTourRevised**

2. Position the insertion point in the first bulleted item and define a new bullet using this Wingdings 3 symbol.

Now you'll apply the new bullet to the remaining bulleted items.

3. Position the insertion point in the next bulleted item and choose **Home→Paragraph→Bullets menu button ▾**.

The new bullet appears in the Recently Used Bullets category.

4. Click the bullet, scroll through the document, and see that the bullet was applied to the rest of the bulleted items.

Next, you will use nonbreaking spaces to keep a name together on a line.

5. Scroll to the second-to-last line in the *Day 3* paragraph, position the insertion point after *Leonardo*, and delete the space.

6. Choose **Insert→Symbols→Symbol** and choose **More Symbols**.

7. Choose **Nonbreaking Space** in the Special Characters tab and finish inserting the character.

Remember the keystrokes for a nonbreaking space: Ctrl + Shift + Space .

8. Position the insertion point after *da*, delete the space, and then press Ctrl + Shift + Space to insert another nonbreaking space.

9. If necessary, display formatting marks and notice the symbol used for nonbreaking spaces.

Navigate in a Long Document

Next, you will insert a bookmark for navigating in the document.

10. Create a bookmark for the text *Day 6*, using **Day6** as the bookmark name.

11. Move to the top of the document and then use the Bookmark feature to jump to Day 6.

    Now you will locate a term in the document.

12. Open the Navigation pane, type **Day 1** in the search field, and position the insertion point in the **Day 1** page.

13. If necessary, click the **Headings** button at the top of the Navigation pane; click the **Day 4** heading to jump to that location and then close the Navigation pane.

    Next you will split the window so you can compare different parts of the document.

14. Choose **View→Window→Split** and then scroll the top window to **Day 1** and the bottom window to **Day 6**.

15. Double-click the **split bar** to return to one window.

16. Save and close the file.

Work with a Large Table

You will make some modifications to a table to improve its readability. You'll begin by increasing the cell margins and then repeat the header row for each page.

17. Open **W7-A2-Chateaux** from your **Word Chapter 7** folder and save it as: **W7-A2-ChateauxRevised**

18. Position the insertion point in the table, choose **Table Tools→Layout→Alignment→Cell Margins**, and change the top and bottom margins to **0.08**.

19. With the insertion point in the first row of the table, choose **Table Tools→Layout→Cell Size dialog box launcher**.

20. Use the **Row** tab in the Table Properties dialog box to repeat the header row on each page.

21. Scroll to the top of page 2 to see the repeated header row.

22. Save and close the file.

APPLY YOUR SKILLS: W7-A3

Prepare Cuban Travel Information for a Client

Universal Corporate Events has asked you to research information about travel to Cuba, and your research has been approved. In this exercise, you will format the document so it can be presented to clients.

1. Open **W7-A3-CubaTravel** from your **Word Chapter 7** folder and save it as: **W7-A3-CubaTravelRevised**

2. Apply the Heading 1 style to the *Cuba Background* heading at the top of the document.

    Hint: If necessary, display the Styles task pane.

3. Apply the Heading 2 style to the headings *U.S.–Cuba Relations*, *U.S. Assistance to Cuba,* and *Bilateral Economic Relations*.

4. Scroll down to the *Outdoor Activity* heading and apply the Heading 1 style.

5. Scroll down to the *Top-Rated Cuban Tourist Attractions* heading and apply the Heading 1 style.

   Next, you will modify the heading styles.

6. Position the insertion point in the **Cuba Background** heading and modify the Heading 1 style by changing the font color to **Brown, Accent 3**.

7. Scroll to page 3 and notice that the other Heading 1 styles were updated.

8. Position the insertion point in the **U.S.–Cuba Relations** heading and modify the Heading 2 style to use the font color **Brown, Accent 3**.

9. Close the Styles task pane and then scroll down to see that the other Heading 2 headings are updated.

10. Scroll to page 3, position the insertion point in the first bulleted item, and define a new bullet using this Wingdings symbol character.

Format a Table for Readability

11. Scroll to the table and change the top and bottom cell margins to **0.08**.

12. Repeat the header row on all pages.

    Now you will add a caption to the table.

13. Scroll to the bottom of the table and position the insertion point on the first blank line below the table.

14. Use the New Label dialog box to insert **Excerpt from PlanetWare Website** as the table caption.

    Notice the number 1 appears at the end of the caption. Because there is only one table in the document, the number is not necessary.

15. Delete the number **1** at the end of the caption.

16. Save and close the file; exit Word.

Project Grader

If your class is using eLab (labyrinthelab.com), you may upload your completed Project Grader assignments for automatic grading. You may complete these projects even if your class doesn't use eLab, though you will not be able to upload your work.

PROJECT GRADER: W7-P1

Using Themes, Styles, and Other Tools

This project combines learning objectives from chapters 6 and 7. In this exercise, you will apply formatting to an existing document by using tools that simplify formatting tasks.

1. Download and open your Project Grader starting file.
   - *Using eLab:* Download **W7_P1_eStart** from the Assignments page. You *must* start with this file or your work cannot be automatically graded.
   - *Not using eLab:* Open **W7_P1_Start** from your **Word Chapter 7** folder.

2. Use these guidelines to insert a Quick Part:
   - Quick Part to insert: **Document Property, Title**
   - Insert it in the empty paragraph at the top of the document.
   - After insertion, the title *The History of Board Games* should be displayed.

3. Insert the **Semaphore** cover page and make these changes to the fields:
   - Date: Enter today's date.
   - Document Subtitle: **Games That Changed the World**
   - Author: Enter your name.
   - Company Name: **Taylor Games**
   - Company Address: Delete the Address field.

4. Apply the **Metropolitan** theme.

5. Apply the **Blue Warm** theme color.

6. At the top of page 2, apply the **Title** style to **The History of Board Games** Quick Part text.

7. Apply the **Basic (Stylish)** style set (the fourth option in the Style Sets list).

8. On page 5, apply the **checkmark** ✓ bullet style (located in the Bullets Library) to the five games below the *Other Famous Games in History* heading.

9. On **page 3**, insert a bookmark named **Mansion** in front of *The Mansion of Happiness (1843)* heading.

10. Save your document.
    - *Using eLab:* Save it to your **Word Chapter 7** folder as **W7_P1_eSubmission** and attach the file to your eLab assignment for grading.
    - *Not using eLab:* Save it to your **Word Chapter 7** folder as: **W7_P1_Submission**

History of the Chevrolet Corvette

This project combines learning objectives from chapters 6 and 7. In this project, you will use formatting tools and other features to enhance the Corvette history document.

1. Download and open your Project Grader starting file.
   - *Using eLab:* Download **W7_P2_eStart** from the Assignments page. You *must* start with this file or your work cannot be automatically graded.
   - *Not using eLab:* Open **W7_P2_Start** from your **Word Chapter 7** folder.

2. Use these guidelines to insert a Quick Part:
   - Quick Part to insert: **Document Property, Title**
   - Insert it in the empty paragraph at the top of the document.
   - After insertion, the title *History of the Chevrolet Corvette* should be displayed.

3. Insert the **Ion (Dark)** cover page and make these changes to the fields:
   - Year: Enter the current year
   - Document Subtitle: `Eight Generations`
   - Author: Enter your name
   - Company Name: Change *Car* to `Cars`.
   - Address: Delete the Address field.

4. Apply the **Berlin** theme.

5. Apply the **Red Violet** theme color.

6. At the top of **page 2**, apply the **Title** style to the **History of the Chevrolet Corvette** Quick Part text.

7. Apply the **Lines (Simple)** style set (the twelfth style on the Built-In style set list).

8. On **page 7**, insert a bookmark named **C5** in front of the *Fifth generation (C5; 1997–2004)* heading.

9. On **pages 7** and **8**, change the bullets in all 20 of the bulleted paragraphs to the **checkmark** ☑ bullet located in the Bullets Library.

10. At the end of the text on **page 12**, insert the **Registered Sign** ® just to the right of the phrase *Registered Trademark*. The symbol should be between the *k* in *Trademark* and the period at the end of the sentence.

11. Save your presentation.
    - *Using eLab:* Save it to your **Word Chapter 7** folder as `P7_P2_eSubmission` and attach the file to your eLab assignment for grading.
    - *Not using eLab:* Save it to your **Word Chapter 7** folder as: `P7_P2_Submission`

✈ Extend Your Skills

These exercises challenge you to think critically and apply your new skills in a real-world setting. You will be evaluated on your ability to follow directions, completeness, creativity, and the use of proper grammar and mechanics. Save files to your chapter folder. Submit assignments as directed.

W7-E1 · That's the Way I See It

You have just started your own personal training business and will advertise your business with an informative brochure (maximum two pages) to be distributed through local businesses in the community. Decide on a name for your business. Include a mission statement and a description of your background qualifications. Create a bulleted list of the services you offer and another bulleted list of the benefits your clients will enjoy. Customize the bullets using a symbol of your choice. Use Word's built-in heading styles to make your brochure professional looking and easy to read. Create a table listing classes you offer, short descriptions of the classes, and the days and times the classes will meet. Apply the table style of your choice and increase the cell margins to add white space. Don't forget your contact information. Feel free to use an Internet search to gather ideas to assist you with content. Save your file as: **W7-E1-Exercise**

W7-E2 · Be Your Own Boss

You want to increase your customer base at Blue Jean Landscaping, so you will create a one- or two-page flyer advertising your business. Write an "About Us" paragraph describing the services you offer and include a mission statement. Also, write a paragraph or two about your background qualifications. Include another paragraph about the pesticide safety techniques you employ at your company. Blue Jean Landscaping saves customers money by having them provide the labor for their projects. Create a bulleted list of the physical tasks customers will accomplish to take advantage of your cost-cutting offer. Create a table listing classes you offer, such as "How to Plant Roses," to educate your customers in the skills they need to provide the labor for their gardens. Use built-in heading styles to section off the different parts of the flyer and modify the styles to suit your taste. Customize the bullets for your bulleted list, format the table with a table style, and add white space to the table by increasing cell margins. If necessary, search the Internet for information about landscaping companies to help you with the content. Save the file as: **W7-E2-Landscape**

W7-E3 · Demonstrate Proficiency

As the owner of Stormy BBQ, you are proud of serving only locally grown, organic vegetables and free-range, farm-raised pork and beef. Create a two-page flyer to distribute to customers at the cash register. Include a mission statement and a paragraph or two describing the history of Stormy BBQ, and include one or two customer testimonials. Create a bulleted list of the benefits of eating locally produced food. Insert a menu in the form of a table that spans two pages and add a caption to the table. Use custom styles that you create from scratch to section off the topics in your flyer and create custom bullets for your list. Apply a table style to your menu, add white space for ease of reading, and repeat the header row at the top of page 2. Conduct an Internet search if you need help with the menu or benefits of the healthy food you serve. Save the file as: **W7-E3-BBQ**

8 | Organizing Long Documents

Plowing through a long document can be challenging for the reader if it is not well organized. Word offers several great tools for organizing documents. A table of contents and an index help readers locate specific topics and terms. Headers and footers display important information, such as page numbers and chapter names. In this chapter, you will work with these tools, organizing long documents and making them more accessible to the reader.

LEARNING OBJECTIVES

- ▸ Create a table of contents
- ▸ Work with multiple headers and footers
- ▸ Insert an index
- ▸ Keep text together
- ▸ Add a watermark

Project: Organizing a Long Document

The Raritan Clinic East Policies and Procedures Manual contains principles and guidelines adopted by the clinic to reach its long-term goals. It influences all major decisions and activities in day-to-day operations. You recently accepted a position in the human resources department at Raritan Clinic. You have been tasked with reviewing the current Policies and Procedures Manual, and you have identified numerous "finishing" features that need to be added to the manual to make it easier to use. By adding a table of contents, index, and headers and footers, you believe the document will be more user-friendly.

Creating a Table of Contents

Readers appreciate a good table of contents. It outlines the document and adds a professional appearance. And if the document is electronic, the table of contents links provide Internet-like navigation.

The Table of Contents (TOC) feature automatically builds a table of contents by gathering up the headings that are formatted with heading styles. The headings in the TOC are organized in the sequence in which they appear in the document. In addition, TOC styles are applied that correspond to the heading levels. The styles then format the table entries. For example, Heading 2 entries are subordinate to Heading 1 entries. You can automatically update a table of contents created with the built-in heading styles.

You can apply a predesigned table of contents format from the Table of Contents gallery, or you can create a custom table of contents, which gives you more control over the formatting.

≡ References→Table of Contents→Table of Contents 📄

Creating a Page for the Table of Contents

In most documents, the table of contents appears either at the beginning of the document or just after the title page in documents containing a title page. Because the table of contents is often created after the document is complete, you may need to create a new page to hold the table.

When headers and footers or other page-level formatting such as page numbering appear in a document, it is better to use a section break to create a page to hold the table of contents. This allows flexibility, such as numbering the table of contents page(s) with Roman numerals (i, ii, iii) and the rest of the document with Arabic numerals (1, 2, 3).

Table of Contents Links

A table of contents is inserted as a large field composed of various table entries. Each entry within the table functions as a hyperlink. You can use the links to quickly navigate in the document.

Table of Contents
Mission Statement ....
Scope of Services Current Document Ctrl+Click to follow link ....
Patient Management Procedures ....

In this exercise, you will open the Raritan Clinic East Policies and Procedures Manual and review its heading styles. Then you will create a table of contents and use the links to navigate in the document. Finally, you will remove the table of contents.

1. Start Word, open **W8-D1-RaritanP&P** from your **Word Chapter 8** folder, and save it as: **W8-D1-RaritanP&PRevised**

2. Choose **Home→Styles dialog box launcher** 🔲.

3. Scroll to the first page of the body of the document and position the insertion point in the heading *Mission Statement*.

   Notice that Heading 1 in the Styles task pane is highlighted, indicating that it is the style used to format the heading.

4. Position the insertion point in several additional headings on page 2.

   Notice that both Heading 1 and Heading 2 styles are on the page.

5. Close the Styles task pane and then position the insertion point in front of the heading *Mission Statement*.

   Now you will insert a section break to create a blank page for the table of contents.

6. Choose **Layout→Page Setup→Breaks** 🔲 and then choose **Next Page**.

7. If necessary, display formatting marks; then, scroll up and position the insertion point to the right of the paragraph symbol, just in front of the section break, and tap [Enter].

8. Choose **References→Table of Contents→Table of Contents** 🔲 and then choose **Automatic Table 2** from the gallery.

9. Scroll up and review the table of contents.

   You can see that the headings in the document are used as the table of contents entries.

Navigate Using Hyperlinks

10. Hover the mouse pointer over the *Initial Diagnostic Evaluation* entry in the table and notice the pop-up message.

11. Press [Ctrl] and click the link.

    Word jumps to that heading in the document.

12. Scroll up to the top of the table of contents and click the table to select it.

13. Click the **Table of Contents** 🔲 button in the upper-left corner and choose **Remove Table of Contents** at the bottom of the menu.

14. Save the file.

The Update Table Button

When you make changes to headings or move text in a document, you need to update the table of contents. The Update Table button makes this task easy. Whenever the insertion point is anywhere in the table of contents, two buttons appear in the upper-left corner of the table.

The Table of Contents button displays the Table of Contents gallery, including a command to remove the table.

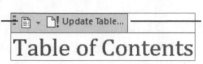

The Update Table button updates the table of contents with the latest changes.

When you click the Update Table button, a dialog box presents options for updating page numbers only or the entire table. Choose the page numbers option if you have been adding text but haven't changed any headings.

Tip! *You can right-click a table of contents and choose Update Field from the menu.*

≣ References→Table of Contents→Update Table | F9

The Table of Contents Dialog Box

The Table of Contents gallery provides the fastest method for creating a table of contents, but if you wish to have more control over the formatting of your table, you can use the Table of Contents dialog box. When you use the dialog box, you must also manually add the title that precedes the table. In addition, there are no Table of Contents or Update Table buttons at the top of the table as there are for a table generated from the Table of Contents gallery. To update a manual table of contents, you can use the F9 shortcut keystroke.

View the video "Create a Custom Table of Contents."

DEVELOP YOUR SKILLS: W8-D2

In this exercise, you will use the Table of Contents dialog box to insert a custom table of contents. Then you will edit a heading and update the table of contents.

1. Save your file as **W8-D2-RaritanP&PRevised** and, if necessary, display formatting marks.

   The insertion point should be just to the left of the section break at the top of the blank table of contents page, before the paragraph mark.

2. Tap Enter to create a new, blank line.

   The blank line will hold the title. Next you will reformat its paragraph symbol with your desired title formatting.

3. Follow these steps to format and add the table title:

Ⓐ Select this paragraph symbol.

Ⓑ Choose **Home→Font→Clear All Formatting**.

Ⓒ Change the font size to **14 pt**.

4. Type `Table of Contents` and tap ⌨Enter⌨.

5. Choose **References→Table of Contents→Table of Contents** 📑.

6. Choose **Custom Table of Contents** at the bottom of the gallery to open the Table of Contents dialog box.

7. Follow these steps to generate a table of contents:

Ⓐ Make sure these checkboxes are checked.

Ⓑ Make sure dots are chosen here.

Ⓒ Choose **Formal** as the format.

Ⓓ Click **OK**.

8. Scroll to the bottom of the table and delete the extra paragraph symbol.

Edit a Heading and Update the Table of Contents

9. Locate the heading *Patient Attendance and Billing* on page 4 of the document and change **Attendance** to: **Appointments**

Now that you have made a change in a heading, you need to update the table of contents.

10. Scroll up and position the insertion point in the table of contents.

There is no Update Table button in the upper-left corner of the table.

11. Tap F9 to begin the update; when the Update Table of Contents dialog box appears, choose **Update Entire Table** and click **OK**.

The word Attendance *changed to* Appointments.

12. Save your file.

Multiple Headers and Footers

Initially, the header and footer content is the same throughout a document because the Link to Previous feature is turned on by default, as shown in this illustration.

When a document contains multiple sections, you can break the link between sections and thereby create a new header and footer for each document section. For example, suppose you want to number the front portion of a long document using small Roman numerals and the body of the document using Arabic numerals. Separating the document into sections is the first important step before creating multiple headers and footers within a document.

Restarting and Formatting Page Numbers

When you have more than one section in a document, you may wish to control the starting page number within a section. Typically, the body of a document should start at page 1 rather than continuing the Roman numerals from the front matter. You may also want to control the page number formats. The Page Number Format dialog box provides options to restart numbering and to modify the number format, such as changing from Roman numerals to Arabic numerals.

You can choose from a variety of page numbering formats.

You can continue page numbering from the previous section or restart numbering with a specific number.

Different First Page Header or Footer

There may be times when all you want to do is set up a different header or footer on the first page of a document. For example, suppose you want all pages of a document numbered in the footer area of each page except for the cover page. You can set a different first page header or footer simply by choosing the Different First Page option in the Header & Footer Tools Design contextual tab.

DEVELOP YOUR SKILLS: W8-D3

In this exercise, you will insert header text that will appear in both sections of the document. You will also break the connection between footers so you can have different footers in each section, and then you will change the starting page number on the second page of the document.

1. Save your file as **W8-D3-RaritanP&PRevised** and, if necessary, display formatting characters.

2. Position the insertion point in **section 2**, which begins with *Mission Statement*.

3. Choose **Insert→Header & Footer→Header** and then choose **Edit Header**.

4. Take a moment to observe the header area.

Header -Section 2- **Mission·Statement¶**　　　　　　　　　　Same as Previous

The Header -Section 2- tab indicates that the insertion point is in the header area of section 2; the Same as Previous tab indicates that text you type in section 2 will carry over to the previous section. In other words, the sections are linked. You want the header sections to be linked in this instance because the word DRAFT should appear on all pages. You'll add that next.

5. Tap `Tab` to position the insertion point at the center of the header area and type: **DRAFT**

6. Format the header text with **Bold**, **14 pt**, and then double-click in the body of the document to close the header area.

7. Scroll up to the table of contents.

   Notice that the word DRAFT appears in the header. That's because the headers in both sections are linked. Now you will add a footer that appears in only one section.

8. Scroll down and position the insertion point in **section 2**.

9. Choose **Insert→Header & Footer→Footer** 📄 and then choose **Edit Footer**.

   Notice the Same as Previous tab in the footer area. You don't want the footer text to appear on the table of contents page, so you will break the link.

10. Choose **Header & Footer Tools→Design→Navigation**.

    The Link to Previous button is highlighted, meaning it is turned on and the footers in sections 1 and 2 are linked.

11. Click the **Link to Previous** 🔲 button to turn it off and break the link between the two sections.

    The Same as Previous tab at the right side of the footer area disappears.

12. Choose **Header & Footer Tools→Design→Header & Footer→Footer** 📄 and then choose **Blank**.

13. Click **Type Here** and type: **Policies & Procedures Manual**

14. Tap `Tab` to position the insertion point in the center of the footer area and then type: **Raritan Clinic East**

15. Tap `Tab` to position the insertion point at the right side of the footer.

16. Choose **Header & Footer Tools→Design→Header & Footer→Page Number** 🔢.

17. Choose **Current Position** and then choose **Plain Number**.

Change the Starting Page Number

You want to start numbering with a 1 on the first page of the document body.

18. Choose **Header & Footer Tools→Design→Header & Footer→Page Number** 🔢.

19. Choose **Format Page Numbers** and then choose **Start At**.

    Number 1 is chosen automatically, but you could change it if you needed to.

20. Click **OK** to restart page numbering with a 1 and then double-click in the document body to close the header and footer areas.

21. Scroll up and notice the footer does not appear on the table of contents page.

22. Scroll down and observe the footer text in the rest of the document.

    Because the page numbering changed, you need to update the table of contents again.

23. Scroll to the table of contents and position the insertion point in the table of contents.

24. Tap ⌐F9⌐, choose **Update Entire Table**, and click **OK**.

25. Save your file.

Creating an Index

Adding an index to a document gives the reader an easy way to find important words. To create an index, you mark the entries and then generate the index. The entries you mark are sorted alphabetically, and their page numbers are inserted.

Marking Index Entries

Marking index entries and subentries is a case-sensitive action. If you mark all occurrences of a word such as *Billing* for inclusion in the index, only those occurrences of the word in which the *B* is capitalized are included. So it's important to consider which occurrences you want marked before selecting Mark All.

⊙ View the video "Main Entries and Subentries."

≡ References→Index→Mark Entry 🗎 *or* References→Index→Insert Index 🗎 *or* References→
Index→Update Index 🗗

DEVELOP YOUR SKILLS: W8-D4

In this exercise, you will mark index entries and subentries in preparation for generating an index.

1. Save your file as: **W8-D4-RaritanP&PRevised**

2. Go to the first page of the body of the manual and select the heading **Mission Statement**.

3. Choose **References→Index→Mark Entry** 🗎.

   Now you will edit the main entry text.

4. Type **Goals** in the Main Entry field to replace the text that was automatically inserted in the Mark Index Entry dialog box.

   The text that was in the field came from the words you selected in the document. You can always replace or edit the suggested entries in this manner.

5. Click **Mark** at the bottom of the dialog box.

   Now you will examine an index code.

6. If necessary, drag the dialog box to the side and notice that the code *{ XE Goals}* was inserted into the document.

   This code identifies Goals *as a main index entry.*

7. Select the word **specialties** at the end of the second line in the second paragraph under the *Mission Statement* heading.

8. Click the **Mark Index Entry** dialog box to activate it and then click **Mark** to use the proposed text as the main entry.

9. Select **General Medicine** in the first line of the third paragraph below *Scope of Services*, click the dialog box to activate it, and click **Mark**.

10. Scroll down and select **Patient** in the heading *Patient Appointments and Billing,* click the dialog box, and click **Mark**.

Mark All Entries

Depending on the nature of the document you are marking, there may be text you want to mark every time it appears.

11. Select **Billing** in the heading *Patient Appointments and Billing* and then click the dialog box.

12. Click **Mark All** to mark all occurrences of *Billing* for inclusion in the index.

Remember, it only marks Billing if it begins with a capital letter.

13. Select **billing** toward the end of the first line in the third paragraph below *Patient Appointments and Billing,* click the dialog box, and click **Mark All**.

Mark Subentries

14. If necessary, scroll down to the *Patient Records* heading; then follow these steps to mark records as a subentry:

Ⓐ Select **Patient** in the heading.

Ⓑ Click the **Mark Index Entry** dialog box to activate it.

Ⓒ Type **records** in the Subentry field and click **Mark**.

15. Navigate to the second paragraph below the *Patient Records* heading, select **files** in the first line, and click the dialog box to activate it.

16. Double-click **files** in the Main Entry field and then press Ctrl+X.

17. Click the **Subentry** field and press Ctrl+V to paste *files* into the field.

18. Type **Patient** in the Main Entry field and click **Mark**.

19. Close the Mark Index Entry dialog box.

20. Save your file.

Generating Index Entries Using a Concordance

If a document is extremely long, marking index entries can be overwhelming. There is an automatic option for marking words and phrases to be included in an index. This option allows you to create a list of words and phrases you want to include and saves it as a separate file that acts as a concordance file.

When you use a concordance file to generate an index, it's important to know how it works. These guidelines will provide you with some basic information:

▸ The list of words and phrases to be included as main entries should be typed in one column straight down the left margin of the document or in the first column of a table.

▸ The document should contain only the words and phrases to be marked.

▶ To mark entries with subentries, create the concordance using a table layout. In the first column, type the words you want to mark as the main entry. In the second column, type the main entry followed by a colon, followed by the text for the subentry, without spaces.

| patient | patient:records |

▶ Entries can be listed in any order in the concordance. They will be sorted and grouped alphabetically when you generate the index. However, sorting the words helps identify duplicate words in the concordance.

DEVELOP YOUR SKILLS: W8-D5

In this exercise, you will mark index entries using a concordance document.

1. Save your file as: **W8-D5-RaritanP&PRevised**
2. Open **W8-D5-P&PConcordance** from your **Word Chapter 8** folder.
3. Scroll through the document, review its contents, and then close the document.
4. Position the insertion point anywhere on the title page at the top of the document.
5. Choose **References→Index→Insert Index** 📄.
6. Click **AutoMark** at the bottom of the dialog box to display the Open Index AutoMark File dialog box.
7. Navigate to your **Word Chapter 8** folder and double-click **W8-D5-P&PConcordance**.

   Although nothing appears to happen, the list of words and phrases in the concordance is compared with the manual list. When a word is located, the entry is automatically marked in the manual list.

8. Scroll through and review the document.

   Notice the numerous index marks that were added from the concordance in addition to the individual marked items from the previous exercise.

9. Turn off formatting marks.

   Because index codes can be quite lengthy, displaying them can cause text to roll onto other pages. Turning off formatting marks ensures that page numbers are accurate.

10. Save the file.

Inserting and Updating the Index

After all the index entries are marked, you can use the Index dialog box to insert the index. You can choose the overall format for the index and select several other formatting options. You can update an index in the same manner as a table of contents.

There are several ways to modify an index once you create it:

▶ Use the Index dialog box to change various formatting options.

▶ Format the index directly.

▶ Change the text of an entry by replacing it directly in the code that was originally created and then update the index.

▶ Delete an entry by removing the code and updating the index.

Note! *The format that's active in the Index dialog box will be reapplied if you update the index.*

☰ References→Table of Contents→Update Index | F9

In this exercise, you will generate and format an index.

1. Save your file as: **W8-D6-RaritanP&PRevised**
2. Press ⎡Ctrl⎤+⎡End⎤ or scroll down to move to the end of the document.

   An index should begin on a blank page.
3. Type the heading **Index** and tap ⎡Enter⎤.
4. Select the heading and format the text as **Bold, 16 pt**.
5. Position the insertion point on the blank line below the Index heading and choose **References→Index→Insert Index** 📄.
6. Choose **Formal** from the Formats list at the bottom of the dialog box and click **OK**.

Modify the Index Format

7. Click anywhere in the index and choose **References→Index→Insert Index** 📄.
8. Choose **Modern** from the Formats list and then choose **Run-In** at the top-right corner.
9. Click **OK**; click **OK** again when the message appears asking if you want to replace the index.

   The new index is inserted with the Run-In number style. Notice how the style affects the subentries. You've decided you like the previous indented subentries.
10. Click **Undo** ↶ to reverse the change.
11. Save the file.

Keeping Text Together

If you're working on a long document that goes through multiple revision cycles, controlling pagination can be a challenge. Several options in the Paragraph dialog box can be helpful.

▸ **Widow/Orphan Control:** Places at least two lines of a paragraph at the top or bottom of a page; checked by default

▸ **Keep with Next:** Forces a paragraph to appear with the paragraph that follows it; often used to keep a heading with the following paragraph

▸ **Keep Lines Together:** Prevents a page break in the middle of a paragraph

▸ **Page Break Before:** Forces a page break before a specific paragraph

You can further control text by specifying how often Word automatically hyphenates words that are too large to fit at the end of a line. The Hyphenation tool is found in the Page Setup group of the Layout tab. To track how many lines are being used in a page, section, or throughout a document, use the Line Numbers tool found in the same group.

DEVELOP YOUR SKILLS: W8-D7

In this exercise, you will use the Keep with Next option to ensure that specified segments of text stay together when a document is automatically paginated.

1. Save your file as: **W8-D7-RaritanP&PRevised**
2. On the first page of the document body, select the **Patient Management Procedures** heading and the **Entry into Services** subheading.

   A heading should not appear alone at the page bottom. Although that's not the case now, further editing may split a heading from the paragraph that follows.
3. Choose **Home→Paragraph dialog box launcher** ⊡.
4. If necessary, click the **Line and Page Breaks** tab, check **Keep with Next**, and click **OK**.

   This ensures the heading, the subheading, and the paragraph following the subheading will stay together during future edits and automatic pagination.
5. Scroll down to the next page and select the **Patient Appointments and Billing** heading.
6. Choose **Home→Paragraph dialog box launcher** ⊡, check **Keep with Next**, and click **OK**.
7. Save your file.

Watermarks

A watermark is text or a graphic placed behind text or other objects in a document; it is visible only in Print Layout or Read Mode view, and on any physically or digitally printed (such as PDF) versions of the document. Some common watermarks include a faint image of the word *Draft* or *Confidential* in the background.

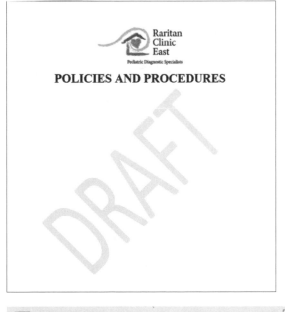

≡ Design→Page Background→Watermark ⊡

The changes made to the Policies and Procedures Manual need to be approved by your manager. Although the word DRAFT appears in the header, you've decided that using the word as a watermark would be more effective. In this exercise, you will delete the term in the header and then add a watermark to the document.

1. Save your file as: **W8-D8-RaritanP&PRevised**
2. Position the insertion point at the top of the document and double-click the header area to open it.
3. Select the word **DRAFT** and tap Delete .
4. Double-click in the body of the document to close the header area.
5. Choose **Design→Page Background→Watermark** and then choose **Draft 1** from the gallery.
6. Scroll through a few pages to view the watermark.
7. Save and close the file.

Self-Assessment

Check your knowledge of this chapter's key concepts and skills using the Self-Assessment in your ebook or online (eLab course or Student Resource Center).

Reinforce Your Skills

Organize a Document with a TOC and Headers and Footers

Kids for Change is providing background reading for its next monthly meeting in which it will brainstorm new ideas to help kids in the community thrive. In this exercise, you will add a table of contents and headers and footers to make the document more accessible to readers.

1. Open **W8-R1-Organizations** from your **Word Chapter 8** folder and save it as: **W8-R1-OrganizationsRevised**

2. If necessary, display formatting marks; then choose **Home→Styles dialog box launcher** to open the Styles task pane.

3. Starting on the first page of the main body of the document, position the insertion point in the headings and notice the heading styles in effect.

4. Close the Styles task pane.

5. On page 2, find the section break at the top of the page and position the insertion point on the blank line above it.

6. Choose **References→Table of Contents→Table of Contents** and then choose **Automatic Table 1** from the gallery.

Modify a Heading

7. Scroll to page 3 and, in the first subheading below *Change for Kids*, select **Tutoring** and replace it with. **Teaching**

8. On page 2, position the insertion point in the table of contents and click **Update Table** at the top of the table of contents border.

9. Choose **Update Entire Table** and click **OK**.

Create a Custom Table of Contents

10. Choose **References→Table of Contents→Table of Contents** and then choose **Custom Table of Contents**.

11. Make sure all three checkboxes are checked and then, if necessary, choose **Formal** from the Formats drop-down list.

12. Click **OK**; when the message appears confirming the replacement, click **OK** again.

Add Multiple Headers and Footers

13. Position the insertion point in **section 2** of the document, which begins with *Introduction*.

14. Choose **Insert→Header & Footer→Header** and then choose **Edit Header**.

Notice the Same as Previous tab at the right side of the header area. You will now break the link between sections 1 and 2.

15. Choose **Header & Footer Tools→Design→Navigation→Link to Previous** 🔳.

Notice that the Same as Previous tab no longer appears at the right side of the header.

16. Tap [Tab] to position the insertion point in the center of the header and type: `Kids for Change`

17. Double-click in the body of the document to close the header area.

18. Scroll up and notice that the header doesn't appear on pages 1 and 2; scroll down and observe the header on pages 3 and 4.

19. If necessary, position the insertion point in the page starting with *Introduction*, which is in section 2.

20. Choose **Insert→Header & Footer→Footer** and then choose **Edit Footer**.

Notice the Same as Previous tab at the right side of the footer area.

21. Choose **Header & Footer Tools→Design→Navigation→Link to Previous** 🔳 to break the link between sections 1 and 2.

22. Choose **Header & Footer Tools→Design→Header & Footer→Footer** and then choose **Austin**.

Notice that the Austin format placed a border around the page and that page numbering starts at page 2. You will now change the numbering to start on page 1.

23. Choose **Header & Footer Tools→Design→Header & Footer→Page Number** 🔳 and then choose **Format Page Numbers**.

24. Choose **Start At** from the bottom of the Page Number Format dialog box.

The number defaults to 1, which is what you want.

25. Click **OK** and then double-click in the body of the document to close the footer area.

26. Scroll down and notice the numbering on pages 3 and 4; scroll up and notice that there are no footers on pages 1 and 2.

27. Save and close the file.

REINFORCE YOUR SKILLS: W8-R2

Add an Index to a Document

The leader for the next Kids for Change monthly meeting is providing members with a document containing ideas for how kids can promote sustainability, which is the topic of the meeting. In this exercise, you will create an index for the document so members can easily locate important terms.

1. Open **W8-R2-Sustainability** from your **Word Chapter 8** folder and save it as: `W8-R2-SustainabilityRevised`

2. If necessary, display formatting marks; then select **wood products** in the first bullet point.

3. Choose **References→Index→Mark Entry**.

This places wood products *in the Main Entry field.*

4. Type **salvaged** in the Subentry field and click **Mark**.

   Notice the colon between wood products *and* salvaged *in the index code in the document. This indicates that* salvaged *is a subentry of* wood products.

5. Select **salvaged** in the Subentry field, type **recycled** in its place, and click **Mark**.

   This adds another subentry for wood products.

6. Select **light bulbs** in the third bullet point and then click the dialog box to activate it.

7. Type **fluorescent** in the Subentry field and click **Mark**.

8. Change the subentry text to **standard** and click **Mark**.

   This adds another subentry for light bulbs.

9. Select **paper products** in the fifth bullet point, click the dialog box, and click **Mark**.

10. Select **recycle** in the second line of the sixth bullet point and then click the dialog box.

11. Mark these terms as subentries for *recycle:*
    - **wood products**
    - **paper products**
    - **plastic containers**
    - **cell phones**
    - **electronics**

12. Close the dialog box.

Insert an Index

13. Press Ctrl + End or scroll down to move to the end of the document and then press Ctrl + Enter to insert a page break.

14. Type **Index** and tap Enter ; format the heading with bold, 16 pt; and position the insertion point on the blank line below the heading.

15. Turn off formatting marks.

    Remember, displaying index codes can affect page numbering.

16. Choose **References→Index→Insert Index** 📄.

17. Follow these guidelines to complete the index:
    - Choose **Classic** in the Formats list.
    - Check the **Right align page numbers** checkbox.
    - Choose **dots** in the Tab Leader field.

    ☑ Right align page numbers
    Ta**b** leader: ....
    Forma**t**s: Classic

18. Click **OK**.

Modify an Entry and Update the Index

19. Scroll to the second-to-last bullet point and select **Computer Takeback Campaign**.

20. Choose **References→Index→Mark Entry**.

    This phrase will be a subentry under recycle, *so you will cut the term and paste it into the Subentry field.*

21. Press ⌊Ctrl⌋+⌊X⌋, position the insertion point in the **Subentry** field, and press ⌊Ctrl⌋+⌊V⌋.

22. Type **recycle** in the Main Entry field and click **Mark**.

23. Close the dialog box and scroll down to the index.

24. Turn off formatting marks.

    Formatting marks were turned on when you marked the last entry.

25. Hover the mouse pointer over the index, right-click, and choose **Update Field**.

Finalize the Document

This document will go through some revisions, so you want to be sure the lines in the second-to-last bullet point don't split between pages if repagination takes place.

26. Scroll up and select the bullet point that begins with *Recycle old electronics*.

27. Choose **Home→Paragraph→dialog box launcher**.

28. If necessary, click the **Line and Page Breaks** tab, check **Keep Lines Together**, and click **OK**.

    Now you will insert a DRAFT watermark so this document isn't mistaken for the final version.

29. Choose **Design→Page Background→Watermark** 📄 and choose **Draft 2** from the gallery.

30. Save and close the file.

REINFORCE YOUR SKILLS: W8-R3

Organize a Long Document

Kids for Change is planning a fair, Sustainability for the Twenty-First Century. One of the members has prepared a report of background information that will be used to kick off the planning session. You have been asked to organize the document to make it more accessible for the reader. In this exercise, you will create a table of contents and an index and insert headers and footers.

1. Open **W8-R3-WikiSustain** from your **Word Chapter 8** folder and save it as: **W8-R3-WikiSustainRevised**

2. If necessary, display formatting marks; then scroll through the document and observe the heading styles.

    You will insert a new page and generate the table of contents.

3. On the second page, position the insertion point in front of *Introduction*.

4. Choose **Layout→Page Setup→Breaks** and insert a Next Page section break.

5. Scroll up and position the insertion point in front of the section break (to the right of the paragraph symbol) and tap ⌊Enter⌋.

6. Choose **References→Table of Contents→Table of Contents→Automatic Table 2**.

Update the Table of Contents

7. Hover the mouse pointer over the *Energy* link in the table of contents and then press ⌊Ctrl⌋ and click the link to jump to that heading in the document.

8. Position the insertion point at the end of the *Energy* heading, tap ⌊Spacebar⌋, and type: **consumption**

9. Update the entire table of contents.

Now you'll change the table of contents format.

10. Choose **References→Table of Contents→Table of Contents→Custom Table of Contents**, choose the **Formal** format if necessary, click **OK**, and then choose **Yes** to replace the table of contents.

Add Headers and Footers

11. Scroll down and position the insertion point in **section 2**, which begins with *Introduction*.

12. Choose **Insert→Header & Footer→Header→Edit Header** and break the link between sections 1 and 2.

13. Tap Tab twice to position the insertion point at the right side of the header area and then type **Sustainability in the Twenty-First Century** and close the header area.

The header appears throughout section 2 but not in section 1.

14. Position the insertion point in **section 2**, choose **Insert→Header & Footer→Footer→Edit Footer**, and break the link.

15. Choose **Header & Footer Tools→Design→Header & Footer→Footer→Austin**.

Now you will set the page numbering to start at 1 in section 2.

16. Choose **Header & Footer Tools→Design→Header & Footer→Page Number** and then choose **Format Page Numbers**.

17. Set the numbering to start at 1 and then close the footer area.

Create an Index

18. Select the **Atmosphere** heading toward the top of the new page 1 and mark it as an index entry.

19. Type **global warming** in the Subentry field and click **Mark**.

20. Select the text in the Subentry field, type **carbon reduction** in its place, and click **Mark**.

21. Select the **Subentry** text, type **air pollution:nitrogen oxides** (no spaces surrounding the colon), and click **Mark**.

Whether you're creating a concordance or marking entries in the Mark Index Entry dialog box, the word to the right of the colon is a subentry of the word on the left.

22. Now mark these items in the Subentry field:
    - **air pollution:sulfur oxides**
    - **air pollution:photochemical smog**
    - **air pollution:acid rain**
    - **air pollution:sulfate aerosols**

23. Click in the document, scroll down and select **Management of human consumption** toward the bottom of page 2, and then click the dialog box to activate it.

24. Type **Energy Consumption:increase in CO2** in the Subentry field and click **Mark**.

25. Mark these entries in the Subentry field:
    - `Energy Consumption:fossil fuel emissions`
    - `Energy Consumption:climate change`
    - `harvesting rainwater`
    - `ethical consumerism`
    - `local food production`
    - `circular material flow`
    - `renewable sources`
    - `industrial ecology`

26. Close the dialog box.

27. Position the insertion point at the end of the document, create a new page for the index, and then turn off formatting marks.

    Remember, the index codes can cause a change in pagination.

28. Type **Index** and tap Enter; format the text with bold, 14 pt; and then position the insertion point in the blank line below the text.

29. Insert an index using the Modern format, right-align page numbers, and use dots as the tab leader.

    Notice the subentries under air pollution *and* Energy Consumption. *Now you'll mark another entry and then update the index.*

30. Scroll to page 1, select the **Freshwater and oceans** heading, and mark it as an index entry.

31. Click in the document, select the **Land use** heading on page 2, mark it as an index entry, and then close the Mark Index Entry dialog box.

32. Turn off formatting marks.

    Word turned on formatting marks when you marked the new index entries.

33. Position the insertion point in the index and tap F9.

Keep Text Together

If this document is revised, using some pagination features will simplify the process. In this example, you want the Management of human consumption *heading to always be at the top of a new page.*

34. Scroll to page 2 and position the insertion point in front of *Management of human consumption*.

35. Choose **Home→Paragraph dialog box launcher** and, if necessary, click the **Line and Page Breaks** tab.

    Some pagination options are already in place for this text.

36. Check the **Page break before** checkbox and click **OK**.

    This ensures that this heading will always start on a new page. Because pagination has changed, it's a good idea to update the table of contents and the index.

37. Position the insertion point in the table of contents and update the entire table.

38. Position the insertion point in the index and tap F9.

39. Save and close the document.

📎 Apply Your Skills

Finalize a Report

Universal Corporate Events sent you to Munich on a familiarization trip. You have completed the content for your report on the trip and now will apply some formatting. In this exercise, you will create a table of contents to make it easy to locate specific topics in the report and will also add a header and footer.

1. Open **W8-A1-Munich** from your **Word Chapter 8** folder and save it as:
   W8-A1-MunichRevised

2. Open the Styles task pane, scroll through the document to observe some of the heading styles in use, and then close the task pane.

3. Position the insertion point in front of *Introduction* on the first page of the body and insert a **Next Page** section break.

4. If necessary, display formatting marks, scroll up and position the insertion point in front of the section break before the paragraph mark, and tap Enter.

5. Insert an **Automatic Table 1** table of contents and use the **Parks** hyperlink to jump to that heading.

6. Position the insertion point at the end of the heading, tap Spacebar, and type: **and recreation**

7. Update the table of contents to reflect the change.

8. Open the Table of Contents dialog box, apply the **Classic** format, choose the dots from the Tab Leader drop-down list, and click **OK**.

9. When the message box appears confirming the replacement, click **Yes**.

10. Position the insertion point in **section 2**, which begins with *Introduction*, edit the header, and break the link between sections 1 and 2.

11. Insert a header using the **Banded** style from the Header gallery; close the header area.

12. With the insertion point in section 2, edit the footer to break the link between sections 1 and 2, and then insert a footer using the Banded style.

13. Set up the page numbering to start at **1** in section 2 and then close the footer area.

14. Scroll to the Table of Contents and update it.

15. Save and close the document.

Create an Index and Use Pagination Options

Universal Corporate Events has asked you to do some research on Bangalore for a client. Now that you've completed the research, you will add an index to make it easy for the client to locate important terms. In this exercise, you will mark entries and subentries and use a concordance to create the index. Then you will make additions to the index and update it.

1. Open **W8-A2-Bangalore** from your **Word Chapter 8** folder and save it as:
   W8-A2-BangaloreRevised

2. If necessary, display formatting marks; then mark the three main headings on page 1 (**Background**, **Climate**, and **Get in**) as main index entries.

3. Mark **By plane** as a subentry of *Get in*.

4. On page 6, mark **Landmarks** and **Temples** as main index entries.

5. Navigate to your **Word Chapter 8** folder and open **W8-A2-Concordance**; examine the file to see which entries will need to be marked in the next step and then close it.

6. Use the **AutoMark** button in the Index dialog box, together with **W8-A2-Concordance**, to mark additional index entries; turn off formatting marks.

    Now you'll insert an index.

7. Scroll to the end of the document and insert a page break to create a blank page for your index.

8. Type **Index** at the top of the new, blank page and tap Enter.

9. Format *Index* with bold, 14 pt; position the insertion point on the blank line below the heading; and insert an index using the **Formal** format.

10. Scroll up to page 1 and select **Background**.

11. Choose **References→Index→Mark Entry**.

12. Mark these terms as subentries of *Background*:

    - **population**
    - **Garden City of India**
    - **IT industry**

13. Turn off formatting marks and update the index.

14. On page 1, select the **Background** heading.

15. Open the Paragraph dialog box and check **Keep with next** on the Line and Page Breaks tab.

16. Select the **Climate** heading and apply the **Keep with next** option.

17. Select the **Get in** and **By plane** headings and apply the **Keep with next** option.

18. Save and close the file.

APPLY YOUR SKILLS: W8-A3

Organize a Long Document

A Universal Corporate Events agent wrote a report on Basque country. Now it's time to enhance the document's readability. In this exercise, you will create a table of contents and an index. You will work with headers and footers and set up a page break pagination option.

1. Open **W8-A3-Basque** from your **Word Chapter 8** folder and save it as:
    W8-A3-BasqueRevised

2. If necessary, display formatting marks; then open the Styles task pane.

3. Scroll through the document, observe the heading styles, and then close the task pane.

4. To create a new page for the table of contents, insert a Next Page section break just before the heading *The Basque Country* on page 2.

5. Scroll up, position the insertion point in front of the section break, tap Enter, and insert an Automatic Table 2 table of contents.

6. Use the **Climate** link in the table of contents to jump to the *Climate* heading; type **Basque** in front of *Climate* and update the table of contents to reflect the change.

7. Create a custom table of contents by applying the **Distinctive** format.

8. Position the insertion point in section 2 (begins with *The Basque Country* heading), edit the header, break the link between sections 1 and 2, and insert a header using the **Blank style**.

9. Type **The Basque Country** in the Type Here area; close the header area.

10. With the insertion point in section 2, edit the footer and break the link between sections 1 and 2.

11. Insert a footer using the **Austin** style and format the starting page number to start at page 1; close the footer area.

Mark Entries and Create an Index

12. Mark index main entries and subentries using the headings indicated in this table:

Main Entry	Subentry
Features	Atlantic Basin
	Middle section
	Ebro Valley
Basque Climate	
Transport	Road
	Rail
	Airports
	Seaports

13. Turn off formatting marks, position the insertion point at the end of the document, and insert a page break.

14. Type **Index** and tap Enter; format the text with bold, 14 pt; position the insertion point on the blank line below the heading; and insert a Formal index.

15. Mark the **Cuisine** heading (page 4) as a main entry, turn off formatting marks, and then update the index.

Keep Text Together

16. Position the insertion point in front of the *Transport* heading (page 2) and insert the **Page Break Before** pagination option.

17. Because you changed pagination, update the table of contents and the index.

18. Save and close the file.

⊟ Project Grader

If your class is using eLab (labyrinthelab.com), you may upload your completed Project Grader assignments for automatic grading. You may complete these projects even if your class doesn't use eLab, though you will not be able to upload your work.

PROJECT GRADER: W8-P1

Enhancing the History of Board Games Document

In this exercise, you'll put some finishing touches on the History of Board Games document by adding a table of contents and an index. You'll then change heading levels and add index entries and follow by updating the table of contents and index.

1. Download and open your Project Grader starting file.
   - *Using eLab:* Download **W8_P1_eStart** from the Assignments page. You *must* start with this file or your work cannot be automatically graded.
   - *Not using eLab:* Open **W8_P1_Start** from your **Word Chapter 8** folder.
2. On **page 2**, insert the **Confidential 1** watermark.
3. On **page 8**, use the **Keep with Next** pagination setting to keep the last two paragraphs together (the paragraph starting with *Additionally* and the quotation paragraph below it).
4. On **page 2**, insert a table of contents in the empty space near the top of the page using the **Automatic Table 2** format.
5. Change the following headings to the Heading 2 style:
   - **United States** heading on **page 4**.
   - **21st Century** heading on **page 5**.
6. Update the table of contents using the **Update Entire Table** option.
7. On **page 9**, insert an index in the empty paragraph below the *Index* heading using the **Classic** format and leaving all other index settings at the default values.
8. Mark the following index main entries, leaving all other Mark Index Entry settings as the defaults:
   - **Catan** (two instances)
   - **Stratego** (one instance)
9. Update the index.
10. On **page 1**, insert a **Built-in Banded** footer with the **Different First Page** option turned on.
11. Replace the footer page number with the text: `TAYLOR GAMES`
12. On **page 2**, insert a **Built-in Banded** footer with the **Different First Page** option turned on.
13. Save your document.
    - *Using eLab:* Save it to your **Word Chapter 8** folder as `W8_P1_eSubmission` and attach the file to your eLab assignment for grading.
    - *Not using eLab:* Save it to your **Word Chapter 8** folder as: `W8_P1_Submission`

Enhancing the Corvette History Document

You've been asked to add large document enhancement features to the Corvette History document. In this exercise, you'll use footers, a table of contents, and index features to do so.

1. Download and open your Project Grader starting file:
   - *Using eLab:* Download **W8_P2_eStart** from the Assignments page. You *must* start with this file or your work cannot be automatically graded.
   - *Not using eLab:* Open **W8_P2_Start** from your **Word Chapter 8** folder.

2. On **page 2**, insert the **Confidential 1** watermark.

3. On **page 2**, insert a table of contents using the **Automatic Table 1** format.

4. Open the **W8_P2_Concordance** document from your **Word Chapter 8** folder.

5. Add these entries to the end of the concordance document:
   - **Boattail**
   - **Ramjet**
   - **Wonderbar**

6. Save the concordance document to your **Word Chapter 8** folder as **W8_P2_ConcordanceEdited** and then close the document.

7. Use the **Index AutoMark** feature to open **W8_P2_ConcordanceEdited** as the Index AutoMark file.

8. On **page 15**, insert an index in the empty paragraph below the *Index* heading using the **Classic** index format. Leave all other index settings at the defaults.

9. On **page 2**, insert the **Built-in Banded** footer with the **Different First Page** option turned on.

10. In **Section 1**, change the header & footer page number format to roman numerals (i, ii, iii...).

11. In **Section 2**, insert a **Built-in Banded** footer making the footer the same on the first page.

12. In **Section 2**, start the footer page numbering at: **1**

13. Update the table of contents using the **Update Page Numbers Only** option.

14. Update the index.

15. Save your document.
    - *Using eLab:* Save it to your **Word Chapter 8** folder as **W8_P2_eSubmission** and attach the file to your eLab assignment for grading.
    - *Not using eLab:* Save it to your **Word Chapter 8** folder as: **W8_P2_Submission**

◢ Extend Your Skills

These exercises challenge you to think critically and apply your new skills in a real-world setting. You will be evaluated on your ability to follow directions, completeness, creativity, and the use of proper grammar and mechanics. Save files to your chapter folder. Submit assignments as directed.

W8-E1 That's the Way I See It

As a small-business owner, you want to offer your customers a document that provides an in-depth, categorized overview of your products. If you were a bookstore owner, for example, you might categorize books by genre (e.g., history, biography, fiction). Start a new document and save it as: **W8-E1-ProductDescriptions**

Decide on the type and name of your business. Type an introduction (three to four sentences) for each main product category, providing longer content for the subcategories. Format main categories with Heading 1 and give each at least three subcategories (Heading 2). Your document should be at least seven pages, including a cover page, a table of contents, and index (ten main entries and at least three subentries). Be sure to insert a Next Page section break between the table of contents and the body of the document. Also include multiple footers (page numbering starting at page 1 in section 2, no footers in section 1) and the Keep Text Together option (keep heading lines together with the paragraph following headings; apply this feature at least twice). You may copy content from the Internet, but cite your sources.

W8-E2 Be Your Own Boss

As the owner of Blue Jean Landscaping, you want to provide your customers with in-depth information for their spring gardens, focusing on fruits, vegetables, and legumes. Start a new document and save it as: **W8-E2-SpringPlanting**

Create an introduction (three to four sentences). Do online research to create at least three subcategories for each category. Format the category headings with Heading 1 and the subcategories with Heading 2. Provide detailed information, such as the best growing conditions for a particular type of tomato. Your document should be at least seven pages, with a cover page, table of contents, and index. You may copy content from the Internet, but cite your sources. Insert a Next Page section break between the table of contents and the document body. Use page numbers in the section 2 footer, starting at page 1; use no footer in section 1. Your index should include twenty main entries and at least five subentries.

W8-E3 Demonstrate Proficiency

Stormy BBQ is planning to sell a book about BBQ cooking, and you have been asked to provide the research, which you will do online. Feel free to copy content from online sources—just remember to cite your sources. Start a new document and save it as: **W8-E3-BBQBook**

The book will include three main categories: BBQ Grills and Tools, BBQ Tips and Techniques, and BBQ Recipes. Each category heading should be formatted with the Heading 1 style. Create a short introduction (three to four sentences) for each main category. Based on your research, identify at least two subcategories for each category; format the subcategory headings with the Heading 2 style. Use a Next Page section break to designate a cover page and table of contents as section 1 and the rest of the document as section 2. Insert a header with the company name that appears only in section 2. Insert a page number footer that appears only in section 2 and that starts numbering at page 1. Create an index of at least fifteen terms of your choice, including main entries and at least five subentries.

9 | Collaborating in Word

The Internet makes it easy for project teams to collaborate when drafting documents. Team members can exchange documents across the country as easily as across the hall. Several features make collaboration activities more efficient. For example, you can track all of the changes made to a document by each team member and combine these changes into a single document for review. In this chapter, you will work with these collaboration tools.

LEARNING OBJECTIVES

▸ Use the highlighter tool

▸ Track your changes to a document

▸ Review tracked changes from others

▸ Send emails from Word

▸ Review changes from multiple reviewers

▸ Compare documents with no tracked changes

📁 Project: Collaborating on a Manual

As a member of the human resources department, you have been working to finalize the Raritan Clinic East Policies and Procedures Manual. It's now ready for review by personnel in the human resources department. As others review the manual, they will use collaboration tools to mark suggested changes. Some reviewers will insert comments to identify their recommendations, while others will use the Track Changes feature to mark suggested edits. Some will highlight text to identify wording that needs revising. Your task will be to review all suggested edits and comments and finalize the document for printing.

The Highlighter

The highlighter pen works just like its real-life counterpart (except you can easily erase the highlighting). The pen applies a transparent color to the text background and offers a variety of highlighting colors. You can color-code the highlights you use in a document if you wish, such as highlighting notes to yourself in yellow and "waiting for information" reminders in green.

There are multiple highlighter colors to choose from.

≡ Home→Font→Text Highlight Color 🖊️

DEVELOP YOUR SKILLS: W9-D1

In this exercise, you will highlight a note to yourself and a reminder that you are waiting for additional information from the Finance department.

1. Open **W9-D1-PolicyManual** from your **Word Chapter 9** folder and save it as:
   `W9-D1-PolicyManualRevised`

2. With the insertion point at the beginning of the document, do a search for: **Pediatric General Medicine**

3. On page 2, position the insertion point in front of *Pediatric*.

4. Type this text: `Chin has more information about these specialties.` Spacebar

5. Choose **Home→Font→Text Highlight Color** [aby] **menu button** ▾ and then choose **Bright Green** from the gallery.

   When the mouse pointer is in the body of the document, it looks like a highlighter pen.

6. Drag the pen across the text you just added to highlight it.

7. Click **Text Highlight Color** [aby] to turn off the pen.

   Notice that the color on the button face reflects the most recently used color.

Tip! *Tapping* Esc *also turns off the pen.*

8. Press Ctrl + End or scroll to the end of the document and type this text: `Check with Finance to see if they have information to add.`

9. Select the sentence and choose **Text Highlight Color** [aby] **menu button** ▾ →**Yellow**.

   This highlights the selected text and changes the button color to yellow.

10. Save the file.

Tracking Changes to a Document

Track Changes is one of the most useful tools for collaborating with team members as you pass documents back and forth. Reviewers can track changes while they edit, and the originator can see who is making what changes in the document and either accept or reject the suggested changes.

Reviewers can also use the Comment feature to leave messages in a document as a means of collaborating with the originator. For example, reviewers may want to explain to the originator why they are making a particular change.

≡ Review→Tracking→Track Changes [icon]

Review and Collaboration

In today's world, when requests for instant feedback are the norm, knowing the typical online reviewing process can ensure that you're well prepared to be a valuable contributor. Reviewers use Track Changes to mark edits and add comments. It's important to use Track Changes so the originator can see all of the proposed edits. Files may be passed back and forth among team members via email, cloud storage, or other means.

Viewing Tracked Changes

You have options for viewing edits made to documents using Track Changes. The method you choose is a matter of personal preference.

▸ **Inline:** Edits are marked directly within sentences and paragraphs. Deleted text is colored and marked through with a line; added text is underlined and in a different color.

▸ **Balloons:** Comments and edits appear in balloons on the right side of the document (called the markup area). Each balloon identifies the person who made the edit and the type of edit made—inserted text, deleted text, etc.

Note! *The balloons method is the primary method used in this chapter.*

View the video "Display Options for Track Changes and Comments."

Setting the Username and Initials

Track Changes uses information set up in the Word Options dialog box to identify the username for edits made to a document. For this reason, whenever you collaborate on a document in which Track Changes is used, make sure your username and initials are set correctly.

≡ Review→Tracking dialog box launcher →Change User Name

Setting Reviewer Ink Colors

Track Changes can display different colors to distinguish the edits of each reviewer who works on the document. Each reviewer can specify colors for his or her comments and tracked changes. This makes it easier to rapidly identify changes submitted by a specific reviewer. It also allows you to keep a consistent color for a reviewer you work with frequently, rather than settling on colors that may be assigned automatically.

Warning! *Changing your reviewer ink colors in this way will change these settings permanently until you change them again.*

≡ Review→Tracking dialog box launcher ⌐ →Advanced Options

DEVELOP YOUR SKILLS: W9-D2

In this exercise, you will turn on Track Changes, change the tracking colors, and set the user's name and initials for the revised Raritan Clinic East policy manual.

1. Choose **Review→Tracking dialog box launcher** ⌐ and click the **Advanced Options** button.

2. Follow these steps to choose options for your reviewer ink color settings:

(A) Set the color for insertions to **Blue**.

(B) Set the color for deletions to **Red**.

(C) Set the color for comments to **Teal**.

(D) Click **OK**.

3. Click the **Change User Name** button at the bottom of the Track Changes Options dialog box and, if necessary, enter your username and initials.

4. If you want to override the settings from the current Microsoft Account, click the checkbox below the Initials field for **Always use these values regardless of sign in to Office**, and click **OK** twice.

Adding Comments to a Track Changes Document

The Comment feature is a great collaboration tool to use in conjunction with Track Changes. The Reply button in the comment balloon allows reviewers and originators to communicate back and forth during the editing and reviewing process. For example, a reviewer might want to point out the reason for a deletion. The Resolve button is meant for reference only, meaning a user may mark a comment as resolved so other users know the issue has been corrected.

≡ Review→Comments→New Comment 🗏

DEVELOP YOUR SKILLS: W9-D3

In this exercise, you will choose the balloon display for tracking changes, and then you will insert a comment and make revisions to the document.

1. Save your file as: **W9-D3-PolicyManualRevised**

2. If necessary, choose **Review→Tracking→Display for Review** 🖺 and then choose **All Markup**.

3. Choose **Review→Tracking→Track Changes** and, if necessary, display formatting marks.

4. Choose **Review→Tracking→Show Markup→Balloons** and, if necessary, choose **Show Revisions in Balloons**.

    Deleted text, comments, and formatting changes will appear in balloons in the markup area. Added text will be underlined in the body.

5. Scroll to page 2. In the last paragraph on the page, select **Referral** at the beginning of the paragraph.

6. Choose **Review→Comments→New Comment**.

7. Type this text in the comment balloon: **Indent to match other paragraphs.**

8. In the same paragraph, locate and select the text **(see Appendix A)** in the next line; delete it.

    The deleted text appears in a balloon in the markup area, and a gray change bar appears in the left margin to help reviewers locate changes.

9. Follow these guidelines to continue with deletions:
    - Search for the word **see** to locate each additional cross-reference to an appendix.
    - Delete the ten other cross-references for Appendices B–K.
    - Delete extra spaces between words where appropriate.

10. Search for **Patient Management Procedures** and then position the insertion point at the end of the heading.

11. Follow these steps to insert introductory text for the heading:

    Ⓐ Tap [Enter].

    Ⓑ Tap [Tab] and then type the text shown here.

    Ⓒ Notice the gray change bar in the left margin that helps locate changes.

    Notice the formatting balloons in the markup area. Although the font is the same for the other body text, the style is different from the heading; therefore, the difference is noted.

12. Close the Navigation pane and save the file.

Reviewing Tracked Changes

Reviewers' tracked changes are only suggestions; tracked changes don't become permanent unless the originator accepts them. Originators can also reject a reviewer's suggestions.

This rejects the currently selected change.

Navigate to the previous or next change using these buttons.

Use this to accept the currently selected change.

These options appear when you click the Accept menu button ▼. Similar choices are available on the Reject button.

> **Tip!** *You can right-click a proposed change and choose an Accept or Reject command from the pop-up menu.*

Displaying Tracked Changes

You can display tracked changes in four distinctive views. Depending on the type of detail you want to focus on, each view offers specific advantages.

VIEWS FOR TRACKED CHANGES

Markup	Description
Simple Markup	This shows where a change occurred with a red change bar in the margin. Clicking the change bar displays the markup details.
All Markup	This option shows all markups.
No Markup	This hides all markups and displays a final document appearance with the proposed changes.
Original	This shows the original document and hides all markups.

☰ Review→Changes→Accept ☑ or Reject ☒

☰ Review→Tracking→Display for Review 🗏

Lock or Unlock Tracking

You can use a password to lock tracking in a document. Doing so will prevent anyone from turning Track Changes on or off, or accepting or rejecting any changes. To unlock this feature, you'll need the password you initially used when locking.

≡ Review→Tracking→Track Changes 📝 menu button ▾→Lock Tracking

---

DEVELOP YOUR SKILLS: W9-D4

In this exercise, you will use different markup views to display the document. Then you will review tracked changes to the document, accepting some changes and rejecting others.

1. Save your file as: **W9-D4-PolicyManualRevised**
2. Choose **Review→Tracking→Display for Review** 📝→**Original** and then scroll through the document.

   The document now appears as it did before changes were made.

3. Choose **Display for Review** 📝→**All Markup** and then scroll through the document.

   Notice the balloons in the markup area on the right. Deleted text, comments, and formatting changes appear in balloons, while inserted text is underlined in the body.

4. Choose **Display for Review** 📝→**Simple Markup** and then scroll through the document.

   Red change bars appear in the margin where changes occurred. Clicking the change bar displays all the changes in detail; clicking it again hides the details. This is a good view for a document with lots of changes.

5. Choose **Display for Review** 📝→**No Markup** and then scroll through the document.

   This view helps you see what the final document will look like.

Accept and Reject Changes

6. Position the insertion point at the top of the document.
7. Choose **Review→Changes→Next** 🔁.

   This turns on All Markup view and then jumps to and highlights the text you added to the document. This is a good addition, so you will accept it.

8. Choose **Accept** ☑.

   The change marks are removed from the new paragraph, and the focus moves to the next change—the formatting balloon associated with the change you just accepted.

9. Choose **Accept** ☑.

10. Choose **Accept** ☑ again.

Lock and Unlock Tracking

11. Choose **Review→Tracking→Track Changes menu button** ▼**→Lock Tracking**.

12. In the Lock Tracking window that appears, enter **1234** as your password, enter it again in the second box to confirm, and click **OK**.

    Notice that the Track Changes button, as well as the Accept and Reject buttons, are greyed out.

13. Choose **Review→Tracking→Track Changes menu button** ▼**→Lock Tracking**.

14. In the Unlock Tracking window that appears, enter **1234** as your password and click **OK**.

    All buttons related to track changes are once again available.

15. Choose **Next** 🔁 to skip the comment and move to the next change, the deleted reference to Appendix A.

16. Choose **Reject** ☒.

    The deleted text is restored, and you move to the next tracked change.

17. Reject each deleted reference to an appendix.

    The insertion point returns to your comment.

18. Choose **Review→Comments→Delete** 🗙.

19. Choose **Review→Tracking→Track Changes** 📝 to turn off the feature.

20. Position the insertion point at the beginning of the paragraph starting with *Referral* (bottom of page 2) and tap Tab to indent the first line.

21. Save the file.

Saving and Sending Files

Before reviewers can do their jobs, you must get the document to them. You can use the Internet to share your document in several ways:

▸ Email

▸ Microsoft OneDrive

▸ Network drive

This chapter uses email as the method for sharing files.

 File→Share→Email 📧

In this exercise, you will send an email with a copy of the policy manual document attached. For this example, you will send the attachment to your own email address.

1. Choose **Review→Tracking→Track Changes** 📝.

   Turning on the feature helps ensure that the reviewers will use Track Changes.

2. Choose **File→Share→Email** 🖼 and then choose **Send as Attachment**.

3. Follow these steps to complete the email form:

   If your user ID was not set up as a user with an Outlook account, you will see a message saying that no profiles have been created. If so, just dismiss the message, turn off Track Changes, and read through the rest of the exercise.

	To...	Your email address ◀ Ⓐ
	Cc...	
Send	Subject	W9-D4-PolicyManualRevised.docx
	Attached	W9-D4-PolicyManualR... 35 KB Ⓑ

   Please review the attached document. Ensure that Track Changes is active for marking edits. ◀ Ⓒ

   Ⓐ Enter your actual email address here (don't type the text shown).

   Ⓑ Verify that the attachment appears here.

   Ⓒ Add this message for the reviewers.

4. Send the email.

5. Choose **Review→Tracking→Track Changes** 📝 to turn off Track Changes.

Reviewing Changes from Multiple Reviewers

If you set up a document to track changes, you can send copies for review by others. As reviewers make revisions, their changes are tracked. When they send you their edited copies, you can combine the tracked changes into a single document. Each reviewer's changes are marked in a different color so you can recognize each reviewer's input. After the changes are merged, you can navigate through the combined document and accept or reject edits from all users at one time.

The Reviewing Pane allows you to see all your reviewers' changes in a simple list format. You can display the Reviewing Pane either horizontally or vertically. You can jump to specific edits made within the document by clicking them in the Reviewing Pane.

≡ Review→Compare→Compare 📄→Combine

≡ Review→Tracking→Reviewing Pane

Displaying Specific Markups and Reviewers

There are numerous options for displaying tracked changes for combined documents. For example, you may want to look at only the insertions and deletions suggested by reviewers. If you don't need to keep track of formatting changes, you may wish to turn off the Formatting option so you won't be prompted for formatting changes.

Show Markup ▾	
✓	Comments
✓	Ink
✓	Insertions and Deletions
✓	Formatting
	Balloons ▸
	Specific People ▸
	Highlight Updates
	Other Authors

≡ Review→Tracking→Show Markup 🖹

If you combine two reviewer documents with the original, you can choose to see changes from both at once, or, at times, you may wish to focus on just one reviewer. Do that by removing the checkmark in front of the other reviewer's name.

Specific People ▸	✓ All Reviewers
Highlight Updates	☑ John Smith
Other Authors	☑ Brett Reynolds

DEVELOP YOUR SKILLS: W9-D6

In this exercise, you will combine proposed changes from two reviewers with the original document. You will also explore additional features used for working with combined documents.

1. Save your file as: **W9-D6-PolicyManualRevised**
2. Choose **Review→Compare→Compare** 🖹 and then choose **Combine**.
3. Follow these steps to begin combining documents:

Combine Documents ? ✕

Original document
Ⓐ W9-D6-PolicyManualRevised.docx ⌄ 📁
Label unmarked changes with: Jill Murphy

Revised document
W9-D6-Revision1.docx ⌄ 📁 Ⓑ
Label unmarked changes with: John Smith Ⓒ

⇄

Ⓓ More >>   OK   Cancel

- Ⓐ Choose **W9-D6-PolicyManualRevised** here.
- Ⓑ Click **Browse**, select **W9-D6-Revision1** from your **Word Chapter 9** folder, and click **Open**.
- Ⓒ Type **John Smith** here, replacing any existing text if applicable, so you'll know who suggested any unmarked changes.
- Ⓓ Click **More >>** to expand the dialog box.

If Track Changes is not turned on, the reviewer's name doesn't appear with the change. Normally changes are tracked, and the name does not need to be entered in the dialog box.

4. Follow these steps to control document display:

Ⓐ Ensure **Word Level** is active.

Ⓑ If necessary, choose **Original Document**.

The Word Level option causes the entire word to be highlighted, even if only one character or punctuation mark changes. This makes it easier to spot small edits. Now John Smith's proposed edits are embedded in the original document, ready for review.

5. Click **<< Less** to collapse the dialog box and then click **OK**.

Hide Source Documents

6. Click **Compare** 📑, slide the mouse pointer to **Show Source Documents**, and then, if necessary, choose **Hide Source Documents**.

This creates more room on the screen.

7. Choose **Compare** 📑 and then choose **Combine**.

8. In the Original Document field, choose **W9-D6-PolicyManualRevised**.

9. Click the **Browse** button next to the Revised Document field, select **W9-D6-Revision2** from your **Word Chapter 9** folder, and click **Open**.

10. Type **Brett Reynolds** in the Label Unmarked Changes With field and click **OK**.

Brett Reynolds' edits are now displayed with the original and John Smith's edits.

Turn On the Reviewing Pane

11. If necessary, choose **Review→Tracking→Reviewing Pane** 📄 **menu button** ▾, and then choose **Reviewing Pane Vertical**.

The Reviewing Pane (labeled Revisions *at the top) summarizes the proposed changes from both reviewers.*

12. Scroll down the Reviewing Pane to the suggested change by Brett Reynolds, where he deleted *attending*.

13. Click **attending** in the Reviewing Pane and notice that the document scrolls to the location of that change.

Notice the Deleted: attending *balloon in the markup area.*

14. Click **Close** ✕ at the top of the Reviewing Pane.

15. Press Ctrl+Home to move to the top of the document.

16. Review all changes to the document:
- Delete all comments and accept all formatting changes.
- Accept all edits by John and Brett with one exception: On page 3, John deleted a space between *(see Appendix B)* and *Children*. Reject that change.

17. Save the file as **W9-D6-Combined** and then close it.

Comparing Documents

Sometimes documents sent for review are returned with no visible edits. Reviewers might turn off Track Changes so the edits they make are not immediately evident. To determine whether edits have been made, you can use the Compare feature. It enables you to merge two documents into one file; then the documents are examined and automatically marked up using Track Changes so you can locate edits.

To Combine or Compare?

The basic procedures are the same for comparing and combining documents, but each command has a different use.

The Combine command allows you to combine the tracked changes from one or multiple reviewers in one document, and then you can go through the single document to accept or reject the changes.

The Compare command is designed for comparing two documents: one edited version, in which the reviewer did not use Track Changes, and the original. If you attempt to use the Compare feature to add a second reviewer's document, you will be advised that it will automatically accept the first person's changes before comparing the second edited document. Thus, you won't have the option of accepting or rejecting changes from the first reviewer.

≡ Review→Compare→Compare 🗐→Compare

DEVELOP YOUR SKILLS: W9-D7

In this exercise, you will compare an original document with a document received from a reviewer that appears to have no changes in it.

1. Open **W9-D6-PolicyManualRevised** from your **Word Chapter 9** folder and save it as:
W9-D7-PolicyManualRevised

2. Choose **Review→Compare→Compare** 🗐 and then choose **Compare** from the menu.

3. Follow these steps to compare this file with another document:

- (A) Choose **W9-D7-PolicyManualRevised** as the original document.
- (B) Click the **Browse** button for the revised document, navigate to your **Word Chapter 9** folder, and choose **W9-D7-EditedNoMarks**.
- (C) Type **Alice Jackson** here to identify the reviewer.
- (D) Click **OK**; click **Yes** if asked if you want to continue with the comparison.

4. Scroll through the document and observe Alice's edits.

You won't accept and reject changes in this example.

5. Save the file as **W9-D7-AliceEdits** and exit Word.

Self-Assessment

Check your knowledge of this chapter's key concepts and skills using the Self-Assessment in your ebook or online (eLab course or Student Resource Center).

Reinforce Your Skills

Encourage Good Bugs with Companion Planting

Kids for Change is sponsoring a Master Gardener's seminar, and you have researched companion planting. In this exercise, you will use the highlighter to place reminders in your document, add comments, and track and review changes. You will also email your document as an attachment.

1. Open **W9-R1-CompanionPlant** from your **Word Chapter 9** folder and save it as: **W9-R1-CompanionPlantRevised**

2. If necessary, display formatting marks; then position the insertion point at the end of the first paragraph and tap [Enter].

3. Type this text: **Make copies on 3-hole punched paper.**

4. Choose **Home→Font→Text Highlight Color** [aby] menu button ▾ →Turquoise.

5. Drag the mouse pointer, which now appears as a highlighter pen, across the sentence you just typed.

6. Click **Text Highlight Color** to turn off the highlighter and then position the insertion point at the end of the document.

7. Type this text: **Reminder: Check with Ilsa to see if lupine and savory attract lady bugs.**

8. Select the sentence and then choose **Home→Font→Text Highlight Color menu button** ▾ → **Bright Green**.

Customize Your Track Changes

9. Choose **Review→Tracking dialog box launcher** and then click **Change User Name**.

10. If necessary, enter your username and initials, click **OK**, and then click **Advanced Options**.

11. Choose these colors and then click **OK** twice:

Markup Setting	Value
Insertions	**Pink**
Deletions	**Dark Blue**
Comments	**Violet**

Work with Comments and Track Changes

12. Move to the top of the document and select the word **March** in the third line of the first paragraph.

13. Choose **Review→Comments→New Comment** [💬] and type this text: **Do we have a specific date yet?**

14. Scroll down to the *Tomatoes + Cabbage* combination and select the last word, **leaves**.

15. Click the **New Comment** button and type: **Did Ilsa verify that this combination really works?**

    Now you'll turn on Track Changes and make some editing changes.

16. Choose **Review→Tracking→Track Changes** 📝.

17. In the first sentence below the *Companion Planting* heading on page 1, select **makes for** and type **produces** in its place.

18. In the fifth line of the same paragraph, select **mate** and type **pair** in its place.

19. In the first line of the *Radishes + Spinach* section on page 2, select **yor** and type **your** in its place.

20. Scroll down to the *Collards + Catnip* section, position the insertion point at the end of the sentence, tap [Spacebar], and type: `And it will make your cat very happy!`

21. Position the insertion point at the end of the *Marigolds and Melons* section, tap [Enter], and type: `Asparagus + Basil: Seems to encourage lady bugs.`

22. Bold the text **Asparagus + Basil:**.

    Now you'll review the document in various Track Changes views.

23. Choose **Review→Tracking→Display for Review** 📖 **menu button** ▾→**Original** and scroll through the document.

    The document now appears as it was before tracking changes.

24. Use the same technique to experiment with **Simple Markup**, **No Markup**, and **All Markup**, leaving it set at **All Markup**.

    Now you will respond to comments and accept and reject the changes as you are playing the role of the reviewer.

25. Position the insertion point at the top of the document.

26. Choose **Review→Changes→Next** 🔁.

    The insertion point moves to the first comment.

27. Click **Reply** 🔁 in the comment balloon and type: `I'll check with Ilsa.`

28. Choose **Next**.

    The insertion point moves to the tracked deleted words makes for.

29. Choose **Accept** ✅.

    The focus moves to the added word produces.

30. Choose **Accept**.

31. Accept the deletion of *mate* and the addition of *pair*.

    The insertion point moves to the added Asparagus + Basil *information.*

32. Choose **Reject** ❌.

    The insertion point moves to the next comment.

33. Click **Reply** in the bottom of the comment balloon and type: `I'll check with her.`

34. Choose **Next** and accept the deletion of *yor*, the addition of *your*, and the addition of *And it will make your cat very happy!*

35. Make sure Track Changes is still on.

Remember, you want to ensure that reviewers use Track Changes.

36. Choose **File→Share→Email** 📧 and then choose **Send as Attachment**.

If your user ID was not set up as a user with an Outlook account, you will see a message saying that no profiles have been created. If so, just dismiss the message, turn off Track Changes, and read through the rest of this exercise.

37. In the email form, enter your email address in the To field and change the subject to: `Companion planting document attached for review.`

The document is already attached.

38. Type the email body text: `Please be sure Track Changes is turned on when you review the document.`

39. Click **Send** and then choose **Review→Tracking→Track Changes** to turn it off.

40. Save and close the file.

REINFORCE YOUR SKILLS: W9-R2

Combine and Compare Tracked Changes

Kids for Change is planning to participate in California Coastal Cleanup Day. You've researched some information on why this is important, and now your document has been reviewed by two other members. In this exercise, you will analyze the reviewers' edits and comments to finalize your document.

1. Open **W9-R2-CleanCoast** from your **Word Chapter 9** folder and save it as: `W9-R2-CleanCoastRevised`

2. If necessary, choose **Review→Tracking→Display for Review** 📑→**All Markup**.

3. Choose **Show Markup** 📄 and then slide the mouse pointer to **Balloons** and, if necessary, choose **Show Only Comments and Formatting in Balloons**.

4. Choose **Review→Compare→Compare** 📑→**Combine**.

5. Choose **W9-R2-CleanCoastRevised** from the Original Document drop-down list.

6. Click **Browse** on the right side of the dialog box, navigate to your **Word Chapter 9** folder, and open **W9-R2-CleanCoastElla**.

7. Click the **More** button to expand the dialog box and make sure **Word Level** and **Original Document** are chosen, click the **Less** button to collapse the dialog box, and then click **OK**.

8. Click **Compare** 📑, slide the mouse pointer down to **Show Source Documents**, and, if necessary, choose **Hide Source Documents**.

9. Combine the second document, **W9-R2-CleanCoastNed**, with **W9-R2-CleanCoastRevised** and click **OK**.

10. If necessary, position the insertion point at the top of the document and then follow these guidelines to review the changes:
    - Accept all additions and deletions made by Ella and Ned.
    - Reply to Ned's first comment with: `I'll contact one of the Park School teachers.`
    - Reply to Ella's comment with: `We should incorporate that in the report.`
    - Reply to Ned's second comment with: `Are you willing to follow up on this?`
11. Save the file as **W9-R2-CoastEllaNed** and then close it.

Compare Docs

12. Open **W9-R2-Pups** from your **Word Chapter 9** folder and save it as: **W9-R2-PupsRevised**
13. Choose **Review→Compare→Compare→Compare**.
14. Choose **W9-R2-PupsRevised** from the **Original Document** drop-down list.
15. Click **Browse** under Revised Document and open **W9-R2-PupsArthur** from your **Word Chapter 9** folder.
16. Type **Arthur Menendez** in the Label Changes With field on the right and click **OK**.
17. Make sure the insertion point is at the top of the document.
18. Choose **Next** 🗗.

    The first change is a little difficult to see—a comma was added following donors.

19. Accept the change and then continue through the document, accepting each addition and deletion.
20. Click **OK** when the message appears indicating there are no more changes.
21. Save the file as **W9-R2-PupsCompare** and then close it.

REINFORCE YOUR SKILLS: W9-R3

Collaborate in Word

Kids for Change will have a booth at a local farmer's market next month where the group will talk about the importance of buying locally grown food. It is preparing a handout that discusses the significance of buying local, and now the document will be reviewed by two members. In this exercise, you will share the file with reviewers using Word's email and then combine tracked changes from two reviewers. Then you will compare with another document from a reviewer who forgot to use Track Changes.

1. Open **W9-R3-BuyLocal** from your **Word Chapter 9** folder and save it as:
   W9-R3-BuyLocalRevised

   First, you will turn on Track Changes to ensure that the reviewers use it, and then you will email the document.

2. Choose **Review→Tracking→Track Changes** 🖉.
3. Choose **File→Share→Email** 📧→**Send as Attachment**.

   In this example, you will send the email to yourself. If your user ID is not set up as a user with an Outlook account, you will see a message saying that no profiles have been created. If so, just dismiss the message, turn off Track Changes, and read through the rest of the email portion of the exercise.

4. In the email form, enter your email address in the To field and change the Subject to: **Global research attached**

5. Type the following in the email body and then click **Send**: **Please review and propose any changes you would like.**

Combine Tracked Changes from Two Reviewers

6. Choose **Review→Compare→Compare→Combine** and, in the Original Document field, choose **W9-R3-BuyLocalRevised**.

7. On the right side of the dialog box, click **Browse**, open **W9-R3-BuyLocalMarjorie**, and then click **OK**.

8. Choose **Compare→Combine**.

9. In the Original Document field, choose **W9-R3-BuyLocalRevised**.

10. Browse for and open **W9-R3-BuyLocalSerge** and then click **OK**.

11. If necessary, position the insertion point at the top of the document.

12. Use **Next** 🔁 and **Accept** ☑ to review and accept all proposed changes.

13. Reply to Serge's comment about the number of copies with this text: **I'll check to see how many we made last year.**

14. Reply to Marjorie's comment with this text: **I know she is looking into it. I don't think she has heard back from them yet.**

15. Save the document as **W9-R3-BuyLocalCombined** and then close it.

Compare Documents

You've received the last edited document from Margo Meyers, but she did not use Track Changes. You will use the Compare feature to locate the changes.

16. Open **W9-R3-Obesity** and save it as: **W9-R3-ObesityRevised**

17. Choose **Review→Compare→Compare→Compare**.

18. In the Original Document field, choose **W9-R3-ObesityRevised** and, on the right side of the dialog box, browse for **W9-R3-ObesityMargo**.

19. Type **Margo Meyers** in the Label Changes With field and then click **OK**.

20. Scroll through the document and observe Margo's edits.

    You agree with all of the changes, so you'll accept them all at once.

21. Choose **Accept** ☑ menu button ▼→**Accept All Changes**.

22. Save the file as **W9-R3-MargoEdits** and then close it.

✎ Apply Your Skills

Create a Report on Crete

Universal Corporate Events is adding Crete to its Mediterranean tour offerings. You've prepared a report about Crete, and now you're asking a colleague to review it. In this exercise, you will use the highlighter and Track Changes to edit the document and then send it on for further review.

1. Open **W9-A1-Crete** from your **Word Chapter 9** folder and save it as:
   W9-A1-CreteRevised

2. Position the insertion point at the end of the paragraph below the Crete heading and type:
   [Spacebar]**The Roman and Turkish remnants are worth adding to the tour.**

3. Highlight the sentence with pink.

4. Open the Track Changes Options dialog box, click **Change User Name**, and, if necessary, enter your username and initials.

5. Click **Advanced Options** and choose these colors:

Markup Setting	Value
Insertions	**Green**
Deletions	**Red**
Comments	**Turquoise**

6. Select the city name **Heraklion** in the first bullet point.

7. Use the **New Comment** button to insert this comment: **A quick stop in Heraklion to see Knossos would be nice.**

8. Select the city name **Elounda** at the beginning of the fifth bullet point and insert this comment: **A good spot for celebrity watching.**

9. Turn on Track Changes and, in the fourth line of the paragraph below the *Crete* heading, replace *was* with: **were**

10. In the next line, replace *place* with: **island**

11. In the second line of the second bullet point, replace *Brits* with: **British**

12. Scroll to page 2 and locate the second-from-the-last bullet point about the city of Rethymno.

13. Position the insertion point after the space at the end of the paragraph and type: **There is a daily ferry from Athens.**

14. Ensure **All Markup** is active in the Display for Review field and then position the insertion point at the top of the document.

    Now you'll play the role of the reviewer.

15. Use **Next** and **Accept** to find and accept all editing changes.

16. Create an email using these guidelines:
    - Use Word's Email feature to send the file as an attachment.
    - Insert your email address in the To field.

      If your user ID is not set up as a user with an Outlook account, you will see a message saying that no profiles have been created. If so, just dismiss the message, turn off Track Changes, and read through the rest of this exercise.
    - Change the subject to: **Crete Review**
    - Add this message in the body of the email: **I hope my comments are helpful.**
    - Send the email.

17. Save and close the file.

APPLY YOUR SKILLS: W9-A2

Prepare a Report on Whistler Blackcomb

Universal Corporate Events has a client who wants to reward outstanding employees with a ski vacation, and you've been researching Whistler Blackcomb. In this exercise, you will combine the documents from two reviewers into your original. Then you will use the Compare feature with a document that was reviewed without Track Changes.

1. Open **W9-A2-Whistler** from your **Word Chapter 9** folder and save it as: **W9-A2-WhistlerRevised**

2. Ensure the Display for Review feature is set to **All Markup**.

3. Choose **Show Markup→Balloons** and, if necessary, choose **Show Revisions in Balloons**.

4. Combine your original document with Colleen's revised document, **W9-A2-WhistlerColleen**, and enter **Colleen Chase** in the Label Unmarked Changes With field.

5. Combine your original document with Anthony's revised document, **W9-A2-WhistlerAnthony**, and enter **Anthony Nichols** in the Label Unmarked Changes With field.

6. Choose **Compare→Compare**, slide the mouse pointer to **Show Source Documents**, and, if necessary, choose **Hide Source Documents**.

7. If necessary, position the insertion point at the top of the document.

8. Accept all changes made by Colleen, Anthony, and Jill, except the change in the first paragraph of the article where Colleen changed kilometers to miles; reject both the deletion and the addition.

9. Save the file as **W9-A2-WhistlerColleenAnthony** and close it.

   You have received suggested changes from a colleague, Mel. However, Mel did not use Track Changes, so you will use the Compare feature to highlight the changes.

10. Open **W9-A2-SanDiego** from your **Word Chapter 9** folder and save it as: **W9-A2-SanDiegoRevised**

11. Compare **W9-A2-SanDiegoRevised** in the Original Document field with **W9-A2-SanDiegoMel** and type **Mel Johnson** in the Label Changes With field.

12. Scroll through the document, check the changes, and then accept them all at once.

13. Save the file as **W9-A2-SDCompared** and then close it.

Collaborate on a Cabo San Lucas Brochure

Universal Corporate Events has asked you to conduct research for a marketing brochure on Cabo San Lucas. In this exercise, you will make changes to your original document and send it to reviewers. Then you will combine and compare the reviewed documents.

1. Open **W9-A3-Cabo** from your **Word Chapter 9** folder and save it as: `W9-A3-CaboRevised`
2. Make sure **Show Revisions in Balloons** is selected on the Balloons submenu in the Show Markup drop-down list.
3. Open the Track Changes Options dialog box and make sure your username and initials appear in the Word Options dialog box.
4. Change the colors in the Advanced Track Changes Options dialog box as follows:

Setting	Value
Insertions	**Bright Green**
Deletions	**Turquoise**
Comments	**Dark Red**

5. Turn on Track Changes.
6. Below the *See* heading, replace the last word in the first paragraph, *abundant*, with: `plentiful`
7. In the fourth line of the first bullet point, replace *allows for* with: `provides`
8. In the second line of the next bullet point, enter a comma after *old* and delete the word **and**.

   Now you will review your changes.

9. Position the insertion point at the top of the document and then use the **Next** button to move to and reject the *abundant* deletion and the *plentiful* addition.
10. Accept the rest of the changes.
11. Select **Submarine** in the second bullet point below the heading *Scuba Diving & Watersports*, and then add this comment: `This looks like a fun activity. Let's check it out.`
12. Save the file.

Check Track Changes Options and Email Files

13. Check that Display for Review is set to **All Markup**.
14. Use the Email feature and the Send as Attachment option to send the document for review following these guidelines:

    If your user ID is not set up as a user with an Outlook account, you will see a message saying no profiles have been created. If so, dismiss the message and go to the next step.
    - Enter your own email address in the To field.
    - Change the Subject to: `Cabo Review`
    - Enter this email body text: `Please make sure Track Changes is turned on.`
    - Send the email.

Combine Tracked Changes and Compare Documents

15. Use the Combine feature to combine these documents:

- The original document is **W9-A3-CaboRevised**.
- The first revised document is **W9-A3-CaboAudrey** (enter **Audrey Ellis** in the Label Unmarked Changes With field).
- The second revised document is **W9-A3-CaboJose** (enter **Jose Santos** in the Label Unmarked Changes With field).

16. Accept all changes by you, Audrey, and Jose at once.

17. Save the file as **W9-A3-CaboCombo** and close it.

You recently completed a report on Singapore, which was reviewed by your colleague Ellen. She forgot to use Track Changes, so you will use the Compare feature to assess her changes.

18. Open **W9-A3-Singapore** and save it as: **W9-A3-SingaporeRevised**

19. Compare this file with **W9-A3-SingaporeEllen**.

20. Enter **Ellen Pledger** in the Label Changes With field.

21. Review the changes and then accept them all.

22. Save the file as **W9-A3-SingCompared** and then close it.

▤ Project Grader

This chapter does not include Project Grader exercises. Project Grader content is based on the learning objectives for a chapter, and sometimes those learning objectives cannot be accurately graded by the system. Objectives from this chapter that can be accurately graded may be included in later chapters, if applicable.

✈ Extend Your Skills

These exercises challenge you to think critically and apply your new skills in a real-world setting. You will be evaluated on your ability to follow directions, completeness, creativity, and the use of proper grammar and mechanics. Save files to your chapter folder. Submit assignments as directed.

W9-E1 That's the Way I See It

Your business professor has assigned you to prepare a report on the best business opportunities for the coming year. To begin, choose a business that appeals to you. Then create a short introduction (four to five sentences) summarizing your reasons for choosing the business. Search the Internet and copy content of one to two pages on business prospects, citing your sources. Save the file as: **W9-E1-Biz**

Create two copies of the file (give them the names **W9-E1-BizJohn** and **W9-E1-BizJorge**, respectively). Turn on Track Changes and revise the document using your own ideas. Do the same for the "Jorge" document, making different revisions than you did for John. Combine the revised files with your original file. Note that, because you created the John and Jorge files yourself, your name will appear as the reviewer in all cases. Accept and reject revisions as you see fit and then save and close the file.

W9-E2 Be Your Own Boss

As the owner of Blue Jean Landscaping, you are researching recent articles on business opportunities in landscaping to determine future growth potential. Create a report of one or two pages using online content (citing your sources). Provide a short introductory paragraph (four to five sentences) summarizing the outlook for the landscaping business. Save your file as **W9-E2-Landscape** and then make a copy, naming it: **W9-E2-LandscapeArt**

Begin to share the document with Art via email from within Word. Fill out the email form. Make up Art's email address and a subject. When complete, tap PrtScn and paste the screenshot into a new Word document saved as: **W9-E2-Email**

Close the email form without sending. For the "Art" document, revise the document without Track Changes. Insert at least one comment and then save the document. Compare your original with the "Art" file. Note that, because you created the "Art" file yourself, your name will appear as the reviewer. Display the Reviewing Pane in a vertical alignment and then tap PrtScn . Add the screenshot to your "Email" document. Accept and reject revisions as you see fit and include a reply to Art's comment. Save and close the file.

W9-E3 Demonstrate Proficiency

Stormy BBQ plans to hold a BBQ Festival. You've been asked to conduct online research to gather ideas for the festival. Using your own ideas and content from online articles, create a report of one or two pages (citing your sources). Provide an introductory paragraph (four to five sentences) summarizing the purpose of the festival. Save the report as **W9-E3-Festival** and then make a copy, naming it: **W9-E3-FestivalCarla**

Change the reviewer ink setting for insertions, deletions, and comments to red. Take a screenshot and paste it into a new document saved as: **W9-E3-Ink**

Using Track Changes, make revisions to the "Carla" file, including at least one comment, and then save it. Combine the "Carla" file with your original. Note that, because you created the "Carla" file yourself, your name will appear as the reviewer. Accept and reject changes as you see fit and insert a reply to the comment. Highlight one sentence with bright green and then save the file.

10 Sharing and Securing Content

I n this chapter, you will work in Backstage view to control document access. Online storage, such as OneDrive, allows people to store and retrieve documents from any computer with Internet access, and virtual collaboration means that your documents are often in others' hands. There are features that help you control document content and security and guard your personal information.

LEARNING OBJECTIVES

▸ Use file compatibility features

▸ Check documents with the Document Inspector

▸ Restrict formatting and editing in a document

▸ Mark a document as final

▸ Secure documents with passwords and digital signatures

Project: Securing Confidential Information

At Raritan Clinic East, privacy and security of patient records are vitally important. As a Raritan employee, you will explore features that ensure that documents sent outside the clinic remain confidential and contain no information that could enable those receiving the documents to learn more about patients than they need to know. You will use Backstage view and identify some of the security features you can use.

Preparing Documents for Sharing

There are a number of things to think about when sharing documents with colleagues or clients. For one, compatibility issues between the current and earlier versions of Word should be considered. Additionally, documents can contain hidden or personal information about your organization or about the document that you do not want to share publicly. The Document Inspector can help you deal with these matters.

Compatibility Issues

The most recent versions of Word (2007–2019) use the *.docx* file format. Versions of Word prior to 2007 use a *.doc* file format. Benefits of the latter format include smaller file size, improved damaged-file recovery, and more control of personal information. It's important to understand how the current version of Word behaves with documents created in earlier versions. Likewise, you need to make sure your documents can be read by people using earlier versions. There are several things to think about when dealing with compatibility issues:

▶ The latest versions—Word 2019, 2016, and 2013—are compatible.

▶ Word 2007, 2010, 2013, and 2016 can open *.docx* files created in Word 2019.

▶ Documents opened in Word 2019 that were created in Word 2016 or earlier open in Compatibility Mode. The features in Word 2019 are downgraded to be compatible with the older versions. The term *[Compatibility Mode]* appears in the title bar.

▶ To open a Word 2019 document in Word 2010 or earlier, install the Compatibility Pack for Word, which you can download for free from the Microsoft website.

▶ You can convert documents to Word 2019 that were created in versions prior to Word 2016.

▶ You can save a Word 2019 document as a Word 97–2003 document so it can be opened by users of those versions. Some features of the current version either won't be available or will be modified in a manner more compatible with older versions.

In this exercise, you will open a Word 2003 document in Word 2019 Compatibility Mode. You will then try to insert a Word 2019 SmartArt graphic (a new feature) in the 2003 document and see how Compatibility Mode deals with this feature.

Before You Begin: *Download the student exercise files from your eLab course or the Student Resource Center (labyrinthelab.com/office19) and determine your file storage location before beginning this exercise.*

1. Open **W10-D1-2003ProcMan** from your **Word Chapter 10** folder and save it as:
W10-D1-2003ProcManRevised

   Notice [Compatibility Mode] in the title bar at the top of the screen.

   > W10-D1-2003ProcManRevised.doc [Compatibility Mode] - Word

   You will attempt to add a Word 2019 SmartArt graphic to the Word 2003 Compatibility Mode document.

2. If necessary, display formatting marks; position the insertion point in front of the paragraph mark at the top of page 2.

3. Choose **Insert→Illustrations→SmartArt** .

   Word opens the Word 2003 Diagram Gallery rather than the Word 2019 SmartArt gallery because the Compatibility Mode document cannot work with Word 2019's SmartArt feature.

4. Click **Cancel** to close the Diagram Gallery.

   Next you will observe how Word saves the Compatibility Mode document.

5. Choose **File→Save As** and navigate to your **Word Chapter 10** folder.

   Word 2019 defaults to the Word 97–2003 format in the Save As Type field. Word does this unless you purposely convert the document to a .docx format or save it as a Word Document (*.docx) via the Save As Type drop-down list.

6. Click **Cancel** and then click **Back** in the upper-left corner to return to the document.

Note! *Always leave your file open at the end of an exercise unless instructed to close it.*

To Convert or Not to Convert?

If most of the people you share documents with are using pre-2007 versions of Word, it's a good idea to keep their documents in Compatibility Mode. This ensures that documents will look the same in Word 2019 as they do in the older version. It also ensures that the features available in Word 2019 will be limited to, or similar to, the features available in older versions.

Choosing a Conversion Method

If you are working with a Compatibility Mode document that would benefit from the full functionality of Word 2019 features that are currently disabled or limited, you have a candidate for conversion. When you convert the document, Word 2019 turns on the new and enhanced features.

There are two ways to convert an older version (.*doc*) document to a Word 2007–2019 (.*docx*) document:

▸ **Convert:** The Convert command appears on the Info screen in Backstage view when a document is open in Compatibility Mode. Using the command performs a conversion that overwrites the original document. As a result, the older version document is no longer available.

▸ **Save As:** When you resave and rename a document using the Save As command, you are actually making a *copy* of the document. When you perform a Save As with a Compatibility Mode document, you still have the original .*doc* file and you create a new second file, a .*docx* file.

| ☰ File→Info→Convert |
| ☰ File→Save As |

Consider the User

Before converting, keep in mind the person who sent you the document or the person to whom you are sending a document. If you are editing a document that needs to be returned to someone who is using an earlier version of Word, leave the document in its original format instead of converting it.

The Office Compatibility Pack

People who have earlier versions of Word and who need to work with Word 2019 documents can download a free compatibility pack from the Microsoft website to open, edit, and save Word 2019 documents. However, some features will still not be available.

DEVELOP YOUR SKILLS: W10-D2

In this exercise, you will convert a Word 2003 document to the .docx format and then add a Word 2019 SmartArt graphic.

1. Save your file as: **W10-D2-2003ProcManRevised**

2. Choose **File→Info→Convert**.

   A message appears indicating that conversion may cause some minor layout changes. For example, in this document, the pagination is altered slightly when converted.

3. Click **OK** to acknowledge the message.

   Notice that Compatibility Mode *has disappeared from the title bar.*

4. Position the insertion point on page 2 at the beginning of the first paragraph below the *Scope of Services* heading and make sure the insertion point is to the left of the tab that begins that paragraph.

5. Tap Enter and then position the insertion point next to the paragraph mark for the blank line you just created and choose **Insert→Illustrations→SmartArt**.

   Because you converted the document, the SmartArt gallery is now available.

6. Follow these steps to insert a SmartArt graphic:

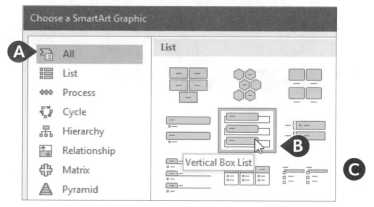

Ⓐ If necessary, choose **All** from the category list.

Ⓑ Choose the **Vertical Box List** graphic.

Ⓒ Click **OK**.

7. If necessary, click the tab at the left side of the graphic to open the Type Your Text Here pane.

8. Type this text:

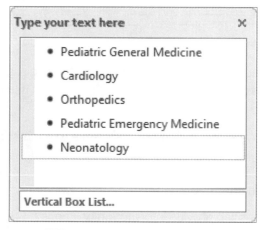

9. Close ⊠ the Type Your Text Here pane.

10. Save the document.

Preparing Backward-Compatible Documents

If you know you'll be working with people who have older versions of Word, and if it's important that all features are compatible among the versions, you might start your new document by saving it as a Word 97–2003 document. This way you avoid using features unavailable in older versions.

WORD

The Compatibility Checker

If you save a Word 2019 document to an older Word version, the Compatibility Checker notifies you if the document contains features unique to newer versions of Word. You can also manually run the Compatibility Checker before saving the document in older versions.

> **Microsoft Word Compatibility Checker** ? ✕
>
> ⓘ The following features in this document are not supported by earlier versions of Word. These features may be lost or degraded when you save this document in an earlier file format. Click Continue to save the document. To keep all of your features, click Cancel, and then save the file in one of the new file formats.
>
> | Summary | Occurrences |
> |---|---|
> | SmartArt graphics will be converted into a single object that can't be edited in previous versions of Word. | 1
Help |

The Compatibility Checker alerts you to how Word 2019 features will be handled if you save a document to an earlier version of Word.

≡ File→Info→Check for Issues→Check Compatibility

Round-Tripping Documents

You may hear the term round-tripping as you work with documents created in various versions of Word. Round-tripping refers to the practice of converting a document to a different format and then saving it back to the original format. For example, you may open a Word *.doc* file, convert it to a *.docx* file, and then decide to save your changes back to a *.doc* format. Round-tripping can create issues that corrupt the document so that it acts strangely or is damaged beyond repair.

Warning! *Avoid round-tripping to prevent unwanted loss of time and data.*

The Accessibility Checker

The Accessibility Checker checks elements of the document that people with disabilities may find difficult to read and informs you of the issues so you can fix them. The checker issues errors, warnings, and tips:

▸ **Errors:** Elements of the document may be very difficult or impossible to understand.

▸ **Warnings:** Elements of the document may be difficult to understand.

▸ **Tips:** Elements of the document may be better organized for understandability.

Clicking an item in one of these categories will provide information on changing the content to make it more accessible. There is also a link to Help text that describes in detail what you can do to make documents more accessible.

≡ File→Info→Check for Issues→Check Accessibility

DEVELOP YOUR SKILLS: W10-D3

In this exercise, you will begin the process to save a Word 2019 document to a Word 97–2003 format version for people who have not yet upgraded. Then you will check for accessibility issues.

1. Choose **File→Save As** and navigate to your **Word Chapter 10** folder.
2. Click the **Save as Type menu** button ▾, choose **Word 97–2003 Document**, and click **Save**.

   Word displays the Microsoft Word Compatibility Checker with a message indicating that you will not be able to edit the SmartArt graphic, so you've decided not to complete the conversion.
3. Click **Cancel**.
4. Choose **File→Info→Check for Issues→Check Accessibility** to open the Accessibility Checker task pane.

   Notice the two categories: Errors and Warnings. There are no tips for this document.
5. Click the **Read More About Making Documents Accessible** link at the bottom of the task pane to display the Help window.
6. View the Help window content and then close the Help window and the task pane.

Document Properties and the Document Inspector

Valuable information about a document appears in the Properties panel in Backstage view. Among the data Word stores within a document are the author's name, dates for file creation and editing, and the file storage location. Sending this data along with a document can inadvertently reveal to recipients some data that you would rather protect.

If you intend to share a document with colleagues or clients, you may use the Document Inspector to ensure that it contains no hidden or personal information either in the document itself or in the document properties. For example, a document could contain comments and tracked changes that are hidden from view. Document properties could contain information such as the author's name and the company name.

The Document Inspector will display a list of issues found in a document. The only option for removing data for a category is to remove all data within that category. Sometimes you may want to manually review information before deciding which data to remove.

Tip! *To help prevent unwanted data loss, before using Remove All for a category, make a copy of the document, run the Document Inspector on the copy, and remove all issues to see the effect.*

≡ File→Info→Properties

≡ File→Info→Check for Issues→Inspect Document

DEVELOP YOUR SKILLS: W10-D4

In this exercise, you will view document properties and run the Document Inspector. You will remove all personal data from the document.

1. Save your file as: **W10-D4-2003ProcManRevised**
2. Choose **File→Info** and review the properties information in the panel on the right.

   Notice that names appear in the Related People area. You can remove the author's name if desired.

3. Right-click the author's name and choose **Remove Person**.

4. In the Info window, click **Check for Issues** and choose **Inspect Document**.

5. If prompted to save changes, click **Yes**.

   The Document Inspector dialog box opens. You can remove the checkmark from any items you don't want inspected. In this example, you will leave all checkboxes checked except Ink.

6. Click **Inspect** at the bottom of the dialog box and review the results.

Document Inspector	?	×

   Review the inspection results.

   ✓ **Comments, Revisions, Versions, and Annotations**
   No items were found.

   ! **Document Properties and Personal Information**   [Remove All]
   The following document information was found:
   * Document properties
   * Template name

   The inspector found document properties.

7. Click **Remove All** next to Document Properties and Personal Information and then click **Close**.

   If your Document Inspector finds other issues as well, ignore them.

8. Choose **File→Info** and notice that, in the Properties panel, all names associated with the document have been removed.

9. Click **Back** ⊙ and save the file.

Controlling Document Access

When you share documents with colleagues and clients, it can be helpful to control the changes they can make. Several features assist you with protecting documents. For example, you can restrict the kinds of formatting and editing changes a reviewer can make. You can add a password to a document, and you can mark a document as final, thereby discouraging changes to it.

Restrict Editing

The Restrict Editing feature enables you to limit editing changes that reviewers can make. You also have the option to further limit access with a password:

▸ **Restrict for Tracked Changes:** This setting protects a document from having Track Changes disabled. Every change to the document will be noted. In addition, no one can accept or reject changes while the document is protected.

▸ **Restrict for Comments:** This setting permits reviewers to insert and edit comments in the document but not to edit the document itself.

▸ **Restrict for Filling in Forms:** This setting permits users to insert data only in unrestricted areas of a form.

≡ File→Info→Protect Document→Restrict Editing

In this exercise, you will set editing restrictions to allow tracked changes, thus preventing reviewers from disabling the feature.

1. Save the file as: **W10-D5-2003ProcManRevised**
2. Choose **File→Info→Protect Document→Restrict Editing**.
3. Follow these steps to turn on document protection for Tracked Changes:

   Ⓐ Ensure this **checkbox** is checked.

   Ⓑ Ensure **Tracked Changes** is chosen here.

   Ⓒ Click **Yes, Start Enforcing Protection**.

Word displays the Start Enforcing Protection dialog box. At this point, you can either click OK to restrict editing without a password or enter the desired password.

4. Click **OK** to dismiss the password dialog box.
5. On page 2, delete **of Services** in the *Scope of Services* heading.

   The change is marked with Track Changes. No one can alter the document without changes being tracked.

6. Click **Stop Protection** at the bottom of the Restrict Editing task pane.
7. Click **Close** ⊠ in the upper-right corner of the Restrict Editing task pane.
8. Choose **Review→Changes→Next** 🖹 and click **Accept** ☑.
9. Click **OK** when the message appears.
10. Save the file.

Allow Changes to Part of a Document

If you choose No Changes (Read Only) in the Editing Restrictions list, the Exceptions option appears. This option lets you specify certain areas of the document that a person can edit freely. For example, if a document is in its final version except for one section, you can exempt the incomplete section so it can be edited. You can also choose the people you want to allow to edit.

In this exercise, you will specify the document as read-only; however, you will apply an exception to three paragraphs so reviewers can make changes to them.

1. Save your file as: **W10-D6-2003ProcManRevised**
2. Choose **File→Info→Protect Document→Restrict Editing**.
3. Follow these steps to restrict editing:

   Ⓐ Make sure a checkmark appears here.

   Ⓑ Set the restriction level to **No Changes (Read Only)**.

4. Scroll to page 3 and select the three paragraphs below the *Entry into Services* heading.
5. Place a checkmark in the **Everyone** checkbox under Exceptions (Optional).

   This specifies that all reviewers will be able to edit these paragraphs.

6. Click **Yes, Start Enforcing Protection** at the bottom of the task pane.
7. Click **OK** to bypass setting a password.
8. Click to deselect the paragraphs.

   The editable paragraphs are shaded to make them easily visible to reviewers.

Attempt to Edit in a Restricted Area

9. Select a word anywhere there is no shading and tap Delete.

   Nothing happens because you are restricted to editing only the shaded paragraphs.

10. Delete the third paragraph in the shaded area.

    The deletion is allowed because it's in the area that was specified as an exception.

11. Click **Stop Protection** at the bottom of the task pane.
12. Select the two remaining shaded paragraphs and then remove the checkmark from the **Everyone** checkbox in the task pane.
13. Click in the document and notice the shading has been removed.
14. Save the file.

Restrict Formatting

When you share a document with multiple reviewers, it's easy to imagine a jumble of formats if there are no restrictions. You can restrict reviewers to applying only the Word styles you choose. Formatting is restricted to a list of specified styles, thus providing formatting consistency and preventing anyone from indiscriminately formatting the document.

DEVELOP YOUR SKILLS: W10-D7

In this exercise, you will use the Restrict Editing task pane to apply formatting restrictions.

1. Save your file as: **W10-D7-2003ProcManRevised**
2. Choose **File→Info→Protect Document→Restrict Editing**.
3. Follow these steps to open the Formatting Restrictions dialog box:

Ⓐ Place a checkmark here.

Ⓑ Click the **Settings** link.

4. Follow these steps to set specific restrictions:

Ⓐ Click **None** to uncheck all the checkboxes at once.

Ⓑ Scroll down and place checkmarks in the **Heading 1** and **Heading 2** checkboxes.

The only formatting change a reviewer can make is to add Heading 1 or Heading 2 formatting.

5. Click **OK**; when Word displays a message asking if you want to remove other styles, click **No**.

Removing other styles from the document would reformat the entire document, possibly with unexpected results.

6. In section 2 of the Restrict Editing task pane, remove the checkmark next to **Allow only this type of editing in the document**.

If a dialog box appears asking if you want to remove the ignored exceptions, click No.

7. Click **Yes, Start Enforcing Protection** in the Restrict Editing task pane.

   In this example, you will not add a password.

8. Click **OK** to dismiss the password dialog box.

   Notice that the task pane now contains a link to Available Styles.

   Restrict Editing ▾ ×

   Your permissions

   This document is protected from unintentional editing.

   You may edit in this region, but all changes will be tracked.

   You may format text only with certain styles.

   Available styles...

9. Click the **Available Styles** link to display the Styles task pane.

   In addition to the Normal style, the only styles available are Heading 1 and Heading 2.

10. Scroll to the top of page 2 and apply the **Heading 1** style to **Our Mission**.

11. Close the Styles task pane and then display the **Home** tab.

    All the Font and Paragraph formats are grayed out in the Ribbon because formatting is restricted to two heading styles.

12. Click **Stop Protection** at the bottom of the Restrict Editing task pane and then close the task pane.

    The Font and Paragraph formats are restored on the Ribbon.

13. Save the file.

Passwords and Encryption

Using commands on the Backstage view Info screen, you can set an additional password that is required to open the document. If you use both passwords, the reviewer would need one password to open the document and another password to edit it.

Adding a document password also encrypts the document. Encryption means Word uses a code or mathematical algorithm to alter information so it is inaccessible to unauthorized readers. When you encrypt a document, Word prompts you for a password.

Note! *Passwords are case-sensitive.*

≡ File→Info→Protect Document→Encrypt with Password

DEVELOP YOUR SKILLS: W10-D8

In this exercise, you will set a document password and then remove it.

1. Choose **File→Info→Protect Document→Encrypt with Password**.

2. Type **pass** in the Encrypt Document dialog box and click **OK**.

3. Type **pass** in the Confirm Password dialog box and click **OK**.

   Notice that the security setting is displayed in the Info screen.

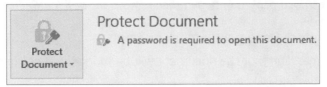

4. Click **Back** and then save and close the document.

   If you receive a message asking whether you would like to increase security on your computer, click No.

   Now you'll open the document with a password.

5. Choose **File→Open** and click **W10-D7-2003ProcManRevised** at the top of the Recent Document list.

   In some classrooms, the Recent Documents list may be cleared upon rebooting the computer. If so, navigate to your Word Chapter 10 folder to open the document.

6. Type **pass** in the password box and click **OK**.

   Now you will remove the password.

7. Choose **File→Info→Protect Document→Encrypt with Password**.

8. Select the characters in the password field, tap Delete , and then click **OK**.

9. Click **Back** and then save the file.

Marking a Document as Final

Another way to control edits and access to content is to mark the document as final. Using the Mark as Final command makes a document read-only. As a result, readers and reviewers will know that this document appears as it did when it went to a client, was filed electronically, or was in some other way beyond the point where edits would be useful. Marking as final also prevents accidental altering of the document. When a document is marked as final, the following message appears in the Info tab in Backstage view:

Protect Document
This document has been marked as final to discourage editing.

Editing Documents Marked as Final

When the Marked as Final feature is turned on, a yellow bar appears at the top of the document. The message in the bar lets you know that the document has been marked as final to discourage editing, and the Ribbon is hidden. Note that the feature only *discourages* editing. It is not as secure as a password would be. The button in the message bar enables you to edit the document anyway.

MARKED AS FINAL An author has marked this document as final to discourage editing. | **Edit Anyway**

 File→Info→Protect Document→Mark as Final

In this exercise, you will mark a document as final and then remove the designation to re-enable editing.

1. Choose **File→Info→Protect Document→Mark as Final**.
2. When Word displays a message that the document will be marked as final and saved, click **OK**.

   Word displays additional information about this setting.
3. Take a moment to read the information and then click **OK**.

   The security setting is displayed on the Info screen.
4. Click **Back** ⬅ to return to the document.

   Notice the Marked as Final *bar at the top of the screen.*
5. Select the heading **Our Mission** on page 2.
6. Tap ⌷Delete⌷ and see that the text is not deleted.
7. Choose **File→Info→Protect Document→Mark as Final** to turn off the feature.
8. Click **Back** ⬅ and notice that the Marked as Final bar at the top of the screen has disappeared.
9. Save the file.

Attaching Digital Signatures

With the ability to rapidly transmit documents globally, security concerns arise. How can a client know for certain that a critical document originated in your office? A digital signature is a secure means of stamping a document as authentic and originating from you. Other people cannot modify a signed document without causing the digital signature to be removed or the document to be marked as invalid.

You may use a digital signature when passing documents to others as an email attachment, as a downloadable file on your organization's intranet, from a website, or on a flash drive. You add a digital signature to a file by first attaching a digital certificate.

Digital Certificates

You may obtain digital certificates from third-party vendors who check identification before issuing a certificate. If you post documents on an intranet or the Internet, your network administrator will usually provide you with an authentic digital certificate.

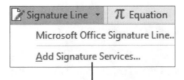

This option on the Signature Line
menu links to a Microsoft website,
where you can choose a third-party vendor.

You may also create your own digital certificate, although its use is limited. Self-made certificates are not verified by any outside agency; therefore, they're not necessarily a reliable measure, but they are the most convenient.

DEVELOP YOUR SKILLS: W10-D10

In this exercise, you will create a temporary digital certificate on your local computer. You will start by locating the SELFCERT application on your computer, which is installed as part of the Microsoft Office 2019 package.

1. Open **File Explorer** 📁 and navigate to the **SELFCERT** application through a path such as C:\Program Files (x86)\Microsoft Office\root\Office16.

Note! *This will be the correct file path for most computers. If yours is an exception, ask for assistance. And note you may not have user permission to create digital certificates on computers that are for general use by multiple people.*

📜 **SELFCERT.EXE**

2. Scroll to locate the SELFCERT application.

3. Double-click the file. When the Create Digital Certification dialog box opens, type **James Elliott** in the Your Certificate's Name field.

> Your certificate's name:
>
> | James Elliott |
>
> [OK] [Cancel]

4. Click **OK**; when a message appears indicating that a certificate was successfully created for James Elliott, click **OK** again.

   You have now created a digital certificate that can be used to apply a digital signature to your files.

5. Close the File Explorer window and then save the file.

Digital Signatures

There are two ways to add a digital signature to a document:

▸ You can add a visible signature line to a document and then capture the digital signature when the document is signed.

▸ If a visible signature line is not necessary, you can add an invisible digital signature. A signature button appears on the status bar at the bottom of the screen, so the recipient can verify that the document has a digital signature.

≡ Insert→Text→Signature Line

DEVELOP YOUR SKILLS: W10-D11

In this exercise, you will add a signature line to a document and add a digital signature. You will then attempt to modify the signed document. Finally, you will remove the visible signature and add an invisible digital signature.

1. Save your file as: **W10-D11-2003ProcManRevised**

2. Press Ctrl+End to move to the end of the document and then tap Enter twice.

3. Choose **Insert→Text→Signature Line** 🖉 to display the Signature Setup dialog box.

4. Complete the information as shown:

The Instructions to the Signer *text is provided by default. You can modify it if necessary. In this exercise, you'll leave the text as is.*

5. Click **OK** to complete the signature setup.

A signature line appears with the signer's name and title below. Now you'll sign the document.

6. Right-click the signature line and choose **Sign**.

7. Follow these steps to sign the document:

Ⓐ Type **James Elliott** here.

Ⓑ If the Signing As name isn't James Elliott, click **Change**, choose **James Elliott**, and click **OK**. Click **Yes** when the message appears to use the certificate.

Ⓒ Click **Sign**.

If you didn't change the Signing As name, a message appears indicating the certificate cannot be verified and asking whether you want to use this certificate. Remember, a self-created certificate is not verified by a third-party agency.

8. If necessary, click **Yes** to use the certificate.

9. When a message appears indicating your signature has been saved, click **OK**.

A yellow bar at the top of the document indicates the document is marked as final. The Recoverable Signature note above the signature is notifying you that the signature is not verified by an outside agency. A signature button appears on the status bar indicating a digital signature in the document.

Page 7 of 7   2031 words

10. Attempt to delete a word in the paragraph above the signature line.

A message briefly appears on the status bar indicating that you can't make a change because the selection is locked.

Now you will remove the signature so you can add an invisible signature. Remember, you can use an invisible signature when a visible signature is not required; however, a signature button will still appear on the status bar.

11. Click the **Signature** button on the status bar to display the Signatures task pane.

You may notice the term Recoverable Error *at the top of the task pane. This is because you are using a self-created certificate.*

12. Right-click the **James Elliott** signature in the task pane and choose **Remove Signature**.

A message appears, asking you to verify that you want to remove the signature.

13. Click **Yes** to remove the signature.

14. When a message appears indicating the signature was removed, click **OK**.

Remove the Signature Line and Add an Invisible Digital Signature

15. Select the signature line and tap Delete to remove it.

16. Close the Signatures task pane.

Now you will add an invisible signature, which you do in Backstage view.

17. Choose **File→Info→Protect Document→Add a Digital Signature**.

18. Follow these steps to add the signature:

Ⓐ Choose **Created and Approved This Document**.

Ⓑ Type **Raritan Procedure Manual** here.

Ⓒ Click **Sign**.

A message appears indicating the certificate cannot be verified. Again, a self-created certificate is not verified by a third-party agency.

19. Click **Yes** to use the certificate.

20. When a message appears indicating the signature has been saved with the document, click **OK**.

    Notice the Marked as Final note in the yellow bar at the top of the screen and the signature button on the status bar.

    Because you cannot edit a document after a signature has been attached, there is no option to save the document. When you close the document, the signature will still be attached.

21. Close the file and exit Word.

Self-Assessment

Check your knowledge of this chapter's key concepts and skills using the Self-Assessment in your ebook or online (eLab course or Student Resource Center).

⊥ Reinforce Your Skills

REINFORCE YOUR SKILLS: W10-R1

Plan for Trout in the Classroom

Kids for Change hopes to get involved in the "Trout in the Classroom" project, in which kids raise fish from eggs until they're ready to be released in streams. A team member created a research report in Word 2003, but the rest of the team is using Word 2019. In this exercise, you will convert an older document to Word 2019 format and work with backward compatibility, document properties, and the Document Inspector.

WORD

1. Open **W10-R1-Trout** from your **Word Chapter 10** folder and save it as: **W10-R1-TroutRevised**

   Notice Compatibility Mode *in the title bar. Now you will attempt to add a SmartArt graphic to the document.*

2. Press Ctrl + End to position the insertion point at the end of the document and choose **Insert→Illustrations→SmartArt** 🖼.

   The Word 2003 Diagram Gallery opens because a Word 2003 document is not compatible with the SmartArt feature.

3. Click **Cancel** to close the Diagram Gallery.

   Now you will convert the document to the Word 2019 format.

4. Choose **File→Info→Convert** and click **OK** when the conversion message appears.

   Notice that [Compatibility Mode] *no longer appears in the title bar; the document is now in Word 2019 format. Now you will insert a SmartArt graphic.*

5. Choose **Insert→Illustrations→SmartArt** 🖼.

6. Choose the **Process** category on the left, choose **Continuous Block Process**, and click **OK**.

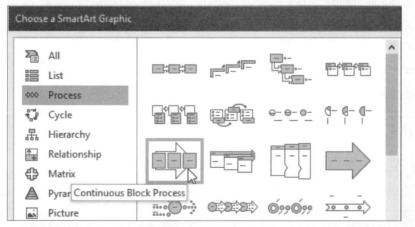

7. Click the tab to the left of the graphic and type the following in the Type Your Text Here pane; close the text pane when you're finished:
   - First bullet: **Hatch**
   - Second bullet: **Release**

8. Click the third text box in the graphic to select it and tap Delete.

9. Position the mouse pointer on the graphic's upper-right corner sizing handle and drag down diagonally toward the center of the image until it's about half its original size.

Prepare a Backward-Compatible Document

You want to make sure that the originator of the file will have access to it. You will format a Word 2019 document to be compatible with earlier versions.

10. Choose **File→Save As** and navigate to your **Word Chapter 10** folder.

11. Click the **Save As Type menu** button ▼, choose **Word 97-2003 Document (*.doc)**, and click **Save**.

    The Microsoft Word Compatibility Checker opens, indicating that SmartArt graphics are not supported in earlier versions of Word. You will cancel the conversion so the SmartArt graphic will work as intended.

12. Click **Cancel**.

Inspect the Document

13. Choose **File→Info** and observe the Properties panel on the right.

    Names appear in the Related People area.

14. In the Info screen, choose **Check for Issues→Inspect Document**.

    A message appears indicating that you should save your changes because the Document Inspector may remove data that can't be restored.

15. Click **Yes** to save the file and open the Document Inspector.

    In this example, you will leave all checkboxes checked.

16. Click **Inspect**.

    The inspector found properties and personal information, which you will remove.

17. Click the **Remove All** button next to Document Properties and Personal Information and then close the dialog box.

    If the Document Inspector found other issues as well, ignore them.

18. Choose **File→Info** and notice that the names were removed from the Related People area in the Properties panel.

19. Click **Back** to return to the document.

20. Save and close the file.

REINFORCE YOUR SKILLS: W10-R2

Help in a Backyard Bee-Counting Project

The bee population has declined, and Kids for Change plans to help gather data by taking part in a bee-counting project. One of the members has researched methodologies for doing this. The research will be the basis of discussion for the next monthly meeting. In this exercise, you will use document protection features to prevent the document from being modified accidentally.

1. Open **W10-R2-Bees** from your **Word Chapter 10** folder and save it as:
   W10-R2-BeesRevised

2. Chose **File→Info→Protect Document→Restrict Editing** and place a checkmark in the checkbox below the Editing Restrictions heading in the task pane.

3. Choose **Tracked Changes** from the drop-down list and then click **Yes, Start Enforcing Protection**.

4. When the dialog box opens, enter `pass` in both password fields and click **OK**.

5. Select **method** in the first line of the first paragraph below the *Counting the Vanishings Bees* heading and type `technique` in its place.

   The changes are marked because no one can modify the document without changes being tracked.

6. Click **Stop Protection**; when the Unprotect Document box appears, type `pass` in the Password field and click **OK**.

   Now you will accept the changes you made.

7. Choose **Review→Changes→Next** 🔁.

8. Accept both changes and click **OK** when the message appears.

Apply Editing Restrictions

Now you will apply editing exceptions and specify only certain parts of the document that can be edited. You will, however, allow reviewers to add comments anywhere in the document.

9. Choose **Comments** from the drop-down list in the Editing Restrictions section of the task pane.

10. Select the first three paragraphs in the main article and then place a checkmark in the **Everyone** checkbox below the Exceptions (optional) heading in the task pane.

11. Click **Yes, Start Enforcing Protection** and then click **OK** to close the dialog box without setting a password.

12. Deselect the paragraphs and notice the unprotected area is shaded, making it easy for reviewers to locate.

13. Select any word outside the shaded section and attempt to delete it.

    The deletion doesn't work because only the shaded area can be edited.

14. In the first line of the third shaded paragraph, select **decline in** and replace it with: `waning`

    The change is allowed because it's in the area specified as an exception. Now you will add a comment, as comments were specifically permitted in the Restrict Editing task pane.

15. In the fifth paragraph of the article, select **$200 billion**.

16. Choose **Review→Comments→New Comment** 🗨.

    Comments are allowed, not only in the exceptions area, but anywhere in the document.

17. Type this text: `Can anyone verify this dollar amount?`

18. Click **Stop Protection**.

19. Select the shaded paragraphs, remove the checkmark from the **Everyone** checkbox in the task pane, and then close the task pane.

20. Right-click the comment in the markup area and choose **Delete Comment**.

Set a Document Password and Mark a Document as Final

21. Choose **File→Info→Protect Document→Encrypt with Password**.

22. Type `pass` in the Encrypt Document dialog box and click **OK**.

23. Type **pass** in the Confirm Password dialog box, click **OK**, and then save and close the document.

24. Choose **File→Open** and click **W10-R2-BeesRevised** at the top of the Recent Documents list.

25. Type **pass** in the password box and click **OK**.

26. In the Backstage Info screen, choose **Protect Document** again and choose **Mark as Final**; when the message appears, click **OK**.

27. When additional information about this setting appears, click **OK**.

28. Click **Back** to return to the document.

    Notice the Marked as Final bar at the top of the screen.

29. Select the first paragraph in the main article and tap Delete .

    The text is not deleted because the document is marked as final.

30. Choose **File→Info→Protect Document→Mark as Final** to turn off the feature.

31. Click **Back** to return to the document.

    The Marked as Final bar at the top of the document has disappeared.

Create a Digital Certificate and Add a Digital Signature

Now you will generate a self-created digital certificate so you can apply a digital signature to your document. Remember, a self-created certificate is not verified by an outside agency.

32. Open File Explorer and navigate to the SELFCERT application through a path such as C:\Program Files (x86)\Microsoft Office\root\Office16.

Note! *Seek assistance as necessary to determine the path on your computer. And remember that you may not have permission to create a digital certificate on computers for general use by multiple people.*

SELFCERT.EXE

33. Scroll to locate the SELFCERT application.

34. Double-click the file; when the Create Digital Certification dialog box opens, type **Charles Eng** in Your Certificate's Name field and click **OK**.

35. When the message appears indicating the certificate was successfully created, click **OK** and then close the File Explorer window.

36. Position the insertion point at the end of the document and choose **Insert→Text→Signature Line** .

37. Follow these guidelines to complete the information in the dialog box:
    - Suggested Signer: **Charles Eng**
    - Suggested Signer's Title: **Project Manager**
    - Suggested Signer's E-mail Address: **CharlesEng@Kids.com**.
    - Click **OK** to complete the setup.

38. Right-click the signature line and choose **Sign**; type **Charles Eng** next to the X in the Sign dialog box.

39. If the Signing As name at the bottom of the dialog box is not Charles Eng, follow these steps:
    - Click the **Change** button, choose **Charles Eng**, and click **OK** to close the dialog box.

      A message appears indicating the certificate cannot be verified because a self-created certificate is not verified by an outside agency.
    - Click **Yes** to use the certificate.

40. Click the **Sign** button to close the Sign dialog box; click **Yes** to acknowledge that the certificate cannot be verified.

41. Click **OK** when the next message appears.

42. Attempt to delete a word in the document.

    The deletion does not work because you cannot edit a signed document.

43. Close the document.

REINFORCE YOUR SKILLS: W10-R3

Learn About 4-H

Kids for Change is thinking about partnering with the 4-H organization on a project. One of the members has researched the organization, and the research document will be the basis for discussion in the next monthly meeting. In this exercise, you will prepare a document for sharing by considering compatibility issues and controlling access to the document. Finally, you will apply a digital signature to the document.

1. Open **W10-R3-4H** from your **Word Chapter 10** folder and save it as: **W10-R3-4HRevised**

   Notice Compatibility Mode *in the title bar. Next you will convert this Word 2003 document to a Word 2019 document.*

2. Choose **File→Info→Convert**.

3. In the message box indicating the conversion may cause changes, click **OK**.

   Compatibility Mode *no longer appears in the title bar. Now you will work with the Document Inspector.*

4. Choose **File→Info** and notice that names appear in the Related People area of the Properties panel.

5. In the Info screen, choose **Check for Issues→Inspect Document**.

6. When the message to save changes appears, click **Yes**.

7. When the Document Inspector opens, leave all checkboxes checked and then click **Inspect** and review the results.

   The inspector found properties and personal information in the document.

8. Click the Document Properties and Personal Information **Remove All** button and then close the Document Inspector.

9. Choose **File→Info** and notice that the names have been removed in the Related People area of the Properties pane.

Restrict Editing and Apply Editing Exceptions

10. In the Backstage Info screen, choose **Protect Document→Restrict Editing**.

11. If necessary, click the checkbox below the Editing Restrictions heading in the task pane and choose **Tracked Changes** from the drop-down list.

12. Click **Yes, Start Enforcing Protection** and then click **OK** to close the dialog box without setting a password.

13. In the first paragraph below the *About 4-H* heading, position the insertion point in front of *universities* and type: `colleges and` Spacebar

The changes are marked with Tracked Changes because that was chosen in the Restrict Editing task pane.

14. Click **Stop Protection** and then right-click the change and choose **Accept Insertion**.

15. Choose **No Changes (Read Only)** from the drop-down list in the Editing Restrictions section of the task pane.

16. Select the three paragraphs below the *Cooperative Extension System* heading on page 1 and then check the **Everyone** checkbox in the task pane.

17. Click **Yes, Start Enforcing Protection** and click **OK** to bypass setting a password.

18. Click in the document to deselect the text and notice that the exceptions text is shaded.

19. If necessary, display formatting marks; position the insertion point next to the paragraph symbol at the end of the third line in the second paragraph.

20. Tap Delete twice to combine the paragraphs and then tap Spacebar .

21. Click **Stop Protection**, select the shaded paragraphs, and then remove the checkmark from the **Everyone** checkbox.

22. Close the Restrict Editing task pane.

Mark the Document as Final

23. Choose **File→Info→Protect Document→Mark as Final**.

24. When a message appears indicating that the document will be marked as final and saved, click **OK**.

25. In the message box with additional information about this setting, click **OK**.

26. Click **Back** to return to the document and notice the Marked as Final bar at the top of the screen.

27. Close the document.

✎ Apply Your Skills

APPLY YOUR SKILLS: W10-A1

Plan a Tour of Mexico City

Universal Corporate Events is planning a tour of Mexico City for a client. The initial research is complete, and now it's time for colleagues to review the article. In this exercise, you will work with compatibility issues, convert a document to different formats, and work with document properties and the Document Inspector.

1. Open **W10-A1-MexCity** from your **Word Chapter 10** folder and save it as:
    `W10-A1-MexCityRevised`
2. Position the insertion point at the end of the document.
3. Attempt to insert a SmartArt graphic and then use the Convert command in Backstage view to convert the document to Word 2019 format.
4. Open the SmartArt Graphic dialog box and then choose the **List** category and the **Vertical Box List** (second graphic, second row).
5. Open the Type Your Text Here pane and add this text at the bullet points:
    *   `History`
    *   `Economy`
    *   `Climate`
6. Close the text pane and then resize the graphic to about half its original size.
7. Use the **Save As** command and navigate to your **Word Chapter 10** folder.
8. Choose **Word 97-2003 Document** from the Save as Type list and click **Save**.

    When the Compatibility Checker opens, notice that the SmartArt graphic will be converted into an object that can't be edited. You may want to edit the object in the future, so you will prevent the conversion.
9. Click **Cancel**.

    Next, you will work with document properties and the Document Inspector.
10. Go to Backstage view and notice the names in the Related People area in the Properties panel.
11. Use the Document Inspector to inspect all categories listed in the dialog box.
12. Remove all document properties and personal information, and then close the dialog box.
13. Go to Backstage view and notice that no names appear in the Related People area of the Properties panel.
14. Save and close the file.

Organize a San Francisco Tour

Universal Corporate Events is adding San Francisco to its West Coast tour options. A Universal Corporate Events rep has done some research, and now some other reps who are familiar with San Francisco will review the document. In this exercise, you will use features for securing the document so accidental changes are not made.

1. Open **W10-A2-SanFran** from your **Word Chapter 10** folder and save it as: **W10-A2-SanFranRevised**

2. Open the Restrict Editing task pane and restrict editing to Tracked Changes.

3. Enforce protection, using **pass** as the password.

   Notice the message in the task pane indicating that all changes will be tracked.

4. Make these edits:
   - In the fourth line of the first paragraph of the main article, delete **road**.
   - Replace *Within* at the beginning of the second paragraph with: **In**
   - In the second line of the same paragraph, delete the comment in parentheses.

5. Stop protection, enter your password, and accept the changes you made.

   Now you will use formatting restrictions.

6. Apply formatting restrictions that limit formatting to the use of the Heading 1 style; do not allow other styles to be removed.

7. Start enforcing protection and bypass using a password.

8. Display the available styles and apply the Heading 1 style to the *Landmarks* and *Neighborhoods* headings.

9. Stop protection and then accept the formatting changes.

   Now you will apply an editing exception.

10. Restrict editing to Comments and then select the **Chinatown** paragraph (starts at the bottom of page 1).

11. Check the **Everyone** checkbox to make the paragraph editable by all reviewers.

12. Start enforcing protection and bypass adding a password.

13. Make these edits:
    - In the first sentence of the *Chinatown* paragraph, delete the phrase **part tourist trap, part**.
    - Select the **Landmarks** heading on page 1 and add this comment: **A trip to Muir Woods to see giant redwoods is a great side trip.**

14. Stop protection, select the **Chinatown** paragraph, and remove the checkmark from the **Everyone** checkbox.

Create a Digital Certificate and Add a Signature

15. Open File Explorer and navigate to the SELFCERT application.

16. Double-click **SELFCERT** and then type **Ella Mae Chang** in the field at the bottom of the Create Digital Certificate dialog box.

17. Close the File Explorer window.

18. Position the insertion point at the end of the document and tap Enter twice.

19. Use the **Signature Line** command to open the Signature Setup dialog box.

20. Follow these guidelines to enter the information in the dialog box:

Signature Setting	Value
Suggested Signer	`Ella Mae Chang`
Suggested Signer's Title	`Project Manager`
Suggested Signer's E-mail Address	`EllaMae@uce.com`

21. Add `Ella Mae Chang` to the signature line.

    Remember, you may need to change the Signing As name.

22. Attempt to delete a word in the document.

    The deletion is not permitted because a signed document cannot be modified.

23. Delete the signature line in the document.

    Now you will add an invisible signature.

24. Use the Info screen in Backstage view to add a digital signature.

25. In the Sign dialog box, choose **Created This Document** from the Commitment Type list.

26. In the Purpose for Signing This Document field, type: `San Francisco Itinerary`

27. Click **Yes** to use the certificate; when the message appears indicating the signature has been saved, click **OK**.

28. Close the file.

APPLY YOUR SKILLS: W10-A3

Prepare a Cape Town Itinerary

A Universal Corporate Events rep has conducted some research for a Cape Town travel itinerary. Now some colleagues will review the document. In this exercise, you will prepare the document for sharing. You will consider compatibility issues, apply editing restrictions and exceptions, and add a digital signature.

1. Open **W10-A3-CapeTown** from your **Word Chapter 10** folder and save it as: `W10-A3-CapeTownRevised`

2. Choose **Design→Document Formatting→Themes**.

   This feature is not available in a Word 2003 document. Now you will convert the document to the Word 2019 format.

3. Use the **Convert** command to convert the document to the Word 2019 format.

4. Choose **Design→Document Formatting** and notice the Themes feature is now available.

   Now you will apply editing and formatting restrictions and formatting exceptions.

5. Apply the Tracked Changes editing restrictions, but don't add a password.

6. Make these edits:
   - In the first line of the first paragraph in the main article, replace *neighborhood* with: `community`
   - At the end of the same line, replace *inhabited* with: `occupied`

7. Stop protection.

8. Apply formatting restrictions that limit formatting to the Heading 1 and Title styles; don't allow any other formatting styles in the document to be removed.

9. Enforce protection, but don't set a password.

10. Display the available styles and apply the Heading 1 style to the *What to See in Cape Town* heading.

11. Stop protection and accept the formatting change you made.

   Now you will apply editing exceptions to specify an area of the document where reviewers can freely edit.

12. Restrict editing to Comments, select the **Kirstenbosch Botanical Gardens** paragraph at the bottom of page 1, and then check the **Everyone** checkbox.

13. Enforce protection and bypass setting a password.

14. In the fourth line of the editable paragraph, right-click **diverse**, choose **Synonyms**, and choose **varied**.

15. Select **Bo-Kaap** at the beginning of the article and add this comment: `I think we should definitely include this in the tour.`

16. Stop protection.

17. Select the exceptions paragraph, remove the checkmark from the **Everyone** checkbox, and then close the task pane.

Add a Digital Signature

18. Open File Explorer and navigate to the SELFCERT application.

19. Double-click **SELFCERT** and enter `Marty Zane` at the bottom of the Create Digital Certificate dialog box; close File Explorer.

20. Position the insertion point at the end of the document and set up the signature line with this information:

Signature Setting	Value
Suggested Signer	`Marty Zane`
Suggested Signer's Title	`Project Manager`
Suggested Signer's E-mail Address	`MartyZane@uce.com`

21. Sign the signature line by entering `Marty Zane` next to the X in the Sign dialog box.

22. If necessary, change the Signing As name.

23. Close the document and exit Word.

Project Grader

This chapter does not include Project Grader exercises. Project Grader content is based on the learning objectives for a chapter, and sometimes those learning objectives cannot be accurately graded by the system. Objectives from this chapter that can be accurately graded may be included in later chapters, if applicable.

✈ Extend Your Skills

These exercises challenge you to think critically and apply your new skills in a real-world setting. You will be evaluated on your ability to follow directions, completeness, creativity, and the use of proper grammar and mechanics. Save files to your chapter folder. Submit assignments as directed.

W10-E1 That's the Way I See It

As the owner of a small business, you are considering adding a new product to your line. Decide on the type of business you are in and what the new product will be. Conduct online research of the new product.

Create a short introduction (three to five sentences) describing why you think the new product will enhance your line. Copy content of one to two pages about the product, citing your sources. Include at least two headings. Save the file in Word 97-2003 Document (*.doc*) format as: **W10-E1-NewProd**

Convert the file to the current format. Insert a SmartArt graphic from the List category and list three benefits of your new product. Restrict formatting to Heading 1 and Heading 2 styles and then apply heading styles to all of the headings. Restrict editing to Comments. Select one paragraph and make it exception text that all reviewers may freely edit. Add a comment to text that is not part of the exception text.

W10-E2 Be Your Own Boss

As the owner of Blue Jean Landscaping, you are researching online marketing articles specifically targeted to the landscaping business. After researching several articles, decide which marketing approach you will use and write a short introduction (five to six sentences) describing the benefits of your chosen approach. Copy the article as the basis for your research document, citing your source. Save the document as: **W10-E2-Market**

Because you will be distributing this document to current and potential customers, you want to check it for personal information. Examine the document properties to determine whether your name is visible in the Properties panel. Use the Document Inspector to remove all personal information. Set a document password (**pass**). Finally, create a digital certificate in your name, and then apply a visible digital signature to the end of the document and sign it.

W10-E3 Demonstrate Proficiency

The owner of Stormy BBQ is considering expanding the business to include a BBQ food truck. Conduct online research regarding how to start a food truck business. Create a one- to two-page report, copying information from the Internet and citing your sources. Write a short introduction (four to five sentences) summarizing why you think a food truck is a good or bad addition to the business. Save the document as: **W10-E3-FoodTruck**

Because you will distribute this document for the Stormy BBQ marketing staff to review, you will prepare it for sharing. Examine your document's properties and use the Document Inspector to remove all personal information. Select a paragraph in the document and apply the exception that makes the paragraph available to all reviewers to edit. Apply editing restrictions, making it read-only. Enforce protection and assign the password (**pass**). Finally, create a digital certificate in your name and apply an invisible digital signature to the document.

WORD

11 | Personalizing Word

You can increase productivity by customizing Word to work the way you want it to work. In addition, you can use built-in accessibility features whenever the default methods are not serving your needs. In this chapter, you will work with Word options, AutoCorrect, and document properties to enhance the way you work. You will also work with translation and accessibility settings to make your documents easier to use for those who speak other languages or have disabilities.

LEARNING OBJECTIVES

▸ Customize Word options

▸ Use AutoCorrect to insert customized text

▸ Modify document properties

▸ Implement and use accessibility features

▸ Use language translation features

Project: Setting Up Word to Work the Way You Do

You have been working with Raritan Clinic East for several months. By examining the types of documents you have created during this time, you have some ideas for setting up Word to make it more efficient. You have learned that most documents are saved in folders in a specific location, and you want to set the default directory to access your main folder. You plan to pin documents you use all the time to the Recent Documents list so they're always at the top of the list, and you have discovered that document properties can be helpful in searching for files located in a large group of files. You've also identified ways to make Word easier to use for employees with disabilities. Finally, you've been informed that several employees speak other languages, so you decide to translate some of the company documents.

Setting Word Options

The Word Options dialog box includes many options for you to control the way Word acts. In the Proofing category, you can set up your own AutoCorrect terms to print. In the Save category, you can change the AutoRecover time interval and identify the default folder you want to use to store files. You can use the Advanced category to set the number of documents that appear in the Recent Documents list.

Note! *Word Options are program-level settings, meaning they're settings for Word as a program—they don't affect individual documents. It also means any changes you make in Word Options remain in place until you change them.*

≡ File→Options

Customizing AutoCorrect

In addition to correcting errors, AutoCorrect lets you automatically insert customized text and special characters. It's also useful for replacing abbreviations with full phrases. For example, you could set up AutoCorrect to insert the name of your company whenever you type an abbreviation for it.

You can also delete built-in AutoCorrect entries that may interfere with your writing; however, this is not recommended when working on public or shared computers. If you use these program-level settings to improve your own productivity, you may inadvertently complicate that of others.

View the video "An Overview of the AutoCorrect Dialog Box."

≡ File→Options→Proofing→AutoCorrect Options button

You can designate exceptions to AutoCorrect so it doesn't alter text as it normally would. For example, AutoCorrect assumes that a period indicates the end of a sentence and, therefore, capitalizes the first letter of the next word. But, in some cases, such as after abbreviations, you don't want the next word capitalized. The Exceptions feature lets you handle this easily.

View the video "AutoCorrect Exceptions."

In this exercise, you will create a custom AutoCorrect entry. You type Raritan Clinic East *over and over in your work, so it's an ideal candidate for an AutoCorrect shortcut.*

1. Open **W11-D1-DraftProc** from your **Word Chapter 11** folder and save it as: **W11-D1-DraftProcRevised**

2. Choose **File→Options**, click the **Proofing** category in the left panel, and then click **AutoCorrect Options** to open the AutoCorrect dialog box.

3. Follow these steps to create an AutoCorrect shortcut:

A Type **rce** in the Replace field.

B Type **Raritan Clinic East** in the With field.

C Click **Add**.

4. Click **OK** twice.

5. Press ⌈Ctrl⌉+⌈End⌉ to move to the end of the document and then scroll to the top of the page.

6. In the first line of the first paragraph, position the insertion point in front of the word *share* and type: **at**⌈Spacebar⌉**rce**⌈Spacebar⌉

7. In the first line of the second paragraph, delete **the Clinic**, type **rce**⌈Spacebar⌉, and correct any spacing if necessary.

   Now you will delete the AutoCorrect term so the next person who uses the computer will have the same experience.

8. Choose **File→Options**, click the **Proofing** category in the left panel, and then click **AutoCorrect Options**.

9. Type **rce** in the Replace field to scroll the list to that term.

10. Click **Delete** and then click **OK** twice.

11. Save the file.

Changing the AutoRecover Interval and Default File Location

If you're concerned about power failures or are working on an important document, you may wish to reduce the amount of time between automatic saves. Your documents are saved every ten minutes by default.

When Word and other Office programs are installed on a computer, default file locations are set up. The default save location is your OneDrive; however, you can change the default file location to a folder on your local computer. Doing so reduces the time it takes to navigate to that location. The new save location applies to new, unsaved documents. A document that was previously saved will default to the folder in which it was originally saved.

 You may not have user permission to change the AutoRecover interval or the default file location on a public or shared computer. The settings changes made in this section are program level and permanent.

≡ File→Options→Save→Save AutoRecover Information Every x Minutes

≡ File→Options→Save→Default Local File Location

DEVELOP YOUR SKILLS: W11-D2

In this exercise, you will set the AutoRecover time interval to five minutes. Then you will change the default file location where files are saved.

Before You Begin: *Ask assistance as necessary to determine whether you have user permission to change the AutoRecover interval or default file location. If you do, verify the procedure for restoring the original AutoRecover interval and default file location. If you don't, read the steps to familiarize yourself with the process.*

1. Choose **File→Options** and click the **Save** category on the left.

 As you make changes, first make a note of the current settings so you can reset them to the original state later in this chapter.

2. Follow these steps to change the AutoRecover interval:

Ⓐ	Save documents	Ⓑ
	Save files in this format:	Word Document (*.docx)
	☑ Save AutoRecover information every	5 ⬍ minutes

Ⓒ

Ⓐ Locate the Save Documents section at the top of the dialog box.

Ⓑ Write down the current AutoRecover interval so you can reset it later.

Ⓒ Use the **spin box controls** to set the time to **5** minutes.

Your documents will now automatically save every five minutes.

3. In the same section of the dialog box, check the **Save to Computer by default** checkbox.

4. To specify a particular folder, click **Browse** to the right of the Default Local File Location field.

5. In the Modify Location dialog box, scroll in the left column to and choose **Desktop** and then click **OK** twice.

   The Desktop is now your default save location. Next you will test the change.

6. Press ⎡Ctrl⎤+⎡N⎤ to start a new, blank document.

7. Choose **File→Save As** and notice that *This PC* is highlighted rather than Recent.

8. Click **Browse** at the bottom of the Save As panel on the left.

The Save As dialog box opens with the Desktop as the target save location.

9. Click **Cancel** to close the Save As dialog box and then click **Close** in the left panel to close the blank document.

If you made changes in this exercise, you will reset them to their original state later in this chapter.

Modifying the Recent Documents List

The Open screen in Backstage view displays a list of recent documents accessed on the computer. By default, the Recent Documents list shows the last 50 documents opened on the computer. When a document appears in this list, you can open it by clicking the document name. You can turn off the feature so that no documents are listed or change the number of documents shown in the list.

If you move a document to a different folder using an application such as Windows Explorer, the link to the document in the Recent Documents list is broken. After moving a document, you need to re-navigate to the new location to open the file.

Changing the Number of Files in the Recent Documents List

If you find that you primarily work with the last few documents in the Recent Documents list before moving on to new documents, you may want to change the number of documents shown to reduce the number of documents you have to select from. Setting the number of documents to display in the list is controlled by settings in the Word Options dialog box. Settings range from 0 to 50.

 View the video "Set the Number of Recent Documents to Display."

≡ File→Options→Advanced→Show This Number of Recent Documents

Pinning a File to the Recent Documents List

Periodically, you may find yourself modifying a document over an extended period of time. To ensure that the document always appears in the Recent Documents list, you can pin it to the list. Pinned documents appear at the top of the list and remain in the list regardless of how many additional documents you access.

 View the video "How to Pin a File to the Recent Documents List."

Clearing the List of Recently Used Documents

If you perform tasks associated with specific projects, you might enjoy the ability to clear all unpinned items from the Recent Documents list, thus displaying only the documents you purposely pinned. In addition, if you are using a computer you share with others, you may want to clear the list so others won't have easy access to the documents you used, especially if you work with confidential documents.

Note! *You may not have user permission to change the Recent Documents list on a public or shared computer. The setting changes made in this section are program level and permanent.*

 View the video "Setting the Recently Used List to Zero."

In this exercise, you will change the number of documents that appear in the Recent Documents list. You will also pin a document to the list.

Before You Begin: *Seek assistance as necessary to determine whether you have user permission to change the Recent Documents list. If you do, verify the procedure for restoring the original Recent Documents settings. If not, read the steps to familiarize yourself with the process.*

1. Choose **File→Options** and then follow these steps to change the number of documents shown in the Recent Documents list:

- Ⓐ Choose the **Advanced** category.
- Ⓑ Scroll down to the Display options.
- Ⓒ Write down the value in this box and then change it to **10**.

2. Click **OK**, choose **File→Open**, and note that a maximum of ten documents appear in the Recent Documents list. (Your list may have fewer than ten documents.)

3. Right-click any document in the list and notice (but don't click) the Clear Unpinned Documents command.

   Clicking this would clear all unpinned documents from the list.

4. Tap ⎵Esc⎵ to close the menu.

   Now you will pin, and then unpin, a document in the list.

5. Right-click any document in the list and choose **Pin to List**.

   The document moves to the Pinned category at the top of the list and a pushpin icon appears on the right.

6. Click the **pushpin** icon of the document you just pinned to unpin it.

7. Return to the document window.

Restoring Default Settings

Setting custom options for the way you work is a great practice if using a computer that is assigned to you. However, these settings are permanently applied to Word on a program level, and when you are working on a computer you share with others, it's generally a good idea to restore the default settings you have changed.

In this exercise, you will restore the default settings in the Word Options dialog box. By restoring the options to their original state, you also will review the features just covered.

Before You Begin: *Retrieve the default settings you wrote down when you modified options earlier.*

1. Choose **File→Options** and then follow these steps to restore your AutoRecover interval:

Ⓐ Choose the **Save** category.

Ⓑ Reset the AutoRecover duration to **10** or enter the setting you wrote down when you made the change in this field.

Ⓒ Check this box if it was previously unchecked.

Ⓓ Enter the file location path you wrote down earlier.

Leave the dialog box open.

2. Follow these steps to restore your Recent Documents list:

Ⓐ Choose the **Advanced** category.

Ⓑ Reset the number of recent documents to **50** or enter the original setting you wrote down when you made the change in this field.

3. Click **OK**.

Document Properties

Each time you create a new document, properties information is pulled from options set on your computer as well as information detected about the document. Properties information appears in the Properties panel of the Info screen in Backstage view. Information includes such items as the file size, the date on which it was created/modified, and the author's name. The Advanced Properties feature contains more data about your document, and this is where you can create custom properties.

The Advanced Properties dialog box contains the widest array of properties.

W11-D5-DraftProcRevised.docx Properties

General | Summary | Statistics | Contents | Custom

Title: Draft Procedures Manual
Subject:
Author:
Manager:
Company:

Category:
Keywords: Staff, Nurses, Aids, Doctors
Comments: Sent for review early in April.

Hyperlink base:

Template: Normal.dotm

☑ Save Thumbnails for All Word Documents

OK | Cancel

Entering information in the Properties panel also populates fields in the Advanced Properties dialog box.

Checking the "Thumbnails" checkbox fills in the Contents tab with headings (Heading 1 through Heading 3 styles) that appear in the document.

Following are descriptions of the tabs in the Advanced Properties dialog box:

▸ **General:** Contains some of the same information as the Properties panel in Backstage view, as well as additional information, including location and file attributes, such as Read Only

▸ **Summary:** Contains the same text boxes as the Properties panel, including Title, Keywords (Tags), and Comments; checking the Save Thumbnails for All Word Documents checkbox fills in the Contents tab with headings (Heading 1 through Heading 3 styles) that appear in the document

▸ **Statistics:** Contains many of the same statistics as the Properties panel in Backstage view as well as additional fields, such as Paragraphs, Lines, and Characters

▸ **Contents:** Contains the document headings (Heading 1 through Heading 3 styles) when the Save Thumbnails for All Word Documents checkbox is checked on the Summary tab

▸ **Custom:** Allows you to define additional fields, which can be useful when searching for a document in a large group of documents

DEVELOP YOUR SKILLS: W11-D5

In this exercise, you will add comments and keywords (tags) to the procedures manual.

1. Save your file as: **W11-D5-DraftProcRevised**
2. Choose **File→Info** and review the document properties in the Properties panel on the right side of the screen.

3. Enter the information shown in the Title, Tags, and Comments fields, and then enter your name in the Author field.

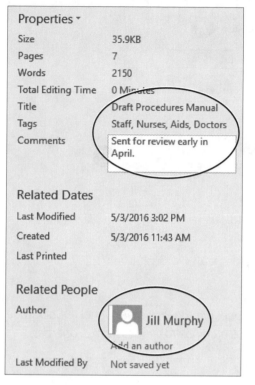

4. Click the **Properties menu** button ▾ at the top of the Properties panel and choose **Advanced Properties**.

The properties you entered in the Properties panel are replicated in the Summary tab.

5. Click **OK** and then return to the document.

6. Save the file.

Creating a Custom Property

When there is no existing property to meet your needs, you can create a custom property and define the type of data you plan to place in the field, including Text, Date, and Number. A list of suggested names is provided for custom fields, but you can also define your own property names. For example, if you want to include a due date for a document, you can create a new Due Date property and assign Date as the data type. These custom properties don't appear in the Properties panel in the Backstage Info view. To view them, you need to refer to the Custom tab of the Advanced Properties dialog box.

DEVELOP YOUR SKILLS: W11-D6

In this exercise, you will create a custom property for the procedures manual to hold the due date for the final version of the document.

1. Save your file as: **W11-D6-DraftProcRevised**

2. Choose **File→Info**, click the **Properties menu** button ▾ at the top of the Properties panel, and choose **Advanced Properties**.

3. Follow these steps to create a new custom property:

(A) Click the **Custom** tab.

(B) Type **Due Date** in the Name field.

(C) Select **Date** from the Type list.

(D) Type **7/31/2021** in the Value field.

(E) Click **OK**.

Remember, custom properties do not appear in the Properties panel in Backstage view. Refer to the Custom tab in the Advanced Properties dialog box to view custom properties.

4. Save the document.

Accessibility

Word offers several options to enhance accessibility, making it more user-friendly for those who have difficulty with the default settings. For those with reading difficulties, Word provides tools to enhance document readability and can also read documents aloud in a variety of digital voices.

One of the most useful Accessibility features is the Tell Me box, which allows users to simply enter the command they are looking for instead of using the Ribbon to find it. Word also works well with a variety of screen reader software, and it can adapt easily to various types of keyboards.

"Tell me what you want to do" box

≡ View→Immersive→Learning Tools 📖

Add Alternative Text

Using alternative text helps people with limited vision understand the meaning of pictures and graphics. Although traditionally used with web pages, you can also add alternative text to regular Word documents for greater accessibility.

≡ Picture Tools→Format→Accessibility→Alt Text 🖼

DEVELOP YOUR SKILLS: W11-D7

In this exercise, you will view the document in the Immersive Learning Tools feature using the Tell Me box. You'll also add alternative text to the image at the top of the document.

1. Save your file as: **W11-D7-DraftProcRevised**

   Choose the View tab on the Ribbon to see the location for Immersive→Learning Tools. Return to the Home tab before proceeding to the next step.

2. Click anywhere inside the **Tell me what you want to do** box next to the Help tab on the Ribbon and type: **learning tools**

3. Choose the **Learning Tools** option at the top of the results list.

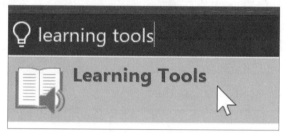

   The command is executed just as if you had selected it from the View tab in the Ribbon. The Tell Me box can execute any ribbon command; all you have to do is type it in.

4. If necessary, in the Immersive Learning Tools view, choose **Immersive→Learning Tools→ Learning Tools→Column Width menu button ▾ →Narrow**.

5. Choose **Immersive→Learning Tools→Learning Tools→Syllables** to turn on syllable breaks.

6. Place the insertion point at the beginning of the first paragraph in the main document and choose **Immersive→Learning Tools→Learning Tools→Read Aloud**.

7. Choose **Immersive→Learning Tools→Close→Close Learning Tools** to close the Immersive view and stop the read aloud feature.

   Next, you'll add alternative text to the logo image at the top of the document.

8. Scroll to the top of the document's cover page and select the **Raritan Clinic East** logo image.

9. Choose **Picture Tools→Format→Accessibility→Alt Text 🖼**.

10. In the Alt Text panel, click **Generate a description for me** to have Word try to analyze the image and generate an automatic description.

If this is the first time you're using this feature, you may see a box that asks if you want to Use Intelligent Services. If the box appears, click Turn On.

Alt Text   ▾ ✕

How would you describe this object and its context to someone who is blind?

(1-2 sentences recommended)

```
┌──────────────────────────────────┐
│ |                                │
│                                  │
│                                  │
│                                  │
└──────────────────────────────────┘
```

┌─────────────────────────────────┐
│   Generate a description for me │
└─────────────────────────────────┘

☐ Mark as decorative

Word generates the description A close up of a logo *with high confidence. If this were inaccurate, you could type in your own alt text description or modify the automatically generated description.*

11. Close the Alt Text panel and then save and close the file.

Global Content Standards and Language Options

Word uses language settings to determine how to proof your documents or where to make suggestions concerning spelling and grammar. In addition, Word can translate words and phrases you type into a variety of languages. Word can also translate entire documents with a single click.

☰ Review→Language→Language 🌐 menu button ▾→Set Proofing Language

☰ Review→Language→Translate 🔠 menu button ▾→Translate Selection or Translate Document

DEVELOP YOUR SKILLS: W11-D8

In this exercise, you'll check the default proofing language to make sure it's set to English. Then, you'll use Word's Translator to translate a simple phrase from English to Spanish and then translate an entire document into Spanish.

1. Open a new, blank document.

2. Choose **Review→Language→Language** 🌐 **menu button** ▾→**Set Proofing Language**.

English (United States) *is selected and the checkbox for detecting the language automatically is checked.*

3. Click **Cancel**.

4. Type this text into the blank document: **Hello! How are you?**

5. Highlight the phrase **How are you?** and choose **Review→Language→Translate** 🈂 **menu button ▾→Translate Selection**.

   If this is the first time you're using the Translation feature, you may see a box that asks if you want to Use Intelligent Services. If so, click Turn On.

6. In the Translator panel that appears, change the To language to **Spanish**.

   To Spanish ▾

   ¿Cómo estás?

7. Close the document without saving and then open **W11-D8-Newsletter**.

8. If necessary, choose **Review→Language→Translate→Set Document Translation Language**.

9. In the Translator panel, set the From language to **English** if necessary, set the To language to **Spanish**, and click **Translate**.

   Selection   **Document**

   Create a translated copy of this document with the Microsoft Translator service.

   From English ▾

   To Spanish ▾

   Translate

   After a few moments, the translated document will appear.

10. Save the translated file as **W11-D8-NewsletterSpanish** and then close it.

11. Close the English version of the file without saving.

Self-Assessment

Check your knowledge of this chapter's key concepts and skills using the Self-Assessment in your ebook or online (eLab course or Student Resource Center).

Reinforce Your Skills

Streamline Kids for Change Office Procedures

Kids for Change is streamlining its office procedures. Staff members will review various options to determine which changes will help them be more efficient. In this exercise, you will prepare screenshots of the features you would like staff members to consider for personalizing Word.

1. Open **W11-R1-WordOptions** from your **Word Chapter 11** folder and save it as: **W11-R1-WordOptionsRevised**

    First, you will create an AutoCorrect shortcut for a Kids for Change Nature Hikes project.

2. Choose **File→Options→Proofing** and click **AutoCorrect Options**.

3. Type **kfcnh** in the Replace field, type **Kids for Change Nature Hikes** in the With field, and click **OK** twice.

4. Position the insertion point at the end of the document and then type **AutoCorrect Shortcut: kfcnh** and tap ⏎ **Enter**.

    Now you will work with Save options.

5. Choose **File→Options**, choose the **Save** category, and change the AutoRecover interval to **15** minutes.

Save documents		
Save files in this format:	Word Document (*.docx)	
☑ Save AutoRecover information every	15 ⊝	minutes

6. Check the **Save to Computer by default** checkbox.

7. Click **Browse** to the right of the Default Local File Location field.

8. In the Modify Location dialog box, navigate to the **Desktop** and click **OK**.

    Now you will take a screenshot of the Word Options dialog box and paste it into your Word Options document.

9. Press ⎇ **Alt** + **PrtScn** to take a screenshot of the dialog box and then click **OK** to close the dialog box.

10. Press **Ctrl** + **V** to paste the screenshot; resize it to about a third of its original size.

11. Create a new, blank document so you can test the default local file location.

12. Choose **File→Save As** and click **Browse** at the bottom of the left-hand panel.

    The path at the top of the dialog box leads to the Desktop. The change worked!

13. Click **Cancel** to close the Save As dialog box.

14. Click **Close** in the far-left panel to close the blank document without saving it.

Customize the Recent Documents List

15. Choose **File→Options→Advanced**.

16. Scroll down to the Display options and change the number of recent documents to **8**.

Display		
Show this number of Recent Documents:	8	⊕ ⓘ

17. Press [Alt]+[PrtScn] to take a screenshot and click **OK**.

18. Ensure the insertion point is at the end of the document, tap [Enter], and paste the screenshot; resize it to about a third of its original size.

19. If necessary, resize the screenshots until they both fit on the first page of the document.

20. Choose **File→Open** and notice that a maximum of eight documents appear in the Recent Documents list.

Now you will pin a document to the Recent Documents list.

21. Hover the mouse pointer over a filename to display the pushpin icon at the right and then click the **pushpin** to pin the document to the list.

The document will remain in the list until it is unpinned.

22. Right-click the document you just pinned and choose **Unpin from List**.

You can clear all documents, except pinned documents, from the list.

23. Right-click any document in the Recent Documents list and notice (but don't click) the Clear Unpinned Documents command.

24. Tap [Esc] to close the menu.

Now you will restore the settings you changed in the Word Options dialog box.

25. Retrieve the list of changes you noted earlier and, if necessary, restore these options to their original settings:

- AutoRecover interval
- Save to Computer by Default checkbox
- Default Local File Location path
- Number of Recent Documents displayed

Create a Custom Property

26. Choose **File→Info**, click the **Properties menu** button ▼ at the top of the Properties panel, and click **Advanced Properties**.

27. Click the **Custom** tab and follow these guidelines to create a custom property:

- Choose **Checked By** from the Name list.
- Leave the data type as Text.
- Type **Reviewer Sean Oct 17** in the Value field.

You have requested that each reviewer sign in here so you can easily track who has already reviewed the document and when.

28. Take a screenshot of the dialog box and click **OK**.

29. Return to the document and make sure the insertion point is at the end of the document.

30. Tap ⌈Enter⌋, paste the screenshot in your Word Options document, and resize it to about a third of its original size.

This screenshot will appear on page 2.

31. Save and close the file.

REINFORCE YOUR SKILLS: W11-R2

Make Kids for Change Documents Accessible

Kids for Change is making their documents accessible for users with disabilities. They are also translating their documents to increase readership. In this exercise, you will activate accessibility features in a newsletter and translate the newsletter into French.

1. Open **W11-R2-Vaccine** from your **Word Chapter 11** folder and save it as: **W11-R2-VaccineRevised**

2. Choose **View→Immersive→Learning Tools**.

3. If necessary, set the width to Wide by choosing **Immersive→Learning Tools→Learning Tools→Column Width menu button ▾→Wide**.

4. If necessary, choose **Immersive→Learning Tools→Learning Tools→Syllables** to turn on syllable breaks.

5. Choose **Immersive→Learning Tools→Close→Close Learning Tools**.

Use the Tell Me Box to Add Alternative Text to an Image

6. Select the vaccine image at the end of the second column and then click in the **Tell Me** box.

7. Type **alt text** and choose **Display the Alt Text Pane** from the list of results.

8. In the Alt Text pane, click **Generate a description for me**.

The automatically generated description needs just a little extra detail.

9. Place the insertion point after the word *person* in the generated description.

10. Tap ⌈Spacebar⌋ and type: **being vaccinated**

11. Close the Alt Text pane and save the file.

Translate the Document

12. Place the insertion point anywhere in the text and choose **Review→Language→Translate menu button ▾→Set Document Translation Language**.

13. In the Translator panel that appears, set **French** as the To language and click **Translate**.

14. Save the French version of the document as `W11-R2-VaccineRevisedFrench` and close it.

15. In the English version of the document, close the Translator panel and close the document.

REINFORCE YOUR SKILLS: W11-R3

Personalize Options and Translate a Document

Kids for Change will participate in an after-school tutoring program. In this exercise, you will personalize Word to work more efficiently. You'll add alt text to the image and then translate the document into Italian.

1. Open **W11-R3-WaterPollution** from your **Word Chapter 11** folder and save it as: `W11-R3-WaterPollutionRevised`

2. Choose **File→Options→Save** and change the AutoRecover interval to **5** minutes.

3. Check the **Save to Computer by default** checkbox.

4. Click **Browse** to the right of the Default Local File Location field, navigate to the Desktop, and click **OK** twice.

Now you will observe the change to the default file location.

5. Start a new, blank document.

You saved the tutoring file outside of the default location, so if you click Browse, you will access its original storage location. You will use the new, blank document to test the storage location you just set.

6. Choose **File→Save As** and note that *This PC* is highlighted.

7. Click **Browse** and notice that the path at the top of the Save As dialog box leads to the Desktop.

8. Click **Cancel** to close the Save As dialog box and then close the blank document without saving it.

Pin a Document to the Recent Documents List

9. Choose **File→Open**, hover the mouse pointer over a filename, and notice the pushpin icon to its right.

10. Click the **pushpin** to move the file into the Pinned category at the top of the list.

11. Click the **pushpin** again to unpin the document and return it to the main list.

Now you will restore the default settings that you noted earlier.

12. Click **Options** on the left and restore these items to their original settings:
- AutoRecover interval
- Save to Computer by Default
- Default Local File Location

Add Alt Text and Translate the Document

Now you will add alt text to the image and translate the document into Italian.

13. Select the image at the bottom of the second column and choose **Picture Tools→Format→ Accessibility→Alt Text**.

14. In the Alt Text box, type **Two children fishing by a lake** and then close the Alt Text panel.

15. Place the insertion point anywhere in the document text, click the **Tell Me** box, and type: **translate**

16. In the results, hover the mouse pointer over Translate, and in the submenu that appears, choose **Set Document Translation Language**.

17. Set the To language to **Italian** and click **Translate**.

18. Save the translated document as **W11-R3-WaterPollutionRevisedItalian** and close it.

19. In the English version of the document, close the Translator panel.

20. Save the file and exit Word.

✎ Apply Your Skills

APPLY YOUR SKILLS: W11-A1

Review Office Efficiency

The Universal Corporate Events office manager is reviewing various options to determine whether it's possible to make work more efficient for the company. In this exercise, you will create an AutoCorrect shortcut, change options for saving, and work with document properties.

1. Open **W11-A1-Efficiency** from your **Word Chapter 11** folder and save it as: **W11-A1-EfficiencyRevised**

2. Open the Word Options dialog box, choose the **Proofing** category, and click **AutoCorrect Options**.

3. Enter **uce** in the Replace field and **Universal Corporate Events** in the With field; click **OK** twice.

4. Position the insertion point at the bottom of the document and type **uce** Enter to test the shortcut.

5. Open the Word Options dialog box; in the Save category, change the AutoRecover interval to **30** minutes.

6. Check the **Save to Computer by default** checkbox.

7. Use the **Browse** button to the right of the Default Local File Location and set the path to the Desktop.

8. Take a screenshot ([Alt]+[PrtScn]) of the Word Options dialog box, paste it at the end of your document, and resize it to about a third of its original size.

9. Create a new, blank document and choose **File→Save As**.

10. Click **Browse** to test your default file location (Desktop) and then cancel the dialog box and close the blank document.

    Now you will restore the default settings.

11. Retrieve the list of default settings you wrote down earlier and reset the defaults in the Word Options dialog box.

12. In the Properties panel in Backstage view, type **Efficiency** in the Tags field.

13. Use the **Properties menu** button ▼ to open the **Advanced Properties** dialog box.

14. Follow these guidelines to add a custom property:

Property	Value
Property Name	**Checked By**
Property Type	**Text**
Property Value	**Matt Robinson**

As staff members review the potential procedural changes, they will enter their names in the Properties dialog box so you can tell when everyone has completed the review.

15. Take a screenshot of the Properties dialog box and click **OK**; return to the document.

16. Position the insertion point at the end of the document, generate a blank line, and paste the screenshot, resizing it to about a third of its original size.

17. Save and close the file.

APPLY YOUR SKILLS: W11-A2

Universal Corporate Events Expansion

Universal Corporate Events is preparing to expand into Mexico. To do so, it needs to be ready to translate documents into Spanish. In this exercise, you will activate Learning Tools, add alt text to the images in a document, and translate the document into Spanish.

1. Open **W11-A2-Multitasking** from your **Word Chapter 11** folder and save it as: **W11-A2-MultitaskingRevised**

2. Open the document in the Immersive Learning Tools view.

3. If necessary, set the column width to **Wide** and turn *off* the Syllables breaks; then close the Immersive Learning Tools view.

4. Select the image at the beginning of the document and open the Alt Text panel.

5. Type **Cartoon image of a man doing six things with six arms** in the Alt Text box.

6. Select the image at the end of the document and click **Generate a description for me** in the Alt Text box.

7. In the automatically generated description, replace the word *Water* with **Rocks** and close the Alt Text panel.

8. Place the insertion point anywhere in the document text, set the translation language to **Spanish**, and translate the document.

9. Save the translated document as **W11-A2-MultitaskingRevisedSpanish** and close it.

10. Close the Translator panel.

11. Save the English version of the file and close it.

APPLY YOUR SKILLS: W11-A3

Get Ready for the Corporate Trainer

Universal Corporate Events staff will be reviewing advanced Word features with a corporate trainer. The staff will practice using the features and record questions for the trainer. In this exercise, you will work with an AutoCorrect shortcut and the Word Options dialog box. You will also translate a document into Spanish.

1. Open **W11-A3-TravelTips** from your **Word Chapter 11** folder and save it as **W11-A3-TravelTipsRevised**

   First you will create an AutoCorrect shortcut. You anticipate frequently typing the name of a new client, Morgan, Alexander, and Swift, so a shortcut will be a real time saver.

2. Open the Word Options dialog box, choose the **Proofing** category, and click **AutoCorrect Options**.

3. Enter **mas** in the Replace field and **Morgan, Alexander, and Swift** in the With field; click **OK** twice.

4. Click the insertion point at the end of the document, type **mas**, and tap [Enter].

5. Open the Word Options dialog box, choose the **Save** category, and change the AutoRecover interval to **20** minutes.

6. Check the **Save to Computer by default** checkbox.

7. Use the **Browse** button to change the default local file location to the Desktop.

8. Take a screenshot of the **Word Options** dialog box, click **OK**, and paste it at the end of your document.

9. Create a new, blank document so you can test your changes.

10. In the Backstage, Save As screen, click **Browse** and check that the path at the top of the Save As dialog box targets the Desktop.

11. Click **Cancel** to close the Save As dialog box and then close the blank document without saving.

12. Restore the default settings in the Word Options dialog box.

Add Alt Text and Translate the Document

Now you will add alt text to the document's image and translate it into Spanish.

13. Select the image at the end of the document and add this alt text: **ClipArt image of two travelers in an airport**

14. Translate the document into Spanish, saving the Spanish version as: **W11-A3-TravelTipsRevisedSpanish**

15. Close the Translator panel, save the English version of the file, and exit Word.

📋 Project Grader

This chapter does not include Project Grader exercises. Project Grader content is based on the learning objectives for a chapter, and sometimes those learning objectives cannot be accurately graded by the system. Objectives from this chapter that can be accurately graded may be included in later chapters, if applicable.

Extend Your Skills

These exercises challenge you to think critically and apply your new skills in a real-world setting. You will be evaluated on your ability to follow directions, completeness, creativity, and the use of proper grammar and mechanics. Save files to your chapter folder. Submit assignments as directed.

W11-E1 That's the Way I See It

As the owner of a small business, you know it's important for your staff to operate as efficiently as possible. You're a whiz with Word, and you want to show your employees some features that can help them effectively organize the Word environment. Write a one- to two-page document explaining how the following might help them:

▸ When would it be beneficial to change the AutoRecover time interval?

▸ Under what circumstances would it be helpful to change the default file location?

▸ What is the benefit of pinning documents to the Recent Documents list?

▸ How can custom properties be useful?

Add two or three screenshots to help make your concepts come alive. Add your own Title and Comment to the Properties panel in Backstage view for the document you create. Save your file as: **W11-E1-WordIdeas**

W11-E2 Be Your Own Boss

As the owner of Blue Jean Landscaping, you've noticed your business has been increasing lately among the Latino community. To better serve your customers, you decide to start translating your monthly newsletters into Spanish. You also decide to further improve the usability of your newsletters by adding alt text to your images.

Do some research on new landscaping technologies. Write a one- to two-page newsletter about the company's expansion and some of the new landscaping technology you plan to adapt at Blue Jean Landscaping. Be sure the newsletter includes at least one image and add alt text to that image. When finished, translate the newsletter into Spanish. Save your English file as **W11-E2-BJLNewsletter** and your Spanish file as **W11-E2-BJLNewsletterSpanish**

W11-E3 Demonstrate Proficiency

The owner of Stormy BBQ just attended a Microsoft Word class at the local community college, and it opened his eyes to some of the beneficial features that he had not been aware of. Knowing that you are a very experienced Word user, he has asked you to record some ideas about how Word options, accessibility features, and translation options can benefit the business. Write a one- to two-page paper explaining what Word options (at least three) you would modify and why. Insert two images into the document and add alt text to both of them. Translate the document into another language so you can show the owner an example of Word's translation feature. Use the Properties panel to add a Title and Tag. Save your English file as **W11-E3-StormyWordFeatures** and your translated file as **W11-E3-StormyWordFeaturesTranslated**

12 Creating Custom Forms and Using Macros

Word allows you to create custom forms for others to fill out. Creating forms gives you significant control over what information is entered and where. You can also automate repetitive tasks by recording macros, which can execute a long list of steps with a single click. In this chapter, you will work with creating custom forms and macros to enhance the way you work.

LEARNING OBJECTIVES

▸ Activate and use hidden Ribbon tabs

▸ Create and use custom forms

▸ Create and run macros

▸ Edit created macros

▸ Use macros across documents

📁 Project: Automating Tasks in Word

As a long-time employee of Raritan Clinic East, you've been entrusted with several new responsibilities. The clinic will be using a new electronic system for patients to enter their information, instead of using traditional pen and paper. Doing so will help automate patient information, as reception personnel will not have to take what patients have written on a form and type it into the computer. You've been tasked with creating the form that patients will use. However, this is just one of many tasks you've been given, and you realize that you can be far more efficient by automating several of the tasks in Word. After doing some research, you've learned that macros are a great way to create personalized automation tasks.

Creating a Custom Form

When you create a custom form, you increase control over where other users may enter information. Word's content controls allow you to create a form with check boxes, text fields, drop-down lists, and other items. For example, when users must enter a date, a Date Picker Content Control gives users the option to pick a date from a drop-down calendar instead of typing it into the field.

Each content control has specific properties. The Check Mark properties allow you to specify which symbol (for example, a checkmark or another symbol) is used to fill in the box, while the Drop-Down List properties allow you to add a series of choices to the drop-down menu attached to the field.

Once you've set up the main body of the document, you can then enter the necessary content controls. Content controls do not include spaces before or after the field, so remember to include them where needed. Finally, you can restrict editing to prevent others from making changes to your document's main body, while still allowing users to fill out the form fields generated by the content controls.

☰ Developer→Controls

Preparing to Add Content Controls

The Developer tab is hidden by default; it doesn't appear on the Ribbon until you activate it, which is necessary to create custom forms. To activate the Developer tab, open Word Options and check the necessary box under the Customize Ribbon tab.

To prevent inadvertently adding content to your forms as you're building them (for example, accidentally checking a box), it's a good idea to use Design Mode. Doing so will prevent any changes to form field content.

☰ File→Options

☰ File→Developer→Controls→Design Mode ☑

In this exercise, you will build a patient form. First, you will activate the Developer tab so it appears on the Ribbon and turn on Design Mode. Then you'll add content control fields and change their properties. Finally, you'll restrict editing of this document to prevent patients from making changes to anything but the form fields.

1. Open **W12-D1-PatientInfo** from your **Word Chapter 12** folder and save it as:
   W12-D1-PatientInfoRevised

2. Choose **File→Options→Customize Ribbon**.

3. In the Customize Ribbon pane, check the **Developer** box and click **OK**.

The Developer tab now appears in the Ribbon.

4. Turn on Design Mode by choosing **Developer→Controls→Design Mode**.

Add Content Controls

5. Place the insertion point after the colon at the end of the first form line, labeled *Today's Date*, tap Spacebar , and choose **Developer→Controls→Date Picker Content Control** 📅.

Because you are in Design Mode, Word inserts a noneditable Date Picker Content Control field. When you turn off Design Mode, as you will later in the exercise, you will see how the final editable field will wlook.

> **Today's Date:** Click or tap to enter a date.

6. Implement the controls as shown, remembering to place the insertion point after the colon at the end of each line, tap Spacebar , and choose the control:

Line	Implement Control
Patient Name	**Developer→Controls→Rich Text Content Control** Aa
Patient Phone Number	**Developer→Controls→Rich Text Content Control** Aa
Patient Date of Birth	**Developer→Controls→Date Picker Content Control** 📅
Yes	**Developer→Controls→Check Box Content Control** ☑
No	**Developer→Controls→Check Box Content Control** ☑

> **Today's Date:** Click or tap to enter a date.
>
> **Patient Name:** Click or tap here to enter text.
>
> **Patient Phone Number:** Click or tap here to enter text.
>
> **Patient Date of Birth:** Click or tap to enter a date.
>
> **Do you have insurance?**   Yes ☐ No ☐

Edit Content Control Properties

7. Place the insertion point after the colon at the end of the last line, tap Spacebar , and choose **Developer→Controls→Drop-Down List Content Control** 📋.

A drop-down list doesn't do much good without list entries, so you will use content control properties to add these entries as well as adjust other options.

8. If necessary, place the insertion point anywhere in the *Choose an item* text in the new content control field, and then choose **Developer→Controls→Properties** 📄.

9. Follow these steps to adjust properties in the Content Control Properties dialog box:

Ⓐ Type **Doctor** as the Content Control title.

Ⓑ Check **Use a style to format text typed into the empty control**.

Ⓒ From the Style drop-down menu, choose **Strong**.

The Drop-Down List Properties at the bottom of the dialog box allow you to enter the list entries that patients will be able to choose from.

10. Click **Add**; in the Add Choice dialog box, type: **Dr. Morgan** in the Display Name box and click **OK**.

The same text, Dr. Morgan, *will also appear in the Value box.*

11. Repeat the process to enter three additional choices:
- **Dr. Yung**
- **Dr. Baylor**
- **Dr. Bundt**

You decide to list the doctors in alphabetical order.

12. Select **Dr. Baylor** and click **Move Up** twice.

13. Select **Dr. Bundt** and click **Move Up** twice.

Display Name	Value
Choose an item.	
Dr. Baylor	Dr. Baylor
Dr. Bundt	Dr. Bundt
Dr. Morgan	Dr. Morgan
Dr. Yung	Dr. Yung

Drop-Down List Properties

Add...
Modify...
Remove
Move Up
Move Down

14. Click **OK** to close the Content Control Properties dialog box.

15. Choose **Developer→Controls→Design Mode** to turn off Design Mode.

Patients will see this form when they open the file. They'll be able to use the date pickers to choose dates, enter text in the text fields, check the boxes where appropriate, and choose from the list of doctors.

Restrict Editing

Finally, you'll restrict editing so patients cannot edit the main body of the form.

16. Choose **Developer→Protect→Restrict Editing**.

17. In section 2 of the Restrict Editing panel that appears, check the **Allow only this type of editing in the document** box and select **Filling in forms**.

1. Formatting restrictions

☐ Limit formatting to a selection of styles

Settings...

2. Editing restrictions

☑ Allow only this type of editing in the document:

Filling in forms ▼

3. Start enforcement

Are you ready to apply these settings? (You can turn them off later)

Yes, Start Enforcing Protection

18. In section 3, click **Yes, Start Enforcing Protection**; in the password box, leave both boxes blank and click **OK**.

The file is ready for patients to use.

19. Turn off the Developer tab by opening the Word options window and unchecking Developer under the Customize Ribbon.

20. Close the Restrict Editing panel and then save and close the file.

Automating Tasks with Macros

Macros are useful for automating routine tasks, especially those that involve many steps. You can record a series of steps using the macro recorder and then play them back automatically when needed. For example, you may need to switch to a color printer frequently. You can record the steps of the process in a macro, and, when it's time to switch printers, the macro can quickly perform the steps. Whenever you find yourself doing the same thing over and over, you have a candidate for a macro.

≡ View→Macros→Macros

Assigning Macros to a Toolbar or a Keyboard Shortcut

If you intend to use a macro frequently, you can assign it to a keyboard shortcut or a button on the Quick Access toolbar for easy access. This isn't required, though. You can always run a macro directly from the Macros dialog box.

Storing Macros

Macros can be stored within individual documents or entire templates, including the Normal.dotm template, which is the default location for storing macros. The *m* in the *.dotm* file extension indicates the template can contain macros. Macros stored in the Normal.dotm location are available to all documents on the system, meaning you can create a macro using one document, save it under the Normal.dotm template as shown in this image, and then run the macro on other documents. No matter where you choose to store your macro, keep in mind that the macro name cannot contain spaces but will accept other characters, such as the underscore.

Macro names cannot contain spaces. ──

You can assign a macro to run from a Quick Access toolbar button or a keyboard shortcut. ──

You can choose the document name or the Normal.dotm template in which to store the macro.

Recording Limitations

Certain mouse motions such as scrolling, selecting options from drop-down lists, and resizing windows cannot be recorded in macros. You may also find that certain commands are grayed out on the Ribbon or in the drop-down list during the macro recording. You can overcome these limitations by choosing alternative techniques. For example, if selecting an item from a drop-down list doesn't record in a macro, display the dialog box containing the feature and make the selection there. Instead of scrolling in a document, use arrow keys to position the insertion point (keystrokes are recorded). Likewise, when selecting text with the mouse fails to record, try ⎡Shift⎤ plus arrow keys or other keyboard shortcuts.

When you record a macro and change settings in a dialog box using arrow keys, the change normally sticks until you exit Word; this means the dialog box doesn't reset to its default state. As a result, running the macro again in the same session may change the setting to the *next* option in the dialog box.

 When necessary, reset the dialog box to its default state as part of the macro.

DEVELOP YOUR SKILLS: W12-D2

In this exercise, you will record a macro that sets up the orientation, margins, and page size for a survey form. The macro will also insert and format text.

1. Create a new, blank document.
2. Choose **View→Macros→Macros** 📇 **menu button** ▾ **→Record Macro**.
3. Follow these steps to name the macro and begin the recording process:

| Record Macro | ? | ✕ |

Macro name:
Ⓐ SurveyForm

Assign macro to

🔨 Button   ⌨ Keyboard

Store macro in:
Ⓑ All Documents (Normal.dotm)

    Ⓐ Type **SurveyForm** (no spaces) in the Macro Name field.

    Ⓑ Ensure the storage location is the **Normal.dotm** template, which makes the macro available to all documents on your computer, and click **OK**.

The mouse pointer now has a cassette tape attached to it, indicating that your steps are being recorded. Now you will perform the steps to record.

4. Choose **Home→Styles** and click the **No Spacing** style in the Quick Styles gallery.

This sets line spacing at 1.0 and removes the after-paragraph spacing.

5. Choose **Home→Font→Bold** B .
6. Type: **Raritan Clinic East Pediatric Diagnostic Specialties**
7. Choose **Layout→Page Setup→Orientation** 🔲 and then choose **Landscape**.
8. Choose **Layout→Page Setup→Margins** 🔲 and then choose **Custom Margins**.

9. Set the top and bottom margins to **0.4"** and the left and right margins to **0.5"**.

10. Click the **Paper** tab at the top of the dialog box and then set the width to **7"** and the height to **5"**.

11. Click **OK** to apply the settings.

Stop Recording and Run the Macro

12. Choose **View→Macros→Macros** [icon] **menu button** ▼ **→Stop Recording**.

    The macro is now ready for playback.

13. Close the document without saving it and then create a new, blank document.

14. Choose **View→Macros→Macros** [icon].

15. Follow these steps to run the macro:

Ⓐ Choose your **SurveyForm** macro.

Ⓑ Click **Run**.

Your macro creates a copy of your survey form. The heading line is selected. You can click to deselect. If you made an error in the macro, you could delete the incorrect macro and record it again. Later in the chapter, you will learn to make minor edits in the VBA Editor.

16. Close the document without saving it and then create a new, blank document.

Editing Macros with the VBA Editor

Visual Basic for Applications (VBA) is a macro programming language that runs in Office 2019 applications. When you record a macro, you are creating a Visual Basic module containing program instructions that execute when you run the macro. This topic provides a brief introduction to Visual Basic, but a complete discussion is beyond the scope of this course.

You can edit a macro by displaying the Visual Basic module and modifying the code. The editor has its own menus, toolbars, and commands, which allow you to develop, edit, and test Visual Basic applications.

DEVELOP YOUR SKILLS: W12-D3

In this exercise, you will open the Visual Basic editor and revise your macro. Then you will run the modified macro.

1. Choose **View→Macros→Macros** [icon].

2. Choose your **SurveyForm** macro and click **Edit**.

3. Follow these steps to modify the code:

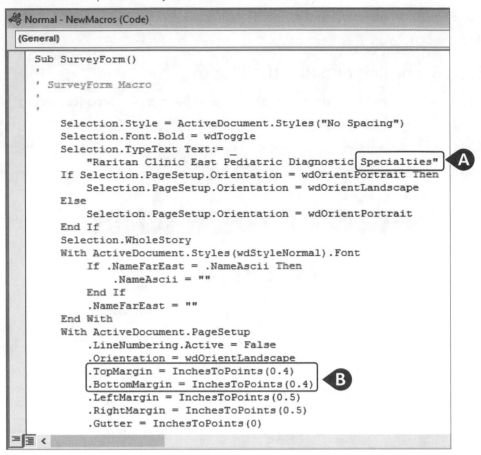

Ⓐ Change the word *Specialties* to: **Specialists**

Ⓑ Change the top and bottom margin settings from *0.4* to: **0.5**

4. Choose **File→Close** and return to Microsoft Word.

The changes are saved automatically. Now you will test the edited macro.

5. Choose **View→Macros→Macros** 🖼, choose **SurveyForm** in the Macro Name list, and click **Run**.

Notice that the word Specialties *has changed to* Specialists.

6. Choose **Layout→Page Setup→Margins** ⊞→**Custom Margins**.

Notice that the top and bottom margins are now set to 0.5.

7. Close the dialog box.

8. Close the document without saving and then create a new, blank document.

Running Macros from the Quick Access Toolbar

When you create a macro to automate repetitive tasks, you are trying to increase efficiency. To make macros run more efficiently, you can assign them to a button on the Quick Access toolbar or to a shortcut keystroke. By taking advantage of these time-saving tools, you alleviate the tedious nature of displaying the Macros dialog box and selecting the macro each time you want to run it.

You can assign a toolbar button or keyboard shortcut to a macro as you record it. In addition, you can assign a toolbar button to an existing macro using the Quick Access toolbar commands in the

Word Options dialog box. Word offers numerous button images you can choose to help identify your macro buttons.

View the video "Assign a Macro to the Quick Access Toolbar."

DEVELOP YOUR SKILLS: W12-D4

In this exercise, you will assign the SurveyForm macro to a Quick Access toolbar button.

1. Choose **File→Options→Quick Access Toolbar**.
2. Follow these steps to assign a macro button to the Quick Access toolbar:

Choose commands from:ⓘ

Macros ◀ Ⓐ

<Separator>
Normal.NewMacros.SurveyForm Ⓑ

Customize Quick Access Toolbar:ⓘ

For all documents (default) ◀ Ⓒ

   Ⓐ In the Choose Commands From menu, choose **Macros**.

   Ⓑ Select the **Normal.NewMacros.SurveyForm** macro.

   Ⓒ Ensure **For All Documents (Default)** is chosen here.

3. Click **Add** in the middle of the dialog box and then click **OK**.

   Notice that a new button appears on the Quick Access toolbar.

4. Hover the mouse pointer over the button to see the button name in a ToolTip and then click the button to run the macro.

Macro Security

Macro attacks were more prevalent in earlier versions of Microsoft Office. Added security features in recent versions have caused virus creators to pursue other avenues; however, it's always better to be safe than sorry. The Trust Center in the Word Options dialog box contains security settings.

Macro Settings

○ Disable all macros without notification
◉ Disable all macros with notification
○ Disable all macros except digitally signed macros
○ Enable all macros (not recommended; potentially dangerous code can run)

MACRO SETTINGS OPTIONS

Option	What It Does
Disable all macros without notification	Word disables all macros and does not notify users
Disable all macros with notification	The default setting; gives the user the option to enable or disable a macro
Disable all macros except digitally signed macros	Allows users to enable or disable only digitally signed macros
Enable all macros (not recommended; potentially dangerous code can run)	Significantly reduces security and could cause serious damage

WORD

Deleting Macros

You may create a macro for use in a special project, and when the project is complete, you no longer need the macro. Deleting a macro when it's no longer required helps keep the list of macros from becoming unwieldy.

DEVELOP YOUR SKILLS: W12-D5

In this exercise, you will review security settings and delete the macro you previously created. Finally, you will remove the macro button from the Quick Access toolbar.

1. Choose **File→Options→Trust Center**.
2. Click **Trust Center Settings** and review the Macro Settings options at the top of the dialog box.

   You will not make any changes to security settings.
3. Click **Cancel** twice to close the dialog boxes.

   Now you will delete your macro.
4. Choose **View→Macros→Macros** .
5. Choose the **SurveyForm** macro in the Macro Name list, click **Delete**, and click **Yes** to verify the deletion; close the dialog box.

   Now you will remove the macro button from the Quick Access toolbar.
6. Right-click the **macro** button and choose **Remove from Quick Access Toolbar**.
7. Exit Word without saving the document.

Self-Assessment

Check your knowledge of this chapter's key concepts and skills using the Self-Assessment in your ebook or online (eLab course or Student Resource Center).

Reinforce Your Skills

Create a Volunteer Form

Kids for Change is always looking for volunteers to help with its various community projects. You've been asked to create a form to help streamline the volunteering process. In this exercise, you will add content control fields to the form and restrict editing so volunteers can fill out the form but not change the form itself.

1. Open **W12-R1-VolunteerForm** from your **Word Chapter 12** folder and save it as: **W12-R1-VolunteerFormRevised**

2. Choose **File→Options→Customize Ribbon**.

3. In the Customize the Ribbon pane, check the **Developer** box and click **OK**.

4. Turn on Design Mode by choosing **Developer→Controls→Design Mode** .

5. Place the insertion point after the end of the first form line (*What is your name?*), tap Spacebar , and choose **Developer→Controls→Rich Text Content Control** Aa .

6. Implement the controls as shown, remembering to place the insertion point after the colon at the end of each line, tap Spacebar , and choose the control:

Line	Implement Control
Best phone number	**Rich Text Content Control** Aa .
Which project	**Drop-Down List Content Control**
What date	**Date Picker Content Control**
Yes	**Check Box Content Control** .
No	**Check Box Content Control** .

Edit Content Control Properties

7. Place the insertion point anywhere in the drop-down list content control at the end of the third line and choose **Developer→Controls→Properties** .

8. Using the **Add** button toward the bottom of the Content Control Properties dialog box, add these three items as choices for the drop-down list:
   - **Recycling Initiative**
   - **Scholarship Fund Drive**
   - **School Transportation**

9. Click **OK** to close the Content Control Properties dialog box.

10. Choose **Developer→Controls→Design Mode** to turn off Design Mode.

Restrict Editing

11. Choose **Developer→Protect→Restrict Editing** .

12. In section 2 of the Restrict Editing panel, check the box and select **Filling in Forms** from the drop-down menu.

13. In section 3, click **Yes, Start Enforcing Protection**; in the password box, leave both boxes blank and click **OK**.

14. Turn off the Developer tab, close the Restrict Editing panel, and save and close the file.

REINFORCE YOUR SKILLS: W12-R2

Create Kids for Change Carbon Footprint Macro

Kids for Change operates on a tight budget, so it types its own document header information instead of having it printed professionally. The group is working on a carbon footprint project and wants that information to appear in the headers of documents related to the project. Because this is something the group will do over and over, it knows it has a good candidate for a macro. In this exercise, you will create and test the macro.

1. Create a new, blank document.

2. Choose **View→Macros→Macros** 🔲 **menu button ▼→Record Macro**.

3. Name the macro **Header** and verify the Normal template is chosen in the Store Macro In field.

4. Click **OK** to start recording.

The mouse pointer now has a cassette tape attached to it so you know your steps are being recorded.

5. Choose **Insert→Header & Footer→Header** ▯ and then choose **Edit Header** at the bottom of the gallery.

6. Tap Tab to position the insertion point in the center of the header and type: **Kids for Change**

You can't double-click in the document body to close the header area. This is one of the mouse movements that the macro recorder can't record.

7. Choose **Header & Footer Tools→Design→Close→Close Header and Footer** ☒.

8. Choose **View→Macros→Macros menu button ▼→Stop Recording**.

9. Close the document without saving; start a new, blank document.

Now you will run the macro.

10. Choose **View→Macros→Macros**, make sure the Header macro is chosen, and click **Run**.

11. Close the document without saving; start a new, blank document.

Use the VBA Editor to Modify the Macro

12. Choose **View→Macros→Macros**, verify the Header macro is chosen, click **Edit**, and locate the *Kids for Change* text.

```
End If
ActiveWindow.ActivePane.View.SeekView = wdSeekCurrentPageHeader
Selection.TypeText Text:=vbTab & "Kids for Change"
ActiveWindow.ActivePane.View.SeekView = wdSeekMainDocument
```

13. Position the insertion point before the quotation mark and after the word *Change*, tap Spacebar , and type: **Carbon Footprint Project**

14. Choose **File→Close** and return to Microsoft Word.

Now you will assign the macro to a keyboard shortcut and run the macro to verify your editing changes.

Assign the Macro to a Keyboard Shortcut

15. Choose **File→Options→Customize Ribbon**.

Notice the Customize button next to Keyboard Shortcuts at the bottom of the left-hand panel.

> Keyboard shortcuts: Customize...

16. Click **Customize...** and then scroll down and choose **Macros** from the Categories list on the left.

17. Choose the **Header** macro in the field on the right.

18. Position the insertion point in the **Press New Shortcut Key** field and press Ctrl + 9.

Below the Current Keys field at left, notice that the shortcut you entered is currently unassigned.

19. Click **Assign** to assign the shortcut to your macro, click **Close**, and then click **OK**.

Now you will test the macro.

20. Press Ctrl + 9 to run the macro and then notice the editing change you made.

Review Macro Security and Delete the Macro

21. Choose **File→Options→Trust Center**, click **Trust Center Settings**, and review the Macro Settings at the top of the dialog box.

You will not change any security settings.

22. Click **Cancel** twice to close the dialog boxes.

23. Choose **View→Macros→Macros** 🖳, verify the Header macro is chosen, and click **Delete**.

24. Click **Yes** to confirm the deletion and then close the Macros dialog box.

25. Save the file as **W12-R2-Header** in your **Word Chapter 12 folder** and then close it.

REINFORCE YOUR SKILLS: W12-R3

Create a Form and Use a Tutoring Schedule Macro

Kids for Change needs your help with its after-school tutoring program. In this exercise, you will create a form for tutoring volunteers and create a macro that generates a table in which you can set up the weekly tutoring schedule.

1. Open **W12-R3-Tutoring** from your **Word Chapter 12** folder and save it as:
W12-R3-TutoringRevised

2. If necessary, use the Word Options window to activate the Developer tab in the Ribbon.

3. Turn on **Developer→Controls→Design Mode** ☒.

4. Place the insertion point after the colon at the end of the first form line (*Your Name*), tap Spacebar, and choose **Developer→Controls→Drop-Down List Content Control** 🔲.

5. Choose **Developer→Controls→Properties** 🔲 and enter these items as choices for the drop-down list:
- **Max**
- **Allison**
- **Manuel**
- **Margarita**
- **Other**

6. Click **OK** to close the Content Control Properties dialog box.

7. Insert a **Rich Text Content Control** `Aa` at the end of the next line, remembering to include the space.

8. Insert a **Check Box Content Control** `☑` after the word *Yes* in the next line, remembering to include the space.

9. Turn off **Developer→Controls→Design Mode** `☒`.

Record and Run a Macro

Now you will create a table macro that Kids for Change can use each week to set up the tutoring schedule.

10. Position the insertion point in the blank line at the end of the document.

11. Choose **View→Macros→Macros** `▦` **menu button ▾ →Record Macro**.

12. Name the macro **TutorTable** and verify the Normal template is chosen in the Store Macro In field.

    Now you will assign the macro to a keyboard shortcut.

13. Click **Keyboard**.

14. Ensure Macros appears in the left column and then choose the **Normal.NewMacros. TutorTable** macro on the right.

15. Position the insertion point in the **Press New Shortcut Key** field and press `Ctrl`+`8`.

    Notice that the shortcut is unassigned.

16. Click **Assign** and then click **Close**.

17. Choose **Insert→Tables→Table** `▦` and drag in the grid to create a **5x7** table.

    The insertion point should be in the first table cell. Macro recording limitations don't allow you to drag the mouse pointer to select cells, so you will use keystrokes.

18. Press `Shift` and tap `→` five times to select the first row.

19. Choose **Table Tools→Layout→Merge→Merge Cells** `▦`.

20. Choose **Table Tools→Layout→Alignment→Align Center** `▤` and type: **Weekly Tutoring Schedule**

21. Enter the remaining text, using arrow keys to position the insertion point.

    Remember, macro recording limitations don't allow you to position the insertion point with the mouse pointer.

Weekly Tutoring Schedule				
	Max	Allison	Manuel	Margarita
Monday				
Tuesday				
Wednesday				
Thursday				
Friday				

22. Choose **View→Macros→Macros** `▦` **menu button ▾ →Stop Recording**.

    Now you will remove the table so you can recreate it with the macro. Nelly is replacing Allison while she is out of town, so you'll make that change to the macro first.

23. Right-click the table and choose **Delete Table**.

24. Choose **View→Macros→Macros** `▦`, make sure the TutorTable macro is chosen, and click **Edit**.

25. Locate Allison's name. (You may need to enlarge the Visual Basic window—Allison is near the bottom.)

```
End With
Selection.MoveRight Unit:=wdCharacter, Count:=5, Extend:=wdExtend
Selection.Cells.Merge
Selection.SelectCell
Selection.ParagraphFormat.Alignment = wdAlignParagraphCenter
Selection.Cells.VerticalAlignment = wdCellAlignVerticalCenter
Selection.TypeText Text:="Weekly Tutoring ScheduleMax"
Selection.MoveRight Unit:=wdCell
Selection.TypeText Text:="Allison"
```

26. Double-click **Allison** to select it and type: **Nelly**

27. Choose **File→Close** and return to Microsoft Word.

Now you will run the macro to see your editing changes.

28. If necessary, place the insertion point in the last blank line on the page and then press Ctrl + 8 to run the macro.

Notice Nelly's name in the table. Now you will delete the macro.

29. Choose **View→Macros→Macros** 🖳.

30. Make sure the TutorTable macro is selected and click **Delete**; click **Yes** to confirm.

31. Close the Macros dialog box, remove the Developer tab from the Ribbon, and save and close the file.

Apply Your Skills

Create a Customer Satisfaction Survey

Your supervisor at Universal Corporate Events has asked you to create a Customer Satisfaction Survey to be distributed to clients. In this exercise, you will create the survey using content controls and then restrict editing.

1. Open **W12-A1-Survey** from your **Word Chapter 12** folder and save it as: **W12-A1-SurveyRevised**

2. Turn on **Design Mode**.

    Don't forget to include spaces before each of the content controls you will be creating for this exercise.

3. Add **Rich Text Content Controls** for the first and second form lines, labeled **Name** and **Phone Number**.

4. Add a **Check Box Content Control** at the end of the next line.

5. Add a **Drop-Down List Content Control** at the end of the next line.

6. Using the properties window for the Drop-Down List Content Control, add **Yes** and **No** as list choices.

7. In the first line of the survey, labeled *Staff*, place a **Check Box Content Control** after each of the five listed numbers.

Staff:	5 (☐)	4 (☐)	3 (☐)	2 (☐)	1 (☐)

8. Do the same for the remaining four lines of the survey.

9. Turn off Design Mode and restrict editing in the document to Filling Out Forms, leaving the password boxes blank.

10. Close the Restrict Editing panel, deactivate the Developer tab, and save and close the file.

Create a Las Vegas Macro

Universal Corporate Events is preparing a Las Vegas tour for a corporate client. As agents are communicating via email with the travelers, they will paste the macro text into the email as needed. In this exercise, you will create and edit the macro and run it from the Quick Access toolbar.

1. Open **W12-A2-LasVegasMacro** from your **Word Chapter 12** folder and save it as: **W12-A2-LasVegasMacroRevised**

2. Open a new, blank document and then start the macro recorder.

3. Name the macro **LasVegas**, verify the Normal template is chosen, and then click **OK**.

4. Record this text in the blank document: **Upon arrival at the airport, pick up your bags in the luggage area and then look for a limousine driver with a Silicon Tech Group sign. The driver will take you to the MGM Grand where you will stay during your visit.**

5. Stop the macro recorder, tap ⌷Enter⌷, and test your macro to ensure it runs as expected.

   Now you will edit the macro and assign it to a toolbar button.

6. Open the macro editor and locate the word *airport* in the VBA code.

7. Position the insertion point in front of *airport* and type: **Las Vegas**⌷Spacebar⌷

8. Close the macro editor and then open the Word Options dialog box.

9. Choose the **Quick Access Toolbar** category and the **Macros** command.

10. Add your macro to the list on the right and click **Modify**.

11. Choose the envelope button and then change the **Display Name** to **Las Vegas** and click **OK** twice.

12. Tap ⌷Enter⌷ and then run the macro from the Quick Access toolbar.

13. Take a screenshot of the document you used to run your macro and then switch to **W12-A2-LasVegasMacroRevised**.

14. Position the insertion point at the bottom of the document and paste the screenshot.

15. Delete the macro and remove the macro button from the Quick Access toolbar.

16. Save and close the file, and then close the other document without saving it.

APPLY YOUR SKILLS: W12-A3

Create a Form for the Corporate Trainer

Universal Corporate Events staff will be holding a software training potluck lunch with the corporate trainer. You've been asked to put together a sign-up form for the event. In this exercise, you will create the form and create and edit a macro.

1. Open **W12-A3-BrownBag** from your **Word Chapter 12** folder and save it as:
   W12-A3-BrownBagRevised

2. Activate the Developer tab and turn on Design Mode.

   Don't forget to include spaces before each of the content controls you will be creating for this exercise.

3. At the end of the first form line (*Your Name*) add a **Rich Text Content Control**.

4. Add two **Check Box Content Controls** in the next line, one following *Yes* and the other following *No*.

5. Add a **Drop-Down List Content Control** to the end of the third line.

6. Using the properties window for the Drop-Down List Content Control, add these choices:
   - **Brownies**
   - **Chips**
   - **Cookies**
   - **Crackers**
   - **Dip**
   - **Drinks**
   - **Fruit**
   - **Veggies**

7. Turn off Design Mode.

Create, Run, and Edit a Macro

Now you will create a macro that you will use with another client whose employees will visit the Van Gogh Museum in Amsterdam.

8. Position the insertion point in the blank line at the end of the document.

9. Turn on the macro recorder, name the macro **VanGogh**, and ensure the Normal template is chosen.

10. Click **Keyboard** and assign `Ctrl`+`7` to the macro.

11. Record this text: **The Van Gogh Museum is open daily from 9 am to 5 pm. It is located at Amstel 51, Amsterdam, and you can get there by boat shuttle or the Hop on, Hop off bus.**

12. Turn off the macro recorder and tap `Enter` to generate a blank line.

13. Use `Ctrl`+`7` to test the macro.

    Now you will enter additional information in the macro.

14. Open the macro editor and locate the word *bus* at the end of the macro text.

15. Position the insertion point after the period following the word *bus* and tap `Spacebar`.

16. Add this text and then close the macro editor: **Be sure to see The Potato Eaters and Starry Night.**

17. Tap `Enter`, test the macro to verify your change, and then delete the macro.

18. Deactivate the Developer tab, save and close the file, and exit Word.

Project Grader

If your class is using eLab (labyrinthelab.com), you may upload your completed Project Grader assignments for automatic grading. You may complete these projects even if your class doesn't use eLab, though you will not be able to upload your work.

PROJECT GRADER: W12-P1

Creating a Customer Survey Form

You've been asked to create a customer survey form for Taylor Games that customer service representatives can use to gather important information during telephone calls. In this exercise, the form you'll create is a prototype that tests out various content controls and uses a macro.

1. Download and open your Project Grader starting file.
   - *Using eLab:* Download **W12_P1_eStart** from the Assignments page. You *must* start with this file or your work cannot be automatically graded.
   - *Not using eLab:* Open **W12_P1_Start** from your **Word Chapter 12** folder.

2. If necessary, customize the Ribbon to enable the **Developer Tab**, and then enable **Design Mode**.

3. Insert a space after the *Date:* label and insert a **Date Picker Content** control.

4. Insert a space after the *Name:* label and insert a **Plain Text Content** control.

5. Insert a space after the *Age:* label and insert a **Plain Text Content** control.

6. Insert a space after the *Primary Interest:* label and insert a **Drop-Down List Content** control.

7. Add these items to the drop-down list, leaving all other properties for the control set to the default values. The items will appear as both the Display Name and Value:
   - **Books**
   - **Dice**
   - **Games**

8. Insert a space after the *Add to Mailing List?* label and then insert a **Check Box Content** control.

9. Set these properties for the check box control:
   - Title: **Yes**
   - Tag: **Yes**
   - Show As: **Start/End Tag**

10. Insert a space to the right of the check box control and insert another **Check Box Content** control.

11. Set these properties for the second check box control:
    - Title: **No**
    - Tag: **No**
    - Show As: **Start/End Tag**

12. Position the insertion point to the right of the *Comments:* label and record a macro using these guidelines:
    - Macro name: **NoComments**
    - Assign Macro To: Keyboard using the shortcut: **Alt+Ctrl+N**
    - Save Changes In: **W12_P1_eStart** or **W12_P1_Start** if you aren't using eLab.

- Assign the macro and then type an empty space followed by this text: `Customer had no comments`
- Stop recording the macro.

13. Use these guidelines to test your controls and the macro:
    - Use the **Date Picker** control to enter today's date.
    - Enter any name and age in the Name and Age controls.
    - Select any of the choices in the Primary Interest control. The control should display *Books*, *Dice*, and *Games*.
    - Choose either the **Yes** or **No Mailing List** option.
    - Delete the **Customer had no comments** text from the Comments field and use your macro to reenter the text.

Note! *In the next step it is important that you save the document as a Word Macro-Enabled Document type.*

14. Save your form as a macro-enabled document.
    - *Using eLab:* Save it as a Word Macro-Enabled Document (*.docm*) to your **Word Chapter 12** folder as `W12_P1_eSubmission` and attach the file to your eLab assignment for grading.
    - *Not using eLab:* Save it as a Word Macro-Enabled Document (*.docm*) to your **Word Chapter 12** folder as: `W12_P1_Submission`

PROJECT GRADER: W12-P2

Using Content Controls and a Macro in a Business Letter

You've been asked by the Classic Cars Club to send registration follow-up letters to vendors attending the national car show. In this exercise, you will create a letter containing content controls and a macro to individualize and expedite the letter-creation process.

1. Download and open your Project Grader starting file:
   - *Using eLab:* Download **W12_P2_eStart** from the Assignments page. You *must* start with this file or your work cannot be automatically graded.
   - *Not using eLab:* Open **W12_P2_Start** from your **Word Chapter 12** folder.

2. If necessary, customize the Ribbon to enable the **Developer Tab**, and then enable **Design Mode**.

3. Replace the word *DATE* at the top of the letter with a **Date Picker Content Control**. When replacing the word *DATE*, do not remove any of the paragraph marks so that the same spacing is maintained between the logo above the date and the name *David Roberts* below it.

4. Use these guidelines to insert a content control in the first sentence of the large main paragraph:
   - Replace the word *DROPDOWN* with a **Drop-Down List Content Control**.
   - Maintain the spacing of one empty space before and after the content control.

5. Add these items to the drop-down list, leaving all other properties for the control set to the default values. The items will appear as both the Display Name and Value:
   - `5x5 Booth`
   - `10x10 Booth`
   - `Hallway Booth`
   - `Main Floor Booth`

6. Insert a space after the *Mailing List Purchase:* label and then insert a **Check Box Content Control**.

7. Set these properties for the check box control:
   - Title: **Yes**
   - Tag: **Yes**
   - Show As: **Start/End Tag**

8. Insert a space to the right of the check box control and insert another **Check Box Content Control**.

9. Set these properties for the second check box control:
   - Title: **No**
   - Tag: **No**
   - Show As: **Start/End Tag**

10. Insert the same checkbox controls that were created in steps 6–9 next to the *Setup and Tear Down Assistance:* and *Premier Sponsorship Package:* labels.

11. Position the insertion point on the last empty paragraph in the document and record a macro using these guidelines:
    - Macro name: **EarlyBird**
    - Assign Macro To: **Keyboard** using the shortcut: **Alt+Ctrl+E**
    - Save Changes In: **W12_P2_eStart** or **W12_P2_Start** if you aren't using eLab.
    - Assign the macro and type this text in the empty paragraph: **Congratulations! Your Early Bird Registration earned you a 25% discount on your next show!**
    - Stop recording the macro.

12. Use these guidelines to test your controls and the macro:
    - Use the **Date Picker** control to enter today's date.
    - Choose any of the items in the Drop-Down control.
    - Choose **Yes** or **No** in the three sets of Check Box controls.
    - Delete the paragraph you typed while recording the macro (begins with *Congratulations*).
    - Use your macro to reenter the *Congratulations* paragraph in the last empty paragraph.

 Note! *In the next step, it is important that you save the document as a Word Macro-Enabled Document type.*

13. Save your letter as a macro enabled document.
    - *Using eLab:* Save it as a Word Macro-Enabled Document (*.docm*) to your **Word Chapter 12** folder as **W12_P2_eSubmission** and attach the file to your eLab assignment for grading.
    - *Not using eLab:* Save it as a Word Macro-Enabled Document (*.docm*) to your **Word Chapter 12** folder as: **W12_P2_Submission**

◢ Extend Your Skills

These exercises challenge you to think critically and apply your new skills in a real-world setting. You will be evaluated on your ability to follow directions, completeness, creativity, and the use of proper grammar and mechanics. Save files to your chapter folder. Submit assignments as directed.

W12-E1 That's the Way I See It

As the owner of a small business, you know it's essential to stay ahead of the latest trends so you can anticipate your customers' needs. You've decided to create an interest form to distribute to your customers in order to better understand what they are looking for. Create a new document named: **W12-E1-InterestForm**

Add at least five questions to the form, inquiring about which of the latest trends your customers may be interested in. You may decide the subject matter for yourself. Add at least one rich text, one date picker, one check box, and one drop-down list (with choices) content control. Save the document. Remember to turn off the Developer tab and, if you wish, delete any macros created.

W12-E2 Be Your Own Boss

As an administrator at Blue Jean Landscaping, you have found that macros can greatly increase efficiency. You want to create a macro that will rapidly create a letterhead, with the added benefit of avoiding printing costs. Create a new document named: **W12-E2-BJLetterhead**

Record a new macro named **Letterhead** and store it in the Normal template. As part of the macro, type **Blue Jean Landscaping** as the company name and make up the rest of the letterhead content before stopping the recording. Delete the text you used to create the macro and then test it. Delete the letterhead text and then edit the macro to add a comma, ⬚Spacebar⬚, and **Inc.** at the end of the company name. Test the macro again; if it runs as intended, save the document. Remember to turn off the Developer tab and, if you wish, delete any macros created.

W12-E3 Demonstrate Proficiency

The owner of Stormy BBQ has asked you to show him a little more about how to create forms in Word, something he briefly learned about in a Microsoft Word class. You think he would also love macros. Put together a simple online order form with at least one date picker, one check box, and one drop-down list (with choices) content control. Then, think of three different types of Word documents you use at Stormy BBQ and write a few paragraphs at the bottom of your form suggesting at least one macro for each document type. Don't forget to explain why each macro would make creating the document more efficient. Save your file as: **W12-E3-EfficientStormy** and remember to turn off the Developer tab and, if you wish, delete any macros created.

Integrating Word with Excel, PowerPoint, and the Web

One advantage to using a suite of applications is that they're designed to share data and information and work together seamlessly. You can display data stored in an Excel worksheet in a Word document or use Excel data as the source document in Mail Merge. You can send a Word outline to PowerPoint to create a new presentation or insert a PowerPoint presentation in a Word document. You can open a PDF file in Word and edit it, and you can convert a Word document to a web page. In this chapter, you will explore the features that allow Word to interact with other Office programs.

LEARNING OBJECTIVES

- Embed and link Excel objects in Word
- Use an Excel worksheet as a Mail Merge data file
- Create PowerPoint presentations from Word outlines
- Insert PowerPoint presentations in Word documents
- Open a PDF file in Word for editing
- Convert Word documents to web pages

Project: Multitasking with Word, Excel, and PowerPoint

You are an administrative assistant at Raritan Clinic East. An advisory committee meets quarterly to review the budget and clinic activities. In preparation for the upcoming meeting, you will help create the quarterly expense report. The data is in an Excel worksheet, so you will use the Excel data in the report that you will prepare in Word. You will add the chart contained in the Excel file to the report and prepare a PowerPoint presentation using an outline of headings from the clinic's Annual Report. You will generate a letter to all committee members using an Excel name and address file to address the letters. Then you will edit a press release in Word that was saved in PDF format. Finally, you will save your report as a single file web page for posting on the clinic website for others to review.

Embedding and Linking Excel Objects

You can share data and objects among the programs in the Office 2019 suite. Object is a term for an element that you share between files. For example, you can place data and chart objects from an Excel file in a Word document. You embed an object if you don't want it to change when the original source file is updated. On the other hand, if you want the Word document to stay current with any changes in the source file, you link the object to its original file, so your document will be updated when the source file is modified.

Linking or Embedding Data

Whether you are embedding or linking to files, there are two techniques for inserting data from other files:

▶ **Copy/Paste:** Using this procedure, you copy data from a source document, such as an Excel worksheet, and paste it directly into the Word document. Using Paste Special, you can link the data (or not) at the time you paste it. This method is useful when you want to include only a portion of the file.

▶ **Insert Object:** You can insert a file, such as an Excel workbook, from within Word, and you can choose to link the data at the time you insert it. This procedure is useful when you want to include an entire file in a document.

DEVELOP YOUR SKILLS: W13-D1

In this exercise, you will embed an Excel worksheet in a Word document and test its static nature.

1. Start Word, create a blank document, and save it to your **Word Chapter 13** folder as:
   W13-D1-BudgetRpt
2. Type these heading lines:
   Advisory Committee Budget Report
   Third Quarter
3. Tap [Enter] and then select both heading lines.
4. Choose **Home→Styles→More** ⏷ on the Quick Styles gallery and choose **Title**.

5. Position the insertion point in the blank line below the heading lines and type this introductory paragraph:

This report, produced by clinic staff, is in keeping with the Advisory Committee's decision to conduct quarterly reviews of the current year's budget. It provides a snapshot of expenses for the quarter and for the year-to-date.

6. Tap `Enter` and then choose **Insert→Text→Object**.

7. Follow these steps to identify the Excel file from which to embed the data:

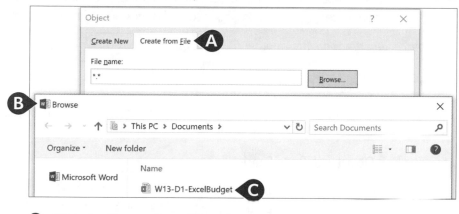

Ⓐ Click the **Create from File** tab.

Ⓑ Click **Browse** and navigate to your **Word Chapter 13** folder.

Ⓒ Double-click **W13-D1-ExcelBudget** and click **OK**.

Modify the Source File

8. Start Excel, open **W13-D1-ExcelBudget**, and save it in your **Word Chapter 13** folder as:
W13-D1-ExcelBudgetRevised

9. Follow these steps to edit a value in the source file:

Ⓐ Click the cell for **14,557** (Q1, Mortgage & Insurance) and tap `Delete`.

Ⓑ Type **10,000** and tap `Enter`.

10. Switch to Word and verify the value of Q1 Mortgage & Insurance remains 14,557.

Because the table is embedded (not linked) in the document, the data in Word is not affected by changes made to the Excel file.

11. Switch back to Excel and click **Undo** twice to return the value to its original amount.

Because you want the report to reflect the most recent data in the worksheet, you will delete the embedded object. You'll link to the data later.

12. Switch back to Word, select the embedded worksheet, and tap `Delete`.

13. Save the Word file and leave all files open.

Linking Objects

When you link data from another application, such as Excel or PowerPoint, to a Word document, the original information resides in Excel or PowerPoint. This is known as the source file because it is the source of the data. When you place the information (object) in a Word document, it becomes the destination file. By linking source files with Word documents, you create a dynamic tie between the two files.

For example, you might start working on a quarterly report before the end of the quarter and, if there's a linked chart in the report, it updates with the current information as the numbers change in Excel. That way, updates are centralized, and you don't have to keep track of making changes in two places.

Note! *Renaming the source file or moving it to another file location will break the link.*

⊕ **View the video "Inserting a Linked Object."**

To link a range of cells or a chart from Excel rather than the entire file, you can copy just that content to the Clipboard and then use the Paste Special command in Word.

⊕ **View the video "Link an Object with Paste Special."**

When pasting objects, multiple options are available, including the option to link the pasted object. Using the Paste Options smart tag, you can link objects to their original files.

⊕ **View the video "Link an Object with the Paste Options Smart Tag."**

≡ Insert→Text→Object→Create from File→Link to File

DEVELOP YOUR SKILLS: W13-D2

In this exercise, you will link Excel data to a Word document using Paste Special. You will then modify the Excel worksheet and observe how the changes update the Word document. Then you will link an Excel chart to the document using the Paste Options smart tag.

1. Save your file as: **W13-D2-BudgetRpt**
2. Switch to Excel and follow these steps to select and copy the Excel data:

A1	▼	× ✓ *fx*	Raritan Clinic East			
	A	B	C	D	E	F
1			Raritan Clinic East Ⓐ			
2			Budget Summary			
3			Q1	Q2	Q3	Q4	Totals
4	Mortgage & Insurance	14,557	14,557	14,557		43,671
5	Utilities	15,201	18,200	21,000		54,401
6	Food	5,480	4,512	3,452		13,444
7	Staff Salaries	87,685	87,685	87,685		263,055
8	Maintenance & Repairs	16,982	17,458	15,225		49,665
9	Fundraising for Donations	820	2,006	67,325		70,151
10	Grand Totals	140,725	144,418	209,244	- Ⓑ	494,387

Ⓐ Click in the merged cell containing the heading *Raritan Clinic East*.

Ⓑ Press ⎖Shift⎗, click the last cell in the worksheet (*494,387*), and choose **Home→Clipboard→Copy**.

3. Switch to Word and, if necessary, position the insertion point at the end of the document.

4. Choose **Home→Clipboard→Paste menu button ▾→Paste Special**.

5. Follow these steps to paste the object:

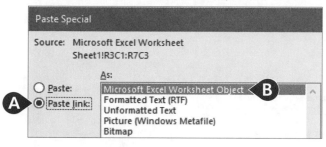

   Ⓐ Choose **Paste Link**.

   Ⓑ Choose **Microsoft Excel Worksheet Object** and click **OK**.

Now you will edit the worksheet and observe the change to the linked object in Word.

6. Switch to Excel and tap ⌷Esc⌷ to remove the marquee (animated dashed line) surrounding the table.

The marquee in Excel identifies the cells copied.

7. Click **cell E4**, which is the Q4 cell for Mortgage & Insurance.

8. Type the Q4 projections, tapping ⌷Enter⌷ after typing each number.

The formulas in the Grand Totals and Totals cells automatically update as you enter the data.

Q4
11,337
1,750
4,975
17,685
2,543
1,529

9. Switch to Word.

The linked table is updated with the additions you made in the Q4 column. If the Excel table failed to update on your computer, right-click the Excel object and choose Update Link.

10. Position the insertion point at the end of the document and tap ⌷Enter⌷ three times.

Link an Excel Chart in Word

Now you will use the Paste Options smart tag to link a chart to Word.

11. Switch to Excel, click the **Sheet 2** tab at the bottom of the Excel window, and click the **pie chart border** once to select it.

The mouse pointer becomes a four-headed arrow, and the selection handles appear in the border.

12. Choose **Home→Clipboard→Copy** 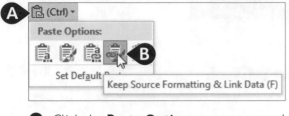 and then switch back to Word.

13. Choose **Home→Clipboard→Paste** .

14. Follow these steps to paste a link for the chart object:

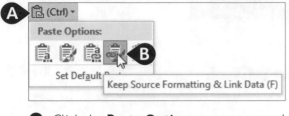

- Ⓐ Click the **Paste Options** smart tag at the bottom of the chart.
- Ⓑ Click **Keep Source Formatting & Link Data**.

15. Save the Word file. Exit Excel, saving changes when prompted.

Opening Excel and Chart Tools from Word

When data or objects from other sources are linked to Word documents, you can open source program tools directly from the Word document and use the tools to edit the object. Or, you can open the Excel application from within Word.

DEVELOP YOUR SKILLS: W13-D3

In this exercise, you will launch Excel from within Word and edit data in the worksheet. Then you will use Live Preview with Excel Chart Tools on the Word Ribbon to view potential formatting changes.

1. Save your file as: **W13-D3-BudgetRpt**

2. Double-click anywhere in the Excel worksheet table object to open the Excel file.

   At this stage, you can make editing changes that will be reflected in the Word document.

3. In Excel, click **cell B7**, the Q1 cell for Staff Salaries, and then type **1,000** and tap Enter.

4. Switch to Word and ensure the data and chart both updated.

   If your table failed to update, right-click the Excel worksheet table and choose Update Link from the menu. It's possible the worksheet table will update but not the chart. If your chart failed to update, double-click the chart and from the Ribbon choose Chart Tools→Design→Data→Refresh Data.

5. Switch to Excel and click **Undo** on the Quick Access toolbar.

6. Switch to Word.

   The chart and worksheet data update to their original values. If your table failed to update, right-click the Excel worksheet table and choose Update Link. If your chart failed to update, double-click the chart and choose Chart Tools→Design→Data→Refresh Data.

7. If you didn't use Chart Tools in the previous step, double-click the chart to display the Chart Tools on the Ribbon.

8. Click the border of the chart to select the chart background.

   You should not see handles on objects within the border.

9. Choose **Chart Tools→Format→Shape Styles→Shape Fill ▨ menu button ▾**.

10. Hover the mouse pointer over several colors to see Live Preview display the effects as they impact the chart area background color.

11. Tap [Esc] to close the gallery and then tap [Esc] again to deselect the chart.

    The Chart Tools tabs disappear from the Ribbon.

12. Save and close the Word file but leave the Excel file open.

Updating and Breaking Links

Linked objects in Word automatically update if the destination file is open at the time the source document changes. Naturally, the destination file is not always open when you modify the Excel source document; however, Word will prompt you to update links when you open a document containing links.

You can break the link between a linked object and its source document without affecting the source document. For example, once the final figures for a period are in, you may want to break the link between Word and Excel so the linked object is converted to an embedded object. Then, the Word report always reflects the closing numbers for that period.

DEVELOP YOUR SKILLS: W13-D4

In this exercise, you will modify the linked Excel file and observe the prompt to update links when you open the Word document. Then you will break the links to the worksheet data and test to see that the links are broken.

1. In Excel, click **cell C4** (Mortgage & Insurance for Q2) and then type **50,000** and tap [Enter].

   You entered an overly large number so the changes in the associated worksheet table and chart will be easy to see.

2. Open **W13-D3-BudgetRpt**, which contains the linked objects.

3. When the message appears prompting you to update links, click **Yes**.

   Observe the change in the worksheet data and in the chart. If your table failed to update, right-click the Excel worksheet table and choose Update Link. If your chart failed to update, click the chart border and choose Chart Tools→Design→Data→Refresh Data.

4. Save the Word file as: **W13-D4-BudgetRpt**

   Now you will break the link between the objects in Word and the Excel file.

5. In Word, right-click in the worksheet data to display a pop-up menu.

6. Choose **Linked Worksheet Object** and then choose **Links**.

7. Follow these steps to break the link for the table:

Ⓐ Make sure the worksheet object is selected.

Ⓑ Click **Break Link**.

8. When the message appears asking if you want to break the link, click **Yes**.

The link disappears from the Links dialog box. The remaining link is already highlighted.

9. Click **Break Link** to break the link between Excel and the chart.

10. When the message box appears, click **Yes**.

The Source File now displays the term NULL, indicating there is no source file attached.

11. Click **OK** to close the Links dialog box.

Now you will test to see that the links are broken.

12. Right-click the worksheet object, review the menu options, and note that the Update Link option is gone.

13. Double-click the chart, choose **Chart Tools→Design→Data**, and notice the Refresh Data button is grayed out, indicating the link is broken.

14. Save and close the Word and Excel files but leave the program windows open.

Using Excel as a Mail Merge Data Source

You may recall that Word's Mail Merge feature is most often used for generating personalized form letters. Word can use a variety of file types as data sources, including Excel files. Whether you type a new data-source list from within Word or create your data source in Excel, the rules for effective data sources apply.

The more data is split into small segments, the more flexibility you have in the merge. Remember that you cannot merge part of a field. For example, if the name field contains the title, first name, and last name, you will not be able to use those elements separately. For instance, in the greeting line, you will not be able to drop the first name and use Dear Title Last Name.

In Excel, the columns are treated as separate fields in a mail merge. Therefore, in a name and address list, it is a good idea to place the title, first name, and last name in separate columns, as shown in the following illustration:

	A	B	C	D	E	F	G
1	Title	First Name	Last Name	Address	City	State	Zip
2	Ms.	Sally	Redding	756 Locust Street	Los Angeles	CA	91025
3	Mr.	Jose	Lopez	7812 Olive Road	Los Angeles	CA	91357
4	Mr.	Charles	Douglas	91 Sycamore Ave.	Los Angeles	CA	91642

Note! *When an Excel worksheet is used as a merge data source file, the first row must contain the field names. Also, all columns and rows must be adjacent to each other for Mail Merge to identify all entries as part of the same data source. You cannot have blank rows and columns within the Excel worksheet data.*

≡ Mailings→Start Mail Merge→Select Recipients→Use an Existing List

DEVELOP YOUR SKILLS: W13-D5

In this exercise, you will begin by examining the Excel worksheet that you will use as the data source. Next you will open a letter and designate it as the main document. Then you will connect the Excel data source to the letter and conduct the merge.

1. In Excel, open **W13-D5-CommAddress** from your **Word Chapter 13** folder.

   Each column represents a mail merge field. Title is a field, First Name is a field, and so forth.

2. Look at the bottom of the Excel worksheet and notice the tab labeled *Sheet 1*.

   This is the name of the page in the Excel workbook that contains the address list. You will see Sheet 1 again later in this exercise.

3. Exit Excel.

4. In Word, open **W13-D5-CommLtr** and save it as: **W13-D5-CommLtrRevised**

5. Choose **Mailings→Start Mail Merge→Start Mail Merge** 🗋 and then choose **Letters**.

   This designates the letter as the main document.

6. If necessary, display formatting marks.

   Being able to see the formatting marks will be helpful later in this exercise. Now you will connect to the Excel data source.

7. Choose **Mailings→Start Mail Merge→Select Recipients** 🖼 and then choose **Use an Existing List**.

8. Navigate to your **Word Chapter 13** folder and open **W13-D5-CommAddress**.

9. In the Select Table dialog box, notice that *Sheet 1* is highlighted.

   Earlier you observed Sheet 1 as the name of the page in the Excel workbook that contains the address list.

10. Click **OK**.

11. In the letter, select the **Today's Date** text; delete it, but don't delete the paragraph symbol at the end of the line.

    Deleting the paragraph symbol would throw off proper business letter spacing.

12. Type the current date in its place.

Insert Merge Codes

13. Select and delete the **Address Block** text, but don't delete the paragraph symbol at the end of the line.

14. Choose **Mailings→Write & Insert Fields→Address Block** .

15. When the Insert Address Block dialog box appears, click **OK** to accept the default settings for the inside address.

16. Delete the **Greeting Line** text but not the paragraph symbol at the end of the line.

17. Choose **Mailings→Write & Insert Fields→Greeting Line** .

18. When the Insert Greeting Line dialog box appears, change the Greeting Line Format from a comma to a colon and click **OK**.

Conduct the Merge

19. Choose **Mailings→Finish→Finish & Merge** and then choose **Edit Individual Documents**.

20. In the Merge to New Document dialog box, click **OK** to merge all records from the Excel file.

21. Turn off formatting marks and scroll through the letters to see the results.

22. Close the merge document without saving it.

23. Save and close **W13-D5-CommLtrRevised**.

Integrating Word with PowerPoint

PowerPoint is another program that Word can share files with. Word outlines can be used to create PowerPoint presentations. This hierarchical structure uses Heading 1 topics as the slide's title, and it uses headings such as Heading 2, Heading 3, and so forth as the bullet and sub-bullet entries in the slide.

Using Word Outline View

The following illustration is an example of an outline created specifically for generating a Power-Point presentation. Clicking or selecting entries in the outline displays the Word heading level in the Outlining tab on the Ribbon.

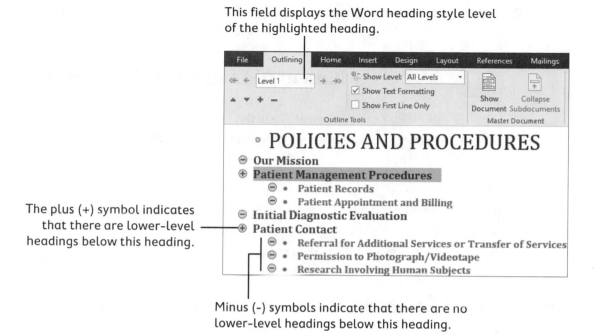

This field displays the Word heading style level of the highlighted heading.

The plus (+) symbol indicates that there are lower-level headings below this heading.

Minus (-) symbols indicate that there are no lower-level headings below this heading.

Although you can use an existing document that contains Word headings to create a PowerPoint presentation, PowerPoint cannot extract body text from a document, so if you use an existing document with body text in addition to the headings, you will have to edit the PowerPoint presentation accordingly.

The procedures used to launch PowerPoint are the same as those used to launch Word. No special knowledge of PowerPoint is required to complete the following exercise.

≡ View→Views→Outline

DEVELOP YOUR SKILLS: W13-D6

In this exercise, you will use a Word outline to create a PowerPoint presentation. Then you will observe how the different heading levels are displayed in the presentation.

1. Open **W13-D6-ProcOutline** from your **Word Chapter 13** folder.
2. Choose **View→Views→Outline** ▣.
3. Click several entries in the outline and notice the Word heading level indicated on the Ribbon.
4. Close the document and start PowerPoint.
5. Click the **Blank Presentation** template on the PowerPoint Start screen.

6. Choose **File→Open** and navigate to your **Word Chapter 13** folder.

7. In the bottom-right corner of the Open dialog box, click the file type drop-down list and choose **All Files**.

8. Double-click **W13-D6-ProcOutline** to open it.

9. Click the **third slide** in the panel on the left to display the slide in the main window.

Patient Management Procedures

- Patient Records
- Patient Appointment and Billing

This title was formatted using the Heading 1 style, and the bullet points were formatted using the Heading 2 style.

10. Exit PowerPoint without saving the file.

Adding a PowerPoint Presentation to a Word Document

When you create a document that will be distributed electronically, it could be useful to include a PowerPoint presentation within the document. For example, suppose you want to distribute a presentation and include a letter with it. You can create the letter and place the presentation in the body of the letter.

Note! *When you insert a presentation into a Word document, only the first slide appears in the document. Double-clicking the slide image plays the show automatically.*

≡ Insert→Text→Object→Create from File

DEVELOP YOUR SKILLS: W13-D7

In this exercise, you will insert a presentation into the letter being sent to board members.

1. Open **W13-D7-AdvisoryLtr** from your **Word Chapter 13** folder and save it as:
   `W13-D7-AdvisoryLtrRevised`

2. Turn on formatting marks and then position the insertion point before the middle paragraph symbol.

3. Choose **Insert→Text→Object** 🗗 and click the **Create from File** tab.

4. Click **Browse** and navigate to your **Word Chapter 13** folder.

5. Double-click **W13-D7-IntroToRCE** (a PowerPoint file) and then click **OK**.

   Word adds a picture of the first slide to the letter. Notice that the image makes the letter extend to two pages. Next you will size the image so that the letter fits on one page.

6. Click the slide image to display the sizing handles.

7. Drag the lower-right sizing handle diagonally up toward the center of the image until the letter fits on one page.

8. Double-click the slide image in the letter to start the slide show.

9. Click the mouse pointer anywhere on the screen to advance the slides.

10. When the black screen appears at the end of the show, click one more time to close it.

11. Save and close the file.

Opening, Editing, and Saving a PDF File

PDF files are popular, thanks to their reduced file size and editing restrictions. You can open, edit, and save a PDF file in Word 2019 without purchasing and learning separate, and often expensive, editing software. After editing the file, you can save it as a Word or PDF file. The file you open is considered a read-only file, so you must save it under a different name.

When you save a PDF file, you can optimize it based on how your audience will likely read it. The Options button lets you choose additional options, such as the range of pages you want to save and the ability to create bookmarks in the PDF file.

Choose additional publishing options here.

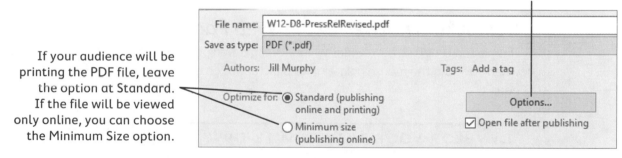

If your audience will be printing the PDF file, leave the option at Standard. If the file will be viewed only online, you can choose the Minimum Size option.

DEVELOP YOUR SKILLS: W13-D8

In this exercise, you will open a PDF file in Word and make editing changes. You will then resave the file as a PDF.

1. Choose **File→Open**, navigate to your **Word Chapter 13** folder, and open **W13-D8-PressRel**.

2. Read the message and then click **OK**.

   The PDF file opens with all the Word editing and formatting tools available.

 When you open a PDF file in Word, there may be formatting issues. Don't worry about that now. Concentrate on learning how to open and edit a PDF file for which you don't have the original Word file.

3. Select the three lines at the top of the page.

4. Choose **Home→Font→Font Color** 🅰 **menu button** ▾ and choose **Blue, Accent 1, Darker 25%**.

5. Choose **Home→Font→Font Size** and choose **16 pt**.

6. Choose **File→Save As**, navigate to your **Word Chapter 13** folder, save the file as **W13-D8-PressRelRevised** and choose **PDF** from the Save as Type list, and then click **Save**.

7. If the PDF file opens in a PDF reader, close the PDF window.

   Remember, the original file is read-only, so saving it under a different name saved the changes in a new file.

8. The original file is still open in Word; close the file without saving.

Creating Web Pages from Word Documents

You can create web pages from Word documents. As you might imagine, this saves you from needing to learn a more specialized web design or coding program. Another advantage is that Word can display a document in Web Layout view so you can make edits before posting the file on the web.

Formatting Web Pages

Web pages are often set up in tables to help align text in multiple columns, and the Table feature works well for this purpose. When you save a document as a web page, Word converts it to hypertext markup language (HTML), the authoring language for web pages. When you convert a document to HTML, some formatting features may be lost. However, most of your documents should translate cleanly into attractive web pages. Saving your files as a single file web page may help to reduce these transition errors.

Using Alternative Text in Web Pages

If a person uses a screen reader while viewing a web page, alternative text appears and is read aloud when hovering the mouse pointer over a picture or graphic. Some users won't see the text, but they'll hear it.

DEVELOP YOUR SKILLS: W13-D9

In this exercise, you will save a document as a single file web page and examine its format. You will also add alternative text to a picture in the document.

1. Open **W13-D9-RCEWalk** from your **Word Chapter 13** folder and save it as: **W13-D9-RCEWalkRevised**

2. If no gridlines appear, choose **Table Tools→Layout→Table→View Gridlines**.

   The document is set up in a table. Gridlines are visible so you can see the column with no content on the left side of the table. Web pages may appear too far to the left in a browser window, so the blank column is acting as a spacer to position the content farther to the right.

   Now you will add alternative text to the picture.

3. Click the picture and choose **Picture Tools→Format→Accessibility→Alt Text**.

4. In the Alt Text box, remove any text that appears and then type:
   Amy Chambers Enter **President, Raritan Clinic East**

5. Close the Alt Text task pane.

6. Choose **File→Save As** and navigate to your **Word Chapter 13** folder.

7. Choose **Single File Web Page** from the Save as Type drop-down list.

   Choosing Single File Web Page from the list will cause a Change Title button to appear below.

8. Click **Change Title** to open the Enter Text dialog box.

9. Type **RCE Walkathon** in the Page Title field and click **OK**; click **Save**.

10. Open the Windows File Explorer, navigate to your **Word Chapter 13** folder, and double-click the MHTML version of **W13-D9-RCEWalkRevised** to open the file in your browser.

    Look closely, and you will see that the MHTML file's icon is very different from the Word file's icon. If the file doesn't seem to open properly in your default browser, right-click on it and choose Open with to try a different browser.

11. Review the document layout and notice the gridlines do not appear in the browser.

12. Close the browser and the Word web page file.

Editing Web Pages in Word

When you create a web page in Word, you can use Word to edit the page. You open the *.htm* page from within Word, make the necessary changes, and then resave the file. When you open it in the browser again, you will see the changes that you made.

DEVELOP YOUR SKILLS: W13-D10

In this exercise, you will open the single file web page you created in the previous exercise and edit it. Then you will reopen the page in your browser and observe the change.

1. Open **W13-D9-RCEWalkRevised.htm**.

2. Change the walkathon date from March 1 to: March **8**

3. Save and close the file, and then restart your browser.

   Steps for opening the file in your default browser may vary slightly. You may need to seek assistance to determine the correct method.

4. Press $\boxed{\text{Ctrl}}$+$\boxed{\text{O}}$ and navigate to your **Word Chapter 13** folder.

5. Double-click **W13-D9-RCEWalkRevised.htm** and click **OK**.

6. Observe the date change you made in the web page.

7. Close your browser and exit Word.

Self-Assessment

Check your knowledge of this chapter's key concepts and skills using the Self-Assessment in your ebook or online (eLab course or Student Resource Center).

✚ Reinforce Your Skills

REINFORCE YOUR SKILLS: W13-R1

Create a Consignment Shop Sales Report

Kids for Change operates a fundraising consignment shop, Collectibles & Curiosities. In this exercise, you will prepare a static sales report and distribute it to the board members. Then you will link the sales report data so you can start collecting data for your year-to-date report.

1. Start Word, open **W13-R1-Q1SalesRpt** from your **Word Chapter 13** folder, and save it as: **W13-R1-Q1SalesRptRevised**

2. Position the insertion point in the first blank line below the paragraph.

3. If necessary, choose **View→Views→Print Layout** 🗒 to change the view.

4. If necessary, turn on formatting marks, choose **Insert→Text→Object** 🗗, and click the **Create from File** tab.

5. Click **Browse**, navigate to your **Word Chapter 13** folder, and double-click **W13-R1-Collectibles**.

   Because you are embedding (not linking) the data in Word, you won't check the Link to File checkbox.

6. Click **OK** to close the dialog box and insert the table.

   Having distributed this report to the board members, you will now link this worksheet table in the Word document so you can begin collecting year-to-date data.

7. Click the embedded worksheet table and tap ⌗Delete⌗.

Link Excel Data to a Word Document

8. Start Excel, click the **Open Other Workbooks** link at the bottom of the Recent list on the left of the Start screen, and navigate to your **Word Chapter 13** folder.

9. Open **W13-R1-Collectibles** and save it as: **W13-R1-CollectiblesRevised**

10. Make sure the *Collectibles and Curiosities* merged cell is selected and then press ⌗Shift⌗ and click the last cell in the table (contains a value of *$1,464.00*).

11. Choose **Home→Clipboard→Copy**, switch to Word, and, if necessary, position the insertion point in the first blank line below the main paragraph.

12. Choose **Home→Clipboard→Paste menu button** ▾ **→Paste Special**.

13. In the Paste Special dialog box, choose **Microsoft Excel Worksheet Object**, click the **Paste Link** option, and click **OK**.

   Now you will edit the worksheet in Excel and observe the change in the linked table.

14. Switch to Excel, tap ⌗Esc⌗ to remove the marquee surrounding the table, and click the cell at the top of the worksheet to select it.

15. Double-click the cell to position the insertion point in the cell and then click and drag to select **Quarter 1**.

A	B	C	D	E
		Collectibles & Curiosities - Quarter 1		

16. Type **Year-to-Date** and tap Enter; switch to Word.

    Notice that the linked table is updated with the change you made. If the table failed to update, right-click it and choose Update Link.

17. Position the insertion point in the blank line below the table.

    Now you will link an Excel chart in Word using the Paste Options smart tag.

18. Switch to Excel, click the **Sheet 2** tab at the bottom of the workbook, and then click the chart to select it.

19. Choose **Home→Clipboard→Copy** and then switch back to Word.

20. Choose **Home→Clipboard→Paste** and click the **Paste Options** smart tag at the bottom of the chart.

21. Click **Keep Source Formatting & Link Data**. (If necessary, use ToolTips to identify the button.)

22. Switch to Excel, exit Excel, and save changes when prompted.

Open Excel and Display Chart Tools from Within Word

23. Double-click in the worksheet table in Word to open the Excel file.

    There is an error in the March sales figure for Glass & Crystal, so you will make that change in the worksheet.

24. Click **cell B7** (*Glass & Crystal, March*) and tap Delete; type **1,500.00** and tap Enter.

25. Switch to Word and ensure that both the table and chart updated.

    If your table failed to update, right-click the Excel worksheet table and choose Update Link from the menu. It's possible the worksheet table will update but not the chart. If your chart failed to update, click the chart and choose Chart Tools→Design→Data→Refresh Data.

26. Save the document and exit Word.

Update Links and Break a Link Between Word and Excel

27. In Excel, click **cell D5** (*Vintage Jewelry, January*) and tap Delete; type **600** and tap Enter.

28. In Word, open **W13-R1-Q1SalesRptRevised**; when the message appears prompting you to update links, click **Yes**.

29. If your table or chart failed to update, use the manual procedures you've used before to update.

30. In Word, right-click the worksheet table to display the pop-up menu.

31. Choose **Linked Worksheet Object** and then choose **Links** from the submenu.

32. With the worksheet selected, click **Break Link**.

33. When the message appears verifying the break, click **Yes**.

34. With the chart selected, click **Break Link**, click **Yes**, and then click **OK**.

    Now you will test to ensure that the links are broken.

35. Right-click the worksheet table in Word and notice that Update Link does not appear in the menu.

36. Select the chart, choose **Chart Tools→Design→Data**, and notice that the Refresh Data button is grayed out.

37. Save and close the Word and Excel files.

Organize an Autumn Garden Cleanup for Seniors

Kids for Change volunteers assist senior citizens with autumn garden cleanup every year, and it's time to get that project rolling again. In this exercise, you will use Excel and Mail Merge to send letters announcing the volunteers' meeting. You will also convert a Word outline to a PowerPoint presentation for the meeting to review garden tasks needed at this time of the year. Finally, you will save a document as a single file web page so volunteers can go online to see which gardening supplies are needed for the project.

1. Open **W13-R2-GardenLtr** from your **Word Chapter 13** folder and save it as:
   W13-R2-GardenLtrRevised

2. Choose **Mailings→Start Mail Merge→Start Mail Merge** ▤→**Letters**.

   Word will now recognize your letter as the main document.

3. If necessary, turn on formatting marks.

   Now you will connect an Excel file as the data source.

4. Choose **Mailings→Start Mail Merge→Select Recipients** and then choose **Use an Existing List**.

5. Navigate to your **Word Chapter 13** folder and open **W13-R2-AddressLst.xlsx** (an Excel file).

6. When the Select Table dialog box appears, make sure Sheet 1, which contains the address list, is selected; then click **OK**.

   Now you will insert the merge codes in your letter.

7. In the letter, delete the **Address Block** text but not the paragraph symbol at the end of the line.

8. Choose **Mailings→Write & Insert Fields→Address Block** ▤.

9. When the Insert Address Block dialog box opens, click **OK** to accept the default formats for the inside address.

10. Delete the **Greeting Line** text but not the paragraph symbol at the end of the line.

11. Choose **Mailings→Write & Insert Fields→Greeting Line** ▤.

12. When the Insert Greeting Line dialog box opens, choose **Joshua** from the drop-down list and click **OK** to insert the Greeting Line code.

    Now you will conduct the merge.

13. Choose **Mailings→Finish→Finish & Merge** ▤→**Edit Individual Documents**.

14. When the Merge to New Document dialog box opens, click **OK** and then turn off formatting marks.

15. Scroll through the documents to see the results of the merge and then close the document without saving it.

16. Save and close **W13-R2-GardenLtrRevised**.

Create a PowerPoint Presentation from a Word Outline

Now you will create the PowerPoint presentation that Kids for Change will use during the meeting to remind team members of the various gardening tasks that must be completed during their cleanup project. You will generate the presentation from a Word outline.

17. Open **W13-R2-GardenTasks** and choose **View→Views→Outline**.

18. Click several entries and notice the heading levels indicated on the Ribbon.

    Level 1 entries will provide slide titles, and Level 2 entries will provide bullet points.

19. Close the outline document.

20. Start PowerPoint and click the **Open Other Presentations** link at the bottom of the Recent list on the left of the Start screen.

21. Navigate to your **Word Chapter 13** folder; in the bottom-right corner, click the drop-down list and choose **All Files**.

22. Double-click **W13-R2-GardenTasks**.

23. Click several slide icons in the left panel and notice that the titles are formed from the Level 1 outline entries and the bullet points come from the Level 2 outline entries.

24. Exit PowerPoint without saving.

Save a Document as a Web Page

In planning for the Kids for Change garden cleanup project, the project manager needs to determine which gardening supplies members can contribute to use during the project.

25. Open **W13-R2-GardenSupplies** from your **Word Chapter 13** folder and save it as: `W13-R2-GardenSuppliesRevised`

    The document is set up in a table, which is common for organizing data in web pages. If you cannot see table gridlines, choose Table Tools→Layout→Table→View Gridlines.

26. Choose **File→Save As**, navigate to your **Word Chapter 13** folder, and choose **Single File Web Page** from the Save as Type list.

27. Click **Change Title**, type `Gardening Supplies` in the dialog box, and click **OK**.

    This text will appear in the title bar or as a tab in your default browser.

28. Click **Save** and note that Word automatically switches to Web Layout view.

    Now you will open the document in your web browser. Steps for opening the file in your default browser may vary slightly. You may need to seek assistance to determine the correct method.

29. Using Windows File Explorer, navigate to your **Word Chapter 13** folder and double-click the MHTML version of **W13-R2-GardenSuppliesRevised**. (If necessary, use the file icon to identify the single file web page file.)

30. Observe *Gardening Supplies* at the top of the browser and then close the browser.

31. Exit all programs.

REINFORCE YOUR SKILLS: W13-R3

Report on a Fundraiser and Work on Pending Projects

Kids for Change sells used books to raise funds for its projects. In this exercise, you will send a letter to the board members containing sales data from Excel. You will also use a PDF file, a PowerPoint presentation, and a single file web page to help pending projects move forward.

1. Start Word, open **W13-R3-BookSalesLtr** from your **Word Chapter 13** folder, and save it as: `W13-R3-BookSalesLtrRevised`

2. If necessary, choose **View→Views→Print Layout** to change from Web Layout view.

3. Start Excel and click the **Open Other Workbooks** link at the bottom of the Recent list on the left side of the Start screen.

4. Navigate to your **Word Chapter 13** folder, open **W13-R3-UsedBookSales**, and save it as: **W13-R3-UsedBookSalesRevised**

5. Press Ctrl+Home to select the first cell in the worksheet; then press Shift and click the last cell in the table (contains *$1,424.00*).

6. Press Ctrl+C to copy the data.

7. Switch to Word, display formatting marks, and then position the insertion point on the second blank line below the letter closing.

8. Choose **Home→Clipboard→Paste menu button ▾→Paste Special**.

9. Choose **Microsoft Excel Worksheet Object** from the list, click **Paste Link**, and click **OK**.

10. Close Excel.

   Now you will open Excel from within Word.

11. Double-click the worksheet table in Word to open the Excel file.

   You need to correct the January sales figure for Historical Fiction.

12. Click **cell C3** (*Historical Fiction, January*); type **$385.00** and tap Enter.

13. Switch to Word and verify that the worksheet table updated.

14. If your table failed to update, right-click the table and choose **Update Link**.

15. Save and close the Word document and exit Excel, saving when prompted.

Add a PowerPoint Presentation to a Word Document

Kids for Change will soon meet to discuss upcoming projects. You will paste a PowerPoint presentation that provides an overview of the projects into a letter to the board members for their review.

16. Open **W13-R3-BoardMtgLtr** from your **Word Chapter 13** folder and save it as: **W13-R3-BoardMtgLtrRevised**

17. Position the insertion point at the end of the document.

18. Choose **Insert→Text→Object** and click the **Create from File** tab.

19. Click **Browse**, navigate to your **Word Chapter 13** folder, double-click **W13-R3-ProjectsPPT**, and then click **OK**.

20. Double-click the slide image to start the presentation and then click the mouse pointer on the screen to advance the slides. (Notice the Beach Cleanup and Golden Retriever Rescue projects as you view the presentation.)

21. When the black screen appears, click again to close the presentation and then save and close the file.

Edit a PDF File in Word

One of the upcoming projects is the Beach Cleanup. Kids for Change wants to get local school kids involved. You will send an online letter to superintendents in the area requesting their support. You will use a PDF file, as it's likely that the letter will be read on computers with varying operating systems and software. The date for the cleanup has slipped a week, so you need to update the file.

22. In Word, open **W13-R3-SuperLtr.pdf** from your **Word Chapter 13** folder.

23. When the message appears, click **OK** and change the date (second line of body paragraph) from *September 3rd* to September: **10th**

24. Save the file as a PDF file naming it: **W13-R3-SuperLtrRevised**

25. If the file opens in a PDF reader, close the reader.

26. Close the Word document without saving.

Create a Web Page from a Word Document

One of the pending projects is the Golden Retriever Rescue project. You've created a flyer announcing the Foster Home Fair for Golden Retriever Rescue, which will take place at the Community Center. You will save the flyer as a single file web page so it can be posted on the Community Center website.

27. Open **W13-R3-FosterHomeFair** from your **Word Chapter 13** folder.

28. Choose **File→Save As** and navigate to your **Word Chapter 13** folder.

29. Name the file **W13-R3-FosterHomeFairRevised** and choose **Single File Web Page** from the Save as Type list.

30. Click **Change Title** and then type **Foster Home Fair** and click **OK**; then click **Save**.

    Now you will add alternative text to the picture.

31. Select the picture and choose **Picture Tools→Format→Accessibility→Alt Text**.

32. If necessary, remove any existing text; in the Description field, type **Olivia needs a good home!** and then close the task pane.

    Seek assistance if you need help opening the file in your browser.

33. Navigate to your **Word Chapter 13** folder using Windows File Explorer and then double-click **W13-R3-FosterHomeFairRevised**.

34. Review the web page and then close the browser.

    Now you will edit the web page. The web page file should still be open in Word.

35. Position the insertion point at the end of the last bullet point, tap ⟦Enter⟧, and type: **Fire Department BBQ Cook-off**

36. Save and close the file.

    Seek assistance if you need help opening the file in your browser.

37. Navigate to your **Word Chapter 13** folder using Windows File Explorer and then double-click **W13-R3-FosterHomeFairRevised**.

38. Observe the change you made to the web page and then close the browser.

Apply Your Skills

Prepare a Report Comparing Tours

In this exercise, you will produce a report for the Universal Corporate Events management team comparing the sales of four tours over three months. You will embed an Excel worksheet table in a Word document and then link an Excel worksheet table and chart in the document. You will update links when changes are made in Excel, and finally you will break the link between Word and Excel.

1. Open **W13-A1-MgmtLtr** from your **Word Chapter 13** folder and save it as: **W13-A1-MgmtLtrRevised**

2. If necessary, choose **View→Views→Print Layout** to change from Web Layout view.

3. If necessary, display formatting marks, and then position the insertion point on the second blank line below the letter closing.

4. Start Excel, open **W13-A1-1stQSales.xlsx** from your **Word Chapter 13** folder, and save it as: **W13-A1-1stQSalesRevised**

5. Press ⌈Ctrl⌉+⌈Home⌉ to select the cell at the top of the table, press ⌈Shift⌉, and click the last cell in the table (value of *$150,000*).

6. Copy the table and then switch to Word and make sure the insertion point is on the second blank line below the letter closing.

7. Click **Paste menu button ▾→Paste Special** and link the **Microsoft Excel Worksheet Object**.

   Now you will make a change to the Excel table and observe the change in the linked table in Word.

8. Switch to Excel and turn off the marquee.

9. Click **cell C3** (*Hawaii Resort, January*) and enter **40,000** to replace the current number.

10. Switch to Word and notice the change you made.

    If your worksheet table failed to update, use the Update Link command. Now you will link an Excel chart from the same file in the document.

11. In Excel, click the **Sheet 2** tab and then click the chart.

12. Copy the chart, switch to Word and paste it at the bottom of the document, and then use the **Paste Options** smart tag and the **Keep Source Formatting & Link Data** button to link the chart in Word.

13. Switch to Excel and save your changes; exit Excel.

    Now you will open Excel from within Word and edit the worksheet.

14. Double-click the worksheet table to open Excel and change the data in **cell B5** (*Bahamas Cruise, March*) to: **45,000**

15. Switch to Word, observe the change, and, if necessary, use **Update Link** to update the worksheet table and **Refresh Data** to update the chart.

16. Save and close the file; exit Word.

    Now you'll make a change in Excel and update links when you reopen the Word document.

17. In Excel, replace the data in **cell D4** (*Florida Spa, February*) with: **40,000**

18. Start Word, open **W13-A1-MgmtLtrRevised** from your **Word Chapter 13** folder, and update the links.

19. If necessary, use **Update Link** to update the worksheet table and **Refresh Data** to update the chart.

    Because you don't want the data to update any more, you will break the link between Word and Excel.

20. In the Links dialog box, break the link for both the worksheet and the chart.

21. Right-click the worksheet table and ensure that the Update Link command is not available.

22. Click the chart, choose **Chart Tools→Design→Data**, and observe that the **Refresh Data** button is grayed out.

23. Save and close all files and exit Excel.

APPLY YOUR SKILLS: W13-A2

Prepare Documents for a Tour to Turkey

Universal Corporate Events reps are planning a tour of Turkey for a client. In this exercise, you will create a PowerPoint presentation from a Word outline. Then you will insert a PowerPoint presentation in a letter for tour members and create a single file web page from a Word document listing side tours in Turkey.

1. Open **W13-A2-TurkeyOutline** and switch to Outline view.

2. Observe the heading levels indicated in the Outlining tab, which will become the title and bullet-point entries in the PowerPoint slides; close the outline document.

3. Start PowerPoint, click **Open Other Presentations** at the bottom of the left panel, and navigate to your **Word Chapter 13** folder.

4. In the bottom of the Open dialog box, choose **All Files** from the drop-down list.

5. Double-click **W13-A2-TurkeyOutline** to open it; click through the slides in the left panel and observe the effect of the different heading levels in the outline.

6. Exit PowerPoint without saving.

    Now you will add a PowerPoint presentation to a letter you're sending as an email attachment to the tour members.

7. In Word, open **W13-A2-TurkeyLtr** from your **Word Chapter 13** folder and save it as: **W13-A2-TurkeyLtrRevised**

8. Position the insertion point at the end of the document, insert **W13-A2-TurkeyPPT**, and view the presentation.

    Now you will save the letter as a PDF file as tour members will likely have different types of computers.

9. Choose **File→Save As**, navigate to your **Word Chapter 13** folder, and save the file as a PDF file.

10. If your file opens in a PDF reader, close the reader.

11. Save and close **W13-A2-TurkeyLtrRevised.pdf**.

    The location for the meeting has changed, so you will edit the PDF file in Word and resave it as a PDF file.

12. Open the PDF file in Word and change *Lakeside* to: **Harbor**

13. Resave the file as a PDF file and name it: **W13-A2-TurkeyLtrRevised2**

14. If the file opens in a reader, close the reader.

15. Save the Word document as **W13-A2-TurkeyLtrRevised2** and make sure to choose Word Document in the Save as Type menu; close the file.

Create and Edit a Web Page in Word

You have been asked to create a web page for the Universal Corporate Events website showing the side tours offered for the tour of Turkey.

16. Open **W13-A2-TurkeyWebPage**, save it as Single File Web Page, and name it **W13-A2-TurkeyWebPageRevised**. Change the title to: **Side Trips in Turkey**

17. Open and observe the web page in your browser, and then close the browser.

    Now you will add a side-tour destination to the web page. The web page document should still be open in Word.

18. Position the insertion point after *Turkish Bath*, tap Enter, and type: **Istanbul**

19. Save and close the file.

20. Open the file in your browser again, observe the change, and then close the browser.

APPLY YOUR SKILLS: W13-A3

Plan an Australian Tour

A Universal Corporate Events representative is preparing an Australian tour for a client. You have been asked to prepare the documents associated with the tour. In this exercise, you will use an Excel name and address list for a mail merge and prepare a letter containing a PowerPoint presentation. Then you will prepare a single file web page about Australia for tour members to view online.

1. Open **W13-A3-AustraliaLtr** from your **Word Chapter 13** folder and save it as: **W13-A3-AustraliaLtrRevised**

2. If necessary, change the view to Print Layout, and then designate the letter as the main document in a mail merge.

3. Designate Sheet 1 of the **W13-A3-AustraliaN&A** Excel file as the recipient list.

4. Replace the **Address Block** placeholder text with the **Address Block code**, accepting the default formats for the inside address.

5. Replace the **Greeting Line** placeholder text with the **Greeting Line code**, accepting the default formats for the greeting line.

6. Finish the merge, choosing **Edit Individual Documents**, and merge all records.

7. Review the merged letters and then close the merged file without saving.

8. Save and close **W13-A3-AustraliaLtrRevised**.

Insert a PowerPoint Presentation in a Word Document

The tour members have now attended an orientation meeting, and the Universal Corporate Events representative has asked you to insert the PowerPoint presentation in a letter to members so they can review the topics covered in the meeting.

9. Open **W13-A3-OrientLtr** from your **Word Chapter 13** folder and save it as: **W13-A3-OrientLtrRevised**

10. Position the insertion point at the end of the letter, insert **W13-A3-AussiePPT**, and view the presentation.

11. Save and close the file.

Create and Edit a Web Page in Word

12. Open **W13-A3-AussieWebPage** from your **Word Chapter 13** folder, save it as a single file web page, and then name it **W13-A3-AussieWebPageRevised** and change the title to: **Australia Overview**

13. View the web page in your browser and then close the browser.

    Now you will edit the web page in Word. The web page file should still be open.

14. Position the insertion point after the word *Territories* and tap ⌨Enter. Type **History** and then save and close the web page file.

15. View the web page in your browser, observe the change, and then close the browser.

16. Exit Word.

📋 Project Grader

This chapter does not include Project Grader exercises. Project Grader content is based on the learning objectives for a chapter, and sometimes those learning objectives cannot be accurately graded by the system.

✈ Extend Your Skills

These exercises challenge you to think critically and apply your new skills in a real-world setting. You will be evaluated on your ability to follow directions, completeness, creativity, and the use of proper grammar and mechanics. Save files to your chapter folder. Submit assignments as directed.

W13-E1 That's the Way I See It

As a sales rep for a small business, you track your quarterly sales in Excel. It's the end of the third quarter, and you will submit the end-of-quarter figures and the associated chart to your boss in a Word file. Create a one-paragraph Word file indicating that you are submitting your third-quarter sales summary. Name the file: **W13-E1-MyLetter**

Link the worksheet table and chart from **W13-E1-3rdQSales**. The product names are generic. Decide which products your company sells and change the product names in the Excel file accordingly, saving it as **W13-E1-3rdQSalesRevised** when finished. Update the linked objects in your Word document, too.

Your boss has asked you to use Mail Merge to send a mailing to customers announcing a new product. Decide on the new product and then write a letter (one to two paragraphs) describing it. Save the file as **W13-E1-MyMergeLtr** and designate the letter as the main document. Designate **W13-E1-Address** (Word Chapter 13 folder) as the recipient list. Add the Address Block and Greeting Line merge codes; conduct the merge. Save the merged file as: **W13-E1-Merged**

W13-E2 Be Your Own Boss

As the owner of Blue Jean Landscaping, you plan to hold a seminar to discuss your products and services. You want a PowerPoint presentation to guide your seminar. Use the Word outline **W13-E2-BJLGardens** to create the slides and save the presentation as: **W13-E2-BJL-PPT**

After the seminar, you will email a Word document to attendees with the presentation inserted. Create a letter (one to two paragraphs) thanking customers for attending the seminar. In your letter, explain that the presentation is included in the email and add instructions on how to play the slide show. Save the Word document as **W13-E2-BJLLetter** and then save it as a PDF using the name: **W13-E2-BJLetterRevised**

W13-E3 Demonstrate Proficiency

Stormy BBQ sponsors an annual rodeo. To encourage a big turnout, you've been asked to prepare a PowerPoint presentation to use as an email attachment for Stormy BBQ's customers. To begin, open **W13-E3-RodeoOutline** in PowerPoint. Save the presentation as: **W13-E3-RodeoPres**

Then, create a two- or three-paragraph Word document describing the rodeo and why people should attend. Save the file as **W13-E3-RodeoWordDoc** and insert a PowerPoint presentation, **W13-E3-RodeoPPT**, in the document. Remember to include instructions on how to run the slide show.

There will be a Rodeo Raffle, and you've been asked to create a web page to put on Stormy BBQ's website listing the prizes. Convert **W13-E3-RodeoWebPage** to a single file web page with the title **Prizes List** and the filename: **W13-E3-RodeoWebPage**

Test the MHTML file in your browser. Add a prize, a $50 Starbuck's Gift Card, to the bottom of the list of prizes in the document. Save the file and then test it again in your browser.

Glossary

Access Database software that helps you quickly retrieve data; allows you to create and enter data into a table and then use forms, reports, and queries to display the desired results

Accessibility Checker Describes possible accessibility issues in your files so you can fix them so someone with a disability can read and access your content

AutoComplete A feature that offers to complete the typing for you when it recognizes certain words or phrases

AutoCorrect Predefined text used for automatically correcting common spelling and capitalization errors; can be customized with user-defined entries

block style Letter style that aligns all parts of a letter with the left margin

bookmarks Selection of text or other objects identified by a name and location; enable quick navigation through long documents

Building Blocks Another term for Quick Parts; usually refers to Quick Parts that provide a traditional part of a newsletter or article, such as pull quotes and sidebars

captions Text added to a figure to describe or explain the figure; text formatted as captions can be used to create a table of figures

cell A box formed by the intersection of a row and column table, in which information is entered and displayed

character styles Styles used to format a single word or selected group of words with text formatting such as font, bold, font size, etc.; no paragraph formatting is included

citation(s) Reference to a source used in a document; contains information to locate the source

Clipboard A location within Microsoft Office that contains thumbnails of what you have recently cut or copied from your Microsoft Office file(s) during your Windows session; used to quickly paste text, pictures, images, or charts into a file

collaborating Working together with other people to edit and complete a document

color sets A subset of themes; determine which colors are applied to various document elements as part of the overall theme aesthetic

column break Manual break of a newsletter column at a specified location; moves text at the break point to the top of the next column

columns Vertical arrangement of cells in a table

comment Electronic note attached to a document

Compatibility Checker When a Word 2019 document is saved down to Word 2010 or an even earlier version, the Compatibility Checker notifies the user how features specific to Word 2019 will be handled

Compatibility Mode Opening a document that was created in Word 2010 or earlier opens it in Compatibility Mode; available features are limited to those found in the earlier versions

Compatibility Pack This free download from Microsoft allows a user to open a Word 2007–2019 document in an earlier version of Word

concordance A list of terms used to mark words or phrases in a document that are to be included in an index

content controls Placeholder fields, entered into forms, that enable users to click on the fields and enter information

contextual tab(s) Hidden Ribbon tabs that only appear when certain types of objects, such as pictures or tables, are selected

convert Feature that allows you to transform documents that were created in an earlier version of an application to the Office 2019 file format

Copy Creates a duplicate of the original selection, which remains in the source location, and places a copy of the selection on the Office Clipboard

cropping Cutting off parts of a picture to make certain other elements stand out or to remove unwanted elements

Cut Removes the original selection from the source location and places the selection on the Office Clipboard

data source In Mail Merge, the variable data that merges with the main document; controlled by merge fields in the main document

demote To increase text indentation so it appears farther away from the left margin and, if numbered or bulleted, reduces the numbering or bulleting level to the next lower level

destination file A file on which an operation is performed or into which data copied from another document is pasted

digital signature Means of authenticating the identity of the originator of a document; a signed document cannot be modified

Document Inspector Reviews documents for hidden data or personal information

document properties Information about a document, such as the date and time it was last modified, the author's name, and the name of the last person who modified it

embed To incorporate within the body of a file or document

encryption Technique for encoding a document so it can only be read by the sender and the intended recipient

endnotes Notes that appear at the end of the document body in which the reference is made; numbered sequentially throughout a document

Excel Worksheet software, arranged with rows and columns, used to create calculations and to make what-if analyses; perfect for preparing a budget or income statement or determining the amount of interest paid on a loan

file format Type of method used for storing information in a file; each application normally has a special file format it uses by default

font sets A subset of themes; determine which fonts are applied to header and body text as part of the overall theme aesthetic

footer Text that usually, but not always, is located toward the bottom of a document and that repeats on all (desired) pages within a document

footnotes Notes that appear at the bottom of the page on which the reference is made; footnote numbers can start with 1 on each page or can be numbered sequentially throughout a document or individually

Format Painter Applies the character and paragraph formatting from the source selection to any characters or text selected

formatting marks Special characters such as spaces, tabs, and paragraph symbols made visible when the Show/Hide button is turned on

handles Small squares or circles on selected graphics that can be dragged to make the graphic larger or smaller

header Text that usually, but not always, is located toward the top of a document, slide, or handout and that repeats on all (desired) pages, slides, or handouts within a document or presentation

hyperlink A block of text or a graphic that takes you to another location in a file, to another file, or to a web page when clicked

insert control Appears when the mouse pointer is outside the table, pointing between columns or rows; click the control to insert a new column or row at that location

Keep Source Formatting Pastes the text and the selection with any formatting (bold, italic, underline) of the selection from the source location to the target location; the selection pasted retains the original formatting from the source location

Keep Text Only Pastes the selection from the source location to the target location; the selection pasted takes on the formatting of the target location

line spacing Vertical space between lines of text

link A code or instruction that connects one part of a source file to a destination file; the destination file can be updated when the source file is modified

Live Preview Feature that allows you to point at formatting commands on the Ribbon to show how the format would appear on selected text and objects without actually applying the format

macro A series of frequently used commands grouped together and saved as a single command; used to speed up repetitive tasks

Mail Merge Feature used to personalize standard letters, envelopes, mailing labels, and other documents by combining a main document with a data source

main document In a Mail Merge, the document that contains the content that remains the same for each recipient; controls the merge with merge fields

manual page break Forced page break created by pressing Ctrl + Enter or choosing Insert→ Pages→Page Break

Mark as Final Command that makes a document read-only; places an icon on the status bar to let readers know they are viewing the final form of the document

merge fields Placeholders in a Mail Merge main document that instruct Word to insert information from a data source

Merge Formatting Pastes the text and selection with any formatting (bold, italic, underline) of the selection from the source location to the target location and combines it with any formatting already at the target location; the selection pasted has formats from both the source and target locations

merged document Document that results when you complete a merge of the main document and the data source

Microsoft account Account that gives you access to your Microsoft settings, files, contacts, and more, as well as to your computer or other devices; can include Bing, Hotmail, MSN, Office, OneDrive, Outlook, Skype, Stores, or Xbox Live

Microsoft Office 2019 Version of Microsoft Office that you purchase one time, for one device, similar to what you may have done to obtain software in the past; anytime there is a new version of Microsoft Office, you need to purchase it if you desire the most recent version (select Office Home & Student 2019 to install Office on one PC)

MLA style *Modern Language Association Handbook for Writers of Research Papers*; shows how to work with sources in expository writing

nonbreaking hyphens or spaces Hyphens or spaces inserted between two or more words to keep those words together on the same line

object Refers to graphical images such as shapes, WordArt, Excel spreadsheets, chart, and pictures; these elements can be shared between documents

Office 365 Version of Microsoft Office that has a monthly subscription rate for one or more devices that offers automatic updates similar to how you purchase apps on your smartphone or tablet (select Office 365 Personal for a monthly subscription for one device—PC or Mac, plus one smartphone and one tablet; select Office 365 Home for a monthly subscription for up to five PCs or Macs, plus five smartphones and five tablets)

Office Online Version of Microsoft Office that is free when you are logged in to a Microsoft account; the online apps include Outlook, Word Online, Excel Online, PowerPoint Online, OneNote Online, and Sway; not all features of Office 365/2019 are available in these apps

OneDrive A service offered by Microsoft that provides free online storage to those who have a Microsoft Account ID; allows you to get and share files from anywhere on any device

OneNote Notetaking software used to organize notes (handwritten or keyed), audio/sound recordings, screen captures, or sketches you have collected or created to share with others

orientation Direction in which the page is turned for viewing and printing, either portrait (short edge on top) or landscape (long edge on top)

Outlook Personal information manager software used to create, send, and receive emails, record tasks, maintain one or more calendars, schedule meetings and appointments, manage contacts, and take notes

paragraph In Word, this is created anytime you tap Enter; it can consist of several lines, a single line, or a blank line

paragraph style Style used to format a paragraph or selected group of paragraphs; may include character formatting

Paste Inserts a copy of the most recent item found on the Office Clipboard at the target location, or destination; there are usually at least three paste choices: Keep Source Formatting, Merge Formatting, and Keep Text Only

PowerPoint Presentation software used to create, edit, revise, format, and share slides designed to tell a story, market a product, or explain a concept

promote To reduce text indentation so it appears closer to the left margin and, if numbered or bulleted, to elevate the item to the next higher level of bullet

Publisher Desktop publishing software used to design and lay out text and images, often for newsletters or brochures

Quick Parts Reusable text and/or graphic elements that can be customized and inserted into documents

round-tripping Converting a document created in Word 97-2003 to Word 2019 format and then saving it back to the Word 97-2003 document format

rows Horizontal groups of cells in a table

section break Position in a document where one section ends and another begins because page formatting is going to change, such as from single- to multiple-column layout

select To drag over the desired text with the mouse pointer; also called highlighting

shapes Tool for drawing graphics in documents

Show/Hide button Feature that displays nonprinting characters such as tabs, spaces, and paragraph symbols onscreen for easy access

Skype Web communication software that utilizes the Internet to share audio, video, text, messages, files, or desktops via a webcam on both the sending and receiving devices

smart tag Context-sensitive option button that appears on menus

SmartArt Predesigned graphic designs added to a document; categories include List, Hierarchy, Pyramid, and so forth

software suite Collection of applications generally produced by the same manufacturer and bundled together for a better price that provides a common user interface throughout each application

sort Process used to arrange data in a specific order, such as alphabetic, numeric, by date, or in ascending or descending order

source Original location of text that has been cut or copied

source file The document in which data or copied text originally appeared

split To create two or more table cells from a single table cell

style Group of formats that allows you to quickly apply multiple formats at once; when a style is modified, all text with the style applied is updated with the modification; also known as Quick Styles

style sets Used to change font and paragraph properties, interact with themes; most effective when used in conjunction with the Styles gallery

tab stops Preset stops along the horizontal ruler set at every half inch to control and align text; can be customized

table styles Styles applied to table cells, rows, or columns to ensure formatting consistency

target Destination location for pasted text

template A preformatted document or workbook layout used as the basis for new documents to maintain consistency among documents and save the user time and that usually contains text, paragraph, table, graphical, and other types of formatting

theme Preset formatting selections you can apply to a document or presentation; include colors, graphic elements, and fonts all designed to work well together and quickly achieve the look of a professional design

thumbnails Small images that represent an application, file, etc.

title bar Appears across the top of the application window; contains the name of the application and the name of the current file

toggle Selecting a button once to turn it on and again to turn it off

Track Changes Feature that, when activated, marks each change to a document; the changes can then be reviewed and either accepted or rejected

view Onscreen layout of a document optimized for performing specific tasks or for determining how the document will look in final form

Visual Basic for Applications (VBA) A programming language used by Office programs that creates modules containing macros

watermark Text or images placed in the header of a document so it appears faintly behind document text and graphics

widow/orphan control Prevents placing the last line of a paragraph at the top of the next page (widow) or the first line of a paragraph at the bottom of a page (orphan); ensures there are at least two lines of a paragraph at the top or bottom of a page

wildcard characters Special characters used in place of unknown characters when conducting a search

Word Word-processing software for creating, editing, revising, formatting, and sharing documents

WordArt Feature for creating stylized formatting of text; often used for headings

Word Wrap Automatic moving of text to a new line when it extends beyond the right margin of a paragraph; eliminates the need to tap Enter at the end of lines within a paragraph

Index

NOTES

NOTES

NOTES

NOTES

NOTES

NOTES

NOTES

NOTES